Eliot Now

Eliot Now

Edited by
Megan Quigley and David E. Chinitz

BLOOMSBURY ACADEMIC
LONDON • NEW YORK • OXFORD • NEW DELHI • SYDNEY

BLOOMSBURY ACADEMIC
Bloomsbury Publishing Plc
50 Bedford Square, London, WC1B 3DP, UK
1385 Broadway, New York, NY 10018, USA
29 Earlsfort Terrace, Dublin 2, Ireland

BLOOMSBURY, BLOOMSBURY ACADEMIC and the Diana logo are trademarks of
Bloomsbury Publishing Plc

First published in Great Britain 2024

Copyright © Megan Quigley, David E. Chinitz, and contributors, 2024

Megan Quigley, David E. Chinitz, and contributors have asserted their right under the
Copyright, Designs and Patents Act, 1988, to be identified as Authors of this work.

Cover design by Rebecca Heselton
Cover image: TS Eliot at Love Beach, New Providence Island, while on his honeymoon in
the Bahamas, 1957 © Slim Aarons/Getty Images

All rights reserved. No part of this publication may be reproduced or transmitted
in any form or by any means, electronic or mechanical, including photocopying,
recording, or any information storage or retrieval system, without prior
permission in writing from the publishers.

Bloomsbury Publishing Plc does not have any control over, or responsibility for, any
third-party websites referred to or in this book. All internet addresses given in this
book were correct at the time of going to press. The authors and publisher regret any
inconvenience caused if addresses have changed or sites have ceased to exist,
but can accept no responsibility for any such changes.

A catalogue record for this book is available from the British Library.

Library of Congress Cataloging-in-Publication Data
Names: Quigley, Megan, editor. | Chinitz, David, editor.
Title: Eliot now / edited by Megan Quigley and David E. Chinitz.
Description: London; New York: Bloomsbury Academic, 2024. |
Includes bibliographical references.
Identifiers: LCCN 2023058260 (print) | LCCN 2023058261 (ebook) |
ISBN 9781350173927 (hardback) | ISBN 9781350471733 (paperback) |
ISBN 9781350173934 (pdf) | ISBN 9781350173941 (ebook)
Subjects: LCSH: Eliot, T. S. (Thomas Stearns), 1888–1965–Criticism and interpretation. |
Eliot, T. S. (Thomas Stearns), 1888–1965–Archives.
Classification: LCC PS3509.L43 Z67173 2024 (print) | LCC PS3509.L43
(ebook) | DDC 821/.912–dc23/eng/20240226
LC record available at https://lccn.loc.gov/2023058260
LC ebook record available at https://lccn.loc.gov/2023058261

ISBN: HB: 978-1-3501-7392-7
ePDF: 978-1-3501-7393-4
eBook: 978-1-3501-7394-1

Typeset by Newgen KnowledgeWorks Pvt. Ltd., Chennai, India

To find out more about our authors and books visit www.bloomsbury.com
and sign up for our newsletters.

Contents

Notes on Contributors	vii
Abbreviations for Works by T. S. Eliot	xii

Part I New Eliot

1	Introduction: Eliot New *Megan Quigley and David E. Chinitz*	3
2	The New *Poems of T. S. Eliot* *Mark Ford*	11
3	*The Complete Prose*: The Critic's Workshop *Anthony Cuda*	23
4	Eliot's Divided Life *Frances Dickey*	37
5	Eliot as Public Intellectual *Jeremy Noel-Tod*	51

Part II Eliot in Theory

6	"No empty bottles": Eliot's Ambivalent Anthropocene *Julia E. Daniel*	67
7	T. S. Eliot and Translation *Vera M. Kutzinski*	79
8	Whiteness and Religious Conversion in *Four Quartets* *Ann Marie Jakubowski*	93
9	Tiresias and TERFism Today: *The Waste Land*'s Modernist Feminine, Cis and Trans *Emma Heaney*	107

10	Eliot in the Dadabase *Elyse Graham and Michelle A. Taylor*	119
11	Of Corpses, Corpuses, and Career Capital: Eliot and Print Culture *Michael H. Whitworth*	131
12	The Always Inconvenient Dead: Lyric Theory and Eliot's Early Poetry *Paul Franz*	143
13	Eliot's Political Theology *C. D. Blanton*	155
14	The Perfect *Post*-Critic? *Sumita Chakraborty*	169

Part III Looking Ahead

15	T. S. Eliot and the Humanities to Come *Simon During*	183
16	Eliot, Brexit, and the Idea of Europe *Jason Harding*	195
17	Mature Fans Steal: Eliot's Fictions *Megan Quigley*	207
18	Afterword: Strange God—Eliot, Now *Urmila Seshagiri*	221
19	*The Waste Land* Centenary: Poets on Eliot *James Longenbach, Carl Phillips, Lesley Wheeler, Craig Raine, Hannah Sullivan, and Alison C. Rollins*	233

Selected Bibliography of Recent T. S. Eliot Scholarship	253
Index	261

Contributors

C. D. Blanton is a member and former chair of the Program in Critical Theory at the University of California, Berkeley. He is the author of *Epic Negation: The Dialectical Poetics of Late Modernism* (2015) and coeditor of *A Concise Companion to Postwar British and Irish Poetry* (2009). He has published essays in *PMLA*, *South Atlantic Quarterly*, the *Yale Journal of Criticism*, and several edited collections.

Sumita Chakraborty is Assistant Professor of English and Creative Writing at North Carolina State University. Her scholarship has appeared in *Cultural Critique*, *Interdisciplinary Studies in Literature and the Environment*, *Modernism/modernity*, *College Literature*, and other journals, and her monograph, *Grave Dangers: Poetics and the Ethics of Death in the Anthropocene*, is under contract. Her first collection of poems, *Arrow*, was published in 2020.

David E. Chinitz, Professor of English at Loyola University Chicago, is the author of *T. S. Eliot and the Cultural Divide* (2003) and *Which Sin to Bear? Authenticity and Compromise in Langston Hughes* (2013). His *Complete Prose of T. S. Eliot, Volume 6: The War Years, 1940–1946* (coedited with Ronald Schuchard) won the 2019 MLA Prize for a Scholarly Edition. He has served as president of the Modernist Studies Association and the International T. S. Eliot Society.

Anthony Cuda is Professor and Associate Head of English at the University of North Carolina, Greensboro. He is the author of *The Passions of Modernism: Eliot, Yeats, Woolf, and Mann* (2010) and coeditor of *The Complete Prose of T. S. Eliot: The Critical Edition, Vol. 2: The Perfect Critic, 1919–1926* (2014). He is secretary of the International T. S. Eliot Society and executive director of the T. S. Eliot International Summer School.

Julia E. Daniel is an associate professor at Baylor University and a past coeditor of the *T. S. Eliot Studies Annual*. She is the author of *Building Natures: Modern American Poetry, Landscape Architecture, and City Planning* and coeditor of *Modernism in the Green: Public Greens in Modern Literature and Culture*. Her work has also appeared in *Ecomodernism*, *Modernism in the Anthropocene*, *Critical Quarterly*, and *The Cambridge Companion to "The Waste Land."*

Frances Dickey is Associate Professor of English at the University of Missouri, Columbia; author of *The Modern Portrait Poem from Dante Gabriel Rossetti to Ezra Pound* (2012); and editor of *The Complete Prose of T. S. Eliot, Vol. 3: Literature, Politics, Belief, 1927–1929* (2015) and *The Edinburgh Companion to T. S. Eliot and the Arts* (2016). She served a term as president of the International T. S. Eliot Society and as coeditor of the *T. S. Eliot Studies Annual*.

Simon During is a professorial research fellow at the University of Melbourne. His books include *Foucault and Literature* (1992), *Modern Enchantments: The Cultural Power of Secular Magic* (2002), and *Against Democracy: Literary Experience in an Era of Emancipations* (2012). He is currently collaborating with Amanda Anderson on a book entitled *Humanities Theory*.

Mark Ford is a professor in the English Department at University College London. Recent publications include *Woman Much Missed: Thomas Hardy, Emma Hardy, and Poetry*; *Lunar Solo* (a parallel-text edition of the poetry of Jules Laforgue); and *A Guest Among Stars: Essays on Twentieth-Century Poets* (all 2023).

Paul Franz completed his doctorate in modern British literature at Yale in 2020 and has since taught at Yale, the Cooper Union, and the Royal Military College of Canada, where he currently holds a term appointment in the Department of English, Culture, and Communication.

Elyse Graham is Professor of English and Digital Humanities at Stony Brook University. She has published with McGill-Queen's University Press, Oxford University Press, and Stanford University Press and has a book under contract with HarperCollins.

Jason Harding is Professor and Head of the Department of English at City University of Hong Kong. He is the author or editor of seven books, including *"The Criterion": Cultural Politics and Periodical Networks in Interwar Britain* (2002), *The New Cambridge Companion to T. S. Eliot* (2017), and (with Ronald Schuchard) volume 4 of *The Complete Prose of T. S. Eliot: The Critical Edition* (2015).

Emma Heaney is currently the associate director of XE: Experimental Humanities and Social Engagement, a master's program at New York University, for which she also serves as a clinical associate professor. She is the author of *The New Woman: Literary Modernism, Queer Theory, and the Trans Feminine Allegory* (2017) and the editor of *Feminism Against Cisness* (forthcoming in

2024). Her collection of essays about gestation and economy, *This Watery Place*, is forthcoming.

Ann Marie Jakubowski is a PhD candidate in English at Washington University in St. Louis. Her dissertation explores the relationship between religious conversion and modernist form, arguing that conversion is a paradigmatic event in global modernism and that it is shaped and determined by questions of literary form. Her writing has also appeared in the *Journal of Modern Literature*, *Salon*, *Avidly*, and *The Millions*.

Vera M. Kutzinski, the Martha Rivers Ingram Professor of English and Professor of Comparative Literature at Vanderbilt University, has published widely on the nineteenth- and twentieth-century literatures of the Americas and on translation. She is the author of *The Worlds of Langston Hughes: Modernism and Translation in the Americas* (2012) and coeditor (with Anthony Reed) of *Langston Hughes in Context* (2022).

James Longenbach was the Joseph Henry Gilmore Professor of English at the University of Rochester. His books of literary criticism include *Stone Cottage: Pound, Yeats, and Modernism*; *The Resistance to Poetry*; *How Poems Get Made*; and *The Lyric Now*. His award-winning poetry appeared in the *Nation*, the *New Yorker*, and the *Paris Review*. Longenbach's poetry collections include *Threshold*, *The Iron Key*, *Earthling*, and *Forever*. He passed away in 2022.

Jeremy Noel-Tod is an associate professor in the School of Literature, Drama and Creative Writing at the University of East Anglia, and serves as academic director of the British Archive for Contemporary Writing. His poetry criticism has been widely published, and his books as editor include *The Oxford Companion to Modern Poetry* (2013), the *Complete Poems of R. F. Langley* (2015), and *The Penguin Book of the Prose Poem* (2018). He writes a weekly poetry Substack, *Some Flowers Soon*.

Carl Phillips is the author of sixteen books of poetry, including *Then the War: And Selected Poems 2007–2020*, which won the 2023 Pulitzer Prize. His most recent prose book is *My Trade Is Mystery: Seven Meditations from a Life in Writing* (2022). He lives on Cape Cod, in Massachusetts.

Megan Quigley, Associate Professor of English at Villanova University, is the author of *Modernist Fiction and Vagueness: Philosophy, Form, and Language* (2015) and the editor of two clusters of essays on #MeToo, T. S. Eliot, and modernism in *Modernism/modernity* Print Plus (2019, 2020). She has published essays in the *James Joyce Quarterly*, *Modernism/modernity*, *Philosophy and Literature*, *Poetics Today*, *LARB*, the *T. S. Eliot Studies Annual*, and *nonsite*.

Craig Raine is a poet, dramatist, librettist, novelist, and literary critic. He was Fellow in English at New College, Oxford, for twenty years, and retired in 2010. His study *T. S. Eliot* was published in 2006. He writes a monthly column for the *TLS*.

Alison C. Rollins is Assistant Professor of English at the University of Wisconsin–Madison. Her works of poetry have appeared or are forthcoming in *American Poetry Review*, *Gulf Coast*, *Iowa Review*, and the *New York Times Magazine*. Her first poetry collection, *Library of Small Catastrophes*, was published in 2019. She was the winner of a Pushcart Prize in 2020 and was awarded a 2023–4 Harvard Radcliffe Institute Fellowship.

Urmila Seshagiri is Professor of English Literature at the University of Tennessee. She is the author of *Race and the Modernist Imagination* (2010) and editor of Virginia Woolf's *Jacob's Room* (2022). Her work has appeared in *PMLA* and *Modernism/modernity*, and she is the recipient of grants from the National Endowment for the Humanities, the Mellon Centre for Studies in British Art, the American Philosophical Society, and the Robert B. Silvers Foundation.

Hannah Sullivan teaches English at New College, Oxford. She is the author of *The Work of Revision* (2013) and is currently writing a book about meter and free verse. Her first collection of poetry, *Three Poems*, was awarded the T. S. Eliot Prize for 2018. Her second collection, *Was It for This*, was published in 2023.

Michelle A. Taylor received her PhD in English from Harvard in 2021 and has held postdoctoral fellowships at the University of Oxford and Emory University. Her book manuscript in progress, *Clique Lit: Coterie Culture and the Making of Modernism*, proposes new methods for reading and understanding coterie culture and practice in the modernist period. She has published essays and articles in, among other venues, *College Literature*, *Modernist Cultures*, *The Point*, *FT Magazine*, and the *New Yorker*.

Lesley Wheeler is the author of *Poetry's Possible Worlds* (2022), a hybrid book about reading contemporary poetry during a time of crisis. Her other works include the novel *Unbecoming* (2020) and five poetry collections; the sixth, *Mycocosmic*, will appear in 2025. Her poems and essays appear in *Poetry*, *American Poetry Review*, and *Poets & Writers*, and she is poetry editor of *Shenandoah*.

Michael H. Whitworth is Professor of Modern Literature and Culture in the Faculty of English, University of Oxford, and a tutorial fellow of Merton College, Oxford, where he teaches Victorian and modern literatures in English. His books include *Einstein's Wake: Relativity, Metaphor, and Modernist Literature* (2001), *Virginia Woolf* (2005), and *Reading Modernist Poetry* (2010). He has also written essays and chapters on Hugh MacDiarmid, Herbert Read, C. Day Lewis, and Mina Loy.

Abbreviations for Works by T. S. Eliot

Eliot–Hale   "The Letters of T. S. Eliot to Emily Hale." 2022. tseliot.com.

Letters1–9   *The Letters of T. S. Eliot*. Ed. John Haffenden et al. 9 vols. (in progress). London: Faber, 2009–.

Poems1–2   *The Poems of T. S. Eliot*. Ed. Christopher Ricks and Jim McCue. 2 vols. London: Faber; Baltimore: Johns Hopkins University Press, 2015.

Prose1–8   *The Complete Prose of T. S. Eliot: The Critical Edition*. Ed. Ronald Schuchard et al. 8 vols. (online). Baltimore: Johns Hopkins University Press, 2014–19.

Part I

New Eliot

1

Introduction: Eliot New

Megan Quigley and David E. Chinitz

> I would meet you upon this honestly.
> I that was near your heart was removed therefrom
> To lose beauty in terror, terror in inquisition.
> I have lost my passion: why should I need to keep it
> Since what is kept must be adulterated? (*Poems1* 32–3)

Drafted by a thirty-year-old Eliot, "Gerontion" (1920) is a youthful poem pondering the ravages of time.[1] It asks "honestly" to meet the reader face-to-face to inquire what can be preserved from change. If beauty, terror, passion, and even love are destined to wither and die, what can be salvaged? And is what remains even worth saving? This dramatic monologue issues from the mouth of an elderly, even an ancient, man, a characteristic Eliotic persona. Embodying what "Tradition and the Individual Talent" calls "the mind of Europe"—his recollections include Thermopylae, the Passion, the Inquisition, and the Reign of Terror—Eliot's speaker belongs to a past that, even for himself, lacks glory; in the present, it is merely a "decayed house" he no longer owns. Is this voice, after such knowledge, one we care to hear, much less forgive? And how is reading T. S. Eliot in 2023 different from sitting with the aged Gerontion?

For different it is! Eliot studies is an intellectually vibrant, methodologically adventurous, and politically and philosophically exciting field, as *Eliot Now* aims to demonstrate. "Gerontion," the dramatic monologue, asks readers to confront their assumptions, prejudices, and nostalgia for some sort of golden age of reason, which Gerontion himself laments. The poem is thematically and pragmatically the perfect test case for thinking about Eliot now. Steeped in allusion and irony, and generically recognizable, it remains a beloved icon for New Critical exegesis; it also exemplifies what makes Eliot, the subject of Eliot studies now, different from the "Old Possum" of yore. Since 2009, the published letters, new editions, and revelations from formerly closed archives have made Eliot nearly unrecognizable.

These fresh resources shed light on the meaning of "Gerontion" in ways never possible before. The poem is notoriously difficult in part because of the diversity of names that populate it, which have tortured critics for a century. "Mr Silvero," "Hakagawa," "Madame de Tornquist," and "Fraulein von Kulp" inhabit Gerontion's memories and lead readers down a rabbit hole of source-hunting. The recently published *Complete Poems* fortunately offers (among many other responses) Eliot's own exasperated retort, in a letter, to this kind of reading:

> As for the etymologies you drive me to despair. Anybody nowadays has the right to attribute anything he likes to anyone else's unconscious and if you choose to think that I knew all these etymologies you are at liberty to do so. All I can say is that these names came to me spontaneously as suitable for certain persons whom I had known.[2]

Echoing Wordsworth's "spontaneity" as the method of poetry, romantic Eliot directs us away from source-hunting. We can see Eliot doubling down on his rejection of readers who believe him a font of scholarly knowledge—and believe his poetry to require such erudition to be enjoyed—in "English Poets as Letter Writers," a reconstructed lecture published in the *Complete Prose*: "I have been trying for some years, indeed, ever since I provided one of my poems with notes, to shatter the fiction that I was a man of vast erudition. I have denied this at every opportunity, at first rather diffidently, finally rather querulously, and I have found that no one believes me" (*Prose4* 846). These two recent sources provide a wealth of information about Eliot's sources and ideas—one available at a mouse-click to any reader with access to the digital *Complete Prose*—which were previously accessible only through archival labor.

Eliot's letters to Emily Hale provide further insight into the cast of characters in "Gerontion." On January 27, 2023, Eliot's estate published these letters on tseliot.com, the T. S. Eliot Foundation website. Altogether unavailable for sixty-four years, the letters opened in 2020 to readers with physical access to Princeton's Firestone Library. Now any reader with internet access can read Eliot's thousand letters to his longtime love. One encounters there his offhand assertion, in a letter of March 24, 1931, that the name "Mr. Silvero" referred to Matthew Prichard, an art historian and assistant director at the Boston Museum of Fine Arts. Eliot had told Herbert Read in April 1926 that Prichard's "sensibility to art is greater than that of anyone I have ever met" (*Letters3* 133), and he reported to Hale that he had been "very much under [Prichard's] influence" during his 1910–11 year in Paris.[3] Although Eliot confesses "a great debt" to Prichard, he adds:

> I felt simultaneously a fascination and an aversion which was a great mental strain and precipitated at one moment a kind of mystical crisis which was awful. I felt afterwards that the man had an abnormal love of power over younger men which sprang from some sexual distortion.

One thinks immediately of Mr. Silvero's "caressing hands" in "Gerontion" and about the sexual-"mystical" nexus that features in earlier poems by Eliot. But fascinatingly, Eliot's letter isn't only expressing a younger man's erotic aversion to an older one, nor is it simply homophobic. His letter about Prichard, written in response to Hale's concern about her own connection with a female student, reassures her that such mutual regard is "perfectly good normal and right." What seems "abnormal" about Prichard is his love of power and domination over the young. Is it possible that these themes have lain unnoticed in "Gerontion" for a hundred years? In a later letter to Hale dated March 6, 1933, Eliot elaborates:

> [Prichard] wanted to dominate, to possess, a young man as no one I have ever known has wanted to possess a young man's soul. And then there were, I estimate, about twenty seconds when I was alone in my room in a Paris boarding house, when I just was sure that I had gone over the edge: and I had a vision of hell which I must believe few people ever get: I just hung on, but thinking that *I* was completely gone, blown to pieces.

Here, Eliot appears to be thinking about his own homoerotic temptations. He is also—and just as importantly—thinking about the spiritual evil of wanting to control the soul of any other person. Mirroring the fears of the governess in Henry James's "The Turn of the Screw," a story he tells Hale he is lecturing on the next day in a Harvard undergraduate class, "Evil" is about the desire to possess another's will.[4]

Although these revelations can hardly be said to resolve the obscurities of "Gerontion," they just as certainly open provocative new windows into the poem and what Frances Dickey has called its "vocabulary of fear and sin—'depraved,' 'confusion,' 'fear,' 'unnatural vices,' 'impudent crimes,' 'wrath,' and 'terror' (twice)." This language, Dickey argues, "suggests that the power struggle with Prichard and his vision of hell remained with Eliot and infuse the poem."[5] Without reducing "Gerontion" to autobiography, Eliot's letters to Hale have altered the poem's meaning in ways that can be debated but not effaced. "Henceforward in discussions of 'Gerontion,'" writes Jayme Stayer, "the complexity of Eliot's relationship to Prichard will add depth to these lines … What biographical facts remain hidden, what became transformed into Mr. Silvero, and what elements were wholly invented by Eliot are now open questions."[6] John Haffenden's editorial notes to the Eliot–Hale letters, available only since 2023, direct readers to Prichard as a source for "Gerontion" as well.

"Gerontion" also contains some notoriously anti-Semitic lines, beginning "My house is a decayed house, / And the Jew squats on the window-sill, the owner" (*Poems1* 31). Eliot's letters to Hale expose more of his casual (and occasionally caustic) prejudice than either his poems or his other correspondence. They also indicate its limits. The potentially programmatic anti-Semitism suggested in "Gerontion"—the notion that Jews are expropriating a moribund Europe—fortunately goes undeveloped; in fact, Eliot rejects the fascist version of that idea, ridiculing Oswald Mosley for "declaiming at the Jews in the Albert Hall."[7] Later, in a published essay, he expresses "the gravest anxiety" over the treatment of French Jews by the Vichy regime and hopes that the French Church will "rise to protest" (*Prose6* 180).[8] We also see, though, that even the limits to Eliot's anti-Semitism have their limits, as when he tells Hale he is "distressed for the fate of the Jews in Vienna" but quickly adds that he would prefer, nevertheless, that not *too* many Austrian Jewish academics settle in England (March 29, 1938). In this case, the "new" texts do not significantly change our reading of "Gerontion." If anything, they confirm what most readers already thought the lines about the Jewish landlord meant, and "Gerontion," instead, takes its place as part of an evolving pattern of prejudice in Eliot's thinking whose outlines the new texts allow us to discern more precisely.

This collection seeks to guide readers through the new materials that are available for the first time outside of restricted archives and to welcome unabashedly fresh approaches to Eliot. The paragon of literary modernism, Eliot continues to be an author whom critics love to hate (Misogynist! Reactionary! Anti-Semite!) and readers love to devour (Profound! Revolutionary! Resonant!). Why does one figure elicit such different responses? While Eliot's influence on literary studies and modern poetry is immense, 90 percent of Eliot scholarship has been conducted without knowledge of 90 percent of what Eliot actually wrote in his lifetime, as Ronald Schuchard, the general editor of the *Complete Prose*, has colorfully estimated. *Eliot Now* collects emerging and established voices in Eliot studies to begin to correct that oversight, integrating contemporary critical approaches with sustained attention to the newly published materials. Whether grappling with the controversial two-volume *Poems*, narrating the experience of opening Eliot's letters in the Emily Hale papers, or rereading Eliot's works through ecocritical or trans studies lenses, *Eliot Now* shows how this most renowned twentieth-century literary catalyst continues to change the way we read literature today.

There are reasons why "Eliot Now" may seem an untimely slogan. In many minds, Eliot remains the embodiment of the European canon, of a dated model of historical literary progression, of ideas of greatness and influence that have grown increasingly unpalatable since the 1970s. For Cynthia Ozick in 1989, Eliot represented a tarnished yet nostalgic concept of "the power and prestige of high art"; today, as English departments talk of decolonizing their curricula, Eliot appears to stand at the center of the empire.[9] No less for us than for Ozick, numerous keywords of literary study as we learned it are associated with Eliot's direct and indirect influence. Today, amid many innovative and evolving ways to think through literary analysis, history, and values, Eliot's idea of literature may well seem, like Gerontion's, a "decayed house." What place, if any, can Eliot take in a renovated, reconceived, globalized, decolonized literary culture and the scholarship that attends to it?

Since 1980, Eliot has gone from being virtually the epitome of modernism to being an important modernist. That is appropriate in an expanding canon. The new Eliot texts tend to humanize and demystify him further. "Eliot" often appears in these materials as a work in progress, not the arbiter of literary taste, making us ask how and why he came to fill that role, a question as much about literary studies as it is about Eliot. The essays in *Eliot Now* are no hagiography: instead, they endeavor to place what we now know of Eliot—his poetry, his criticism, his life—in contemporary discussions about the value of the humanities, of literature, of canon-formation and canon-dismantling. As the debates about what constitutes an education continue, his focus on the value of the humanities for living a meaningful life remains pivotal. For some of our contributors this book's title could end in an affirmative exclamation point—*Eliot Now!*—for others more of a dubious question mark—*Eliot, Now?*—but for all, and we hope for our readers, thinking through Eliot remains a dynamic and productive method of literary-critical self-scrutiny.

This book is divided into three sections, "New Eliot," "Eliot in Theory," and "Looking Ahead." In "New Eliot," experts shed light on the recently published materials—the poems, prose, and correspondence—and how Eliot as poet, critic, and historical figure has been transformed by their revelations. Our contributors ask us to note that they could have written so much more, had we given them the space, about what we've learned of Eliot through the new publications; yet their work shows clearly what profound difference those texts have made already. The second section, "Eliot in Theory," takes advantage of these new materials to read Eliot in conjunction with contemporary literary approaches. Engaging topics urgent for our literary fields—for example, lyric theory and post-critique—as well as urgent for our world—environmentalism, race, and gender—this section builds on Eliot as a critical monument to show his relevance today. We strove to include critics at various stages of their careers, representing different and sometimes conflicting views. The final section looks ahead, beyond "Eliot" (hence his disappearance from the section title), to his immense influence on the humanities in the academy and on culture at large. We include two additional timely political and politicizing topics in "Eliot, Brexit, and the Idea of Europe" and "Afterword. Strange God: Eliot Now" to think through the importance of a healthy Europe in Eliot's worldview for global stability and the relationship between Eliot's Christian Europe and historical racism. Urmila Seshagiri's "Afterword" acts as one concluding gesture of our collection, asking what becomes of Eliot's poetry in light of the disturbing elements of his social theory.

Finally, to illustrate Eliot's continued relevance for twenty-first-century verse, the volume ends with six poets' commentary on one hundred years of *The Waste Land*. This section too is sustained by our theoretical impetus, balancing critique with creative response. This forum on *The Waste Land*'s centenary honors the memory of James Longenbach, who contributed an essay not long before his death. The volume thus aims to use new theoretical approaches, examine new texts, and elicit the voices of poets themselves in order to show how Eliot now is Eliot new.

* * *

The editors are grateful to those who have made the publication of *Eliot Now* possible. Ben Doyle and Laura Cope at Bloomsbury worked with us patiently and valiantly, even through a pandemic. The International T. S. Eliot Society, the Modernist Studies Association, the Modern Language Association, and the T. S. Eliot International Summer School provided venues where a number of the chapters received first hearings. Our generous colleagues Jean Lutes, Seth Pollins, Kamran Javadizadeh, and Jayme Stayer offered thoughtful readings, advice, and encouragement, and several Villanova graduate students (particularly Nicholas Manai and Jamie Wojtal) rendered valuable research assistance. A visiting faculty fellowship at St. Edmund Hall, University of Oxford, provided time and space for germinating the project. Grants from the Subvention of Publication Program at Villanova University and the Office of Research Services at Loyola University Chicago underwrote the indexing and supplemental editing of the volume. Sheri Vandermolen went far beyond the call of duty in her copy editing of the text. Our sincere appreciation to all who are mentioned here, to the many other friends and colleagues who fortified us in these challenging times, and to our families for their love and support.

Notes

1 See *Poems1* 467 for textual history and arguments about the dating of the first TS, and *Poems2* 339–41 for additional textual details.
2 Eliot to Grover Smith, July 4, 1949 (*Poems1* 468).
3 March 24, 1931 (Eliot–Hale). On Prichard's critical philosophy and its relation to Eliot, see John D. Morgenstern, "The Modern Bacchanal: Eliot and Matisse," in *The Edinburgh Companion to T. S. Eliot and the Arts*, edited by Frances Dickey and John D. Morgenstern (Edinburgh: Edinburgh University Press, 2016), 51–68.
4 We now have access to these lecture notes in the *Complete Prose* (*Prose4* 758–809).
5 Frances Dickey, "Outing Mr. Silvero," presented at *International T. S. Eliot Society: 41st Annual Meeting*, online, October 2, 2020.
6 Jayme Stayer, "The Temptations of the Hale Archive," *Time Present: The Newsletter of the T. S. Eliot Society* 103 (2021): 1–2.
7 March 25, 1935 (Eliot–Hale).
8 *The Christian News-Letter* 97 (September 3, 1941).
9 Cynthia Ozick, "T. S. Eliot at 101," *New Yorker*, November 20, 1989: 119–54.

2

The New *Poems of T. S. Eliot*

Mark Ford

In a wide-ranging lecture entitled "Fifty Years of American Poetry," delivered in 1962, Randall Jarrell dwelt briefly but memorably on the strange case of T. S. Eliot, and on the academic industry that his poetic oeuvre and critical tenets had spawned. Jarrell exclaims:

> Won't the future say to us in helpless astonishment: "But did you actually believe that all those things about objective correlatives, classicism, the tradition, applied to *his* poetry? Surely you must have seen that he was one of the most subjective and daemonic poets who ever lived, the victim and helpless beneficiary of his own inexorable compulsions, obsessions? From a psychoanalytical point of view he was far and away the most interesting poet of your century. But for you, of course, after the first few years, his poetry existed undersea, thousands of feet below that deluge of exegesis, explication, source listing, scholarship, and criticism that overwhelmed it. And yet how bravely and personally it survived, its eyes neither coral nor mother-of-pearl but plainly human, full of human anguish!"[1]

Over the six decades since Jarrell's acute formulation of the division between the "human anguish" conveyed by Eliot's poetry and the multiple competing interpretations that it has inspired, Eliot's poetic canon has been greatly expanded: first by a trade edition of *Poems Written in Early Youth* (1967) and the drafts of *The Waste Land* (1971); then, in 1996, by Christopher Ricks's copiously annotated edition of the early notebook that Eliot provisionally entitled *Inventions of the March Hare*, a volume of over four hundred pages that also includes in an appendix a selection of the "improper" Columbo and Bolo verses; and finally (in all senses of the word), in 2015, by Ricks and Jim McCue's definitive *Poems of T. S. Eliot*, whose two volumes run to nearly two thousand pages and gather up every squib and clerihew penned by the master's hand.

And meanwhile the "deluge of exegesis," to use Jarrell's term, has ebbed and flowed in all manner of peculiar and unlikely waves. Certain critics writing in the 1980s and 1990s, for instance, posited a shadowy queer Eliot, whose most famous poem was the result of an erotically charged encounter between a dominant *miglior fabbro* and a submissive hysteric; "The male modernist anus," argued Wayne Koestenbaum, for instance, "a barren, intrinsically unprocreative zone, achieves a weird flowering—lilacs out of the dead land—when men collaborate: Pound penetrates Eliot's waste land, and fills the hollow man with child."[2]

Maybe so, but Eliot's *Poems* now ends on a vigorously heterosexual note, with a limerick culled from *Valerie's Own Book* (the title Eliot gave to two notebooks in which he wrote out for his second wife selections of his published and unpublished poems).[3] The first of these notebooks concludes, as does Ricks and McCue's edition of his poetry, with "The Blameless Sister of Publicola," a poem dated September 16, 1959, some two and three-quarter years after Eliot had married his secretary, Valerie Fletcher. It begins:

> I know a nice girl named Valeria
> Who has a delicious posterior (*Poems2* 290)

A note points us to the relevant passage in *Coriolanus* from which Eliot derived his title, knowledge of which adds a piquant literary sauciness to the poem, for the Valeria in Shakespeare's play is famous for her modesty:

> The noble sister of Publicola,
> The moon of Rome, chaste as the icicle
> That's curdied by the frost from purest snow,
> And hangs on Dian's Temple—dear Valeria![4]

The contrast between Shakespeare's paragon of modesty and her less inhibited namesake clearly affords the still relatively newly wedded couple an added thrill.

"The more we know of Eliot," Pound famously declared of his protégé, "the better"—a quote used by Faber & Faber as jacket copy for Volume I of Ricks and McCue's awe-inspiringly thorough and authoritative edition. I suppose, to be truly "complete," the editors had no choice but to include even verses so clearly meant for private consumption as "The Blameless Sister of Publicola" and "Sleeping Together" ("My fingers move softly below, to her navel, / And touch the delicate down beneath her navel, / Coming to rest on the hair between her thighs" [*Poems1* 317]) or "How the Tall Girl's Breasts Are" ("like ripe pears that dangle / Above my mouth / Which reaches up to take them" [*Poems1* 318]). Yet there can surely be no doubt that Eliot himself would have been appalled and enraged had any Tiresias-style seer predicted to him the publication—and by the firm that he made famous!—of such frank and intimate commemorations of the sexual acts performed on his own divan or bed.

"I am Lazarus, come from the dead," Eliot's first haunted protagonist, J. Alfred Prufrock, wistfully imagines declaring, over tea, to a Boston society hostess, "Come back to tell you all" (*Poems1* 8). Eliot's personal obsession with the posthumous, with the traffic between the living and the departed that features so prominently in all periods of his work—"this pendulum in the head / Swinging from life to death," as he puts it in *The Waste Land*-related fragment "Song" (*Poems1* 284)—can't help but frame the literary resurrection of all the drafts and fragments and discarded poems that Eliot chose not to publish in his life. There is always an element of the Lazarus-like in editions that significantly alter the lineaments of a canonical author's work, perhaps especially so for a poet-editor who had exerted such complete control over the presentation of successive editions, including the publication of two *Collected Poems*—that of 1936, which ends with *Burnt Norton*, and that of 1963, which remained, until 2015, the standard means of consuming Eliot. Like the edition of Ricks and McCue, the 1963 *Collected* concludes with a poem addressed to Valerie, but "A Dedication to My Wife"—a poem apparently so disliked by F. R. Leavis that in his copy he stapled up the page—evinces a guarded awareness of the boundary between private and public wholly absent from the Tall Girl poems: "But this dedication," it concludes, "is for others to read: / These are private words addressed to you in public" (*Poems1* 219). After so much psycho-sexual speculation about the sources of Eliot's poetry, "A Dedication to My Wife" registers as Eliot finally settling a troubling canard, or as at long last washing his clean linen in public. In a letter of August 1964 to Cyril Connolly, thanking him for mentioning this poem in his review of the *Collected*, Eliot muses: "It would almost seem that some readers were shocked that I should be happy" (*Poems1* 1061).

But even the more relaxed Eliot of the years of his second marriage was unequivocally opposed to annotated editions of his poetry. In November 1962 he made clear in a letter addressed to Henry Willink, the Master of Magdalene College, Cambridge, that he was unmovable on this point—notwithstanding the fact that he had himself provided the mock-scholarly notes to *The Waste Land*: "I will not," he declared, "allow any academic critic (and there are plenty of these in America only too willing) to provide notes of explanation to be published with any of my poems" (*Poems1* xvi–xvii). This aversion is perhaps best glossed by his discussion of meaning in *The Use of Poetry and the Use of Criticism* of 1933: "The chief use of the 'meaning' of a poem, in the ordinary sense, may be … to satisfy one habit of the reader, to keep his mind diverted and quiet, while the poem does its work upon him: much as the imaginary burglar is always provided with a bit of nice meat for the house-dog" (*Prose4* 690). This suggests a high romantic or even mystical concept of poetry as capable of accomplishing its true, if inexplicable, "work" only at those moments when it is successful in tranquilizing the rational quest for meaning; and fussing around with footnotes can only dilute the potency of this primary experience. Eliot undoubtedly believed that "genuine poetry can communicate before it is understood," to quote from his 1929 essay on Dante, in which he reflects at length on the complex ratio between "enjoyment" and "understanding," between "the direct shock of poetic intensity" and rational comprehension:

> In my own experience of the appreciation of poetry I have always found that the less I knew about the poet and his work, before I began to read it, the better … I was passionately fond of certain French poetry long before I could have translated two verses of it correctly. With Dante the discrepancy between enjoyment and understanding was wider still. (*Prose3* 700–1)

So it is possible that Eliot would not have wholly agreed with Pound's statement that the more we know of him, the better.

The dialectic between letting go, between dreamy immersion in the numinous but half-understood—*The Waste Land*'s "awful daring of a moment's surrender" (*Poems1* 70)—and its antithesis, the "great labour" involved in acquiring what "Tradition and the Individual Talent" calls the "historical sense" (uncompromisingly defined as knowledge of both "the whole of the literature of Europe from Homer" and of "the whole of the literature of [the poet's] own country" [*Prose2* 106]), was as central to Eliot's imaginative processes as the dialogue between the living and the dead. And it is a dialectic that makes its presence felt in almost every engagement with his poetry: is one responding to the "human anguish" or piecing together his allusions to Joseph Conrad or St. John of the Cross or his use of anthropological references?

This brings me to the exhaustive parade of possible echoes or sources or revealing analogues that Ricks and McCue append to almost every word and phrase in Eliot's poetry. By now Eliot scholars will have come—at least partially—to grips with the truly breathtaking erudition marshaled by Ricks and McCue and the dizzying range of links that they adduce between Eliot's deployment of even the most ordinary words and these words' appearance in previous—and subsequent—texts of all kinds. In a review of these volumes for the *London*

Review of Books,[5] I cited examples from Ricks and McCue's annotations to the opening lines of "The Love Song of J. Alfred Prufrock," which include quotations from texts as diverse as *Acts and Resolutions of the 29th General Assembly of Iowa* (1902), which records a payment made to one R. D. Bennett "for sprinkling a certain street"; from *High Sierra* (1940), by the crime novelist W. R. Burnett, which uses the phrase "one-night stand"; and from *The Secrets of the Great City: A Work Descriptive of the Virtues and the Vices, the Mysteries, Miseries and Crimes of New York City* (1868), in which the phrase "cheap hotels" occurs (*Poems1* 377, 379). The net they cast, in other words, is very, very wide. In the years since this review was published, however, I have come both to treasure and to respect the only slightly insane thoroughness with which they weave a context for every aspect of the Eliotic—even his pronunciation of particular words on his recordings: we are told, for instance, that in his readings of "Prufrock" Eliot always sounds the final *t* in restaurants and, further, that the "OED also gives a pronunciation in which it is not sounded, and the spelling of its first citation, from Fenimore Cooper, 1827, points to the French derivation: 'At the most renowned of the Parisian restaurans' (*The Prairie* II ii 28)" (*Poems1* 379). "Well," to borrow a line from Philip Larkin's "Wild Oats," "useful to get that learnt."[6]

One grows accustomed, then, to the initially mind-blowing compendiousness of this edition's commentary, rather as one does to, say, Wikipedia or the *OED*. I would never have known, or thought to find out, that dogfighting was outlawed in England and Wales in 1835, had I not looked up Ricks and McCue's note to "who sharpen the tooth of the dog, meaning / Death" ("Marina," *Poems1* 777); nor that a snifter of brandy, if taken medicinally, did not violate America's prohibition laws, had I not turned to their gloss on the last line of "Sweeney Erect" ("And a glass of brandy neat" [*Poems1* 506]); nor that "the de Courtenays were feudal holders of the East and West Coker manors from the thirteenth to the sixteenth centuries and enjoyed mixed fortunes over generations," were I not curious about the source of the phrase "Houses rise and fall" in *East Coker* (*Poems1* 929); nor that ether was first used for pain relief at Massachusetts General Hospital in 1846 (Prufrock's "etherised upon a table" [*Poems1* 377]); nor that sulfate of iron was prescribed for constipation by Edward John Waring in his *Manual of Practical Therapeutics* (3rd edition, 1871), a fact deemed relevant to the juxtaposition of "iron" and "merds" in "Gerontion" (*Poems1* 473); and so on. A number of notes, such as the one concerning the de Courtenays, are crowdsourced; that is, they derive from personal communications to the editors from a busy cadre of allusion-spotters. In this, these volumes again resemble the *OED* or Wikipedia, for they are in part a collective enterprise. Inevitably the poet himself is also a major, if inadvertent, contributor to the vast web of intertextuality underlying his work that the commentary presents, and every nook and cranny of his archive has been scoured for possible clues: in Scofield Thayer's copy of *Ara Vos Prec*, for instance, in which "Gerontion" was first published, Eliot added a number of penciled marginalia. Beside the line "The goat coughs at night in the field overhead," he wrote "Cf. Wyndham Lewis: *The Enemy of the Stars*," referring to a 1914 play by Lewis published in *Blast* in which Lewis uses the phrase "coughing like a goat" (*Poems1* 473).

It should be stressed that the parallels posited by Ricks and McCue and their band of disciples rarely, in practice, work to demystify the Eliot line or image in question. This may in part be because the transformation achieved is complete ("Those are pearls that were his eyes' "); the fragment, that is, is so saturated with the emotional charge it receives from its new context that it strikes the reader as successfully stolen, to use Eliot's own critical phraseology, rather than merely borrowed. Certainly their notes nudge toward a particular interpretation far less than those of B. C. Southam, whose *A Student Guide to the Selected Poems of T. S. Eliot* (first published in 1968, now in its sixth edition) shaped the attempts of generations of undergraduates to decode Eliot and sent them scurrying off to read Laforgue and Corbière and Baudelaire and Donne and Webster and Dante and Lancelot Andrewes, to name some of the most obvious, in the hope of somehow getting the *echt* Eliot experience. This edition exponentially expands these further reading lists. The immensely valuable index to the editorial material itself runs to twenty-five pages in double columns, and it seems that all sorts of writers whom Eliot either rarely referred to in his critical prose or treated somewhat disdainfully contributed to the process of seeding the seabed of his memory, to generating whispers in the labyrinthine echo chamber of his auditory imagination. This is particularly true when one looks up his American forebears, who, when mentioned in his critical prose, tend to be damned, at best, with faint praise: Whitman garners some thirty entries, Emerson twenty, and even John Greenleaf Whittier and Henry Wadsworth Longfellow are credited as possible poetic influences on a handful of occasions each.

Textually, these volumes also aim at inclusiveness. Ricks and McCue felt compelled, surely rightly, to preserve the 1963 *Collected Poems*, although it is likely to bemuse those who aren't paid-up Eliot buffs to register that this "deathbed" edition of his poetry occupies a little over a tenth of the total page count. The "Uncollected Poems" section of Volume I brings together *Inventions of the March Hare* (including the excised leaves on which Eliot had copied out ribald pieces such as "The Triumph of Bullshit" and "Ballade pour la grosse Lulu," although a case might have been made for relegating them to the "Improper Rhymes" section of Volume II); all the rejected drafts relating to the composition of *The Waste Land*, such as "The Death of the Duchess," "Exequy," and the exceedingly unpleasant "Dirge" ("Full fathom five your Bleistein lies / Under the flatfish and the squids. / Graves' Disease in a dead jew's eyes!" [*Poems1* 285]); a range of not particularly amusing occasional poems addressed to such as John Hayward and Geoffrey Faber; various *Cats* outtakes; the never-before-seen Tall Girl poems; as well as a second dedication to Valerie that ends, like *The Waste Land*, with three spaced-out—but far less ambiguous—words:

> Love   adoration   desire (*Poems1* 319)

In Volume II, which really *is* for hard-core Eliot aficionados only, we get *Old Possum's Book of Practical Cats* (amazingly, the commentary is two pages longer than the text itself!); *Anabasis* (in parallel text with the original French); pages and pages of clubman Eliot's "witty" rhymes; and all forty-nine stanzas of the tediously scatological and racist *The Columbiad*—the first time it has been published in full. I rather wish I didn't know that Eliot copied out stanzas such as the following—which in the current climate should probably come with a trigger-warning—into *Valerie's Own Book* for their shared delectation:

> One day King Bolo from the shore
> Began to cheer and chortle.
> He cried "I see Columbo's ass
> A shitting through a porthole."
> His big black queen set up a shout
> And all his swarthy vassals
> And the band stuck up the national hymn
> Of "Hairy Balls and Ass-Holes." (*Poems2* 276)

It is odd, and possibly revealing, that when compiling *Valerie's Own Book* he chose to interleave such verses with poems in which he seems at his most earnest: he interrupts, for example, his transcription of part V of *East Coker* with four stanzas from *The Columbiad*, clearly enjoying the intercutting of such high-minded pronouncements as "Love is most nearly itself / When here and now cease to matter" (*Poems1* 191) with King Bolo's address to his "Big Black Queen":

> "For," said he, "who is there on our isle
>   At once so sweet and sooty?
>   At once so fresh and fruity?
>   At once so rough and rooty?" (*Poems2* 283)

Behind those "features of clerical cut" stirred a "thousand sordid images" ("Lines for Cuscuscaraway and Mirza Murad Ali Beg," *Poems1* 143; "Preludes," 16).

These volumes, then, present Eliot the poet, or rather Eliot the poet/versifier, warts and all. A poem like "Dedication II" might easily serve for a Hallmark Valentine's Day card, while, at the other extreme, the King Bolo saga casts a lurid light on his racial anxieties, to use the kindest possible term, as well as his schoolboy delight in sharing with fellow connoisseurs such as Conrad Aiken, Pound, Lewis, Bonamy Dobrée, and then his second wife, the offensive and obscene. The publication in full of Eliot's gleeful but dispiriting "improper" rhymes does, however, accentuate the extent to which, especially from "The Hollow Men" on, his imagination achieved moving and meaningful poetic expression by sublimating the base and physical and traumatizing into their antithesis: the abstract, the rarefied, the mystical. The poems themselves often dramatize this process, as in "Eyes that last I saw in tears":

> The golden vision reappears
> I see the eyes but not the tears
> This is my affliction. (*Poems1* 139)

The transition into the overlapping realms of poetry, death, and dream causes the tears to vanish, but at a price that is not easy to calculate: this poem, initially published in 1924 as the first of "Doris's Dream Songs," results in the ominous but vague "affliction"; by the end of *Little Gidding* of nearly twenty years later, it has escalated into an all-consuming mystical self-abnegation, "costing," as Eliot the ascetic puts it, "not less than everything" (*Poems1* 209). What the adept receives in compensation are "golden vision[s]" like the trance-state of the first section of *Burnt Norton*, in which desire is sublimated as we watch, transformed into the symbols of calm and perfection:

> And the pool was filled with water out of sunlight,
> And the lotos rose, quietly, quietly,
> The surface glittered out of heart of light (*Poems1* 180)

The metaphysical redemption gestured toward in such moments is a far cry from the visceral agony endured by more directly masochistic early Eliot saints, such as St. Sebastian, who flogs himself until his blood shines in the lamplight, or St. Narcissus, who achieves a satisfaction that is almost sexual by willfully submitting to physical pain.

"The Love Song of St. Sebastian" and "The Death of Saint Narcissus" (whose opening lines were reworked for *The Waste Land*) are likely the two most significant Eliot poems not to feature in his 1963 *Collected*. Eliot was clearly troubled by the implications of the latter. It was submitted by Pound to *Poetry* in May of 1916 and accepted for that year's September edition, only for instructions to be issued for its withdrawal (the galleys are scored through, and "Kill" written on them). Eliot claimed not to have "the foggiest recollection" of the piece when Hayward was putting together material for the twelve-copies-only edition of *Poems Written in Early Youth* of 1950 (where it is rather out of place, for it was probably composed in 1915), but he agreed to its inclusion, and presumably proofread it—only to have second thoughts, reflecting in a 1953 letter that he wished he had destroyed it (*Poems1* 1066, 1154). The angst it displays is of a piece with that animating poems such as "The Love Song of J. Alfred Prufrock," especially the excised "Prufrock's Pervigilium" material, or "Rhapsody on a Windy Night," particularly in lines such as "If he walked in city streets / He seemed to tread on faces, convulsive thighs and knees" (*Poems1* 270); but the possible solutions tried out are far more extreme: a series of Ovidian transformations allows the poem's protagonist to imagine himself first as a tree solipsistically "tangling its roots among each other," then as a fish whose "slippery white belly" is "held tight in his own fingers, / Writhing in his own clutch," and finally as a young girl raped by a drunken old man. This experience schizophrenically divides him, forcing him to taste "his own whiteness / The horror of his own smoothness," but also makes him feel "drunken and old." Only by deploying the desert-hermit-martyr imagery, toward which Eliot would so often be drawn, can this schism be resolved:

> He danced on the hot sand
> Until the arrows came.
> As he embraced them his white skin surrendered itself to the redness of blood, and satisfied him. (*Poems1* 271)

The poem entwines the self-infatuated classical Narcissus with his Christian namesake, the second-century Bishop of Jerusalem, who for many years lived as a desert recluse; and it is the religious self-sacrifice prompted by the example of the bishop that at last puts an end—but again, at what cost?—to the "inexorable compulsions, obsessions," to borrow Jarrell's terms, acted out in the poem: "Now he is green," it ends, "dry and stained / With the shadow in his mouth."

Eliot included "The Love Song of St. Sebastian" in a letter to Conrad Aiken of July 25, 1914, in which he expresses a worry that the poem is "morbid, or forced" (*Poems1* 1142). It is certainly morbid, and much rude forcing happens in it. Reprising Robert Browning's "Porphyria's Lover," its speaker is one of those

Eliot characters, like Sweeney of *Sweeney Agonistes*, compelled to confess to his urge to "do a girl in" (*Poems1* 124). His motivations are more complex, however, than those of Sweeney or of Browning's outrageously boastful psychopath, for he oscillates between the poles of deadly mastery and utter submission, between active self-torture and clinically denoted violence against his beloved. "I would come in a shirt of hair," he proclaims in the opening line, as one might plausibly expect from a saint; his masochism extends, however, to hour after hour of self-flagellation at the foot of her stair, as if he were enacting some bizarre initiation ritual, at the end of which protracted "torture and delight," he arises her "neophyte," ready to follow where she leads (*Poems1* 265–6). The poem reveals Eliot at his most gothic and gruesome—as both "victim and helpless beneficiary" of the circuitry of his imagination:

> Then you would take me in
> Because I was hideous in your sight
> You would take me in without shame
> Because I should be dead (*Poems1* 266)

The speaker's self-mutilation and imagined death appear to be a precondition of his being taken in "without shame," and also to license his fantastical murder of the woman in the poem's second paragraph. The strangling in which the poem climaxes is achieved slowly and quasi-erotically—and it is the protagonist's hideousness or "infamy" that seems to underlie it, as if he were some latter-day De Flores, driven to make her his "semblable," as Middleton and Rowley's disfigured henchman does Beatrice-Joanna at the conclusion of *The Changeling*:

> And I should love you the more because I mangled you
> And because you were no longer beautiful
> To anyone but me. (*Poems1* 266)

Elements of this ghoulish zero-sum transaction can be found in figurations of the erotic throughout Eliot's poetic oeuvre—until, that is, the arrival into his life of Valerie, a turn of events as miraculous as the denouement of any of the late Shakespeare plays that meant so much to him.

Although it has been many decades since such poems were known only to Eliot cognoscenti, it is good to have them assembled in the volumes that will operate for the foreseeable future as the standard text of his poetry. In fact all of the poems collected in *Inventions of the March Hare* offer fascinating perspectives on the young dandy's development, and his overwhelming infatuation (there can be no other term) with Jules Laforgue. It can feel almost like watching a game of transatlantic poetic tennis, as Eliot, with elegant *politesse*, deftly returns Laforgue's cunningly flighted serve, settles into a steady rally of self-mocking ironies, or advances *faux*-boldly to the net to volley away the sublime:

> And Life, a little bald and gray,
> Languid, fastidious, and bland,
> Waits, hat and gloves in hand,
> Punctilious of tie and suit
> (Somewhat impatient of delay)
> On the doorstep of the Absolute. (*Poems1* 239)

On occasion Eliot could be somewhat coy about his early debt to Laforgue, whom he never, for instance, quite gets around to naming in the 1919 piece in the *Egoist*, "Reflections on Contemporary Poetry," where he expresses most fully the "ineffaceable" impact of the French poet's work on him, a force he compares to an all-transforming love affair:

> This relation is a feeling of profound kinship, or rather of a peculiar personal intimacy, with another, probably a dead author. It may overcome us suddenly, on first or after long acquaintance; it is certainly a crisis; and when a young writer is seized with his first passion of this sort he may be changed, metamorphosed almost, within a few weeks even; from a bundle of second-hand sentiments into a person. (*Prose2* 66)

A few of Ricks's *Inventions of the March Hare* notes have actually been trimmed in the process of their transposition to this new edition, but there are still plenty of cross-references to help flesh out the "profound kinship" that Eliot felt with the most decisively invigorating of his early precursors.

Eliot reported himself pleased to learn that this notebook, which had been acquired by John Quinn in 1922, along with the manuscript of *The Waste Land*, had disappeared at some point after Quinn's death a couple of years later. Both eloquently testify to his shrewdness as a self-editor—although it goes without saying that Pound also played a crucial role in the excisions and improvements made to the latter. The fascination exerted by Eliot's draft material, even when one can see that he was right not to publish it, might be taken as an index of the fascination of the literary persona that he constructed in both poetry and prose, and which has made even his juvenilia and false starts resemble an old master's preliminary sketches or pentimenti, to be pored over and deciphered and related to the work that he did eventually bring to the public's attention. Eliot was conscious that, as far as his own reputation was concerned, less was more, and that making a splash with his very best efforts at judiciously chosen intervals was the way to increase both market share and market value. Ever since Pound read "The Love Song of J. Alfred Prufrock" in 1914 and trumpeted his find by declaring that Eliot had, in some uncanny way, "modernized himself ON HIS OWN," those who have fallen under its spell have sought to understand the alchemical processes that resulted in his poetry (*Poems1* 365). As far as sources go, these volumes indubitably gather all the data, but the transformation remains uncanny, unsettling, unforgettable:

> 'That corpse you planted last year in your garden,
> 'Has it begun to sprout? Will it bloom this year?
> 'Or has the sudden frost disturbed its bed?
> 'O keep the Dog far hence, that's friend to men,
> 'Or with his nails he'll dig it up again!
> 'You! hypocrite lecteur!—mon semblable,—mon frère!' (*Poems1* 57)

Notes

1 Randall Jarrell, "Fifty Years of American Poetry," in *The Third Book of Criticism* (London: Faber), 314–15.
2 Wayne Koestenbaum, *Double Talk: The Erotics of Male Literary Collaboration* (London: Routledge, 1989), 123.
3 The contents are given in *Poems2* 304–5.
4 William Shakespeare, *Coriolanus*, in *The Riverside Shakespeare*, 2nd ed., edited by G. Blakemore Evans et al. (Boston: Houghton Mifflin, 1997), 1480.
5 Mark Ford, "I gotta use words." Rev. of *The Poems of T. S. Eliot*, edited by Christopher Ricks and Jim McCue. *London Review of Books*, August 11, 2016. 9–12. https://www.lrb.co.uk/the-paper/v38/n16/mark-ford/i-gotta-use-words.
6 Philip Larkin, *Collected Poems*, edited by Anthony Thwaite (London: Faber, 1988), 143.

3

The Complete Prose: The Critic's Workshop

Anthony Cuda

Even for a writer whose calculated reserve earned him an unforgettable and lifelong sobriquet, Eliot could be surprisingly insistent upon reticence and restraint in his criticism. More than once he asserts that the good critics should say less, that they should point and be silent, or that they should merely put the reader "in possession of facts" ("The Function of Criticism," *Prose2* 466). And for many years, the austere, compact volumes of his *Selected Essays* and *Selected Prose* seemed models of principled self-discipline: judicious, concentrated, parsimonious even. But now, with the publication of eight new mammoth volumes of his nonfiction prose over the last decade, one begins to wonder. It's a bit like touring a towering, glass-and-metal high rise accompanied by its architect, who professes to deal only in miniatures. This much we know is true: Eliot wrote much more than most readers believed, and scholarship must begin to give an account of it.

As a coeditor of the *Complete Prose*, I feel obliged to rise to this occasion and offer a grand synthesis of his critical corpus; as a scholar and a realist, I know that would be folly. I offer, instead, pertinent background and facts about the edition, including salient through lines that strike me as significant, revelatory, or rich with potential. In short, from the point of view of his critical prose, "Eliot now" is becoming profoundly different from Eliot a decade ago. We are on the cusp of something quite rich and strange.

His influence on subsequent criticism is unassailable, and his essays have long been compulsory reading, but Eliot was never sanguine about the prospect of collecting and reprinting his prose writings. In fact, especially when he was young, he regarded much of his work in the genre as mere journalism, meant to bolster his income and sometimes help him secure an entrée into another circle of London's insular literary culture. Nearing his fiftieth birthday, he wrote to John Hayward, whom he had asked to be his literary executor, in February 1938:

> I have had to write at one time or another a lot of junk in periodicals the greater portion of which ought never to be reprinted. If any of this came to light, you would have to decide … you could take it in general that what I have not published in books by the time of my death I don't consider worth publishing. F[aber] & F[aber] might be tempted, and your job would be to say no. (*Letters8* 800)

Fortunately, his gruff prohibition proved neither lasting nor absolute. Though Eliot suggested, "I can never re-read any of my own prose writings without acute embarrassment" ("The Music of Poetry," *Prose6* 310), he did indeed recognize the value of his front-page *TLS* essays, and he was keenly aware of how much time and intellectual energy he expended on short, occasional pieces, like the regular *Criterion* chronicles of cultural and literary life in London and Europe. In fact, he begins to reconsider almost immediately after forbidding the exhumation of his buried prose, in the same letter to Hayward: "possibly a careful selection might be made of the best commentaries. I don't know." Two decades later, time and the bell had softened his reserve. He told one potential editor: "It may be that there are some of my uncollected contribution to periodicals that are worth preserving, but I feel that it is premature to consider any definitive collection."[1] These and other decisions about uncollected and unpublished writing ultimately fell to Valerie Eliot, who brought out *The Waste Land: A Facsimile* (1971) and volume 1 of the *Letters* (1988) herself, before authorizing Ronald Schuchard and Christopher Ricks to edit and publish *The Varieties of Metaphysical Poetry* (1993) and *Inventions of the March Hare* (1996), respectively. But she had promised Eliot before his death that she would collect and edit his literary remains on her own, and her resolute sense of responsibility prevented her from letting other publications proceed. Scholarship abhors a vacuum, though, and this delay unintentionally encouraged writers to fill the waiting space with partial, skewed, and incomplete portrayals of Eliot. The task facing scholars now is to take stock of his expanded corpus and gauge accurately whether and how it differs from that which we've known.

Background: Filing Cabinets and Parsimony

Although Eliot showed resolute generosity to other poets from behind his desk at Faber, he was a severe and miserly editor of his own work. He oversaw only four major collections of essays during his lifetime: *The Sacred Wood* (1920), *For Lancelot Andrewes* (1928), *On Poetry and Poets* (1957), and, most important, *Selected Essays* (1932, 1934, 1951); the final collection, *To Criticize the Critic*, appeared posthumously, in 1965. Minor collections and printed lectures appeared in several shorter volumes, including *Elizabethan Essays* (1934) and *The Idea of a Christian Society* (1939), which were either incorporated into the larger collections or allowed to go out of print. There were other, minor books, but by the late twentieth century, Eliot's prose canon had dwindled to a mere fraction of his life's work in the genre. The thirty-eight prose pieces assembled in *Selected Essays* (1951) remained the only reliable collection in England.[2] And with even that book unavailable in the United States, readers relied for decades on the thirty-one pieces (some heavily excerpted) reprinted in Frank Kermode's edition, *The Selected Prose of T. S. Eliot* (1975). For most of us, these are the principal sources for reading and teaching Eliot's ideas, which have taken hold as some of the most influential critical perspectives of the last century. *Yet they comprise less than 4 percent of the prose that he wrote during his lifetime.* The majority of scholars who write about Eliot haven't had the chance to read the majority of what he wrote.

It was an old letter from Ted Hughes, who regarded Eliot as "an utterly new species" of poet, that sparked a renaissance in the publication of the poet's criticism.[3] At a private tea in 2004, Ronald Schuchard reminded Valerie Eliot of Hughes's letter to her in 1988, congratulating her on publishing the first volume of the *Letters* and expressing the hope that she would assemble Eliot's prose. After years of reluctance, she agreed that the time had come. "There could not have been for her a more difficult 'yes,'" Schuchard recalls: "after 40 years of devoting herself to the collecting, preserving, transcribing and editing of her husband's works for a complete edition, time and declining health were overtaking her in the task."[4] Schuchard, whom she appointed as general editor, began to assemble an editorial team for the *Complete Prose*, and in the following years the *Letters* and the *Poems* were also commissioned. With support from the Guggenheim Foundation, the Hodson Trust at Johns Hopkins, the T. S. Eliot Editorial Project in England (funded by the Arts and Humanities Research Council), and others, the *Prose* editors set to work collecting the hundreds of articles, reviews, and occasional writings that Eliot composed over the course of his career.

An essential guide to this stage of the project was the revised 1969 edition of Donald Gallup's bibliography, the singular resource upon which Eliot scholars had long relied to track down extant prose items for their own research. The photocopies packed our hanging file folders and jammed our cabinet drawers.

Certain pieces had always been easy to find: his *TLS* leaders, articles from the *Egoist*, broadcast transcripts from the *Listener*, for instance. Others, though, were accompanied by considerable obstacles. To read "Modern Tendencies in Poetry" in its original venue, for instance, the industrious scholar needed to book a flight to one of the three worldwide libraries in possession of the first issue of *Shama'a: A Magazine of Art, Literature & Philosophy*—an obscure Indian journal with ties to the Theosophical Society in Chennai—where the only published version appeared, in April 1920, replete with dozens of typos and misspellings. The Gallup bibliography was a starting point, but the editors discovered its record to be much less complete than expected. With access to numerous archives—especially the newly organized Faber day files and correspondence—editors uncovered an array of unknown, forgotten, or misplaced prose items. Eliot's private archives yielded long-sought gems. And a number of Eliot's letters contain evidence of unknown prose: invitations to speak, letters of gratitude sent after a lecture, and references to unrecorded events, occasions, and one-off publications.

Take, for instance, the lecture on George Chapman that Eliot gave to the Cam Literary Club at Cambridge, in November 1924. He despaired about its rough and unworthy state to Richard Aldington (*Letters2* 531), and four days after delivering it, he told Virginia Woolf that it was "after all my labours … unworthy of subsequent publication" (537). Yet months afterward, the lecture remained on his mind. He still hoped to revise it and publish it in the *Criterion*; he even advertised it in a subscription flyer.[5] Unlisted in Gallup and finally discovered among his private papers, this fugitive lecture sketches out a set of ideas that Eliot revisited and refined for the next decade in his plays, a theory that explains why some characters seem to be "listening for other voices and … conducting a conversation with spectres" ("A Neglected Aspect of Chapman," *Prose2* 553). Other correspondence led to the discovery of an unrecorded publication that was printed in the *Chichester Diocesan Gazette*, composed after Eliot spent a weekend in Chichester at the invitation of G. K. A. Bell. In the essay "If I Were a Dean," he proposes to make every "cathedral the centre of religious and artistic activity in its diocese" and to bring all of the "resources of art" to bear upon it (*Prose4* 298). Yet another passing reference provided the clues for uncovering an address he gave for the Save the Children Fund at the invitation of its president, Noel Buxton. After the talk, Eliot casually handed Buxton the sole copy of his script, which was later printed (and promptly forgotten) in their periodical, *The World's Children*. Letters to editors, unsigned reviews, fugitive lectures: in the final tally, the editors unearthed several hundred items that were not in the Gallup bibliography.

In Possession of Facts

Bearing in mind Eliot's admonition about facts, I would be remiss if I neglected to offer some basic factual dimensions of an edition so recent and massive (*Prose2* 466). In its hardcover and PDF versions, the eight-volume *Complete Prose* contains 6,540 pages. The volumes assemble a total of 1,077 prose items, ranging from book reviews and chronicles to essays, lectures, letters to the editor, even short fiction. Of those, 116 had not been previously published anywhere: they appear in the *Complete Prose* for the first time. And an additional 171 were not recorded in the Gallup bibliography; many of these were unsigned reviews, so even Eliot specialists were often unaware of their existence.

Eliot really began his career as a prose writer in 1916, when he went from laboring over arcane graduate essays and dissertation chapters to publishing some twenty-five reviews on topics ranging from nihilism and epic poetry to Bergson and Euripides. From 1916 until his death, the only year in which he wrote fewer than ten pieces of prose was 1922, when he was still recovering from a breakdown, suffering a series of illnesses (*Letters1* 666), and navigating the complex emergence of two landmark publications: the first issue of the *Criterion* and, of course, *The Waste Land*. His most prolific year (measured by publication count alone) came shortly thereafter: 1927 features no fewer than fifty-four pieces of prose.

Publication of the *Complete Prose* occurred over the course of five years, with the first two volumes appearing in digital form in 2014; the last, in 2019.[6] An updated version of the full edition was released in hardcover in March 2021, with numerous slight errors revised throughout and, more important, an appendix added to volume 8 to contain the unanticipated written statement that Eliot directed his estate to publish upon the unsealing of his letters to Emily Hale, which occurred at Princeton in January 2020.

In the abstract, editorial decisions can seem both fussy and overbearing. But at their best, they quietly guide and reshape the reading experience of a text in illuminating and revelatory ways. For instance: the decision to arrange Eliot's prose writings in chronological order, rather than dividing the edition into published and unpublished prose, or maintaining the integrity of previous collections (i.e., *The Sacred Wood* or *For Lancelot Andrewes*). This seemingly minor decision exerts immediately an effect, integrating Eliot's best-known ideas back into the historical and personal contexts whence they arose, long before his reputation made them seem inevitable. From an early stage, he cultivated an ethos of authority in his reviews, even striking an "occasional note of arrogance" and "cocksureness" that he later regretted ("To Criticize the Critic," *Prose8* 459). This imperious, sometimes churlish tone—along with the thematic arrangement of *Selected Essays*—has lent his prose an unapproachable and marmoreal air of finality and completion. In the *Complete Prose*, readers encounter Eliot's best-known essays in their original contexts—alongside dozens of minor reviews, letters to the editor, broadcasts, and lectures—and they recognize how profoundly contingent and provisional these essays really were, how firmly embedded in history, biography, and circumstance. The irrefutable unity of "The man who suffers" and "the mind which creates" has never been more evident ("Tradition and the Individual Talent," *Prose2* 109).

A prime example: his most widely read and influential essay, "Tradition and the Individual Talent," appears in the *Complete Prose* not as an ungainsayable statement of high modernist aesthetics. Instead, it's part of a continuum, one installment in a series of roughly contemporaneous pieces approaching a similar set of issues. He adopts the same chemistry metaphor in his 1919 lecture for the Arts League of Service ("Modern Tendencies in Poetry," *Prose2* 212–25); he considers the "changing personality of history" in "The Romantic Generation, If It Existed" in July 1919 (*Prose2* 81); and he reflects upon poets who become "bearers of a tradition" in "Reflections on Contemporary Poetry," also published that month (*Prose2* 68). The essays and reviews of these years offer a snapshot of the critic's working studio—containing experiments, fragments, triumphs, early sketches—and afford glimpses into the shifting and unsystematic ideas from which "Tradition" emerged, a pencil drawing that was (in the years to come) inked into print, matted and framed into posterity, and hung upon the wall as abiding doctrine. The chronological arrangement of the *Complete Prose* also allows readers to chart the course of Eliot's intellectual development alongside upheavals in his professional and personal life: the fractious, zealous tone that emerges, for instance, with his conversion to Anglo-Catholicism and is eventually tempered by the war; the profusion of new publication venues after the *Criterion* was shuttered in 1939; the ever-expanding range of his social and political commitments after the war and especially following his Nobel Prize in 1948. During his lifetime, Eliot insisted on including publication dates in his *Selected* editions, in an attempt to offer readers a measure of historical context. Particularly irksome, he writes in "To Criticize the Critic," is how frequently his youthful pronouncements are quoted by critics "as if they had been made yesterday" (*Prose8* 459). In this regard, the *Complete Prose* extends his intention, providing even experienced scholars with a previously impossible glimpse into the processes, changes, and developments of his intellectual commitments, what Eliot himself described as "the chronology, the circumstances under which each essay was written and the motive for writing it" (*Prose8* 456).

General Truths and Rude Jolts

Eliot spent months rereading his own essays and reviews in preparation for a retrospective lecture on his own prose that he was invited to deliver at the University of Leeds in 1961. On October 24, 1960, in the midst of writing the lecture that would become "To Criticize the Critic," he told Eleanor Hinkley that one of his goals was to discern "where my opinions have altered and whether any general truths can be elicited from studying in retrospect the critic I know most about (but I have *avoided* for so many years re-reading my criticism that I may get some rude jolts)" (*Prose8* 470n4).

Without offering either polite truths from on high or rude jolts from below, I will conclude by discussing several territories that I believe the new edition compels us to revisit, either to hone and magnify our maps or to begin redrawing them completely.

Usual Suspects

Dante, Donne, Kipling, and lesser-known seventeenth-century writers—readers already familiar with Eliot's prominent critical interests will find that the *Complete Prose* offers abundant evidence of their sustained and evolving importance to him. For instance, Eliot insistently turned to them to help him think about the relationship between thought and feeling in art. He reserves his greatest praise for those who discern a difficult, reciprocal unity: Donne felt his thought with a sensual immediacy, while Villon thought about feeling with remorseless scrutiny. But less familiar—and therefore even more important—is his repeated insistence that art cannot succeed when it lacks intense feeling. Ben Jonson's satire "fails of the first intensity," he argues, "by not seeming to come out of deep personal feeling" ("The Oxford Jonson," *Prose3* 452). And Dadaism, with its austere sensationalism, demonstrates "a terror of emotion" that derails its aims entirely ("Modern Tendencies in Poetry," *Prose2* 220).

Eliot's abiding admiration for Dante and the Italian Middle Ages is well known, primarily through the slim 1929 pamphlet in which he praises Dante's visual imagination, his psychological acuity, and the "complete scale of the *depths* and *heights* of human emotion" achieved in the *Commedia* ("Dante," *Prose3* 727). But readers of the new edition will also encounter his early review "Dante as a 'Spiritual Leader'" (1919), in which he first reflects on the emotional framework of the *Commedia* and on how its parts are intelligible only against the backdrop of the whole. And they'll find a later unsigned review called "Two Studies in Dante" (1928), in which he explores the psychology of freedom and torment. Even a simple word search of the new edition is illuminating: Dante is a constant and ever-changing touchstone for Eliot in essays, reviews, and writings on all topics, from literary style to religious belief and political conflict. As a Harvard student, he tucked a small copy of the Temple Classics edition of the *Commedia* in his shirt pocket; in many ways, it remained there for the rest of his career.

Eliot spent a lifetime thinking and writing about the Elizabethan Age and the seventeenth century. He developed some of his most influential theories in the course of writing about Shakespeare, Marlowe, and the metaphysical poets. But even seasoned readers of Eliot will be startled by the range of his reviews and the depth of his immersion in detailed scholarly debate about the sixteenth and seventeenth centuries, "perhaps [his] most abiding intellectual passion as a critic" (*Prose3* xxvii). He delivered a series of six weekly BBC broadcasts on Tudor prose in 1929. Adopting a much more accessible tone than usual, these talks range widely over known and unknown writers of the period, with a first-person immediacy that conveys Eliot's sense of them as contemporaries, craftsmen from whom we might still learn. "The Elizabethan age," he asserts in the final broadcast, delivered July 16, "is not something dead and embalmed, or unreal and romantic, but a living age which still lives in ourselves, and an age which had to tackle problems of thought and expression with which we are ourselves vitally concerned" (*Prose3* 688).

Eliot's other distinctive and longtime interests are also on display from new angles and in new lights. He shows an evolving fascination with Baudelaire's sense of morality. He evinces an enduring if mutable interest in the strange, exotic worlds of Rudyard Kipling. He undergoes a remarkable change of mind about the language and versification of John Milton. He demonstrates a persistent, curiously admiring aversion to Algernon Charles Swinburne, who was capable of creating entire worlds out of a profusion of sound without sense. And of course, always prominent and central is Eliot's sense of a living tradition: a past that lives on, invigorated and renewed, in the present, and a present that is "quickened" by the energy and vision of the past (*Prose2* 67).

Enduring Skepticism

Readers accustomed to teaching Eliot from his authoritative perch in anthologies and selections will be surprised by the dogged skepticism and relativism of his early writing. And even those familiar with the relentlessly questioning graduate papers will be startled by how the skeptical habits that he developed at Harvard and Oxford persisted throughout his lifetime. He embraced skepticism as a graduate student, and its intellectual apparatus of doubt, critique, and qualification served him well there and beyond. For instance, as a literary critic, he turned his skepticism on conventional wisdom about "tradition," finding it not chiseled or restrictive but labile and expansive, responsive to the influx of change and transformation at any moment. Throughout his early criticism, he repeatedly chooses to deflect, qualify, and deny—to push arguments toward greater complexity and ambivalence on the topics of doctrine and belief, feeling and form, intention and the unconscious. Early reviewers skewered him for this, accusing him of obscurantism, but it's a testament to his devotion to questions over answers. And though it sometimes wavered, this habit of mind did not vanish with his conversion. In fact, as religious thinker, Eliot dedicates himself to critiques of the norm. "Skepticism for Eliot," write the editors of volume 5, "was not the opposite of faith, but a component of humility" (*Prose5* xxi). In his thinking about social duty and civic responsibility, the skeptic's oppositional stance assumes the status of a moral imperative. It's the responsibility of the writer to "always be in a certain sense in opposition … constantly opposed to current tendencies and to popular values" ("The Responsibility of the European Man of Letters," *Prose6* 542). Even as late as 1953, decades after graduate school, Eliot adapted the skeptic's formula to convey his idea of inspiration. For some writers, inspiration arrives as a sudden gift, a flash of psychic insight leading them to tell a particular story or invoke a specific image. But for others (like himself), these psychic impulses manifest themselves only in negative terms, as refusals, repeating "'not that! not that!' in the face of each unsuccessful attempt at formal organization" ("The Three Voices of Poetry," *Prose7* 828). "Not that! Not that!": skepticism has effectively become an imaginative reflex by this point, at work even before doubt is articulated. For a thinker who underwent such profound and dramatic changes in his midlife, Eliot maintained surprisingly consistent intellectual methods. "[W]e all like to think that we have changed," he wrote of Donne in 1931, which explains why "people shrink from acknowledging that they are exactly the same at fifty as they were at twenty-five" ("Donne in Our Time," *Prose4* 373).

The Public Man

As he wintered into literary celebrity, W. B. Yeats reflected upon himself becoming official, venerable, senatorial even: "a sixty-year-old smiling public man."[7] Eliot's correspondence attests to the many invitations and requests he received as he assumed this polite, public mantle, but the *Complete Prose* also reveals a hitherto unknown and surprisingly persistent aspect of his life after separating from Vivien—namely, an ardent, consuming devotion to local charitable causes in England. Only humility could have prompted him to suggest, in 1951, "it is very rare that I speak in public for good causes and charitable enterprises," because, in fact, the opposite was true: it was rare that Eliot *declined* a request to speak or write on behalf of a charitable cause ("'Those Who Need Privacy and Those Whose Need Is Company,'" *Prose7* 647). The edition is replete with examples. For instance, he delivered an address titled "Some Thoughts on Braille" (1952) to the National Institute for the Blind, on the occasion of the centenary of Louis Braille's death. As the war came to an end, he lectured regularly at the Churchill Club, Ashburnham House, to allied soldiers in rehabilitation or on leave from the front. The edition prints transcripts and summary reports for this and similarly unrecovered lectures in volume 6, along with a synopsis provided by none other than Lieutenant Colonel Donald Gallup, his later bibliographer (*Prose6* 781–92). Eliot fervently engaged students and young people, supporting the International Student Service and repeatedly accepting invitations to give the year-end Speech Day addresses at secondary schools all over England, such as the Truro School in Cornwall ("On Christianity and a Useful Life") and, on the very next day, the West Cornwall School for Girls ("How to Read Poetry"). Perhaps the most memorable of such addresses is the one he delivered on behalf of Cecil Houses, a home for elderly women ("Those Who Need Privacy and Those Whose Need Is Company"). There, he insists that all charities consider the recipients' fundamental need for independence and self-respect: "What matters for the preservation of self-respect … is the relation between the person who gives and the person who receives" (*Prose7* 650). An internationally renowned poet and writer, Eliot found that being a "person who gives" meant, for him, devoting time and energy to writings that he never intended to preserve or collect. For him, it meant years of quiet and unremunerated service undertaken alongside his more public-facing roles, and for us, it means recalibrating our sense of his ethical and professional commitments.

Contemporaries

Though he was no rival to Woolf and her renowned social portraiture, Eliot was much more engaged and animated about the poets and novelists of his generation than we've previously thought. Readers of the *Complete Prose* will be surprised to find that there are, in fact, few contemporaries who do *not* enter the circumference of his awareness. Early reviews such as "Verse Pleasant and Unpleasant" and "The Post-Georgians" stake out his position against older contemporaries J. C. Squire and the Georgian poets, whom he associated with a parochial, sentimental strain of English verse desperately in need of cosmopolitan influx. In essays written for *La Nouvelle Revue française* and subsequently published in English in *Vanity Fair*, he offers rarely cited commentary on May Sinclair, D. H. Lawrence, Wyndham Lewis, and Carl Sandburg. "If one examines the best of contemporary English fiction," he argues, "one finds a tendency towards a style … almost exaggerated in its bareness and simplicity" ("Contemporary English Prose," *Prose2* 451–2). He returns to contemporary prose in "Le Roman anglais contemporain" ["The Contemporary Novel"] (1927), which was never published in English. There he elevates Virginia Woolf's fiction to a greater degree than elsewhere, calling it "the most faithful representative of the *contemporary* novel … perhaps more *representative* than the work of Mr. Joyce": "there is nothing quite like it," he concludes (*Prose3* 92).

Of special significance for their unguarded insights and observations are the notes that Eliot prepared for "English 26: English Literature from 1890 to the Present Day," a class he taught during his visit to Harvard in spring 1933. Some elements are familiar: the influence of Hawthorne on Henry James, or the reliance of modern poets ("Pound and self," Eliot notes) on the style of modern prose stylists (*Prose4* 773). But these notes also reveal an extraordinary combination of close reading and self-commentary, as he pauses to describe certain problems he encountered while writing "Burbank with a Baedeker: Bleistein with a Cigar" and discusses how James overcame similar ones. He then dives headlong into a meticulous reading of a passage in *The Aspern Papers* in which James seems to omit a crucial description of a character's eyes. This is "not a failure," Eliot takes pains to point out: "what is important is not to describe the indescribable, but to note its effect" (*Prose4* 773). Though still serious about Joyce's classicism, he also revels in the "Pure Fun" of reading *Ulysses*; though still averse to Lawrence's psychoanalysis, he applauds his "great powers of observation" and his "immense descriptive and evocative powers" (*Prose4* 791). As the editors observe, the English 26 lectures offer a "more empathetic, literary critique" than the ill-tempered criticisms in *After Strange Gods* (*Prose4* xxix). The *Complete Prose* amply demonstrates that although Eliot may have regarded his essays on classical writers with greater confidence—having consistently chosen to collect them in later editions—he didn't shy away from writing about the distinctive and exciting innovations of his own generation.

The *Complete Prose* is the lynchpin of an extraordinary publishing renaissance of Eliot's work. Along with the voluminous *Letters*, the *Poems*, and the forthcoming *Plays*, it forms part of an editorial undertaking whose scope and scale is simply unmatched in twenty-first-century letters. It lays the foundation for generations of new scholars to enrich and enhance our understanding of Eliot's status as one of the foremost major literary and cultural figures of his time, and an enduring and illuminating influence on ours. It's difficult to imagine, but there is more editorial work to be done on the prose, including promotional blurbs for Faber authors, contributions to the monthly newsletter at Lloyds Bank, and other items. And it's nearly as difficult to imagine the wealth of research and new insight that is to come as readers and scholars begin to recognize *just how much we don't know about Eliot*. There has simply never been a more auspicious time to be a serious student of T. S. Eliot. The urgent need for such wide-reaching, expansive editorial projects is best expressed by Eliot himself:

> It is now becoming understood that Baudelaire is one of the few poets who wrote nothing either prose or verse that is negligible. To understand Baudelaire you must read the whole of Baudelaire. And nothing that he wrote is without importance. He was a great poet; he was a great critic. And he was also a man with a profound attitude toward life, for the study of which we need every scrap of his writing. ("Baudelaire in our Time," *Prose3* 82)

Notes

1 TSE to A. C. Partridge, April 1, 1959. Quoted in *Prose1* xiii.
2 An unrevised second US edition of *Selected Essays* had appeared in 1950, with the essay "John Marston" omitted.
3 Ted Hughes, *A Dancer to God: Tributes to T. S. Eliot* (New York: Farrar Straus Giroux, 1992), 46.
4 Ronald Schuchard, "Goodnight, Mrs. Tom," *Royal Society of Literature Review* (2013): 18–19.
5 For details of the lecture's provenance, see the headnote in *Prose2* 548.

6 Though it was originally conceived as a traditional print project, unexpected changes to editorial and publishing agreements resulted in the *Complete Prose* appearing first digitally—in print-ready PDF format—on the Project MUSE platform, beginning with volumes 1 and 2 in 2014. Subsequent volumes were published in identical format on the same platform, with the final installment appearing in 2019. Johns Hopkins University Press published this revised edition in hardcover, but publishing agreements with UK copyright holders stipulated that it appear solely as limited run, available for purchase only in North America and only as a full set. After close coordination with technical and editorial teams, Project MUSE launched a completely redesigned digital platform in 2023, featuring a full XML version of the text as well as an array of new functionalities, including full-text searching, granular search faceting, hover and lateral annotations, linked cross-references, and continuous page scrolling. There are now three identical versions of the *Complete Prose*—all paginated identically for ease of citation—each serving slightly different sets of user purposes: the XML version, the PDFs, and the hardcover print edition.

7 W. B. Yeats, "Among School Children," in *Yeats's Poems*, edited by A. Norman Jeffares (London: Macmillan, 1989), 323.

4

Eliot's Divided Life

Frances Dickey

"For years I was a divided man": so Eliot described his secret romance with Emily Hale, the American actress and drama teacher with whom he corresponded for a quarter century.[1] From Prufrock's "you and I" to the "compound ghost" in *Little Gidding*, Eliot entertained doubles, internal debates, contradictions, philosophical dialectic, and other divisions.[2] But this frank confession from 1960 places the division within his personal life. Lying sealed until the opening of his letters in 2020, Eliot's posthumous statement exemplifies his instinct for secrecy and control, which drove him to burn Hale's letters and many of his own. The thousands of pages Eliot wrote to Hale between 1930 and 1956 reveal his emotional life with a candor and autobiographical specificity unknown in his other writings.[3] With the steady publication of his collected letters edited by John Haffenden and Ann Pasternak Slater's biography of Vivien Eliot, we are now in a better position to understand his closely protected private life and its intimate connection with his poetry and drama.[4] Eliot experienced his own existence as a series of divisions, rigorously keeping his private and public selves separate by inclination and necessity. Yet his letters to Hale reveal how writing both bridged and thrived on the gaps in his life, revealing the process of "transmutation" by which Eliot turned personal experience into poetry (*Prose2* 110).

Thomas Stearns Eliot was born on September 26, 1888, in St. Louis, Missouri. His parents' house on Locust Street stood on property originally purchased by William Greenleaf Eliot, minister and founder of Washington University, when it was a farm on the outskirts of St. Louis. By the time of young Tom, the youngest of six children, fashion had inexorably marched westward. Anchored by filial duty and proximity to Smith Academy, where Tom attended school until sixteen, his family lingered on the edges of a neighborhood the poet later described to Hale as "a slum" (September 7, 1931). Steps away from the

Eliots' home lay a strip of saloons on Jefferson Avenue known as the "pest hole" of St. Louis.[5] Chestnut Street, three blocks south, was the heart of the city's red light district, now remembered as the birthplace of ragtime.[6] Locust Street thus lay between two neighborhoods whose names seem like allegories for Eliot's young world: "Piety Hill," dotted with churches of every denomination, including his grandfather's Church of the Messiah, and "Death Valley," so called for its violent crime and illness—especially syphilis, at that time an incurable disease leading to premature aging, blindness, paralysis, and insanity.

"It is self-evident that St. Louis affected me more deeply than any other environment has done," wrote Eliot, crediting the influence of his "shabby" environment on his "urban imagery"[7]—such as the cityscape of "Rhapsody on a Windy Night," populated with streetwalkers whose disease-ravaged faces are projected onto a demented, pock-marked moon, or the "evil houses" of "Prufrock's Pervigilium." Jefferson Avenue split his childhood world between good and bad girls, health and illness, life and death. He told Hale that he felt cut off from "other children of my own class," especially girls, who "terrified" him at dancing class (September 7, 1931). Eliot's St. Louis was also racially segregated, a division inscribed on the local geography and repeated in hundreds of venues, gestures, and cultural forms (blackface minstrelsy still influenced Eliot as late as *Sweeney Agonistes*). Eliot grew up at the intersection of hypocritical and damaging divisions: Victorian sexual mores and Jim Crow segregation. Little wonder that as an adult he retained an indelible sense of sin.[8] These experiences may have set the stage for his discomfort with female sexuality and his sense of alienation, central themes of his work even as he attempted to find resolution through poetry, philosophy, religious conversion, and British citizenship.[9]

Eliot also grew up with one foot in New England, where his mother Charlotte took the family for three months every summer, retreating from St. Louis's heat to Eastern Point, a spit of land reaching into the Atlantic Ocean, beyond the fishing town of Gloucester, Massachusetts. While recalling the "long dark river" and the "blue sea" of his two homes, he felt his regional identities conflicted and canceled each other out: "it was not until years of maturity that I perceived that I myself had always been a New Englander in the South West, and a South Westerner in New England" ("Preface to *This American World*," *Prose3* 492); or, as he wrote bitterly to Herbert Read in April 1928, he "was never any thing any where" (*Letters4* 138). Later, as an expatriate in London, he experienced the same sense of dislocation and divided identity on a larger scale. While remaining, as he reminded Mary Hutchinson in July 1919, "a *metic*—a foreigner" in England, he was distanced from his family, even his mother, with whom he shared a special connection (*Letters1* 379).

When Eliot was sixteen, his parents sent him to Milton Academy, outside Boston, for a final high school year, to meet other boys expected to go to Harvard, such as Scofield Thayer, through whom he later met Vivien and received the *Dial* prize for *The Waste Land*. In nearby Cambridge, his aunt Barbara Hinkley and her daughter Eleanor welcomed their young relative, and according to Eliot's recollection (August 18, 1932), here in summer or fall 1905 he first saw Eleanor's friend Emily Hale (1891–1969), then fourteen. Eleanor and Emily were classmates at the Berkeley Street School in Cambridge, and her father led a Unitarian parish in nearby Chestnut Hill. Hale did not recall this early acquaintance, placing their first meeting around 1911.[10] Whether remembering or reconstructing this encounter with Hale as a girl, Eliot treasured photos of Hale at this age, imagining her as Beatrice to his Dante.

The young man with literary gifts and a keen sense of humor followed family tradition by attending Harvard College, whose current president was also an Eliot. He maintained a gentlemanly academic record and entertained friends such as Conrad Aiken with his no-longer-amusing "Bolo" verses. In 1909, his desultory poetic experiments were catalyzed by discovering Jules Laforgue in the pages of Arthur Symons's *The Symbolist Movement in Poetry*, an affinity that drew Eliot to Paris to study in 1910–11. Here he began one of his most creative periods, soon completing "The Love Song of J. Alfred Prufrock," "Preludes," and "Portrait of a Lady." Although we can retrace his intellectual progress through his "temporary conversion" to Bergsonism (*A Sermon Preached in Magdalene College Chapel*, *Prose7* 112), less is known about his friendships in France, such as with his housemate Jean Verdenal, a medical student later killed at Gallipoli. The Hale archive has revealed another person who seems to have made a deep impression on Eliot in Paris: the older Matthew Prichard, formerly the assistant director of the Museum of Fine Arts, Boston—"a strange intense fanatical fellow, who did at that time very much modify my life and influenced deeply my views on art and philosophy … I felt simultaneously a fascination and an aversion which was a great mental strain and precipitated at one moment a kind of mystical crisis which was awful" (March 24, 1931). Eliot told Hale that he referred to Prichard in "Gerontion" as "Mr. Silvero," shedding some light on the anxiety and guilt expressed in that obscure and secretive poem.

Eliot returned to Harvard to study philosophy and Indic languages, an education from which he would draw throughout his career. In what was probably the most significant emotional experience of his adult life, he fell in love with Hale, now a graceful young woman active in amateur theatrical productions around Boston. As Hale recalled, "I was overawed by the quiet, reserved, very brilliant young man whose low voice made all he said very difficult to follow, apart from the content of his already individual thinking. I was given to understand by others that 'I was the only girl he paid any attention to.'"[11] Eliot recalled falling in love with Hale gradually during 1913 and then becoming "completely conscious of it, and quite shaken to pieces" after a performance of *Tristan und Isolde* they attended together (July 24, 1931).[12] The significance of their evening at the opera explains the frame of Wagnerian quotations enclosing the "hyacinth garden" passage in *The Waste Land*, to which Eliot drew Hale's attention as testifying to his love for her (November 3, 1930). The garden scene seems to derive from Eliot's final days in Cambridge, in spring 1914. In his telling, he believed he could not declare himself to Hale, let alone ask her to marry him, until he had an income. Nevertheless, he tried to see her as often as possible, and one afternoon he almost revealed his feelings, a memory he still could not endure without "a kind of dizziness" (July 24, 1931). In the "hyacinth garden," Eliot recast his inability to speak as a moment of possible transcendence, witnessed but narrowly missed: "Looking into the heart of light, the silence" (*Poems1* 56).

His own silence seems to have replayed in Eliot's mind as the great what-if of his life. The question even dominates his posthumous statement, justifying his marriage to Vivien as avoiding "the dull misery of the mediocre teacher of philosophy," as if marrying Hale would have necessitated giving up poetry ("Statement," *Prose8* 598). Eliot left Hale, his family, the United States, and philosophy behind, cutting off anchors one by one during the 1914–15 academic year, but he certainly looked back. Yearning for an alternate universe in which he had married the girl he loved fueled his creativity and gave meaning to his subsequent unhappiness. His posthumous statement that "marrying Hale ... would have killed the poet in me" is deviously accurate and gratuitously slighting, insofar as *not* marrying her revived and sustained his poetic gift for three of his greatest works: *The Waste Land*, *Ash-Wednesday*, and *Four Quartets* (598).

Lithe, vivacious, and daring, Vivien Haigh-Wood (1888–1947) "smoked / And danced all the modern dances" ("Cousin Nancy," *Poems1* 24), meeting Eliot through their mutual enjoyment of dance and the Thayer connection.[13] Neither partner was particularly serious during their short courtship, but a flirtation turned into a lifelong commitment.[14] "All of her actions can be explained by vanity, fear, immaturity, weak physique, weak nerves, drugs and disappointment," Eliot later explained to Hale (August 21, 1931). Drugs were perhaps the most underestimated factor in their unhappy marriage, to which Slater has drawn overdue attention. Vivien had been in the care of doctors for tuberculosis as a child, used "sleeping draughts" for over twenty years (March 4, 1931), and experienced poor health throughout her adult life, with vague complaints that could be related to substance abuse recorded in her diary as early as 1914 ("bad neuralgia," "fearful liver," "splitting headache," and emotional instability).[15] In 1925, doctors uncovered her addiction to chloral hydrate, and she confessed to Sidney Schiff that she had been taking it "for years."[16] As a substance abuser, she suffered from a chronic brain disease, in addition to mental-health issues including eating disorders. An addict's life becomes focused on acquiring and using the addictive substance, depleting the family's resources, and leading their partner into a web of lies and concealment. The trauma of Vivien's disease radiated through their marriage, manifesting itself in classic symptoms including financial stress, disruption of home life, anxiety, depression, guilt, anger, insomnia, substance abuse, weight gain, and illness—all documented in Eliot's letters or others' accounts.[17] Vivien's substance abuse contributed to Eliot's sense of division, not just between the life he chose and the one he might have had but between the appearance and the reality of his marriage. Struggling to explain and contain his wife's erratic behavior without knowledge of the malady, he sought the causes in himself. In April 1925, he wrote to John Middleton Murry: "In the last ten years—gradually, but deliberately—I have made myself into a *machine*. I have done it deliberately—in order to endure, in order not to feel—*but it has killed V*" (*Letters2* 627). Rather than reflecting any wrongdoing, Eliot's constant feelings of guilt toward Vivien may overestimate his role in her suffering and his agency in a series of choices driven by chance and financial necessity. Five years later, as he began writing to Hale, he blamed himself for marrying the wrong woman and blighting the lives of three people:

> It is a greater sin to marry without any feeling at all, I consider, than to marry even from low passion; for a year I was merely dazed and numbed and did not know what was the matter; then, quite suddenly, I awoke. Well, I did not know how much, if any, harm I had done to you; but I could know quite well, the harm I had done which was under my eyes; and I came to see that this at all events I must expiate with the rest of my life. (November 3, 1930)

These words are not far from the question posed in "Gerontion": "After such knowledge, what forgiveness?" While "Gerontion" may seem to brood on the knowledge of Vivien's infidelity with Bertrand Russell,[18] Eliot's expressions of regret for his marriage suggest a different weight: how can he be forgiven for the harm he has done to himself and both women by choosing the one he didn't love? The ambiguity of the poem—its "supple confusions"—mirrors Gerontion's confusion as he searches his past to understand cause and effect, the assignation of blame. In hindsight, chloral hydrate may be the culprit, one whose malign influence Eliot probably did not understand in 1919—and may never have fully understood.

Eliot's personal misery from 1918 to 1922 is well known: working full time at Lloyds Bank, extension lecturing, and writing reviews in the evening, he endured a global pandemic, the death of his father, physical illness and nervous breakdowns, and the dysfunction of his marriage,[19] which he attempted to conceal from his family during their extended visit in summer 1921. Yet Eliot also experienced a surge of creativity, composing "Tradition," "Hamlet," "Dante" (1919), "Philip Massinger," "The Perfect Critic," and other essays collected in *The Sacred Wood* (1920), exploring topics from Elizabethan drama to music hall and Russian ballet, while working on multiple drafts of *The Waste Land*. What inspired this concentration of energy? When Eliot began writing to Hale in 1930, he asked her to reread his poems "and see if they do not convince you that my love for you has steadily grown into something finer and finer. And I shall always write primarily for you" (November 3, 1930). While "Gerontion" seems mired in guilt and contamination for unspecified "vices" and "depravity," burying personal experience in a "wilderness of mirrors," in *The Waste Land*, Eliot clarifies individual figures from his life as speakers and characters rather than obscure pseudonyms. Hale appears bathed in a luminous glow, as if on stage, enclosed in quotations from *Tristan* that capture the circumstances of falling in love with her in 1913 while imagining her as Isolde, the forbidden object of an adulterous love. This idealized portrait stands in contrast to the depiction of his marriage in "A Game of Chess" ("photography," wrote Vivien in the margin).[20] Emotionally polarized between its unsparing representation of a failed marriage and an anguished yearning for another woman, *The Waste Land* is powered not by his feelings toward one woman or the other but by their magnetic opposition.[21]

The publication of *The Waste Land* launched Eliot to international poetic fame and the *Criterion* gave him a platform and an expanding network of writers and intellectuals. However, his private life was desperate. Despite Vivien's brief career writing short fiction for the *Criterion* in 1924, her condition deteriorated, probably due to her spiraling substance abuse. The Eliots moved frequently, and he had little energy or inspiration for poetry. In April 1924, he wrote to his brother, Henry: "I have not been able to leave her for three months. I have gone through some terrible agony myself which I do not understand yet, and which has left me utterly bewildered and dazed" (*Letters2* 379). "The Hollow Men" (1925) sums up this period, as he told Henry: "it is despair, it stands for the lowest point I ever reached in my sordid domestic affairs" (*Letters8* 11).

Caught between incompatible public and private lives, Eliot sought another path with Hale as his guide, as Lyndall Gordon previously surmised.[22] The two met in London's Eccleston Square, probably in 1923, when "I had found myself for a time quite lost … It is from then that my active spiritual life dates, also two years of increasing difficulty, and the rest I do not need to tell" (November 3, 1930).[23] "Eyes that last I saw in tears" (November 1924) may recall their encounter, a "golden vision" of her sympathy, but seen "through division" (*Poems1* 139). As Eliot explained of Dostoevsky's novels in the same month,

> there are everywhere two planes of reality, and that the scene before our eyes is only the screen and veil of another action which is taking place behind it. The characters themselves are partially aware of this division, aware of the grotesque futility of their visible lives, and seem always to be listening for other voices and to be conducting a conversation with spectres. ("A Neglected Aspect of Chapman," *Prose2* 552–3)[24]

Enduring divisions out of his control, Eliot cultivated a spiritual world different from either his "sordid" personal troubles or his tightly buttoned professional persona at the bank. He saw himself following Dante: "deliberately and consciously, with what knowledge of his own needs and limitations he created [Beatrice] as a solution" (*Prose2* 555). Both Gordon and Schuchard intuited Hale's place as his imaginary Beatrice, but the opening of the archive has clarified just how deliberately Eliot drew on his old feelings for Hale to lead himself out of despair.

A new chapter in Eliot's professional life began in 1925, when he joined forces with the publishing house of Faber and Gwyer, meaning a steady income, support for the *Criterion*, publication of anything he wrote, and further influence in the world of letters. Vivien began a series of hospitalizations that, while expensive, periodically relieved Eliot of the burdens of caring for her. In summer 1926, during a disastrous trip to Europe, she became paranoid, probably had a relapse, and later attempted suicide in Paris; in Rome, Eliot fell to the ground before Michelangelo's *Pietà*.[25] These events point toward their different paths: Vivien became a frequent patient at the Malmaison sanatorium outside of Paris, and Eliot was baptized into the Church of England in June 1927. Though Eliot had long contemplated this step, the two events were not unconnected: he put Vivien in the care of professionals and his soul into the hands of God. His conversion and time away from Vivien resulted in a flood of prose, ranging from monthly *Criterion* "Commentaries" to essays on Elizabethan drama, contemporary politics, humanism, and his most cherished author, Dante. He also published his first dramatic work, the fragmentary sections of *Sweeney Agonistes* (1926 and 1927), and new poems, including *Ash-Wednesday* (1927–9). "Loving and adoring you," Eliot told Hale, has "helped me to the Church and to the struggle of the spiritual life … Of course there were many concurrent paths leading me to the Altar—but I doubt whether I should have arrived but for you … And now there is no need to explain 'Ash Wednesday' to you. No one else will ever understand it" (October 3, 1930).

Eliot's emotion in this letter may have taken Hale by surprise, but for him it was the natural extension of a long, silent communion with her various guises. "I was discouraged when he confessed after seeing me again that his affection for me was stronger than ever," recalled Hale in 1965, "though he had assumed years of separation from his home in America and old friends would have changed his attitude toward me."[26] Eliot circumscribed his desire for Hale, however, telling her at the start of their correspondence: "[T]he only kind of happiness now possible for the rest of my life is now with me; and though it is the deepest happiness which is identical with my deepest loss and sorrow, it is a kind of supernatural ecstasy" (November 3, 1930). He sought a soulmate with whom to exchange letters and confidences, but nothing more. As an Anglican, he told Hale, he could not divorce or remarry; he looked forward to twenty or thirty years (or more) of such a relationship with her, promising that "one can (I mean of course two can) make *their* unfulfilled better than the fulfilment of others" (March 12, 1931). Hale found this arrangement "abnormal," a word she used as early as January 7, 1931, and over thirty years later in her final account of their relationship.[27] Idealizing Hale as his Beatrice or Virgin Mary,[28] Eliot created a role for her: a woman in white, the object of his longing, her inaccessibility inspiring his imagination.

In the first years of their correspondence, Eliot lived on at least three separate planes. Writing intimate, self-revelatory letters—often twice a week—he explored his and Hale's past and daily lives, building an understanding he kept secret from all but a few; he also tried to manage Vivien's disorientation and paranoia while concealing the true nature of her illness from others; and working full time as an editor and author, he cultivated his public role as an Anglican poet and cultural critic.[29] This unsustainable situation ended in September 1932, when Eliot departed for a year in America, to deliver the Norton Lectures at Harvard. Over the winter holidays, he traveled by train to California, where Hale was teaching at Scripps College, as she said, to "try to straighten out his emotional life, as he was then separated from his wife."[30] Vivien remained his wife, but Eliot never willingly saw her again. In the coming months and years, Hale sporadically prodded him about remarriage, but he responded firmly, citing the legal and religious impossibility of divorce. Lecturing on Shelley in February 1933, Eliot disapproved of the poet's advocacy of free love in "Epipsychidion," written for a woman named "Emilia" (*Prose4* 647).

In spring 1934, Hale left her job to join her aunt and uncle, Edith and John Perkins, for an extended stay in England and Europe. For the next eighteen months, Eliot and Hale saw each other frequently, in London or at Stamford House, in Chipping Campden, spending happy hours "in the beautiful garden at the rear of the house," from which Hale plucked flowers for Eliot, including roses and the sprig of yew that appears in *Burnt Norton*.[31] While she traveled on the Continent during winter and spring 1935, Eliot drafted *Murder in the Cathedral*, with its theme of temptation, writing to her frequently about dramaturgy (he later told her he began writing plays to impress her [December 1935]). In the summer and fall, Eliot and Hale dined in London, attended concerts and plays, met with friends, took romantic walks and train rides, went sightseeing, relaxed together in his rooms in London and the garden in Campden, and came as close to becoming lovers as his sense of propriety would allow. They exchanged birthday gifts, rings, and vows of love as the time of her sailing drew closer, with an intensity and unanimity of feeling they would not experience again.

On December 5, Eliot sent her the opening lines of *Burnt Norton*, originally written for *Murder* the previous spring, now given new meaning by their time together in the actual rose gardens at Stamford House and the nearby manor of Burnt Norton. Composing the poem, his feelings remained ardent: "I can't tell whether this will be a good poem or a bad one; at any rate, it is I think a new kind of love poem, and it is written for you, and it is fearfully obscure," he wrote on January 13, 1936, adding that he has chosen epigraphs from Heraclitus, "which make the poem more difficult to understand than it would be without them." Not long before, he told Hale: "I have again and again seen the impression I have made, and have longed to be able to cry 'no you all are wrong about me, it isn't like that at all; the truth is perfectly simple and intelligible, and here it is in a few words'" (February 19, 1932). Eliot wanted to be understood, but he also did not want to be—contradictions observed in his feelings for Hale. Soon after completing *Burnt Norton*, he withdrew, in a pattern often repeated during their relationship, harshly criticizing her Unitarian faith and impatiently reiterating the reasons why they could not hope for an earthly union (no matter how desirable and within reach it seemed just two months before). Hale, as he told Jeanette McPherrin, "had a sort of breakdown" (*Letters8* 335) in spring 1936, and when Eliot arrived in New England for a visit at the end of the summer, he found her in a state of "numbness to the external world" (*Letters8* 360). They spent a week at Woods Hole, Massachusetts, where they walked on the beach and heard a tolling bell buoy, one of several memories Eliot worked into *The Dry Salvages*, including the image of her grief-stricken face on the platform as his train departed and her gift of roses, the "withered flowers" in his pocket on the return to England.

As early as "La Figlia Che Piange," the figure of an abandoned woman "compelled [his] imagination," and in this role Hale continued to play his muse (*Poems1* 28). In 1937, as he began work on *The Family Reunion*, Eliot told her he was creating a "nice little part" for her (March 31, 1937): Mary, the cousin/intended bride of Harry, who is tormented by guilt for the death of his wife. As Eliot explained to his director, Martin Browne, in March 1938, Harry's previous marriage "has given him a horror of women as of unclean creatures" (*Letters8* 845), and he feels torn between repulsion and attraction toward Mary, whom he leaves behind when he seeks spiritual enlightenment. It is hard to reconcile the ominous message of the play with Hale's sunny recollections of Eliot proofreading it in the garden at Stamford House. Their last summer holiday in England ended abruptly, with the outbreak of war. With theaters closed, Eliot turned back to poetry, drawing on memories of East Coker, New England, and Little Gidding (all visited in 1936) for three more *Quartets*. As he wrote the poem of the end of their love (especially *The Dry Salvages*), Eliot continued to correspond faithfully with Hale throughout their wartime separation, seven "emotionless / Years of living among the breakage / Of what was believed in as the most reliable— / And therefore the fittest for renunciation" (*Poems1* 195).

Eliot had exchanged one double life for another, but Vivien's unexpected death in January 1947 forced a reckoning: now free to make good on his long-standing promise to marry Hale, he found he could not. He described himself as an Egyptian mummy that crumbles into dust when exposed to air. In a series of painful letters, Eliot probed "a stranger" within himself (February 14, 1947): "I am now facing a division in myself which was created—not perhaps initiated, but brought to a head—by the sudden violent desperate rupture in 1915," he wrote to Hale on March 1, continuing a few weeks later:

I have not been one whole person. So that when you contrast the two aspects of myself the existence of which you recognize, it is not safe to say that one of them (the one you prefer) is the real person, and the other not: the real person must be one in which these are united, and therefore different from either side alone. (March 20, 1947)

Painful to himself and others, self-division defined him and drove his creativity. His marriage to the much younger Valerie Fletcher in 1957, exactly a decade after Vivien's death, brought union to a divided man at the end of his poetic career.

Notes

1. "Statement by T. S. Eliot on the opening of the Emily Hale letters at Princeton University" (*Prose8* 598 and Eliot–Hale); cited henceforward as "Statement."
2. On Eliot's divisions, see Jewel Spears Brooker, *T. S. Eliot's Dialectical Imagination* (Baltimore: Johns Hopkins University Press, 2018) and Nancy Gish, "Discarnate Desire: T. S. Eliot and the Poetics of Dissociation," in *Gender, Desire, and Sexuality in T. S. Eliot*, edited by Gish and Cassandra Laity (Cambridge: Cambridge University Press, 2004), 107–29, and Gish, "A Divided Man," *Time Present: The Newsletter of the International T. S. Eliot Society* 103 (Spring 2021): 10–12.
3. Letters from T. S. Eliot to Emily Hale; Emily Hale Letters from T. S. Eliot, C0686, Special Collections, Princeton University Library; accessible in Eliot–Hale. Cited throughout by date. For background, see Dickey, "May the Record Speak: The Correspondence of T. S. Eliot and Emily Hale," *Twentieth-Century Literature* 66, no. 4 (December 2020): 431–62.
4. See Lyndall Gordon's *T. S. Eliot: An Imperfect Life* and *The Hyacinth Girl: T. S. Eliot's Hidden Muse* (New York: Norton, 1999 and 2022), Robert Crawford's *Young Eliot: From St. Louis to "The Waste Land"* and *Eliot after "The Waste Land"* (London: Jonathan Cape, 2015 and 2022), and Ann Pasternak Slater's *The Fall of a Sparrow: Vivien Eliot's Life and Writings* (London: Faber, 2020).
5. See Dickey, "T. S. Eliot and the Color Line of St. Louis," *Modernism/modernity* Print Plus, vol. 5, cycle 4 (March 9, 2021), https://doi.org/10.26597/mod.0187.
6. David E. Chinitz, *T. S. Eliot and the Cultural Divide* (Chicago: University of Chicago Press, 2003), 38–41.
7. "To the Editor of the *St. Louis Post-Dispatch*" *Prose4* 194; "The Influence of Landscape Upon the Poet," *Prose8* 388–9.
8. Ronald Schuchard, *T. S. Eliot's Dark Angel: Intersections of Life and Art* (New York: Oxford University Press, 1999), 3.

9 Brooker, 1–2.
10 Narrative by Emily Hale (1957), Emily Hale Letters from T. S. Eliot, C0686, Special Collections, Princeton University Library. See "In Her Own Words: Emily Hale's Introduction to T. S. Eliot's Letters," edited by Frances Dickey and Sara Fitzgerald, *T. S. Eliot Studies Annual* 3 (2021): 3.
11 Hale, narrative (1957), 4.
12 The Boston Opera Company gave their first performance on November 29, 1913; Eliot refers to this event on January 20, 1931, January 15, 1932, and August 9, 1934, also addressing Hale as "Isolde" (March 2, 1931).
13 Slater, 13, 20, 8.
14 Slater, 19.
15 Slater, 115, 11.
16 Slater, 216–19, 351–6; *Letters2* 807–8. Aldous Huxley later described Vivien as an "ether addict," a habit that may explain her constant complaints of insomnia and gastric trouble going back to the early 1920s. Anthony Fathman, "Viv and Tom: The Eliots as Ether Addict and Co-Dependent," *Yeats-Eliot Review* 11, no. 2 (1991): 33–6.
17 For the impact of substance abuse on the family, see J. Orford, G. Natera, et al., *Coping with Alcohol and Drug Problems* (London: Routledge, 2005), chapter 5.
18 See Robert Crawford, *Young Eliot*, for detailed examination of evidence for Vivien's adultery, including Russell's description of their one-night stand in 1917 to his lover Constance Malleson (261), and this interpretation of "Gerontion" (321).
19 Slater concludes that by 1919, the couple reached an "understanding" by which both were free to wander (86, 98).
20 *"The Waste Land": A Facsimile and Transcript of the Original Drafts*, edited by Valerie Eliot (New York: Harcourt, 1971), 11.
21 According to David Chinitz, the trope of the failed tryst "magnetised" Eliot's imagination; see "In the Shadows: Popular Song and Eliot's Construction of Emotion," *Modernism/modernity* 11, no. 3 (2004): 449–68.
22 A recurring theme in Gordon's biographies of Eliot. See *An Imperfect Life*, 205–7.
23 Eliot began sending Hale the *Criterion* in September 1923 (*Letters2* 212) and a copy of his 1920 poems, *Ara Vos Prec*, inscribed with Arnaut Daniel's words to Dante, translated "Keep my *Treasure*, where I yet live on, and I ask no more" (Gordon, *Imperfect Life*, 205).
24 Eliot told Ottoline Morrell in November 1924 that he explained the "principles" of "Doris's Dream Songs" in this lecture (*Letters2* 546).
25 Slater, 271–4.
26 Narrative by Emily Hale (1965), Emily Hale Letters from T. S. Eliot, C0686, Special Collections, Princeton University Library.
27 Hale, narrative (1965).

28 Eliot wrote to Hale after Vivien's death: "A woman usually wants a husband: some men want a kind of divinity, a sort of human surrogate for the B.V.M. I have had this" ("Easter Day 1947").
29 Slater, 350.
30 Hale, narrative (1957), 4–5.
31 Hale, narrative (1965); *Poems1* 183.

5

Eliot as Public Intellectual

Jeremy Noel-Tod

Was T. S. Eliot a public intellectual? If we are to avoid anachronism, no. The compound was not in common use when he died in 1965; the earliest *OED* citation is from the *New York Times* in 1967; and in *The Public Intellectual* (2002), Helen Small dates its currency to the 1990s in America and the 2000s in Britain.[1] Moreover, as Stefan Collini has shown, "intellectual" as a noun did not enjoy a securely agreed usage in English in the early decades of the twentieth century—and it was a label that Eliot, at the heart of Anglophone intellectual life, actively resisted.[2] "Let quacks, empirics, dolts debate" (1953)—a piece of light verse inspired by a photograph of a cat on a park bench—is the only poem he published that invokes "intellectuals" as a category, and then with Noël Coward–ish asperity: "Let intellectuals address / The latest Cultural Congress" (*Poems1* 311). The editors of the *Complete Prose* have, of course, employed the term in the now-familiar sense of someone preoccupied with ideas—for example, "Eliot chastised himself for not being more useful as an intellectual" (*Prose5* xxv). But Eliot's dislike of the word invariably implied his anxiety about the modern atomization of knowledge; the fact that the earliest *OED* citation dates from the mid-seventeenth century would have seemed darkly significant to the man who once proposed a never-written three-volume work on "the English Renaissance" called *The Disintegration of the Intellect* (*Prose2* 609). Eliot's "Note of Homage to Allen Tate" in 1959 suggests his alternative ideal:

> By avoiding the lethargy of the conservative, the flaccidity of the liberal, and the violence of the zealot, he succeeds in being a representative of the smallest of minorities, that of the intelligent who refuse to be described as "intellectuals." And what he has written, as a critic of society, is of much greater significance

because of being said by a man who is also a good poet and a good critic of literature. (*Prose8* 362)

Those scare quotes whet "the ironic edge" that *intellectual*, as a noun, retained into the 1960s.³ Eliot here characteristically insists on the value of social criticism when underwritten by literary activity. In one of his last public statements on a political matter—whether the UK should join the European Common Market—he replied to the editors of *Encounter* magazine that he was "neither a scholar nor an intellectual generally" (*Prose8* 529). But if Eliot was not, by 1962, an intellectual, who was? In 1928 he wrote of Julien Benda's post-Dreyfus polemic, *La Trahison des clercs*, that *"clercs"* could only be "feebly" translated as "'intellectuals'" (*Prose3* 345).⁴ Reprising a cadence of learned helplessness from the original phrasing of his final note to *The Waste Land* ("Shantih ... 'The Peace which passeth understanding' is a feeble translation of the content of this word"), Eliot makes clear that he regards the non-equivalence of French and English as a cultural shibboleth (*Poems2* 415). Yet over the course of the review he also argues, *contra* Benda, that "the regiment of the world" should not be given over "to those persons who have no interest in ideas whatever"—a position that implies the need for the category of "[public] intellectual," even as his verbal skepticism declines to name it.

"Clerisy" was the collective noun for intellectuals coined in the nineteenth century by Coleridge as "the learned of all denominations ... all the so-called liberal arts and sciences, the possession and application of which constitute the civilization of a country, as well as the theological" (quoted in *Prose5* 740). In "On the Place and Function of the Clerisy," a 1944 paper for the Moot, the Christian sociological discussion group that met from 1938 to 1947, Eliot considered the contemporary definition of "the clerisy (if it exists)" (*Prose6* 553). But in *The Idea of a Christian Society* (1939), he had already rejected Coleridge's word for proselytizing purposes, noting that the meaning of the term had been "somewhat voided by time" (*Prose5* 701). Instead, he advanced a speculative elite called the "Community of Christians"—as distinct from the "largely unconscious ... Christian Community" (*Prose5* 697)—which "would include some of those who are ordinarily spoken of, not always with flattering intention, as 'intellectuals'" (*Prose5* 703).

Coleridge's coinage arises from the cognate nature of "cleric" and "clerk" (and, indeed, "clerc"), which perhaps adds an extra knowing wink to the self-portrait of 1933: "How unpleasant to meet Mr. Eliot! / With his features of clerical cut" ("Lines for Cuscuscaraway and Mirza Murad Ali Beg," *Poems1* 143). When pressed to say what he was, Eliot often took cover under the old-fashioned mantle of "man of letters"—most notoriously, when he declined to contribute to Nancy Cunard's *Authors Take Sides on the Spanish War* (1937), with "it is best that at least a few men of letters remain isolated," a private reply that was nevertheless printed, under the arch heading "NEUTRAL?" (*Letters8* 783). In 1944, Eliot wrote an article entitled "The Responsibility of the Man of Letters in the Cultural Restoration of Europe," in which he defined this "man" as "the writer for whom his writing is primarily an art." His responsibility, in other words, is to words. But—like the poet who described the latter *Four Quartets* (1943) as "patriotic poems" written under "war-time conditions" (*Poems1* 892)—the world will concern him too:

> [T]he man of letters is not, as a rule, exclusively engaged upon the production of works of art. He has other interests, like anybody else; interests which will, in all probability, exercise some influence upon the content and meaning of the works of art which he does produce. (*Prose6* 519)

Such statements self-consciously modify the severity of the author of *The Sacred Wood* (1920) and his rhetorical air of missionary forbearance: "The temptation, to any man who is interested in ideas and primarily in literature, to put literature into the corner until he cleaned up the whole country first, is almost irresistible" (*Prose2* 295). Eliot's prime example of a poet-critic succumbing to this temptation was Matthew Arnold, who neglected to subcontract his social criticism to "some disciple … in an editorial position on a newspaper" (295). Again the shadow of self-portraiture falls across the page. From 1915, having decided to abandon a career as an academic philosopher and settle in England, Eliot put the intellectual range of his Harvard education to practical use with authoritative (albeit unsigned) book reviews ranging from Indian and French thought to social Darwinism and American education and politics. He also contributed pieces on religion and philosophy to academic journals. It was not until 1917, when his first book of poems, *Prufrock and Other Observations* appeared, that Eliot emerged as an identifiably *literary* critic, writing his first non-review article for *The New Statesman* ("Reflections on *Vers Libre*"). Reporting back to his Harvard classmates that year, however, he mentioned only his philosophical and poetic publications. His early taste for social criticism was not exercised significantly again until after *The Waste Land* (*Prose1* 510), although it occasionally bubbles up as prophetic irony in the acidic cultural commentary of his "London Letters" (1921–2), most notably in the tribute to music-hall performer, Marie Lloyd. When *The Sacred Wood* deprecated Arnold for hunting "game outside of the literary preserve" (*Prose2* 295), Eliot was tacitly setting limits to his own most influential period of literary production.

From 1923, however, having embarked on his editorship of *The Criterion*, he began to chafe at his self-imposed aestheticism, and to develop a sense of himself as an "old-fashioned Tory" (*Letters2* 251).[5] In 1928, as *The Sacred Wood* was reissued, Eliot felt that a status update was needed. Stung by the suggestion from his old tutor, Irving Babbitt, that he was being too secretive—a private intellectual—about his recent conversion to Anglo-Catholicism, he resolved, as Babbitt advised, to "come out into the open" (*Prose6* 187). The result was the notorious preface to *For Lancelot Andrewes: Essays on Style and Order* (1928), in which he tried to "disassociate [himself] from certain conclusions which have been drawn from … *The Sacred Wood*" with the statement that his "general point of view" was "classicist in literature, royalist in politics, and anglo-catholic in religion." Declining to define these terms, Eliot instead pointed to "the small volumes which I have in preparation: *The School of Donne*; *The Outline of Royalism*; and *The Principles of Modern Heresy*" (*Prose3* 513). Readers of the *Complete Prose* looking for *The School of Donne* will find a first draft in Eliot's 1926 Clark Lectures at Cambridge, posthumously published as *The Varieties of Metaphysical Poetry* (1993). *After Strange Gods* (1934), meanwhile, with its subtitle "A Primer of Modern Heresy," was the closest Eliot came to making good (or, in light of his decision to suppress it, bad) on the third title promised. Where, though, is the political wing of the trilogy, *The Outline of Royalism*?

As a political position in England in 1928, royalism, Eliot conceded, was "at present without definition" (*Prose3* 513). It never acquires one in the *Complete Prose*. But fishing for kings in these volumes is one way of tracing what Denis Donoghue calls the "essentially mythical" principle that informed Eliot's vision of social unity as a matter of symbol and ritual, just as it did the "mythical method" of *The Waste Land* (*Prose2* 479).[6] In Volume 1, the terms "royalism" and "intellectual" appear in the outline of his 1916 modern French literature extension lecture on "Royalism and Socialism," where—contrary to the more usual derogatory association of "intellectual" with the anti-Dreyfusard position in French politics—he applied it to, among others, Charles Maurras ("Besides the loyal band of traditional royalists there are several intellectuals who have been led to the royalist position largely as a protest against all the conditions in art and society which seemed to be due to the Revolution" [*Prose1* 473]). In Volume 2, covering the "Perfect Critic" years of 1919–26, "royalism" appears only in the editorial apparatus—a marker of Eliot's suppression of his political views in his literary work at this time. But then, in Volume 3 (1927–9), royalism enjoys a glorious restoration, particularly in the pages of the *Criterion*, as Eliot defends Maurras and his right-wing nationalist movement, the Action Française, following its condemnation by the Catholic Church in 1926, and surveys "The Literature of Fascism" (1928) in an article that states his opposition to totalitarianism as an alternative to democracy, but also remarks: "Most of the concepts which might have attracted me in fascism I seem already to have found, in a more digestible form, in the work of Charles Maurras," whose ideas "have a closer applicability to England than those of fascism" (*Prose3* 547).

His literary admirers were dismayed. The poet Thomas MacGreevy, in his 1931 study of Eliot, excoriated Maurras's ongoing royalism as the belief in "a prince at any price," a journalistic rehashing of "the theories of thirty years ago"; "it is unthinkable," he concluded, "that Eliot should follow the same road."[7] In the same year, Eliot's preoccupation with the relationship between literature and politics prompted the first parts of a new poetic sequence. If, as Evan Kindley has suggested, "Gerontion" (1920)—which was written around the same time as "Tradition and the Individual Talent" (1919)—can be read as a dramatic monologue on the burden of the poet-critic as a cultural administrator ("I an old man / A dull head among windy spaces" [*Poems1* 31]), the unfinished *Coriolan* (1931–2) can be heard as its weary sequel, in which the man of letters who has "come out into the open" about politics has bad dreams about Coriolanus, the reluctant consul of Shakespeare's Roman tragedy ("I a tired head among these heads" [*Poems1* 134]).[8] Ricks and McCue's notes to the *Poems* suggest that Eliot's inspiration for the crowd scene of the first part, "Triumphal March," was the political aftermath of the Great War and the subsequent rise of fascism in Europe. But the jolting switch to French in the final line also pointedly suggests a return to MacGreevy's "theories of thirty years ago." "*Et les soldats faisaient la haie? ILS LA FAISAIENT*" ("And the soldiers lined the streets? THEY LINED THEM"), as Eliot noted, is a quotation, with added emphasis, from "an ironic description of the public funeral of a distinguished man of letters" by Maurras, in *L'Avenir de l'intelligence* (1905) (*Poems1* 829).[9] Eliot bought this book during his formative student year in Paris in 1911, and in his 1928 review of Benda summarized it as "a protest against conditions under which the intellectual, who should be occupied with intellectual matters purely, was forced to mix in the quarrels of the market place" ("Culture and Anarchy," *Prose3* 348). The quoted line is attributed to a "fairly mediocre but representative" man of letters, who rhapsodizes "every time a member of the Republic of letters finds himself touched dead or alive by official honours" (*Poems1* 828–9). The irony of this spectacle, to a royalist, is its debasement of ceremony through liberal democracy's confusion of elites.

"Triumphal March" was followed by "Difficulties of a Statesman," as the intellectual leader flounders among the banal centralized proceduralism of modern bureaucracy ("One secretary will do for several committees" [*Poems1* 133]). Both fragments of *Coriolan* were written in summer 1931. Together, they dramatize Eliot's admirers' reaction to the 1928 preface to *For Lancelot Andrewes*, as summarized in his first extended essay as an Anglican lay commentator, "Thoughts after Lambeth," published in March 1931:

> Somehow I had failed, and had admitted my failure; if not a lost leader, at least a lost sheep; what is more, I was a kind of traitor; and of those who were to find their way to the promised land beyond the waste one might drop a tear at my absence from the roll-call of the new saints. (*Prose4* 227)

The last line of "Difficulties of a Statesman" ("RESIGN RESIGN RESIGN") catches this note of betrayal, as those who once imagined *The Waste Land* would lead them to the Promised Land recant their former chant of "Shantih shantih shantih" (*Poems1* 135, 71). The "hopeful" conclusion that Eliot draws from his supposed apostasy recalls the Maurrasian mockery of "Triumphal March" and its day-tripping crowd on "the way to the temple" (*Poems1* 131). The literary establishment's rejection of his Christianity, he noted with a contrarian's satisfaction, meant that

> the orthodox faith of England is at last relieved from its burden of respectability. A new respectability has arisen to assume the burden; and those who would once have been considered intellectual vagrants are now pious pilgrims, cheerfully plodding the road from nowhere to nowhere, trolling their hymns, satisfied so long as they may be "on the march." (*Prose4* 227)

Eliot the rebel consul would further challenge the "respectable" orthodoxy of his audience with *After Strange Gods* (1934), which attempted ill-advisedly to take the criticism of modern literature into the court of theology, but is now chiefly remembered for the racist remark that, in a unified Christian society, "reasons of race and religion combine to make any large number of free-thinking Jews undesirable" (*Prose5* 20). These words—where "free-thinking" does the prejudicial work that Eliot's scare quotes around "intellectual" would do elsewhere—were central to the argument of Anthony Julius's *T. S. Eliot, Anti-Semitism and Literary Form* (1995).[10] The *Complete Prose* provides new evidence that Eliot also actively opposed the political reality of anti-Semitism: in 1953, he responded to a request for a statement (eventually published in 1963) condemning contemporary Soviet persecution of Jewish citizens. Anti-Semitism, he wrote, is a symptom of profound difficulty, disorder, and maladjustment in the economy and in the spiritual life of that nation; and is exploited by rulers as a desperate remedy which only aggravates, in the end, the malady of which it is a symptom … [A]ny government which persecutes and stigmatizes any body of its own nationals—and most notably the Jews—will in the end have to pay the full penalty for so doing. ("Anti-Semitism in Russia," *Prose8* 550–1)

Full though this is, its detached political analysis echoes another exhibit in Julius's argument: Eliot's qualification of his condemnation of the anti-Jewish Laws of Vichy France with the remark that anti-Semitism "as a symptom the disorder of French society and politics for the last hundred and fifty years" was "a very different thing" to fascism (*Prose6* 180).[11] Unable to resist the flourish of ethnographic nuance again in 1953, Eliot—presumably thinking of the contemporary internecine violence that followed the end of the British Mandate in Palestine and the founding of Israel—distinguishes "true anti-Semitism … from anti-Semitism in Arab countries, which has much more of the nature of ordinary racial, nationalistic and religious conflict" ("Anti-Semitism in Russia," *Prose8* 550). It is hard to see what purpose these intellectual distinctions serve other than to assert the intellectual distinction of their author as he washes his hands with Haines, the English colonial apologist of *Ulysses*: "It seems history is to blame."[12]

Eliot told an émigré audience in London in 1945: "I am not a supporter of any race doctrine, certainly of no philosophy of race superiority and inferiority in the modern sense. It is not blood that I am interested in, but the transmission of *culture*" ("Cultural Diversity and European Unity," *Prose6* 630).[13] But inherited "culture" is exactly how structures of thought, including racial prejudice, are transmitted: as Ngũgĩ wa Thiong'o observes, "Eliot's high culture of an Anglo-Catholic feudal tradition [is] suspiciously close … to the racial doctrines of those born to rule." Eliot's defenders against Julius have often cried "guilt by association." But the evidence for innocence by disassociation is also wanting. As Louis Menand notes, Eliot's "intellectualized politics" led him to publish "Hommage à Charles Maurras" (1948) three years after the Frenchman had been imprisoned for Nazi collaboration; to this, the *Complete Prose* adds a personal "Message on Charles Maurras" to a memorial gathering in 1952, praising Maurras's early writings as "part of the heritage of all European peoples" (*Prose7* 774).[14]

Although Eliot remained loyal to his youthful estimate of Maurras, the reactionary glamour of "royalism" largely disappeared from his public prose after 1930. Privately, he admitted that as a theory it had "always been unformulated in my own mind" (*Letters6* 278).¹⁵ Instead, following his Certificate of Naturalization in 1927, he concentrated on establishing himself as a British public intellectual. Fittingly for a writer whose very name was an anagram of "litotes," Eliot shrank from rhetorical exuberance; contemplating Winston Churchill's prose, he remarked: "at the end of a period we seem to observe the author pause for the invariable burst of hand-clapping" [*Prose5* 4]).¹⁶ Nevertheless, Eliot's prose in the 1930s, like his poetic drama, reflects a shifting of tactics away from "minority journalism" and toward the influential self-fashioning he admired in H. G. Wells: "Through being a popular entertainer, he found an opening as a prophet" ("Views and Reviews: Journalists of Yesterday and Today," *Prose6* 11). In 1929, Eliot wrote to the newly founded BBC proposing a series of talks on "Six Types of Tudor Prose"—not the most obviously entertaining or popular topic but chosen perhaps, as Michael Coyle suggests, for its resonant association with dynastic British history and Eliot's own ancestral connection with the Tudor man of letters Sir Thomas Elyot.¹⁷ In a repeat of his earlier progress from book reviewer to essayist, Eliot applied himself to mastering radio techniques with literary material, making the move to cultural commentator in 1932 for the series *The Modern Dilemma*, with four talks on "the possibility of a Christian society." By the end of the decade, these would become his first extended work of social criticism, *The Idea of a Christian Society* (1939)—a book that is notably silent on the subject of royalism, despite the titular role of the British monarch as the Supreme Governor of the Church of England. Following the Abdication Crisis of 1936 Eliot had warned against reviving the eighteenth-century idea of a "Patriot King," who might become "a kind of Fascist King" ("Mr. Reckitt, Mr. Tomlin, and the Crisis," *Prose5* 453). Now, on the eve of war with Nazi Germany, he warned in *The Idea of a Christian Society* against confusing the idea of a Christian society with a potentially totalitarian "English National Religion," seeking instead the stable but dynamic relationship of authorities ("the Church in England to the Universal Church" [*Prose5* 726–7]), which was the liberal principle that informed his dialectical conservatism from the first (his earliest published review, on books about India, began: "Why is it that so many cultivated British officials in India persist in ignoring what the young and educated Indians of to-day are thinking[?]" [*Prose1* 390]).¹⁸

A decade and a war later, *Notes towards the Definition of Culture* (1948) would go even further in its tactical accommodation of a liberal idea Eliot had long deprecated in Matthew Arnold: "that Culture (as he uses the term) is something more comprehensive than religion" (*Prose7* 206; see also *Prose4* 183). In a famous passage, Eliot's second book of social criticism inverted Arnold's proposition to argue that culture is "*lived* religion" and includes "all the characteristic activities and interests of a people": his illustrative list runs from "Derby Day, Henley Regatta, Cowes, the twelfth of August" via football, pubs, cheese, cabbage, and beetroot to nineteenth-century churches and "the music of Elgar" (*Prose7* 208–9). The first four are all British sporting fixtures associated with the royal family, while Elgar's "Land of Hope and Glory," from his *Coronation Ode* (1902), became a permanent part of the Last Night of the Proms when it was broadcast on BBC television for the first time in 1947.[19] Like the postwar British monarchy itself, Eliot's egalitarian cabbages-and-kings list naturalizes royalism as the ritual annual framing of "everyday" national life, having moved over two decades from a reactionary to a quietist position.[20] As he wrote in the preface to the 1962 edition, "I should not now, for instance, call myself a 'royalist' *tout court*, as I once did: I would say that I am in favour of retaining the monarchy in every country in which a monarchy still exists" (*Prose7* 195).

Philip Larkin once quoted Eliot's evocative mélange of British (or rather, English) life in an essay on John Betjeman, suggesting that the "cultural inclusiveness" of Betjeman's popular poetic Englishness had more in common with Eliot than literary critics might believe.[21] The same might be said of Larkin's own poetry. In 1954, he wrote "Church Going," a poem that expresses an atheist's nostalgia for the community that empty church buildings once symbolized. The verbal parallels between the argument of the poem and Eliot's "The Value and Use of Cathedrals in England Today" (1952) are striking:

> There are, I am sure, people outside of the Church who would gladly see them preserved simply as ancient monuments of historical and artistic interest with turnstiles and admission charges (Eliot)

> ... wondering, too,
> When churches fall completely out of use
> What we shall turn them into, if we shall keep
> A few cathedrals chronically on show (Larkin)

> The increasingly popular midnight corporate communion at Christmas (Eliot)

> Some ... Christmas-addict, counting on a whiff
> Of gown-and-bands and organ-pipes and myrrh (Larkin)

> ... as far as people do come, the cathedral has the responsibility of satisfying the best taste, correcting the imperfect, and educating that which is unformed (Eliot)

> Since someone will forever be surprising
> A hunger in himself to be more serious,
> And gravitating with it to this ground,
> Which, he once heard, was proper to grow wise in (Larkin)[22]

Was Eliot's ephemeral talk to the Friends of Chichester Cathedral a source for "Church Going"? As a university librarian, Larkin was well placed to be aware of its publication in pamphlet form. The resemblance, however, more generally suggests how the pragmatic concerns of Eliot's cultural criticism—caricatured in 1956 by Bernard Bergonzi as those of a "shifty High Church pamphleteer"—informed a dominant tone of intellectual realism about the rituals of national life in postwar English literature.[23] Eliot was always anxious about being seen as too pragmatic, especially on religious matters ("what do we mean by the *use* of a cathedral? For the word *use* can be a very dangerous one to use" [*Prose7* 732]). But when his doctoral thesis, *Knowledge and Experience in the Philosophy of F. H. Bradley*, was finally published in 1964, its conclusion made clear that this was an attitude he had brought into public life from the sphere of philosophy: "If I have insisted on the practical (pragmatic?) in the constitution and meaning of objects, it is because the practical is a practical metaphysic" (*Prose1* 381).

From Raymond Williams's *Culture and Society* (1958) onward, left-wing intellectuals have often dismissed Eliot's claim to be an *engagé* critic of postwar society on the grounds that his politics were a poet's atavistic fantasy: "this Anglo-Catholic classicist-royalist stuff you import from English and want to call sociology," as the academic protagonist of Malcolm Bradbury's *The History Man* (1975) snipes at a stubbornly conservative student.[24] But the *Complete Prose* shows repeatedly how practical Eliot was in the tactics he used to keep his metaphysics warm in the marketplace of ideas, as he moved between literary criticism, social criticism, drama, and poetry, insisting on the coherence of these activities even as their results appeared piecemeal. The leading "man of letters" of his generation was, first and last, a freelancer, writing to the moment even as he lifted his eyes to the eternal. And the activity that originally gave him his authority—his poetry—remained central to his vision, even after he had largely ceased writing it. Colin MacCabe has speculatively explained the scattered nature of Eliot's calls to unity:

> Many books were mooted, but they always ended up as collections of essays or published lectures. My own suspicion is that Eliot never completed a book-length project because he would have had great difficulty in articulating his

belief in a national language as the genuine spirit of a people other than in the elliptical and enigmatic fragments that we have scattered through his essays and poems. Had he done so it might have seemed easier to reconcile the democratic thrust of his poetry with his authoritarian and conservative politics.[25]

Eliot's "belief in a national language as the genuine spirit of a people" was essayed most ambitiously in the public lectures of the 1940s: for example, in "The Music of Poetry" (1942), with its astonishing claim that "at certain moments ... a word can be made to insinuate the whole history of a language and a civilization" (*Prose6* 316), and also in the 1943 and 1945 versions of "The Social Function of Poetry"—the latter delivered in France shortly after VE Day—which propose that poetry's feeling for the collective life of words has a socially unifying function "at every level of education" (*Prose6* 440).

In the early 1960s, Eliot attempted to put these beliefs into action. His last sustained public campaign as a critic, conducted while serving on the committee overseeing the translation of the Revised Psalter (1963), was against the stylistic infelicities of the New English Bible (1961), which threatened to displace resonant cadences of the King James Version (KJV) in England's churches. By taking up this cause, Eliot's intellectual mission once again curiously refashions the liberal prophecy of Matthew Arnold—specifically, Arnold's belief that "the strongest part of our religion today is its unconscious poetry," an idea that found practical application through the Victorian critic's 1872 edition of the KJV Book of Isaiah 40–66 for schoolchildren.[26] Writing in the *Sunday Telegraph*, a newspaper with a much wider circulation than usual for his journalism, Eliot advocated for the socially harmonious uses of Jacobean cadence as ardently as his earliest essay in poetics, "Reflections on *Vers Libre*" (1917), had extolled "the music which can never be recaptured in other words" (*Prose1* 513). Interviewed in 1945 on "the condition of man today," Eliot had expressed the view that "there is too much separation between town and country."[27] But the KJV still bound them together:

> The Complete Oxford Dictionary says that "swine" is now "literary" but does not say that it is "obsolete." I presume, therefore, that in substituting "pigs" for "swine" the translators were trying to choose a word nearer to common speech, even if at the sacrifice of dignity.
>
> I should have thought, however, that the word "swine" would be understood, not only by countryfolk who may have heard of "swine fever," but even by the urban public, since it is still applied, I believe, to human beings as a term of abuse. ("T. S. Eliot on the Language of the New English Bible," *Prose8* 531)

Do public intellectuals feed their pearls to pigs—as the New English Bible would have it—or cast them before swine? For Eliot, defying the proverb in his lifelong effort to sway the wide audience won by his verse with high-minded prose, it was an important distinction.

Notes

Thanks to John Haffenden, Thomas Karshan, Rachel Potter, and Matthew Taunton for intellectual advice during the writing of this chapter.

1 Helen Small, introduction to *The Public Intellectual*, edited by Helen Small (Oxford: Blackwell, 2002), 1.
2 Stefan Collini, *Absent Minds: Intellectuals in Britain* (Oxford: Oxford University Press, 2006), 15–44.
3 Collini, *Absent Minds*, 35–6.
4 Eliot was reviewing the French text in 1927, but Richard Aldington, the English translator of Benda, agreed: "The word 'Clercs' … is defined by M. Benda as 'all those who speak to the world in a transcendental manner.' I do not know the English word for 'all those who speak to the world in a transcendental manner'" (translator's note in Julien Benda, *The Treason of the Intellectuals*, translated by Richard Aldington [New York: William Morrow, 1928], ix).
5 To Ford Madox Ford, October 11, 1923.
6 Denis Donoghue, *Words Alone: The Poet T. S. Eliot* (New Haven: Yale University Press, 2000), 219–21.
7 Thomas MacGreevy, *Thomas Stearns Eliot: A Study* (London: Chatto & Windus, 1931), 65–8.
8 Evan Kindley, *Poet-Critics and the Administration of Culture* (Cambridge: Harvard University Press, 2017), 33–5.
9 To Dudley Sheppard, March 11, 1935.
10 Anthony Julius, *T. S. Eliot, Anti-Semitism and Literary Form*, 2nd ed. (London: Thames & Hudson, 2005), chapter 5.
11 *The Christian News-Letter* 97 (September 3, 1941); Julius, 171–3.
12 James Joyce, *Ulysses* (1922), edited by Jeri Johnson (Oxford: Oxford University Press, 1993), 20. Compare Eliot's private defense of his "free-thinking" remark to J. V. Healey in 1940: "my view does not imply any prejudice on the ground of race, but merely a recognition of what seems to me an historical situation" (quoted in *Prose5* 50).
13 Julius, 216–17.
14 Louis Menand, *Discovering Modernism: T. S. Eliot and His Context* (Oxford: Oxford University Press), 2nd ed., 176.

15 To Charles Smyth, June 8, 1932.
16 "A Commentary," *Criterion* 13 (January 1934).
17 Michael Coyle, "'This rather elusory broadcast technique': T. S. Eliot and the Genre of the Radio Talk," *ANQ* 11, no. 4 (1998): 33.
18 *New Statesman*, 6 (December 18, 1915). For a closely argued account of Eliot's "belief in the efficacy of intellectual discomfort" as the ethical principle underpinning "the apparent inconsistencies of his cultural prose," see Jason M. Coats, "'The Striving': Eliot's Difficult Ethics," *Modernist Cultures* 4, nos. 1–2 (2009): 67–83.
19 "Why Is 'Land of Hope and Glory' at the BBC Proms?," *Classical Music*, accessed June 14, 2021, https://www.classical-music.com/features/articles/last-night-proms-history.
20 On the public appetite for "homely" stories about the royal family in this period, see Richard Hoggart, *The Uses of Literacy* (London: Chatto & Windus, 1957), 111–12.
21 Philip Larkin, *Required Writing: Miscellaneous Pieces 1955–1982* (London: Faber, 1983), 218.
22 *Prose7* 732–6; Philip Larkin, *Collected Poems*, edited by Anthony Thwaite (London: Faber, 2003), 58–9.
23 Bernard Bergonzi, "Truth and Dogma," *Nine* 4, no. 2 (April 1956): 37. Compare A. S. Byatt, *The Virgin in the Garden* (London: Chatto & Windus, 1978) on the "cultural ecstasy" induced in one character by the coronation of Elizabeth II in 1953: "Eliot had said, and she remembered, that the 'English unbeliever conformed to the practices of Christianity on the occasions of birth, death, and the first venture into matrimony …' Now a whole Nation was conforming to an ancient national Christian rite" (242).
24 *The History Man* (1975; repr. London: Arena, 1984), 137. Compare Terry Eagleton, *Criticism and Ideology: A Study in Marxist Theory* (London: NLB, 1976): "it is symptomatic of Eliot's political acumen that the regressive social utopianism of [*The Idea of a Christian Society*] should be offered to the world on the very eve of the Second World War" (147).
25 Colin MacCabe, *T. S. Eliot* (Liverpool: Liverpool University Press, 2006), 67.
26 Matthew Arnold, "The Study of Poetry," in *Selected Poems and Prose*, edited by Miriam Allott (London: J. M. Dent & Sons, 1978), 241.
27 J. P. Hodin, "T. S. Eliot on the Condition of Man Today," *Horizon* 12, no. 68 [July 1945]: 88.

Part II

Eliot in Theory

6

"No empty bottles": Eliot's Ambivalent Anthropocene

Julia E. Daniel

For better or worse, a mention of Eliot often brings to mind his iconic wastes: the barren lands, trashed Thames, and ruins of *The Waste Land*; the atmospheric urban clutter in many of his early pieces; or the oceanic garbage and decaying dung of *Four Quartets*. These abject, visceral images both repel and fascinate readers in ways that reveal Eliot's overlooked ambivalence about the ecological and social life of human detritus. This chapter reconsiders what we would today call Eliot's environmentalism to explore this ambivalence in light of the Anthropocene, particularly through his numerous depictions of anthropocenic waste. They are anthropocenic in terms of their scale, being both massively diffuse and intimately minute at the same time, and their indelibility as phenomena impossible to pass beyond, before, or outside of, let alone to remove. What we discover is that Eliot's response to dwelling in the Anthropocene is ambiguous. Smoke and rubbish both symbolize and manifest cultural and spiritual decay. At the same time, Eliot resists imagining a return to a pure "before," often figured as a clean pastoral. Rather, Eliotic wastes are the inevitable and compounding traces of people who discard material in the act of living. Approaching Eliot through the Anthropocene teaches us that his green investments are more tangled than we might like them to be. And approaching the Anthropocene through Eliot reminds us that living in the "epoch of man" ought not push us into fantasies of impossible purity or prelapsarian agrarianism.

If Eliot's dictum that "mature poets steal" holds true, we might say the same for literary scholars fond of poaching terms from other disciplines ("Philip Massinger," *Prose2* 245). "The Anthropocene" originated in the fields of climate science and geology. It describes "the age of man" in terms of our geologic and global impact, particularly in the era of climate change. It was first used in the

1980s by biologist Eugene Stoermer and gained in popularity in a short paper he coauthored with Paul Crutzen in 2000.[1] In 2016, the Anthropocene Working Group recommended that the term be accepted as a descriptor of a distinct, measurable era in the life of the planet where its natural processes are deeply and irrevocably shaped by human activity. Crutzen and Stoermer argued that the invention of the steam engine inaugurated the Anthropocene, as its creation began centuries of fallout from CO_2-emitting technologies, the aftereffects of which can be measured in core samples of arctic ice and can be felt everywhere in the form of global climate change. Alternate dates and modes of measuring the Anthropocene have been proposed, from atomic radiation to mass-species extinctions. But no matter where they start, all of these proposals posit that human activity created a new era in which we have altered the entirety of earth's systems in ways that leave diffuse, pervasive, indelible traces.

In the hands of environmentalists and literary critics, the Anthropocene floats from its scientific moorings. As Rob Nixon has argued, this material awareness of planet-wide anthropogenic impacts presents us with the daunting problem of even imaging this state of affairs. As such, "new metrics demand new metaphors."[2] In terms of a literary imagination, the Anthropocene is an age in which the pastoral cannot exist. There is no pure natural elsewhere, no place, even hundreds of feet down into the soil or up into the atmosphere, that does not bear some contaminating mark of human activity. For a contemporary reader, this arguably feels a little obvious. But such was not the case for many Western modernists who wrote with the dawning realization that the ocean cannot effortlessly consume everything we throw in it, that garbage reappears rather than disappears, and smoke always blows downwind, never simply "away." And in an era of increasing mechanization, many of the technologies that defined the everyday experience of modernist writers added to that ecological impact, from the widespread use of electrical lighting and automobiles to the dusting of crops with man-made chemical fertilizers and the dumping of industrial pollutants that always lurked behind (or sometimes even within) new mass-market commodities. If we keep the anthropocenic start date near the Victorian era, we might say that the modernist environmental imagination is one that is catching up with the amplifying ecological consequences of an ongoing industrial revolution, with reverberations felt as wide as the globe and as close as one's skin.

As such, ecocritics turned to modernist texts as a body of literary art that testifies to and often reacts against the toxic cultural practices contributing to the age of the Anthropocene. This early green turn toward modernist studies largely valorized the environmental investments of writers like E. E. Cummings, Virginia

Woolf, William Carlos Williams, and T. S. Eliot.[3] For Eliot in particular, recent works by Jeremy Diaper, Gabrielle McIntire, and Etienne Terblanche all explicitly consider Eliot's environmental vision from angles as varied as industrial farming and Buddhist philosophy.[4] The *T. S. Eliot Studies Annual* also recently included a dedicated cluster on Eliot's representation of the biological, with an emphasis on ecological concerns.[5] These studies expanded material cultural approaches that consider the environmental cost of the cars, synthetic perfumes, and garbage that furnish Eliot's work in particular and modernist literature more broadly. But just as ecocriticism moved into more complexity, widening its canon while questioning its own foundational terms, studying an environmental Eliot *now* is an opportunity to revisit those passages that have quietly frustrated our emerald-tinged lenses, my own included. While "Anthropocene" is most often used in a rhetoric of environmental activism, there is also a general sense among scholars that we cannot, as Eliot says, ring the bell backward (*Poems1* 206). It is far too late to reverse most of the traces that define the Anthropocene. The live question then, for contemporary environmental activists and, provocatively, for Eliot himself, is—so now what? How does one live in the Anthropocene? What can we fix, mitigate, come to bear, or even appreciate in the middle of a global wasteland?

A serious problem for greening Eliot is that he has some of the best scenes of garbage and pollution to be found in modern poetry (perhaps after William Carlos Williams). Approaching Eliotic detritus not from an ecocritical perspective but from an anthropocenic one reveals the surprising loveliness, intimacy, and necessity of human waste—a term that I here use broadly to describe the array of cast-off matter produced from human activity—in Eliot's verse.[6] His early Laforguian cityscapes are violet-washed curio cabinets full of garbage: rusted-out springs, rancid butter, and scraps of newspaper. In many ways, the city will remain the *topos* of waste throughout Eliot's career, as the cluttered and crammed dysfunctional center of modern living. The fog of "Prufrock"'s hallucinatory setting is a prime example of how Eliot builds an ambivalent urban anthropocenic atmosphere in the early poetry. As Frances Dickey has recently demonstrated, air pollution was so terrible in Eliot's childhood St. Louis that particulate matter from the factories mingled with domestic soot from chimneys in inky rainfall throughout the city. Atmospheric conditions were so poor that drivers had to honk incessantly during the day to warn each other of oncoming traffic.[7] The Wednesday Club, of which Eliot's mother was a founding member, petitioned that something be done about the industrial smog that often blotted out the noonday sun. Given this real environmental and public-health crisis, it is nothing less than bizarre that the "yellow smoke that rubs its muzzle on the window-panes" in

"Prufrock" is rather disarming (*Poems1* 5). It has a playfulness and tenderness of touch found nowhere else in this poem. Unlike the disembodied (or occasionally dismembered) Prufrock, the pollution rubs, licks, lingers, slips, curls, and ultimately cuddles up for the night. Its composition is an anthropocenic admixture that blends human and natural elements, a commingling of "fog" exhaled from the river and a "smoke" from the chimneys. In its pervasiveness across multiple scales, it is also an anthropocenic reality. The feline toxic fog is, on the one hand, large and diffuse. It roams high and low, from rooftops to gutters, and permeates insides and outsides, slinking through the streets and invading the house. It even nuzzles into the very "corners of the evening," becoming celestial in the process. One cannot imagine any place for a breath of fresh air, and arguably one cannot be had anywhere in the poem. (Even when Prufrock imagines escaping to the sea, at the poem's conclusion, breathing quickly turns to drowning.) And yet, on the other hand, this pollution is also intimate and human-scale. As it coalesces into feline ligature, it bounds off the terrace, where "seeing that it was a soft October night," it curls "once about the house" before settling down to sleep (*Poems1* 5). In the scale of the house, it diminishes into pet-like docility. The image of peaceful sleep here also contrasts with the chemicalized vision of an etherized patient as night sky, a thing technically asleep and yet far from restful. The spreading smog blots out that first simile and offers the speaker (and the reader) some relief. The cat-like pollution even makes the scene slightly beautiful. Its own impressionistic blur makes this October night so "soft" to behold, so welcoming to an animal's repose (*Poems1* 5).

What then are we to do with air pollution in the Prufrockian Anthropocene? It can still, of course, be read as a form of environmental critique. In a world where human contact seems eternally forestalled, the only touch available to our speaker comes from the pollution that spreads into every corner of his world and imagination. As such, pollution is deeply tragic and part of the general atmosphere of malaise throughout the piece. However, even granting that environmental critique, the smoke remains one of the most winsome presences within the poem. One cannot get around the fact that some manifestations of pollution in the Anthropocene can be familiar and eerily lovely. As Joshua Schuster has argued, numerous modern writers celebrate industrial pollution, as far back as Walt Whitman. Schuster critiques that toxic aesthetic and then offers alternatives to be found in the canon of modernism.[8] Eliot's anthropocentric imagination is provocative precisely in the way it makes both moves simultaneously. His smoke is both unhealthy and appealing, impersonal and intimate, beastly and beautiful all at the same time. And most important, there's no escaping it.

If Eliot's feline smoke is disturbingly pleasant for contemporary environmentalist readers, his portrayal of a completely clean Thames in *The Waste Land* is also deeply unnerving. As Gabrielle McIntire and others have thoughtfully demonstrated, *The Waste Land* comfortably lends itself to an ecocritical analysis, depicting as it does a London wreathed in "brown fog," a profoundly polluted Thames that "sweats / Oil and tar" and runs beside a "gashouse," to say nothing of its wider ritual and symbolic architecture stemming from land-based fertility myths. As Richard Lehan has argued, the poem presents readers with the consequences of a Western urbanism that has "lost touch with the land, with the rhythms and the psychic nourishment of nature."[9] Granting this, Eliot's fantasy of a clean, abandoned Thames in "The Fire Sermon" persists as one of the major stumbling blocks for an environmentalist reading. This moment in "The Fire Sermon" pulls heavily from Edmund Spenser's *Prothalamion*, composed for the double marriage of Katherine and Elizabeth Somerset, in 1596. The *Prothalamion* begins by describing the mental state of a speaker overcome by courtly life, seeking refreshment by the flowering banks of the Thames, in classic pastoral mode. He then encounters a pair of river nymphs gathering flowers for the wedding ceremony. An environmental reading might then treat Eliot's refrain, "The nymphs are departed," as a modern lament over the toxic desecration of the river and its environs, yet another wasted land ruined by modernity (*Poems1* 62).[10]

But the dissonances in this node of the mythical method start to compound very quickly. First, the Thames is clean *because* the nymphs and their paramours have abandoned the land. The list of absent trash contains exactly those things cast off by couples enjoying "summer nights":

> The river bears no empty bottles, sandwich papers,
> Silk handkerchiefs, cardboard boxes, cigarette ends
> Or other testimony of summer nights. (*Poems1* 62)

McIntire argues that this scene is a fleeting moment of ecological relief: "the Thames appears for a brief moment as it once might have—as relatively pure and unlittered—although such cleanliness is reported only through negation."[11] However, the emptiness of the Thames jars across almost every register. No bottles or sandwich wrappers means no drinking, eating, or other summer pleasures. Leisure and feasting produce waste, particularly in their modernized prepackaged forms. And such waste would testify to some sort of romantic concourse between the mythic nymphs and the now departed "heirs," yet another set of restless subjects in *The Waste Land* who lack a meaningful connection with the land. No litter means no coupling, and in that equation, Eliot uses the *Prothalamion* against itself. We have *either* a spotless riverside *or* fertility rites, a clean but abandoned Thames *or* a littered one where people actually live. The pastoral promise of both is impossible in the London of *The Waste Land*. Eliot's garbage *via negativa* also writes against any pastoral hope of returning to a preindustrial state of imagined organic flourishing. Where there are "no empty bottles," we do not find green banks, as Spenser presents them "painted all with variable flowers, / And all the meads adorned with dainty gems."[12] Rather, what we find is absence, neither blossoms nor heirs, without a cigarette or anything else in sight. In its lack of human traces, the clean Thames becomes yet another wasteland, a muddy barrenness that testifies to failures of human connection and a rootless, transient culture.

The difficulties of these lines compound when we consider that the Thames was full of this kind of mess during Eliot's lifetime. And it was little better than an open sewer during the life of Spenser.[13] Spenser's pastoral gestures were always illusory, even in his own moment, and Eliot calls them out as such, a move that reflects on the socio-ecological history of the Thames. In the Anthropocene, the nymphs have always already departed. And yet, *The Waste Land* does not celebrate pollution, even in the mitigated manner found in "Prufrock." While the barren riverside is not to be desired, neither is a sullied one to be admired. Eliot clearly does not advocate for using the Thames as a dump, let alone retiring to such a filthy spot for what one assumes would be a similarly degrading throwaway encounter, paralleling the typist's scene. We land in a similar place as in "Prufrock," where we can neither fully discard nor fully embrace the polluting remnants of human culture, though *The Waste Land* captures the same attitude in a slightly different manner. In "Prufrock," we cannot imagine an outside alternative to the cat-like atmosphere of the Anthropocene. By contrast, in *The Waste Land*, we can only imagine a green beyond, before, or elsewhere through emphatically delusional pastoral set-pieces, ones that are quickly revealed to be a sham. And when Eliot shifts the ideal of purity that informs the pastoral onto the contemporary banks of London's great, oily river, the fantasy of a zero-waste culture becomes its own wasteland, a nymphless, trashless muck.

Of course, Eliot did not set himself the task of offering a sustainable alternative to modern living in these poems, and we place an unfair burden on them if we expect as much. Beyond that, as I have argued elsewhere, Eliot's ecological vision in his poetry and drama is largely diagnostic: he offers critique but infrequently gestures toward alternatives.[14] We begin to see some such efforts, however, in his later poetry, coinciding with his increasing involvement in the organicist movement. Jeremy Diaper has provided several detailed studies of Eliot's participation in that movement, the offshoot of which is today's British Soil Association.[15] As Diaper has shown, Eliot was a major critic of modernized Western agriculture, particularly industrialized monocrop farming and the toxic chemical management it requires. Eliot thought a return to village life centered on the rhythms of organic farming had benefits for the cultural, spiritual, civic, and physical health of the English public, as well as for the multigenerational health of English soil, which he, along with the organicists, viewed as a living membrane, not simply inert dirt or parcels of land. At the same time, he knew such a shift back to the land could neither be a slip into an impossible, cheery medieval serfdom nor be mandated by governmental force. Advocating for a sustainable modern agrarian culture in *Notes towards the Definition of Culture*, Eliot explicitly states as much: "[W]hen I say [culture] must grow again from the soil, I do not mean that it will be brought into existence by any activity of political demagogues ... For if any definite conclusions emerge from this study, one of them is surely this, that culture is the one thing that we cannot deliberately aim at" (*Prose7* 199–200). To take true root, such an agricultural revival must evolve from an impulse within the English public (by which he means primarily the working class that would repatriate from the city to the country), one supported by governmental schemes but not forced into existence by them.

Eliot's agrarian scenes in *Four Quartets* come closest to such a vision, as they advocate for a composting culture whose traces participate in healthful cycles of regeneration, rather than in a compounding culture that amasses undigestible piles of lasting trash. The former he links with producers, particularly village-scale farmers, and the latter with exchangers, associated with factory production or other extractive industry. In a 1938 *Criterion* commentary, Eliot quotes from a major organicist text, *Horn, Hoof and Corn*, to critique this tension between factory and field: "Lord Lymington's book is concerned with agriculture, but with agriculture as it concerns everybody. 'Exchangers,' he remarks in his Preface, 'are less important than producers, and among producers it is those who till the soil upon whom civilization is based, more than upon those who mine or manufacture'" (*Prose5* 649). *East Coker* begins with a restrained critique of a culture reliant on such manufacturing, along with the infrastructure and technologies that facilitate it:

> In succession
> Houses rise and fall, crumble, are extended,
> Are removed, destroyed, restored, or in their place
> Is an open field, or a factory, or a by-pass. (*Poems1* 185)

The succession of human habitation rising and falling into different configurations generates another crust of human rubble in the geologic record, as opposed to the images of dynamic composting in the next lines where "old timber" and ashes become earth, which is itself already a healthy composite of composting matter, "cornstalk and leaf." And as fewer people live in the country, houses give way to factories as bypasses keep urban and suburban workers shuttling to and from their extractive labors.

The "bypass" also raises the specter of one of Eliot's least favorite modern innovations: the automobile. While I have elsewhere discussed his concerns about how covered cars disrupted people's relationship with the seasons and the landscape,[16] here the bypass has larger economic consequences for how the widespread use of cars affects land management and population distribution, keeping English workers in city centers that Eliot associates with the inorganic, amassing detritus of modern living. In a March 1931 letter to A. L. Rowse, Eliot writes:

> [N]o one asks, is it for the best that motor-cars should be produced infinitely in Britain *and consumed* [italics original] … When one observes the By Passes of London … this is merely planting out clerks and functionaries in places they could not possibly live unless each had his Small Car; it seems to me the whole present settlement of England is being made to encourage the motor car industry. (*Letters5* 507)

Eliot goes so far to call such an arrangement "morally *indefensible*" (italics original). The economics of the automotive industry becomes an immoral Ouroboros where "we become morally responsible for putting the rest of the population in the morally undesirable position of being able to own motor cars because owing to the motor car industry they have to live in places in which they couldn't live unless they had motor cars" (*Letters5* 508). The shift from human habitation in the countryside to factories, highways, and empty plots at the start of *East Coker* presents this same urban planning concern in verse.

So while Eliot, early in his career, cannot imagine pushing beyond, coming before, or remediating the waste of the Anthropocene, *East Coker* presents some solutions that originate from his work with the organicists. However, it also frames some of those solutions as largely untenable in the modern moment. What follows the factories and highways is a dynamic rendering of soil, inclusive of human habitation and bodies, that is a living force, a process rather than a plot of land:

> Old stone to new building, old timber to new fires,
> Old fires to ashes, and ashes to the earth

Which is already flesh, fur and faeces,
Bone of man and beast, cornstalk and leaf (*Poems1* 185)

Waste, here, does not omnipresently linger, lick, and curl, like Prufrock's polluted atmosphere, nor does it pile up and testify to human activity, like the imagined-yet-absent trash on the Thames. It mutates into new forms that create welcome conditions for new life, a land ethic that Eliot hoped would inform the new shift into village-based organic permaculture.[17]

The difficulty was, how? While organicists were proposing various schemes for moving the urban public and English food systems back to the village, *East Coker* can only present viable agrarian life as an appealing, though tragically remote, form of the past, one we can glimpse only if we "do not come too close" (*Poems1* 185). We can only view a human community moving in tandem with the earth at arm's length and they are rendered in the language of a faded England. Those who are dancing with the rhythms of "The time of milking and the time of harvest" are the same couples who are "Holding eche other by the hand or the arm / Whiche betokeneth concorde," in grammar from the time of Spenser (*Poems1* 186). Here, however, unlike the Spenserian echoes of *The Waste Land*, the fantasy is not quite pastoral. These are actual workers who deal with the mess of real farming, and there is no claim of pastoral cleanliness. "Dung and death" are a necessary part of coupling and harvesting, linked together in a composting cycle where the remnants of one process fertilize and nourish the forms of the next (*Poems1* 186). But it is not a past to which we can simply revert, nor does the poem invite us to do so. We move on with the sea spray to questions more emphatically spiritual and, as we know from the Hale letters, deeply personal. Nor was Eliot naive about the inequitable and unsustainable manorial system upon which such village life was predicated. One of the reasons we can enjoy the peasant dance in its rosy humility is that the lord and lady who actually own the land are notably absent. Eliot had little love for the way the British manorial class had mismanaged the countryside. They were, in theory, responsible for maintaining a robust agrarian life but, in Eliot's opinion, had unethically turned the land under their care into little more than personal pleasure grounds.[18] He had no desire to return to such a system, even if it were possible, which it surely was not in an era when the great houses of the British gentry were being sold or converted into heritage sites.

The problem of being waste-making animals in the vastness of the Anthropocene was one Eliot could not solve, and in that regard, we find in him an intellectual friend, for neither have we. While his anthropocenic imagination resisted the lure of the pastoral, Eliot nonetheless maintained the city/country split upon which it was prefaced. That meant that he, along with proponents of organicism, argued that systemic change in our food and waste systems must be based on a return to the country and a significant dismantling of urban centers. Even as he upheld an understanding of culture as stemming from the inner life of a community, Eliot imagined the urban boom as largely a matter of economics and poor planning. What he failed to consider sufficiently is that people lived in the city because they, like him, mostly enjoyed it. Or, at least, they preferred it to the grueling work of farming. (Eliot himself admitted to being afraid of cows.)[19] Cities offered educational opportunities, cultural amenities, and entertainments, as well as new labor options and mobility for women who would otherwise largely be tethered to domestic spaces in rural communities. As Eliot knew, a true return to agrarian culture had to arise from a deep inclination at the heart of a group of people, a groundswell that simply never occurred. Arguably, one major way to flourish in the Anthropocene is to make cities viable, for human and nonhuman life, both locally and globally, rather than forcing an untenable global de-urbanization. Eliot's own difficulties in imagining a Thames that could be modern, populated, green, and clean persist in debates about the role of urbanism in ecological reform to this day. The city/country, urban/nature split still radically shapes the Western imagination and limits the ways we might reform, design, and inhabit cities as resilient green spaces. The unreal cities of *The Waste Land* need not burn. Rather, we must find ways to make them bloom.

Notes

1 For more on the history of the term and its migration into the humanities, see Carolyn Merchant's *The Anthropocene and the Humanities: From Climate Change to a New Age of Sustainability* (New Haven: Yale University Press, 2020).

2 Rob Nixon, "Anthropocene 2," in *Fueling Culture: 101 Words for Energy and Environment* edited by Imre Szeman, Jennifer Wenzel, and Patricia Yaeger (New York: Fordham University Press, 2017), 44, www.jstor.org/stable/j.ctt1hfr0s3.

3 See, for example, Joshua Schuster, *The Ecology of Modernism: American Environments and Avant-Garde Poetics* (Tuscaloosa: University of Alabama Press, 2015); Bonnie Kime Scott, *In the Hollow of the Wave: Virginia Woolf and Modernist Uses of Nature* (Charlottesville: University of Virginia Press, 2012); Anne Raine, "Ecocriticism and Modernism," in *The Oxford Handbook of Ecocriticism*

(New York: Oxford University Press, 2014), 98–117. See also Julia E. Daniel, *Building Natures: Modern American Poetry, Landscape Architecture, and City Planning* (Charlottesville: University of Virginia Press, 2017).
4 See Gabrielle McIntire, "*The Waste Land* as Ecocritique," in *The Cambridge Companion to "The Waste Land"* (Cambridge: Cambridge University Press, 2015); Etienne Terblanche, *T. S. Eliot, Poetry, and Earth: The Name of the Lotos Rose* (London: Lexington, 2016); Elizabeth Black, *The Nature of Modernism: Ecocritical Approaches to the Poetry of Edward Thomas, T. S. Eliot, Edith Sitwell, and Charlotte Mew* (New York: Routledge, 2017).
5 Julia E. Daniel, ed., "Eliot and the Biological," in *T. S. Eliot Studies Annual*, vol. 3 (Clemson: Clemson University Press, 2021): 47–116.
6 A fuller exploration could consider these wastes in their plurality. For example, the floating oceanic garbage of *The Dry Salvages*, and the ways it serves as a tidal record of human history and human wrongs, including environmental sins, functions differently than the grimy street scenes of the early poems.
7 In her presentation at the 2019 meeting of the International T. S. Eliot Society (St. Louis), Dickey gave evidence of the dire air pollution in Eliot's childhood St. Louis for a reading that situates "Prufrock" squarely in this smoggy atmosphere. One such example Dickey provides comes from the *Post-Dispatch*: "the immense black clouds which hang over our city, and which, by condensation, … drop a continual rain of soot inside, as well as outside of our residences, blackening our finest buildings, damaging our goods, our furniture, … causing so many lung and other complaints by obnoxious gases" ("The People's Forum: The Smoke Nuisance," *STL Post-Dispatch,* June 2, 1887).
8 See Schuster, *Ecology of Modernism*.
9 Richard Lehan, *The City in Literature an Intellectual and Cultural History* (Berkeley: University of California Press, 1998), 134.
10 See "Eliot and the Biological."
11 McIntire, "*The Waste Land* as Ecocritique," 179.
12 Edmund Spenser, *The Yale Edition of the Shorter Poems of Edmund Spenser*, edited by William A. Oram et al. (New Haven: Yale University Press, 1989), 761.
13 As Peter Ackroyd has noted, in the same period when Spenser was extolling the beauties of the Thames, Parliament enacted laws against dumping raw excrement in the river. And while the situation improved with the modernization of London's sewer system in the late 1800s, the Thames was still polluted enough in Eliot's lifetime that Parliament occasionally recessed because of the river's rancid odor. For more on the history of pollution and the Thames, see B. W. Clapp, *An Environmental History of Britain Since the Industrial Revolution* (London: Taylor & Francis, 2014), and Peter Ackroyd, "Filthy River" in *Thames: The Biography.* (New York: Anchor Books, 2008).

14 See Julia E. Daniel, "Wind, Rock, Flower, Glass: *The Family Reunion* as Ecodrama," *The T. S. Eliot Studies Annual* 3 (2021): 69–91.

15 Jeremy Diaper, *T. S. Eliot and Organicism* (Clemson: Clemson University Press, 2019); Jeremy Diaper, "'The Life of the Soil': T. S. Eliot and Organicism," *T. S. Eliot Studies Annual* 3 (2021): 47–68.

16 David E. Chinitz and Julia E. Daniel, "Popular Culture," in *The Cambridge Companion to* The Waste Land, edited by Gabrielle McIntire (Cambridge: Cambridge University Press, 2015), 76–7.

17 For more on Eliot's composting vision in *East Coker*, see Julia E. Daniel's "Modernist Corpses and the Ecology of Burial" in *Eco-Modernism: Ecology, Environment, and Nature in Literary Modernism*, edited by Jeremy Diaper (Clemson: Clemson University Press, 2022), 71–84. This chapter marks a slight shift in my thinking from that piece. While I would still argue that Eliot underscores that modern soil is materially the decayed stuff of generations past, thereby knitting together a largely lost agrarian village life with the dirt beneath his feet in the present, the social and economic arrangement that supported such a composting culture is still framed squarely in the past. In other words, while the soil keeps the materiality of prior generations dynamically present, *Four Quartets* does not successfully imagine a fully modern incarnation of that culture beyond a critique of suburban planning.

18 Eliot frequently criticized the upper classes and the landed gentry in particular for using the British countryside for golf, hunting, extravagant picnics, and leisure drives on Sundays. For more on Eliot's critique of British manorial land management, see Julia E. Daniel's "Wind, Rock, Flower, Glass."

19 In his biography, Peter Ackroyd relates the amusing tales of Eliot's bovine encounters: "He would go on long strolls with Emily—one of them commemorated in the poem 'The Country Walk,' where he expressed his fear of cows and the way in which they stared at him" (229). Ackroyd suspects that this fear began with an earlier encounter in 1935 when Eliot had to flee from a wayward bull and landed in a blackberry bramble. For more, see Ackroyd's *T. S. Eliot: A Life* (New York: Simon and Schuster, 1984), 229–30. See also "The Country Walk," in *Poems1* 296–7.

7

T. S. Eliot and Translation

Vera M. Kutzinski

To write about Eliot and translation is to situate oneself squarely within global modernist studies. This burgeoning field intersects with ongoing debates about world literature(s) in comparative literary studies and postcolonial studies.[1] It has also benefited from the changes in translation studies since the 1970s.[2] Rebecca Beasley is among an increasing number of modernist scholars who consider

> attention to the translation process across cultures and across national and ethnic languages ... vital in order to prevent the grouping of diverse cultural material under the banner of 'modernism' from producing a false sense of homogeneity. For modernist studies to be actively transformed (not only passively informed) by the global turn, we need to be more persistent in asking questions about translation, dissemination, and reception.[3]

Before addressing the dissemination of T. S. Eliot's poetry in translation, however, I want to draw attention to a rather unusual and neglected text, to ask what literary translation actually *is*.

In 1937, when Eliot was already a formidable presence on both sides of the Atlantic, two young Jewish Midwesterners, Isaac Rosenfeld and Saul Bellow, created a little known Yiddish parody of "The Love Song of J. Alfred Prufrock" (1915). Not only does a golem take the place of Eliot's "etherized patient" in "Der shir hashirim fun Mendl Pumshtok" ["The Song of Songs of Mendel Pumshtok"], but Marx and Lenin displace Michelangelo, and the streets and rundown restaurants of an Old World shtetl reek of gefilte fish and wet socks. In this adapted setting, Pumshtok plays the stereotypical role of the lusty Jew as counterpoint to Eliot's sexually repressed Prufrock. The poem survived in oral form, beyond its University of Chicago debut, throughout the 1940s and 1950s; it did not appear in print until 1978, and even then anonymously. It took even longer to identify its authors.[4] Michael Boyden argues that, in contrast to Yiddish modernists, Rosenfeld and Bellow "had no desire to stake out a claim for Yiddish as a language of modernism. By underscoring their alienation from both their European roots and the Anglo-American canon, they indirectly asserted their allegiance to Eliot's poetics."[5] Their allegiance, however, was to the poetics of the early Eliot and not to the Eliot who, in his 1933 lectures at the University of Virginia (collected as *After Strange Gods*), stressed the undesirability of "free-thinking Jews" in his pursuit of cultural and religious unity (*Prose5* 20). Bellow would remark decades later, in "A Jewish Writer in America" (1988), that Eliot would no doubt have consigned him and other Jewish American writers "to a very low place" in his historical consciousness.

Because it is parodic, "Pumshtok" problematizes the concept of translation proper. If translation proper requires the kind of lexical and referential accuracy or equivalence typically seen as markers of fidelity to a source text, "Pumshtok" would qualify as a form of rewriting that violates the source's referents in ways that make it at best what Umberto Eco calls an "anomalous case" of translation.[6] But what some see as referential violence is for others an inevitable part of any translation. Eco prefers "functional equivalence" to equivalence of meaning, admitting that "a translation can express an evident 'deep' sense of a text by violating both lexical and referential faithfulness."[7] André Lefevere agrees that translation is "a shift, not between two languages, but between two cultures,"[8] arguing that translations always "re-write" source texts as they adapt them to their specific cultural circumstances. State ideologies and cultural conventions, he insists, shape *all* translations beyond translators' individual choices, some more visibly so than others.[9] With its resistance to the requirement of translational faithfulness, the "cultural turn" has shifted translation studies away from evaluation and toward detailed analyses of translations' historical and cultural embeddedness and their effects on readers' expectations.[10] This shift has radically changed traditional Western criteria for what a "good translation" may be. Rather than focusing exclusively on how target texts relate back to their sources, the question is now what translations *do*, either by satisfying or resisting readerly expectations.[11] For Eco, "a good translation must generate the same effect aimed at by the original."[12] Eva Hesse, author of a much-maligned German version of *The Waste Land* from the 1960s, takes matters even further by arguing that the purpose of a translation is to show what a given source text might have looked like had it been written in another language.[13] "Pumshtok" is a perfect example of what "Prufrock" might have looked like had it been written in Yiddish; Hesse's controversial *Das wüste Land* (1964), about which I have more to say below, shows what a German *Waste Land* might have looked like. For Hesse, "the truth of a translation is fundamentally not a question of accuracy but of [the] substance" of the source text, which each translator constructs differently.[14] Translation, then, is a function of interpretation, not of linguistic equivalences. Had Eliot himself written about translation, which he did rarely, he might have taken up the following lines from *Burnt Norton* (1935):

> Words strain,
> Crack and sometimes break, under the burden,
> Under the tension, slip, slide, perish,
> Decay with imprecision, will not stay in place,
> Will not stay still. (*Poems1* 183–4)

These lines, even taken out of the context of the poem, speak compellingly to the intralinguistic, interlinguistic, and intercultural dimensions that are all part of translating *and* writing about translation. Words do not stay still.

In what follows, I examine Eliot's reworkings of St.-John Perse's *Anabase*, select critical rereadings of *The Waste Land* as poem-in-translation, and a sampling of non-Anglophone rewritings of that poem. It is not my primary purpose to update the inventory of translations of Eliot's poetry, which Donald Gallup began in 1947 and expanded in 1969.[15] Doing so even with the benefit of the internet would be a prodigious undertaking that requires competence in numerous languages. It is helpful, however, to note just how extensive the global dissemination of Eliot's poetry in other languages has been. First, a baseline. Depending on whether one includes collections and anthologies, Eliot's own poetry publications consisted of forty-seven distinct editions issued in England and the United States between 1912 and 2012.[16] According to Gallup, Eliot's poetic oeuvre had been translated into thirty-eight languages by the late 1960s, from Afrikaans and Arabic to Urdu, Welsh, and Yiddish. The early translations that have received the most attention were, predictably, in French, German, and Spanish. New translations of *The Waste Land* and later poems into European and non-European languages saw print throughout the second half of the twentieth century and well into the twenty-first.[17] As Ghanim Samarrai, for example, points out, *The Waste Land* "has been the most celebrated poem in several Arab countries, especially Iraq, Egypt, and Lebanon."[18] There have been multiple translations of it since 1954, after Iraqi poet Badr Shakir al-Sayyab published *Unshudat al-Matar* [*Hymn of Rain*], a poem that "construct[s] *The Waste Land* … as a counter-discourse to be deployed in testing and weighing, if not breaking open, the monolithic façade comprising the canonical texts of western civilization."[19] Thanks to numerous journal articles and most especially to the essays collected in Elisabeth Däumer and Shyamal Bagchee's *The International Reception of T. S. Eliot* (2007), we now also have a better sense of how many more translations of Eliot's poetry have been circulating in the world-literary system since the 1920s. Along with more recent translations into Arabic, Basque, Bengali, Catalán, Dutch, Icelandic, Korean, Lithuanian, and Malayalam, there are also many earlier ones of which Gallup was unaware, including a Romanian version by Ion Pillat from 1933 and *Dat öde landet*, Erik Mesterton's 1932 Swedish version of *The Waste Land*.[20]

Unlike his friend Ezra Pound, Eliot was not known as a translator, and he had little to say about the one project in which he engaged—a 1924 translation of St.-John Perse's poem *Anabase*. Eliot first translated Perse's poem while working on "Ash-Wednesday" and the Ariel Poems. He revised his 1930 version of *Anabasis* several times, first in 1938, then in 1949, and finally in 1958. For his revisions, he "depended heavily on the recommendations of the author," whom he had already acknowledged as a "half-translator" in his initial preface.[21] "It was felt," Eliot explains in his new prefatory note, "that a greater fidelity to the exact meaning, a more literal translation, was what was needed. I have corrected not only my own licences, but several positive errors and mistakes" (*Prose4* 135). Eliot's appeal to equivalences, fidelity, and license is unsurprising. Most translators at the time subscribed to these concepts. What does surprise, however, is how relatively few changes Eliot actually made to his initial version and how little those changes have to do with making his translation more "literal."[22] He did correct a few grammatical infelicities: "our horses with pure eyes of elders" (for *"nos chevaux purs aux yeux d'ainés"*) is changed to "our pure bred horses with eyes of elders" (53; *Poems2* 113).[23] That "frondage" (for *"feuillages"*) becomes "leaf shadows" (27; *Poems2* 91) gives us probably less pause than the shift from "acridians" (49), a word that Eliot apparently did not know, to the more innocuous "crickets," which then became "locusts" (19; *Poems2* 109).[24] Eliot had also initially domesticated Perse's *"arbre jujubier"* as a "juniper tree," a more obvious geographical displacement because junipers grow in the northern hemisphere. By contrast, the "jujuba tree," or jujube in the more common spelling, for which Eliot opted in his revision (51; *Poems2* 111), hails from southern Asia, perhaps via Lewis Carroll's near-eponymous bird (see *Poems2* 144). Although he does not address these changes, Harris Feinsod, in one of the few analyses of Eliot's *Anabasis* translation, argues, not always convincingly, that Christian theology takes center stage in Eliot's versions.[25] In his enthusiasm for attributing Eliot's effort to relink myth with Old Testament scripture to his conversion to the Anglican Church, Feinsod does not always notice that some of Eliot's more conspicuous "liberties"—notably "the most rapt god-drunken" for Perse's *"le plus ivre"* (*Poems2* 87)—actually predate Eliot's conversion by several years.[26] What makes good sense, however, is Feinsod's claim that Eliot used his translations to pull the Guadalupe-born, future Nobel honoree Alexis Léger into the orbit of a New Critical analytical mindset, even though the ideological priorities of the New Criticism were not easily compatible with modernist "aesthetics of motion and dissonance" that characterize Perse's poem as much as they do Eliot's *Waste Land*.[27]

Perse's *Anabase* certainly fits Eliot's notion of "difficult" poetry. Poets "must be *difficult*," Eliot claims, because "[o]ur civilization comprehends great variety and complexity, and this variety and complexity, playing upon a refined sensibility, must produce various and complex results. The poet must become more and more comprehensive, more allusive, more indirect, in order to force, to dislocate if necessary, language into his meaning" ("The Metaphysical Poets," *Prose2* 381). Although Eliot's geospatial metaphor implicitly registers what Rebecca Beasley calls "the foreignizing aims not only of modernist translations, but of modernist poetry in general,"[28] the complex variety he envisions here also discounts non-European peoples, along with many that at least geographically belong to Europe. They may be part of our world, but they decidedly are not part of what Eliot imagines as "our civilization." Cultures outside of that realm were merely to provide the raw material that "refined sensibilities" were to transform into "modernism's avant-garde rupture of Western bourgeois conventions and art."[29] We encounter a similar displacement in *Notes towards the Definition of Culture* (1943), where Eliot asserts that "the possibility of each literature renewing itself, proceeding to new creative activity, making new discoveries in the use of words, depends on … its ability to receive and assimilate influences from abroad" (*Prose7* 260). This passage speaks most directly to Eliot's own literary practice in *The Waste Land* and even in *Four Quartets*, where his attention to ancient Indian religious texts, such as Brihadaranyaka Upanishad, and traditions, such as Mahāyāna Buddhism, creates an internal diversity that his prose writings tend to eschew. The translations of Indic sources, however "feeble" (to use Eliot's own word from the notes to *The Waste Land*), "formed a part of the heteroglossia from which the poet strives to cross-signify the world," as Edward Upton argues: "The understanding of the self through language necessarily entails an engagement with texts of the cultural Other that have surreptitiously influenced the significations of that language. Therefore, the understanding of all texts changes with the introduction of new texts."[30] Eliot does indeed make this point in "Tradition and the Individual Talent," where he conceives of literary tradition as a living entity that is constantly altered as writers position themselves in relation to their literary forebears such that "[n]o poet, no artist of any art, has his complete meaning alone" (*Prose2* 106). At the same time, however, he contains any underlying cross-cultural sensibility by limiting the "simultaneous existence" of older literary texts to "the whole of the literature of Europe from Homer" (106). This is surely one way of articulating a "poetics of relation," but its exclusivity has little in common with the way in which Édouard Glissant would later conceive of the concept.[31]

When Eliot imagines the literatures of other countries to exist somehow "within" his vision of singular European civilization, which existed neither at the time nor later, we cannot but ask *how* those other literatures came to reside "within," in this cultural space, in the first place. The answer is simple enough: through translation of course, in the same way that Homer, Petronius, and Dante became part of Eliot's "ideal order." Hesse aptly calls them "undeclared translations," that is, texts that have been woven into the linguistic and literary fabric of cultures other than the ones in which they originated, such that they go unacknowledged as sites of intercultural exchanges.[32] *The Waste Land*, in Upton's analysis, "suggests that the presence of Indian texts in European culture, through the process of translation, stimulates dialogical response and leads to cultural innovation ... [making] comparison, however problematic or beneficial, inescapable"; the poem is therefore, according to Christopher McVey, less about a crisis of representation than it is "about globalism and colliding textual traditions ... and about an encounter with alterity or difference that cannot be so easily subsumed into a single worldview."[33] McVey extends Upton's point by stressing that "collocation"—the noun Eliot uses to describe the relation between Augustine's *Confessions* and the Buddha's Fire Sermon—is not synonymous with fusion. Though Eliot (or Tiresias) may long for such a unity, *The Waste Land* fails to make "the West and the East converge into a singular global tradition," transforming it "from a text that tries to knot together a grab bag of varying cultural and religious traditions into a text that registers the necessary acceptance of a world that is too complex, too different, ever to be unified into a whole."[34] What we witness in the multilingual and cross-cultural moments of this poem is not synthesis but a form of "aesthetic syncretism" that McVey regards as high modernism's "sustained and conscious attempt to register the porous and complex relationship between the West and non-West."[35] Eliot's collagic use of translated and untranslated text fragments in *The Waste Land* goes, of course, well beyond the inclusion of Indic texts, making the poem, to adapt Emily Apter's term, a poem-in-translation, in which many languages are at play. That Eliot in his essays consistently pulls back from acknowledging what his own poetry does is something that scholars who evoke "Tradition" and other essays as authoritative frames for reading even his early poetry have not always sufficiently considered.[36] "Classic or not," Nancy Gish reminds us, "Eliot is no longer the authority by which he is read."[37] Many of his translators, even within Europe, had been well aware of this much earlier. For many, Eliot had never been the authority by which they read him.

Although translation is unthinkable without interpretation, a translator, unlike a musician, is "an interpreter categorically barred from interpreting," as Eva Hesse notes.[38] As if in tacit observance of this interdiction, Eliot's translators have rarely granted us any insights into the interpretations that underlie their rewritings. Hesse is a notable exception, and so is Luis Sanz Irles, author of the most recent Spanish translation of *The Waste Land*. To convey the range of possibilities that Eliot's poem opened up for different translators at different times, I want to conclude by bringing Hesse's *Das wüste Land* (1964) into conversation with Sanz Irles's *La tierra baldía* (2020).[39] Two early translations, Ernst Robert Curtius's "Das wüste Land" (1927) and Ángel Flores's *La tierra baldía* (1930), will briefly join my exploration of how different translators decided to rewrite what is known as the seduction scene, the jarringly unerotic sexual encounter at the heart of "The Fire Sermon," which scandalized a number of conservative readers.[40]

Hesse's and Sanz Irles's observations about their respective versions of *The Waste Land* exhibit an extraordinary passion for Eliot's language and how it might function in another cultural context. Sanz Irles's comments about why he rendered Eliot's "Unreal City" in Spanish as "City irreal" rather than "Cuidad irreal" (the more popular choice) are especially illuminating.[41] Both translators probe the intertextual and intercultural dimensions that reside in the poem's sense *and* sound. The different ways in which they read *The Waste Land* as an invitation not to imitate Eliot but to activate unusual and unforeseen resources in their own languages are evident in how each presents Eliot's lower-class male figure. I include a stanza from Curtius, whose translation Eliot admired, to show how his recreation of Eliot's end rhymes is distinct from Hesse's.[42] Curtius and Hesse are among the very few translators in any language to have even attempted to pay homage to Eliot's use of the Shakespearean sonnet form whose ghost hovers above this scene:[43]

> He, the young man carbuncular, arrives,
> A small house agent's clerk, with one bold stare,

One of the low on whom assurance sits
As a silk hat on a Bradford millionaire. (*Poems1* 63)

Der junge Mann, furunkulös, trifft ein,
Ein kleiner Angestellter mit naßforschem Air,
Einer von diesen Lackeln, denen Unverfrorenheit ansteht
Wie der Zylinder einem Ruhrpott-Millionär. (Hesse 25)

Er kommt, der Jüngling mit Pickeln im Gesicht,
Ein kleiner Angestellter, blickt in frecher Glut;
Versicherung sitzt auf ihm und seinesgleichen
Wie auf dem Bradford-Millionär der Seidenhut. (Curtius 25)

Y llega él, el joven purulento,
Pequeño y altanero oficinista,
Tipo vulgar: la arrogancia la sienta
Como una chistera a un ricachón de Bradford. (Sanz Irles 67)

By placing "furunkulös" after the noun and in commas, Hesse turns facial blemishes into character attributes, while Curtius's simply spells out what "carbuncular" means to him: having pimples on one's face. Hesse's next line is even more daring in choosing an unusual singular of the Franco-Anglicism "Air," to pick up the sound of Eliot's "stare" and "millionaire." "Air" also resonates with "Angestell*ter*," pulling the stress from the first to the last syllable and into the semblance of an iamb. Hesse's derogatory colloquialism "naßforsch," more familiar at the time than it is now, inflects lower-class arrogance with inebriation and intensifies "Unver*froh*renheit" ("brazenness"), the noun whose stress picks up the same sound in the following line. Hesse also modifies Eliot's simile. For Eliot's Bradford reference, she substitutes a regionalism that transports the would-be millionaire from northern England to the German Ruhr Valley, cradle of the industrial revolution and of Germany's nouveau riche. That Curtius was more cautious with colloquialisms and especially regionalisms like this one— both deemed unacceptable in a translation—is likely less a sign of his times and more attributable to his academic investments. Sanz Irles, like most Eliot translators, keeps Bradford, connecting it with the colloquialism "ricachón," which I would return to English as "moneybag." Grammatical necessity moves "Bradford" to the end of the line, rendering it all the more foreign because it does not rhyme with anything in Spanish. Instead of worrying about end rhymes, however, Sanz Irles creates distinctive cadences through assonance and alliteration (*p*urulento, *p*equeno, ti*p*o; and *ch*istera, rica*ch*ón).

Where translating *The Waste Land* made Sanz Irles especially attentive to Eliot's prosody, it inspired Hesse to mix seemingly unpoetic colloquialisms and regionalisms with more elevated registers. Contrasting Hesse's version with Curtius's, as well as with Alfred Margul-Sperber's "Ödland" (1926),[44] Elisabeth Däumer demonstrates how Hesse's diction and her mixed registers make male discourse on women's honor the object of parody, "as if to imply the irrelevance, and indeed, hypocrisy, of such discourse … in a world whose governing drive is neither ethical nor spiritual nor erotic, but purely economic."[45] The line "*Wenn schöne Frauen sich verfehlen*," in which Hesse keeps only the italics and not Goldsmith's imported words, stands out because of her archaic use of the verb "sich verfehlen," which indexes a violation of social proprieties about which neither the typist nor her "lover" care. Similarly startling is Hesse's change of register through another archaic verb, "zeihen," in "Sie forscht zerstreut wes sie der Spiegel zeihe" (for "She turns and looks a moment in the glass"). With this verb, Hesse's typist casts a fleeting look in the mirror, assuming that her reflection, a representation of the male gaze, might accuse her. By rhyming "verfehlen" with "strählen" (to smooth), a verb in the same elevated register, Hesse underscores how "automatic" both gestures are before returning to the lower registers when she has her "Tippse," rather than a "secretaria" (Sanz Irles) or a "mecanógrafa" (Flores), put a record on the "Plattenspieler"—rather than on the more conventionally poetic "gramophone" or "gramófono." The issue is not that woman "finds too late that men betray," the line in Goldsmith's sonnet that immediately follows, but that she is complicitous. No victim is she, neither for Hesse nor for Eliot—nor for Sanz Irles, who also replaces Goldsmith's words. Without the italics, the line blends into a linguistic environment in which "locura," feminized in Spanish in a way that the English "folly" is not, stands apart from the masculine end rhymes but still picks up their "o" sounds:

> Cuando una mujer bella comete una locura,
> Y ya sola de nuevo da vueltas por su cuarto,
> Se alisa los cabellos con un gesto automático
> Y se pone a escuchar un disco en el gramófono. (69)

Although Flores's stanza looks similar to Sanz Irles's, it does not attend to either rhyme or rhythm:

> Cuando una mujer hermosa comete tales locuras y
> Vuelve a pasearse por su cuarto, sola,
> Se alisa los cabellos con mano automática
> Y pone un disco en el gramófono. (Flores 43)

Flores seems too preoccupied with denotative meaning to create a translation that not only looks like a poem but also sounds like one.[46]

How willing some Eliot translators have been to push their respective idioms to their cultural limits has depended on historical and ideological factors. When Sanz Irles began his translation in 2018, he did not have to worry about introducing modernist poetry to an audience unfamiliar with it. Nor did he have to legitimate his efforts beyond invoking Octavio Paz, another Nobel laureate, who, like Pablo Neruda and other Hispanic-American poets, had pronounced *The Waste Land* one of the greatest poems of the twentieth century. Rather than lingering over the poem as social critique, Sanz Irles mainly focuses on its literariness: fragmentation, intertextuality, and sound.[47] Hesse, by contrast, was in a very different position in West Germany in the early 1960s. What she hoped would be of interest to younger German audiences at that time was what she herself most admired about *The Waste Land* as a key modernist poem: its radical formal openness and persistent questioning of all received symbolic systems, be they social, religious, or linguistic. Her hopes were dashed when her translation, especially in conjunction with the lengthy analysis that accompanied the reprint edition in 1973, was summarily condemned for intensifying the poem's suppressed erotic dimension and for deploying Freud and Marcuse to portray Eliot as closeted homosexual.[48] In those days, Curtius's older version was a safer choice for most German academics (all of them men), who found Hesse's avant-garde aesthetics, with its anti-authoritarianism, its aversion to hierarchies, and its emphasis on the "dialectic between the aesthetic of ugliness … and the more conventional aesthetic of the beautiful,"[49] distasteful and deeply discomfiting.[50] As a woman who was not part of German academic circles, Hesse was considered a mere interloper. It is only recently that her work, including her translations of Ezra Pound and Langston Hughes, has attracted more serious scholarly attention.[51] In a way, the disparagement of Hesse's *Das wüste Land* in German academia resembles the neglect of Rosenfeld and Bellow's "Pumshtok" in the United States. Both remind us that some of the margins of modernism are closer to home than one might think.

Notes

1 See, for example, Susan Stanford Friedman, *Planetary Modernisms: Provocations on Modernity across Time* (New York: Columbia University Press, 2015).

2 See Susan Bassnett, ed., *Translation and World Literature* (London: Routledge, 2018).
3 Rebecca Beasley, "Modernism's Translations," in *The Oxford Handbook of Global Modernisms*, edited by Mark Wollaeger and Matt Eatough (Oxford: Oxford University Press, 2012), 552.
4 Michael Boyden, "Postvernacular Prufrock: Isaac Rosenfeld and Saul Bellow's Yiddish 'Translation' of T. S. Eliot's Modernism," *Journal of World Literature* 3, no. 2 (2018): 174–95.
5 Boyden, 188.
6 Umberto Eco, *Experiences in Translation*, trans. Alastair McEwen (Toronto: University of Toronto Press, 2001), 106.
7 Eco, 44, 14.
8 Eco, 17.
9 See Lefevere's contributions to Susan Bassnett and André Lefevere, *Constructing Cultures: Essays on Literary Translation* (Clevedon: Multilingual Matters, 1998).
10 Susan Bassnett and André Lefevere, *Translation, History, and Culture* (London: Pinter, 1990), ix.
11 Ayyappa Paniker, "On Translating T. S. Eliot's Poetry into Malayalam," *International Journal of Translation* 3, nos. 1–2 (1991): 81.
12 Eco, 45.
13 Eva Hesse, *Vom Zungenreden in der Lyrik: Autobiographisches zur Übersetzerei* (Aachen: Rimbaud, 2003), 28.
14 Hesse, 18.
15 Donald Gallup, *T. S. Eliot: A Bibliography* (London: Faber, 1969).
16 Ana Mata Buil, "Análisis comparativo de la recepción poética de T. S. Eliot, Marianne Moore y Edna St. Vincent Millay," *Hermēneus* 17 (2015): 154–5.
17 For bibliographical updates see L. S. Ramaiah and Narindar K. Aggarwal, *A Supplement to Indian Responses to T. S. Eliot: A Bibliographical Guide to Writings in English* (Calcutta: Writers Workshop, 1996), and Howard Young, "T. S. Eliot: A Bibliography of Translations of His Works into Spanish, Catalán, Galician, and Basque Plus Selected Studies in Spanish and English (1924–1993)," in *T. S. Eliot and Hispanic Modernity (1924–1993)*, edited by K. M. Sibbald and Howard Young (Boulder: Society of Spanish and Spanish American Studies, 1994), 87–106.
18 Ghanim Samarrai, "Rejuvenating T. S. Eliot's *The Waste Land*," *Canadian Review of Comparative Literature / Revue canadienne de littérature comparée* 41, no. 2 (2014): 113.
19 Terri DeYoung, *Placing the Poet: Badr Shakir al-Sayyab and Postcolonial Iraq* (Albany: State University of New York Press, 1998), 68; see also Hussein N. Kadhim, *The Poetics of Anti-colonialism in the Arabic Qaṣīdah* (Leiden: Brill, 2004).
20 For Eliot's correspondence with Mesterton, see *Letters6* 40.

21 Both prefaces are reprinted in *Prose4* 132–7.
22 See *Poems2* 140–6 for an inventory of variants between the first and the last versions.
23 My first page number refers to the 1930 edition, which is out of print but available online. The 1949 translation is still available in paperback.
24 The French "acridiens" [locusts] should have been "acaridians": "acridians" as a word does not exist in English. The "crickets" appear in the second (and first American) edition from 1938 (last reprint 1977; 63). Eliot made further revisions and corrections in the third edition, published in the United States in 1949: there, he used "locusts" (*Poems2* 109).
25 Harris Feinsod, "Reconsidering the 'Spiritual Economy': Saint-John Perse, His Translators, and the Limits of Internationalism," *Telos* 138 (2007): 139–61.
26 Feinsod, 151. Eliot's translation of "le plus ivre" dates back to 1924 and was unchanged in Eliot's revised translation (23; *Poems2* 87).
27 Feinsod, 153. Peter J. Kalliney, *Modernism in a Global Context* (London: Bloomsbury Academic, 2016), 3.
28 Beasley, 558.
29 Susan Stanford Friedman, "World Modernisms, World Literature, and Comparativity," in *The Oxford Handbook of Global Modernisms*, edited by Mark Wollaeger and Matt Eatough (Oxford: Oxford University Press, 2012), 500.
30 Edward Upton, "Translation, Comparison, and the Hermeneutics of the Fragment in *The Waste Land*," *Journal of Religion* 96, no. 1 (2016): 50–1. According to Upton, *The Waste Land* "meditates explicitly on the question of language and translation in a more provocative way than the later poems," including *Four Quartets* (34).
31 For a different reading of "Tradition," see Viorica Patea, "Eliot's Modernist Manifesto," *Transatlantica* 1 (2016), http://journals.openedition.org/transatlantica/8088.
32 Hesse, *Zungenreden*, 29.
33 Upton, "Translation," 33; Christopher McVey, "Feeble Translations: Failure, Global Modernism, and *The Waste Land*," *South Atlantic Review* 81, no. 2 (2019): 186.
34 McVey, 182.
35 McVey, 186.
36 Hussein N. Kadhim, *The Poetics of Anti-colonialism in the Arabic Qaṣīdah* (Leiden: Brill, 2004), chapter 4. Brian C. Morris, "The Cultural Underground of Eliot, Alberti, and Lorca," in Sibbald and Young, 9–29.
37 Nancy K. Gish, "Eliot's Critical Reception: 'The Quintessence of Twenty-first-century Poetry,'" in *A Companion to T. S. Eliot*, edited by David E. Chinitz (Chichester: Wiley-Blackwell, 2014), 437.
38 Hesse, *Zungenreden*, 23.

39 Luis Sanz Irles and T. S. Eliot, *The Waste Land / La tierra baldía* (Madrid: Olé Libros, 2020). Although space constraints do not allow me to include them in my comparison, Jean de Menasce's "La Terre mise à nu" (1926, reprinted as "La Terre gaste") and Pierre Leyris's *La Terre vaine* (1947) are worth mentioning, in part because Eliot corresponded with both translators.
40 Ernest Robert Curtius and T. S. Eliot, *Das wüste Land: Englisch und deutsch* (Wiesbaden: Insel, 1957; rpt. Suhrkamp, 1975); Ángel Flores and T. S. Eliot, *La tierra baldía* (Mexico: La nave de los locos, 1930; rpt. 1977).
41 Sanz Irles, 38–9.
42 Eliot thanked Curtius for his translation in May 1927: "I flatter myself and you by thinking that it still reads like poetry in translation" (*Letters3* 493).
43 Sanz Irles notes that *The Waste Land* has 140 end rhymes (36).
44 First published in Bucharest in 1968. On Curtius and Margul-Sperber, see Armin Paul Frank, "Some Complexities of European Culture(s) as Manifest in French and German Translations of *The Waste Land*," in *The Placing of T. S. Eliot*, edited by Jewel Spears Brooker (Columbia: University of Missouri Press, 1991), 119–27.
45 Elisabeth Däumer, "(Re)Modernizing Eliot: Eva Hesse and *Das wüste Land*," in *The International Reception of T. S. Eliot*, edited by Elisabeth Däumer and Shyamal Bagchee (London: Continuum, 2007), 46.
46 Interestingly, Eliot wrote to Flores: "certain parts of the poem read very much better in Spanish than in other language except English" (*Letters4* 62).
47 Sanz Irles, 39.
48 Eva Hesse, *T. S. Eliot und "Das wüste Land": Eine Analyse* (Frankfurt-am-Main: Suhrkamp, 1973), 89ff; Däumer, 37, 47.
49 Hesse, *Zungenreden*, 18.
50 See Rainer Emig, "Die Unübersetzbarkeit moderner Lyrik," *"Unübersetzbar?" Zur Kritik der literarischen Übersetzung*, edited by Michael Neecke and Lu Jiang (Hamburg: Verlag Dr. Kovač, 2013), 143–61; also Frank, 124.
51 See Däumer, and Vera M. Kutzinski, "Unspeakable Things Translated: Langston Hughes's Poems in the Post–World War II Germanies," *Atlantic Studies* 13, no. 4 (2016): 535–59.

8

Whiteness and Religious Conversion in *Four Quartets*

Ann Marie Jakubowski

To write about T. S. Eliot and whiteness is, in many ways, to state the obvious. Yet the field of critical whiteness studies has much to say about the obvious, especially once we acknowledge the unremarkability of whiteness as itself an ideological effect.[1] Making whiteness visible entails attention to it as a constructed, racialized category, not the unmarked view-from-nowhere it has long been construed to be. Scrutinizing whiteness decenters it, requiring us to understand race as more than a category relevant only to so-called minority populations. As sociologist Amanda E. Lewis puts it: "in a racialized social system all actors are racialized, including whites. Because all social actors are racialized, at some level they must live and perform or 'do race.'"[2] This chapter asks: how is Eliot "doing race" when he converts to Anglo-Catholicism, is naturalized as a British citizen, and develops the theological poetics that culminates in *Four Quartets*?

Much of the existing work on Eliot and race focuses on his early-career literary representations of racial others—representations that reveal much about his own constructions of whiteness. As Rachel Blau DuPlessis has argued, in Eliot's work, "'Whiteness' is not a clean construct holding an impure Other at bay but a desire to distance *and* confront its own creolized or miscegenated markers."[3] Michael North draws a similar conclusion in his discussion of how the young American poet found in Black dialect a tactically useful way to position himself as an innovative outsider against the contemporary literary mainstream in England.[4] David E. Chinitz has drawn attention to Eliot's ambivalent relation with popular culture, showing how racially fraught were Eliot's engagements with jazz and ragtime.[5] More recently, Anita Patterson has written about Eliot's significant influence on African American poets like

Gwendolyn Brooks and Richard Wright, and Frances Dickey has persuasively connected the alienation abounding in Eliot's early verse to his formative experiences with racial segregation in the St. Louis of his youth.[6] Among Eliot's more infamous poetic engagements with racial others are the Bolo poems, which Gabrielle McIntire describes as "a long cycle of intensely sexual, bawdy, pornotropic, and satirical verse."[7] The privately circulated verses about "King Bolo's big black bassturd kween" are shocking and frequently disturbing, and they cannot be dismissed as mere juvenilia (*Poems2* 252). As Michelle A. Taylor points out, he began writing them while at Harvard, but they continued to provide entertainment throughout his adult life, bringing Eliot "more pleasure more consistently than any of his other works."[8] These approaches have made it clear that race permeates Eliot's poetic imagination, in ways both subtle and overt.

As Eliot's mid- and late-career literary output increasingly tacks toward religious themes, leading up to and extending beyond his 1927 conversion, racialized tropes shape his aesthetic and theological imaginations.[9] Understanding religious conversion as itself a racialized event allows us to see how *Four Quartets* fuses autobiography and theology in a complex meditation on race and identity, pursuing an elusive ideal of whiteness even as it acknowledges that ideal as a fantasy. We can follow Eliot's shifting formulations of whiteness by tracing the racial implications of a key word that emerges again and again in his personal correspondence as well as his published poetry: "valid." The significance Eliot attaches to validity as a criterion for measuring authority and efficacy reveals the extent to which whiteness underwrites his ideas about aesthetic merit and theological orthodoxy. Invocations of validity in Eliot's writing point us to the complex entanglement of religion and race in Eliot's late-career poetics, making it possible to see *Four Quartets* as at once an allegory of re-racination that aims to shore up a coherent white racial identity and a meditation on the follies of its own racial imaginary, renouncing the long-cherished desire for unalienated identity and worldly belonging.

A Valid Way of Writing: Whiteness and Literary Universality

We see Eliot's fraught and fragile sense of his own whiteness in an April 1928 letter to his friend Herbert Read—written less than a year after his conversion—in which he casts himself as a perpetual outsider in explicitly racial terms. He offers a cursory autobiographical sketch describing himself as an American who wasn't an American, ... and who wasn't a Yankee, because he was born in the South and went to school in New England as a small boy with a nigger drawl, but who wasn't a southerner in the South because his people were northerners in a border state and looked down on all southerners and Virginians, and who so was never anything anywhere. (*Letters4* 137–8)

The experience of being geographically adrift fuses with the fear and shame of appearing racially marked, producing a condition of profound alienation. Eliot laments what he hears as his own racially marked speech, but at the same time, as Michael North points out, he gleefully employs Black dialect in correspondence with Ezra Pound as the basis of a sustained, code-like in-joke language.[10] Eliot's polyvalent performance of whiteness negotiates both his shame about his proximity to Blackness and his transgressive desire to co-opt Blackness to take aesthetic advantage of the difference it has been made to signify. Proximity to Black dialect may have been a social handicap in the Boston of Eliot's youth, but the symbolic divide of racial difference also served as an enabling condition for the innovations of his early career work.

At stake here is the poet's access to an idiom of literary universality, capable of rendering local particularities while transcending mere provincialism. Richard Dyer emphasizes the integral link between universality and whiteness, wherein whiteness presents itself as "a human norm," so that while "other people are raced, we are just people."[11] This, Dyer shows, operates as a strategy for securing power: "There is no more powerful position than that of being 'just' human. The claim to power is the claim to speak for the commonality of humanity."[12] Kamran Javadizadeh has written about the implications of such pretensions to universality in lyric poetry, explaining the theoretical assumptions that enable the projection of a stable and coherent lyric subject as "a literary form of white innocence."[13] Eliot's letter to Read seems to lament his inability to access a supposedly unmarked, transcendent vantage point, but concluding the discussion of his hyper-visibility with the assessment that he was therefore functionally *invisible* seems both a genuine lamentation and a bit of wishful thinking. After all, being "never anything anywhere" proves uncannily close to being "always everything everywhere."

"Universality," then, is a quality of enormous significance for Eliot specifically and whiteness generally. In her groundbreaking study of literary whiteness, Toni Morrison shows how white writers rely on the symbolic potential of Black bodies in order to render supposedly universal themes. Using Mark Twain's *The Adventures of Huckleberry Finn* as an example, Morrison writes: "The slave population, it could be and was assumed, offered itself up as surrogate selves for meditation on problems of human freedom, its lure and its elusiveness."[14]

Morrison's reading of Twain demonstrates the extent to which such apparently universal themes as "human freedom" emerge in canonical American literature only through tropes of racial differentiation. Eliot's St. Louis origins, described in explicitly racial terms in the Read letter, made him acutely aware of this distinctively American brand of (white) literary universality.

Twain, a Missouri native like Eliot, seems to have been appealing to the poet as a blueprint to follow in his attempt to alchemize "never anything anywhere" into "always everything everywhere." Eliot praises *Huckleberry Finn* specifically in a 1953 speech titled "American Literature and the American Language," celebrating Twain as "one of those writers, of whom there are not a great many in any literature, who have discovered a new way of writing, valid not only for themselves but for others" (*Prose7* 801). Here, Eliot uses the term "valid" as a proxy for "universal," and he goes on to explain that "the Mississippi of Mark Twain is not only the river known to those who voyage on it or live beside it, but the universal river of human life—more universal, indeed, than the Congo of Joseph Conrad. For Twain's readers anywhere, the Mississippi is *the* river." Eliot's praise for Twain links the validity of Twain's "new way of writing" to his work's "unconscious universality," a quality existing in tandem with its "strong local flavour" but ultimately requiring an unmarked, transcendent vantage point.[15]

That Eliot delivers this speech at Washington University in St. Louis, the institution founded by his grandfather in the city of his birth, intensifies the rhetorical pressure on this discussion of universality. He comments on what makes a way of writing "valid"—or not—from a specific vantage point that he perceives as a threat to his own access to universal literary significance. In giving this speech, Eliot occupies a platform at a place that represents much of what he labored throughout his life to disavow, while at the same time his very presence symbolizes the depth of his attachment to that place. The rhetorical situation out of which this discussion of validity emerges makes it essential to understand this lecture on American literature as a commentary on literary whiteness as well, and a clue about how thoroughly race infuses Eliot's literary vision.

"The only exception to the general rule": Conversion, Validation, Re-racination

Against the backdrop of his anxiously American identity, Eliot's decision to convert to Anglo-Catholicism comes into focus as another strategy for shoring up a white racial identity. He uses "valid" as a proxy for "universal" in his discussion of Twain, but in theological discourse, "valid" carries a precise set of meanings tied up with standards of orthodoxy that ultimately are powerful enough to police boundaries of communal belonging. In a 1927 exchange of letters between Eliot and William Force Stead, the clergyman who would baptize Eliot later that year, "valid" appears again as the two make plans for Eliot to formalize his conversion by undergoing the Catholic sacraments of initiation. Stead's first concern is whether Eliot, who identified himself on February 3 as one "born & bred in the very heart of Boston Unitarianism," has already been baptized, writing: "[F]orgive me if I ask whether you have been baptized? My idea of Unitarians is of austere people who abstain from baptism as well as communion. Perhaps I do them an injustice. Anyway one must be baptized before being confirmed, tho' it is not necessary that one should receive Anglican baptism" (*Letters3* 404). Stead refers to the Catholic doctrine that holds valid any Christian baptism in the name of the Trinitarian God;[16] his tone is tentative perhaps because of the delicacy of determining if Eliot is inside or outside the Christian fold. Eliot responds, on February 7, "I have in short not the *slightest doubt* of my Baptism" (*Letters3* 412). Stead somewhat awkwardly replies that "Unitarian baptism is the only exception to the general rule which I mentioned in my last letter, namely that any baptism whether episcopal or not is recognized as valid, for the one essential is baptism in the name of the Trinity, and that I infer could not be expected in the Unitarian Church" (*Letters3* 428). He offers to consult the bishop to verify, but in his reply of February 28, Eliot readily accepts Stead's conclusion about his baptism's (in)validity: "I do not think that there is any need for you to consult the Bishop on the point you mention: Baptism is obviously necessary" (*Letters3* 428-9). Insofar as baptism defines membership in the Christian community, and Christianity serves as a proxy for whiteness,[17] Eliot's invalid baptism further threatens the coherence of his white racial identity.

This second instance of the word "valid" calls attention to the emphasis placed on continuity in both religious and racial discourses. A respect for continuity as a principle of identity as well as a profound desire to restore it when it appears to have been broken are central to Eliot's religious conversion. Urmila Seshagiri's insight into the constitutive importance attached to matters of continuity and discontinuity in Western racial thinking clarifies this: "the very idea of race—which in this period described biological, national, religious, linguistic, and character difference—invoked the consistent transfer of traits from one generation to the next."[18] Thus, "disruptions in the continuity of racial identity—through miscegenation, geographical displacement, religious conversion, or political upheaval, for example—engendered scientific as well as cultural anxieties about hybridity, contamination, and degeneration." Because religion and race are historically and discursively intertwined, Eliot's conversion must be seen as not only a demonstration of sincere religious belief but also a strategy for re-racination, securing a validly Christian and therefore more coherently "white" identity.

Conceptualizing conversion in this way requires a capacious understanding of race. As Henry Louis Gates, Jr., explains, "the sense of difference defined in popular usages of the term 'race' has both described and *inscribed* differences of language, belief system, artistic tradition, and gene pool … Race has become a trope of ultimate, irreducible difference between cultures, linguistic groups, or adherents of specific belief systems."[19] Gates helps us see religion as an inscription of race, meaning that conversion is, among other things, a racially significant event.[20] The gesture of conversion is a revision of one's religious identity, an identity indelibly shaped by and articulated through racialized tropes of differentiation. If Eliot understands his racial identity as threatened by the geographical discontinuities described in the Read letter, then undergoing formal initiation into an imagined community defined by religion and nation offers one possible way of reconsolidating whiteness.

Thinking of conversion in this way does not minimize or cast doubt upon Eliot's religious beliefs, nor question his commitment to the disciplined ritual practices of his faith. Indeed, Eliot's conversion was motivated by both the sincerity of his beliefs *and* the intensity of his commitment to the spiritual significance of race. Barry Spurr writes that only the Anglican version of Catholicism both "satisfied [Eliot's] requirements regarding the important connection between a Church and the culture of its people" and "offered him the orderliness, wholeness and stability of the understanding of life and its purpose."[21] Indeed, Spurr explains, "There was never any question … that Eliot would become a Roman Catholic, so long as he was an English citizen and a naturalised Briton."[22] Had he remained in Europe, Spurr speculates it is "almost certain" Eliot would have joined the Roman Catholic fold instead, but "in England, this was an impossible allegiance for him, not because of any doctrinal or liturgical reservations, but because of the disconnection from the cultural life of the nation of English Roman Catholics." The yearning for an integral identity, with cohesive religious, national, and racial attributes, directs Eliot's movement toward and through the experience of conversion.

The letters between Eliot and Stead make it clear that "validity" is a criterion that carries specific weight in discussions of sacramental theology while also serving as a metric for determining racial belonging. Converting to

Anglo-Catholicism, then, offers a way of connecting himself to "the cultural life of a nation," as Spurr puts it. For Eliot, "cultural life" is caught up in ideas of race as defined by genealogical continuity. In his case, undergoing a second baptism will ritually restore the continuity of Christian identity that the Catholic tradition perceives to have been broken by the Unitarian church's departure from Trinitarian theology.[23] The theological dubiousness Stead intimates about Eliot's family's Unitarianism dovetails with the dubious whiteness Eliot frets over in the Herbert Read letter—broken continuity, theological and geographical, threatens the validity of Eliot's spiritual and racial identity, requiring intervention to be shored up. If the rejection of his family's Unitarianism enacted by Eliot's conversion to Anglo-Catholicism initially looks like exchanging one variant of white Christianity for another, paying close attention to how each tradition's "validity" is evaluated and guaranteed reveals how his conversion is an essential component of his carefully constructed white racial identity.

"Where prayer has been valid": The Racial Imagination of *Four Quartets*

Whiteness studies can help us see how Eliot is "doing race" when he converts to Anglo-Catholicism and is naturalized as a British citizen, accessing a supposedly more coherent form of whiteness by restoring genealogical continuity defined in both national and religious terms. His last major poetic work, *Four Quartets*, is shaped by the racialized concepts of universality and continuity that underlie Eliot's theological imagination. As he works through these preoccupations in poetry, the intricately layered dynamics of striving and renunciation, desire and withdrawal, understanding and unknowing shatter whatever sense of transcendent security and stability whiteness was supposed to contain. Jed Esty insightfully describes Eliot's conversion and naturalization as "formal acts of affiliation" that are "indicative of Eliot's lust for roots: they make it tempting to think of the poet in these years as an ancient, grim, and determined salmon, swimming upstream against the currents of modernity and diaspora in order to find his beginnings, and of course, his ends."[24] This memorable phrasing elucidates both the motivation at the heart of these dramatic gestures—a "lust for roots"—as well as the all-too-strenuous effort required to pursue that end. Proceeding through a disciplined yet moving sequence of negations, *Four Quartets* is a deeply autobiographical poem that draws on the enormous significance attached to whiteness elsewhere in Eliot's oeuvre, only to set such investments in whiteness aside in favor of a state of spiritual enlightenment within which all vicissitudes of human identity, including race, are contingent, unstable, and illusionary.

Four Quartets relies on and complicates Eliot's biographical and poetic quest for re-racination and securing a stable and unimpeachably white racial identity. Its final section contains a third instance of "valid," the most prominent yet most opaque: "You are here to kneel / Where prayer has been valid" (*Poems1* 202). The word accrues meaning from its other iterations in Eliot's writing, but here, it is evocative rather than evaluative. To understand what valid might mean here, it is essential to contextualize its appearance within *Four Quartets* as a whole. At the macro level, the poem's most significant feature is the geographical movement from England to America and back, spotlighting sites significant to Eliot and his family. This spatial trajectory includes stops at Burnt Norton, in Gloucestershire; East Coker, a village in Somerset; the Dry Salvages, off the Massachusetts coast; and Little Gidding, a small village and civil parish in Cambridgeshire. This locational progression, I argue, maps an allegorical quest for white racial identity onto its pursuit of ever-deeper theological enlightenment. At the same time, though, the poem's micro-level shifts in tone and register undermine that sought-after coherence from within, revealing the pursuit itself to be an exercise in futility.

The second and fourth poems in the sequence, *East Coker* and *Little Gidding*, are especially vital to the *Quartets*' theologically idiosyncratic idea of whiteness. *East Coker* takes readers back to the deep time of the Eliot family tree, named for the village where Eliot's ancestors lived before his distant relative Andrew Eliot left for the Massachusetts Bay Colony in 1668, while *Little Gidding* takes place at a religious community established in 1626 and associated with the royalists during the English Civil War. *East Coker* is where *Four Quartets*' racial imagination is most clearly on display, and the dialectical relations between ends and beginnings, the local and universal, and the historical and transcendent are infused with racial significance. The poem famously opens and closes with a sibylline set of phrases: "In my beginning is my end" and "in my end is my beginning" (*Poems1* 185, 192). This ouroboric symmetry is aesthetically satisfying, epigrammatically reflecting Christian teachings about death and resurrection. Eliot had these lines inscribed on his tombstone at East Coker, making them resonate with personal significance beyond the poem. But at the same time, their powerful coherence is rooted in fantasy, or at least in the suspension of biographical fact that allows the poet to imagine his true beginning not as his actual birthplace of St. Louis but as his ancestors' point of departure from England.

Alluding to those English ancestors, the poem's first section opens a brief and fragile portal of poetic continuity between past and present, just the sort of continuity Eliot lamented the absence of, in his correspondence with Read. Alluding to Sir Thomas Elyot's *The Governour* (1531), the poem veers into Eliot's distant relative's poetic idiom:

> The association of man and woman
> In daunsinge, signifying matrimonie—
> A dignified and commodious sacrament.
> Two and two, necessarye coniunction,
> Holding eche other by the hand or the arm
> Whiche betokeneth concorde. (*Poems1* 186)

This vision is fleeting, though the archaic diction brings the distant past to the visual surface of the page; the words are strange to contemporary eyes and ears, in this moment of verbal intimacy with his ancestors. Their sacramental acts are "dignified and commodious"; their "necessarye coniunction" indicates the reproductive coupling that builds the genealogical line linking them to Eliot himself. It seems all of Eliot's racial angst could be resolved by finding a way to restore this "concorde" to the present, to insert himself into the rhythm they keep "in their dancing / As in their living in the living seasons" (*Poems1* 186). But the vision is strictly conditional: you can see it only "if you do not come too close, if you do not come too close" (*Poems1* 185). Esty writes that "it is part of the poem's discipline that scenes of the past … remain half-glimpsed, crowded with conditionals and negatives."[25] This discipline prevents the poem from lapsing fully into the mirage of perfect genealogical harmony. Opening with this vision thus anchors *East Coker* in the fantasy of racial restoration while simultaneously laying the groundwork for its renunciation.

The ancestral harmony dissolves entirely by the end of the next section, which closes with "The houses are all gone under the sea. / The dancers are all gone under the hill" (*Poems1* 188). Following a pattern shared across the four sections, part three of *East Coker* is focused on imagery of ascetic renunciation, from the descent into the darkness of the London Underground to the allusion to St. John of the Cross. Its opening line, "O dark dark dark. They all go into the dark," echoes the "all gone" of the previous two lines, prompting us to see the village and its dancers as part of what is being negated in this sequence (*Poems1* 188). To read integral racial identity as among the possibilities foreclosed in this section lends new meaning to the lines "I said to my soul, be still, and wait without hope / For hope would be hope for the wrong thing; wait without love /

For love would be love of the wrong thing" (*Poems1* 189). The methodical repetitions "hope … hope … hope" and "love … love … love" emphasize the very qualities the speaker is resolving to deny. Similarly, the intensity of the yearning for genealogical restoration is matched only by the depth of commitment to total dispossession.

When we arrive at Little Gidding, the lines "You are here to kneel / Where prayer has been valid" emerge out of a thicket of conditionals and qualifiers. They offer a clear directive, its forcefulness intensified by the lines that immediately precede it, which explain what you are *not* here to do, namely, "verify, / Instruct yourself, or inform curiosity / Or carry report" (*Poems1* 202). The verbs "verify," "instruct," and "report" differ in tone and in type from the final verb "kneel." In this way, these lines pry apart the quest for *verification* and the gesture of respect for *validity*. The racial anxieties baked into the previous two appearances of "valid" have fallen away at this point; now, unlike in its previous two appearances, validity requires no justification or proof.

If the fleeting glimpses of the ancestors dancing at East Coker or of the broken king arriving in Little Gidding are fragile and qualified ("if you do not come too close," "if you came this way"), the gesture of kneeling here yields a different modality of communion. Its efficacy depends not upon intact lines of succession or continuity with the past but only on the mere contingencies of place and time. Indeed, the poem admits,

> There are other places
> Which also are the world's end, some at the sea jaws,
> Or over a dark lake, in a desert or a city—
> But this is the nearest, in place and time,
> Now and in England. (*Poems1* 202)

This place is significant not because it is the *most* valid, or the *universally* valid, but because it happens to be the nearest. Elsewhere, the poem meditates on the teachings of Hinduism and Buddhism, placing these traditions alongside Christianity and thereby introducing powerful alternatives to whiteness as defined in exclusively Christian terms. Validity in *Four Quartets* is delicate and even arbitrary, not absolute and transcendent but historically determined, as emphasized by the present perfect tense—this is "where prayer *has been* valid." It is the very chanciness of that history that enables its ineffable spiritual efficacy.

In this final iteration, then, validity is historically situated yet theologically potent. If in earlier examples it was a proxy for the abstract transcendence of universal whiteness, here it admits and even embraces its core contingency.

Arriving at this place where prayer has been valid is the endpoint of a journey to the heart of whiteness, but the journey requires the negation of the grounds by which that whiteness would be secured. In this poem, love of race, like love of a country, is finally "love of the wrong thing": it "Begins as attachment to our own field of action / And comes to find that action of little importance / Though never indifferent" (*Poems1* 206).

Reading *Four Quartets* through the prism of whiteness studies helps us understand the extent to which the poem is profoundly shaped by the white racial identity negotiated at its core. Whiteness is yearned for and renounced, embraced and denied, within the poem's intricate movements between the local and universal, the past and present, the historical and transcendent. To grasp the depth of *Four Quartets*' religious implications is to understand its racial imaginary.

Notes

1 Ruth Frankenberg explains that whiteness's status "as unmarked marker is itself an 'ideological' effect that seeks to cover the tracks of its constructedness, specificity, and localness, even as they appear." Given this, Frankenberg argues for the importance of "marking whiteness" across scholarly disciplines, since "whiteness makes itself invisible precisely by asserting its normalcy, its transparency, in contrast with the marking of others on which its transparency depends." Ruth Frankenberg, "Introduction: Local Whitenesses, Localizing Whiteness," in *Displacing Whiteness: Essays in Social and Cultural Criticism*, edited by Ruth Frankenberg (Durham: Duke University Press, 1997), 16, 6.

2 Amanda E. Lewis, "'What Group?' Studying Whites and Whiteness in the Era of 'Color-Blindness,'" *Sociological Theory* 22, no. 4 (2004): 626.

3 Rachel Blau DuPlessis, "'HOO, HOO, HOO': Some Episodes in the Construction of Modern Whiteness," *American Literature* 67, no. 4 (1995): 669.

4 Michael North, *The Dialect of Modernism: Race, Language, and Twentieth-Century Literature* (New York: Oxford University Press, 1994).

5 David E. Chinitz, *T. S. Eliot and the Cultural Divide* (Chicago: University of Chicago Press, 2003).

6 Anita Patterson, "Confronting Racism and *The Waste Land* in the Era of #MeToo," *Modernism/modernity* Print Plus, vol. 5, cycle 2 (September 28, 2020), https://doi.org/10.26597/mod.0171. Frances Dickey, "T. S. Eliot and the Color Line of St. Louis," *Modernism/modernity* Print Plus, vol. 5, cycle 4 (March 9, 2021), https://doi.org/10.26597/mod.0187.

7 Gabrielle McIntire, *Modernism, Memory, and Desire: T. S. Eliot and Virginia Woolf* (Cambridge: Cambridge University Press, 2008): 10.
8 Michelle A. Taylor, "(In)Discreet Modernism: T. S. Eliot's Coterie Poetics," *College Literature* 47, no. 1 (2020): 42.
9 Perhaps the most obvious example of this is the anti-Semitism of *After Strange Gods* (1934). For a fuller discussion of this aspect of Eliot's work, see Anthony Julius, *T. S. Eliot, Anti-Semitism, and Literary Form* (Cambridge: Cambridge University Press, 1995).
10 North, 77–9.
11 Richard Dyer, *White: Twentieth Anniversary Edition* (New York: Routledge, 2017), 1.
12 Dyer, 2.
13 Kamran Javadizadeh, "The Atlantic Ocean Breaking on Our Heads: Claudia Rankine, Robert Lowell, and the Whiteness of the Lyric Subject," *PMLA* 134, no. 3 (2019): 476.
14 Toni Morrison, *Playing in the Dark* (Cambridge: Harvard University Press, 1992), 37.
15 Eliot's reference to Conrad's *Heart of Darkness* invites us to recall Chinua Achebe's famous critique of the racism that enables the supposedly universal qualities of that novel, relying on "Africa as a metaphysical battlefield devoid of all recognizable humanity, into which the wandering European enters at his peril." Achebe, "An Image of Africa," *The Massachusetts Review* 18, no. 4 (1977): 788.
16 In the Anglo-Catholic church, validity is explicitly connected to apostolic succession (mentioned in Stead's letter), or the idea that priests and bishops derive their authority by means of an unbroken chain of succession leading back to Jesus himself. In a contemporaneous monograph, A. E. Manning-Foster explains: "It is impossible to insist too strongly upon this matter of Apostolical Succession, *since the whole theory of the Catholic Church rests upon it,* and no Sacrament can be valid unless it is administered by a validly ordained ministry." Manning-Foster, *Anglo-Catholicism* (London: T.C. & E.C. Jack, 1914), 78.
17 Anthropologist Talal Asad has explored the relationship of Western Christian theology to modern racial ideologies, and religious studies scholars Rachel C. Schneider and Sophie Bjork-James have argued that "it is impossible to fully understand the formation of the racial category of whiteness—or the broader racial order—outside of Christian history." Talal Asad, *Genealogies of Religion: Discipline and Reasons of Power in Christianity and Islam* (Baltimore: Johns Hopkins University Press, 1993); Rachel C. Schneider and Sophie Bjork-James, "Whither Whiteness and Religion? Implications for Theology and the Study of Religion," *Journal of the American Academy of Religion* 88, no. 1 (2020): 178.
18 Urmila Seshagiri, *Race and the Modernist Imagination* (Ithaca: Cornell University Press, 2010): 8.

19 Henry Louis Gates, Jr., "Editor's Introduction: Writing 'Race' and the Difference It Makes," *Critical Inquiry* 12, no. 2 (1985): 5.
20 Gauri Viswanathan also theorizes conversion in these terms, understanding it as "not only a spiritual but also a political activity" that destabilizes both demographic patterns and formulations of modern secularity. Viswanathan, *Outside the Fold: Conversion, Modernity, and Belief* (Princeton: Princeton University Press, 1998), xvii.
21 Barry Spurr, *Anglo-Catholic in Religion: T. S. Eliot and Christianity* (Cambridge: Lutterworth, 2010), 33.
22 Spurr, 108.
23 Robert Crawford offers a brief history of the St. Louis Unitarian community founded by Eliot's grandfather and an overview of their core tenets of belief, highlighting the anti-dogmatic emphasis that Eliot would later come to resent. He concludes dryly that "St. Louis Unitarianism gave [Eliot] much to come to terms with." Crawford, *Young Eliot: From St. Louis to "The Waste Land"* (New York: Farrar, Straus and Giroux, 2015), 41.
24 Jed Esty, *A Shrinking Island: Modernism and National Culture in England* (Princeton: Princeton University Press, 2004), 111.
25 Esty, 155.

9

Tiresias and TERFism Today: *The Waste Land*'s Modernist Feminine, Cis and Trans

Emma Heaney

The Tiresias of *The Waste Land* is a double figure: "though blind," all-seeing and, in Eliot's account, the vantage from which the reader sees "the substance of the poem" (*Poems1* 74). But what do we see of Tiresias? We see "a mere spectator and not indeed a 'character' "; we see their physical body as it exists in the poem's present, with general references to their past experiences. What sort of past? They have zoomed in from another space and time, Hellenic Thebes, to witness the real fleshy lives of the moderns, living their modern lives, in their modern city. In contrast to the rest of the poem's cast, Tiresias has no present, naught but a mythic history, and certainly no conceivable future: unseen seer, man-woman, newly ancient.

In my book *The New Woman* (2017), I position Eliot's Tiresias as one of modernism's many transsexual bodies, tugged between Freud's classical ideation of sex change and the sexologically inspired technocratic future of bodies, stretched on the rack of modernist conceptual capture.[1] Tiresias, like the rest of the coterie of modernist trans femmes, provides an allegorical figure for the woes of changing gender roles, the mechanization of society, and the supposedly castrated condition of womanhood itself. In placing Tiresias in this context, I depart from previous readings, for example, Ed Madden's consideration of Tiresias as Eliot's investigation of ambiguous or changeable gender or Jane Marcus's reading of Tiresias as a comment of modern "emasculation."[2] In contrast, Cyrena Pondrom sees Tiresias as an "avatar" for the sexually unmarked narrator of the poem; the fact that "Tiresias is not androgynous, but alternatively male and female" unsettles both categories.[3] Matthew Scully considers this bodily instability ("plasticity") to be central to understanding the poem's formal instability: "which shifts the critical conversation from a sense of form dependent on the dialectic of order and disorder to a sense of form as 'plastic.'"[4] Almost a century after publication, what effects can we see now of Eliot's assigning any fixed meaning to trans femininity that can help us make a point about history, sex, or form?

The question is important because the first decades of our new century have witnessed another kind of conceptual installation of the trans feminine. Building on a minority (but disproportionately discussed and promoted) strain of 1970s Radical Feminism, finding their origin, perhaps, in Janice Raymond's transmisogynist work *The Transsexual Empire* (1979),[5] a group of feminists called by critics trans exclusionary radical feminists (TERFs) and calling themselves gender-critical feminists have focused their writing and political organizing on the claim that trans women pose a threat to all women's spaces (focusing on domestic-abuse shelters and prisons) and a conceptual impediment to feminist investigation of women's social position and embodied experiences.[6]

Drawing together the structural and conceptual position of the trans feminine in "The Fire Sermon" section of *The Waste Land* and in TERF writing reveals the continued positioning of the trans feminine as merely a conceptual handmaiden to cis femininity, one hundred years after the poem's publication. The poem clarifies the way in which TERFism assesses what trans femininity is assumed to owe cis femininity. This argument allows us to understand the conceptual underpinning of TERFism as long present in the cis approach to trans femininity rather than, as its exponents often claim, as an innovation in thought that fights back the recent development of trans life going mainstream.

Eliot's Trans Feminine Allegory, Then

Eliot detours through queer icons Shakespeare and Baudelaire and bobs and weaves, arguably homophobically, around a racialized merchant who has tried to lure the speaker into joining his dried (currant-like) testicles in a gay weekend at a brothel, before arriving at our stanzas of interest (*Poems1* 63, lines 207–14). We enter the scene "at the violet hour," the mechanized hour of history "when the eyes and back" of all in unison "turn upward from the desk," and in the post-work, pre-afterwork suspension between the bodies that have becomes cogs, collectively, "the human engine waits / Like a taxi throbbing waiting" (*Poems1* 63). As we turn to the Tiresias/typist subsection, the lines become rhythmically mechanical, conforming to a lulling ABAB rhyme scheme against the grain of the willful invention of the previous lineation. We are then introduced to the speaker:

> I Tiresias, though blind, throbbing between two lives,
> Old man with wrinkled female breasts, can see
> At the violet hour, the evening hour that strives
> Homeward, and brings the sailor home from sea. (*Poems1* 63)

Like Athena watching over the homeward-turning sailor of *The Odyssey*, Tiresias looks and sees both the scene and the truths behind the scene. This sight is connected, as in the classical source, to their experience of "throbbing" between male and female existence, between "two lives" defined by an absolute social border impossible (in the logic of the poem) for mortals to transgress. Tiresias's body is exposed to the reader's gaze, presented as the proof of their melancholy condition, which provides both wisdom and pain.

Next, we meet the typist, home after a day of work, clearing away her last meal to make way for the next, served in tins packed by other workers, in factories, who presumably are home opening their own tinned dinners—a modern network of workers all mechanized to afford each other the time to be likewise mechanized. Rather than the structures of her body on display, as with Tiresias, we see her clean laundry flapping on the line ("Out of the window perilously spread / Her drying combinations touched by the sun's last rays") and the architecture of undergarments that industrial manufacture has produced, supposedly, to free the modern woman from that symbol of nineteenth-century repression and bodily containment, the corset: "On the divan are piled (at night her bed) / Stockings, slippers, camisoles, and stays" (*Poems1* 63).

To what use does she put this freedom from Victorian custom? Let her handmaiden seer tell us:

> I Tiresias, old man with wrinkled dugs
> Perceived the scene, and foretold the rest—
> I too awaited the expected guest.
> He, the young man carbuncular, arrives,
> A small house agent's clerk, with one bold stare,
> One of the low on whom assurance sits
> As a silk hat on a Bradford millionaire. (*Poems1* 63)

Perception and foretelling, here, miss the majesty of the classical association—Tiresias doesn't foreknow thanks to divinely bestowed gift. Rather, the humdrum of the gendered sexual encounter is scripted to the point of being "expected," the pocked young man marked, in Eliot's extreme class snobbery, by the repulsive and undeserved "assurance" that he knows how this "scene" will play out. He's a man and she a woman. How else would events unfold? Tiresias's experience grants them the ability to know what will happen and ascertain where the reader's empathy ought to lie: with the woman. In a nihilistic inversion of their response to Hera's question, Eliot's modernist Tiresias judges that it is women who suffer a greater measure of the pain generated by the hopeless state of modern sexuality.

Despite the reliability of the sexual script, the young man carbuncular still needs to be tactical. He gauges that "[t]he time is now propitious," and "bored and tired" as she is, he "endeavours to engage her in caresses" that are "unreproved, if undesired" (*Poems1* 64). Eliot marks the young man's mounting sexual energy:

> Flushed and decided, he assaults at once;
> Exploring hands encounter no defence;
> His vanity requires no response,
> And makes a welcome of indifference. (*Poems1* 64)

Unwanted but not resisted because preordained, inevitable: that's Eliot's view of modern eros organized by the heterosexual idea of "woman" and "man." It is decidedly violent, for women, and, for men, a mindless expression and bolstering practice for an underserved, baseless confidence.

This is all we get of the act of sexual intercourse, because Eliot draws a demure screen across the bodily, technical activities of penetration, of sweat and touch. The form of that screen is the blind seer's empathetic parenthetical. Tiresias is watching, but all we see is the pathos generated when a sexual subject positioned as a woman looks on at the activity that reproduces that positioning on the body of another. From the once-woman, forever feminized prophet/ess, we learn:

> (And I Tiresias have foresuffered all
> Enacted on this same divan or bed;
> I who have sat by Thebes below the wall
> And walked among the lowest of the dead.) (*Poems1* 64)

Here we come to the crux. Observe the play between cis feminine and trans feminine: Tiresias's body is displayed, whereas the typist's is demurely shielded. Eliot's classical trans feminine has already suffered. This assurance is encoded into the peculiar verb formation, "foresuffered," which, although in the past perfect tense, by virtue of its prefix is also tugged toward the past and future continuous. Tiresias suffered in the past what was then the future. Tiresias already suffered the future, even the reader's own. Tiresias will in perpetuity have been always suffering already. Suffering suffuses their bodily predicament, both the suffering of having been cruelly used as a woman and the suffering of being not-quite-woman now, "throbbing" on the brink of womanhood, weighed with "wrinkled breasts," and with all that subject position's atrocious psychic baggage and yet not really in it either, certainly not able to be the object of the kind of empathy of which they are agent. Tiresias is only an object of empathy due to an ontological somatic condition, not, as with their cis counterpart, a historical, that is changeable, one. The suffering is shared, trans to cis, but the recognition goes one way, both within the poem, and for the reader who sees through Tiresias's blind eyes but certainly doesn't see *as* Tiresias. There is no perspectival alignment between reader and speaker, as that speaker is held in her peculiarity, her particularity, her distance from conceivable experience.

This is not the fault of the cis subject of the poem, who doesn't even know Tiresias is on the scene. That's the point. The poem naturalizes the trans feminine Tiresias as not a character in the poem, like the typist, that is, a participant in the action, but in metacritical relation to the typist, a conceptual figure representing and testifying to her miseries, which are presented as emblematic of the real way scores of modern typists live in modern London. There is no equivalent realist representative line drawn between Tiresias and the trans feminine mollies and Maryannes that the typist would pass on her way home through London's violet hour streets.[7] Of course not, my skeptical reader might say. Tiresias is a classical allusion, not a true modern character. Whereas the cis feminine is historical, the trans feminine is out of time, conceptually investigating the relation between the mythical and modern, but in no sense of any particular time, in no way expected to possess the same historicity as a cis subject. Whereas the cis feminine is part of a communal story of womanhood, the trans feminine is an isolate, available for mining for conceptual sustenance. The fact that the trans feminine is routinely presented in this way, beginning with the works of literary modernism, as I argue in *The New Woman*, scripts her role in the psychic drama that is cis depictions of trans femininity in the twentieth century, stripped of the pathos Eliot attributes to her.[8]

As the young man departs, the poem's rhyme scheme breaks briefly. He "bestows one final patronising kiss / And gropes his way, finding the stairs unlit"; the mechanical spell is broken (*Poems1* 64). The young woman gathers herself; she is still caught in the soothing and numbing of the regular rhyme scheme:

> She turns and looks a moment in the glass,
> Hardly aware of her departed lover;
> Her brain allows one half-formed thought to pass:
> "Well now that's done: and I'm glad it's over." (*Poems1* 64)

Sumita Chakraborty reads this ending as censorship: "we hear none of … the typist's 'own' words; Tiresias only permits what he calls 'one half-formed thought' of hers to intrude on his narration," attributing a masculinist gatekeeping role to the blind seer.[9] I propose that here Eliot is shielding his heroine from the indignity of having her violation described and reflecting the extent to which this experience of quasi-consent operates through dissociation, through barely thinking about what is happening, going through the motions mechanically, guided by gendered routine and the man's actions. This kind of interiority, witnessed by Tiresias if not expressed by the typist, is Eliot's defining attribution to this cis woman. The reader understands that she is mired in an intractable situation. But her situation is social, not ontological. The way empathy structures the passage allows us to hope that the typist might, someday, live a less mechanized life, both in the realm of work and in her intimate life.

The trans feminine seer, in contrast, has been "throbbing" in statis for centuries. There's no indication that their situation is changeable; that's the meaning of divinely mandated fate. As we part from the scene, Eliot tells us that "when lovely woman stoops to folly" with a very bad boy, she doesn't have to die, as she evidently did in Oliver Goldsmith's eighteenth century (*Poems1* 64). Rather, she "[p]aces about her room again, alone, / She smooths her hair with automatic hand, / And puts a record on the gramophone" (*Poems1* 64). The modern woman doesn't need art to "wash her guilt away," as Goldsmith had it. Guilt implies thought about one's actions and a period of moral reckoning. On this, she'll pass. She might, however, need a little culture pressed on a disk that circles round and round to return her to a numbed emotional baseline, to "smooth" her where she's rumpled and restore her tenuous self-possession.

Where is the other feminine figure who's made this scene? Apparitional from the beginning, Tiresias has evidently flown the coop still unseen. Can we imagine them leaving the apartment bedchamber, groping down the unlit stairwell, and walking the streets of London, meeting the mollies in scenes of mutual recognition, breaking the spell that modernism cast on trans femininity? Maybe, if we bring such a desire to *The Waste Land*, but not because Eliot's poem authorizes us to do so. "The Fire Sermon" is about the feminized empathy that circulates between Tiresias and the typist, cutting across the border imposed by different bodily predicaments. But it's also about how one of those immiserations is real and one is mythic. The body of Tiresias represents the agony of the typist, the agony of the prosaic, unremarkable, everyday experience of being the object on which another has enacted his personhood. Eliot's famous poem is one of the key texts in which the trans feminine fills the void for a stable eternal symbolic referent, as the cis feminine, through poetic particularization, which is to say humanization, vacates it.

TERFism's Trans Feminine, Now

Many of the tones that characterize Eliot's trans feminine are also sounded in what may seem an unlikely parallel context: contemporary polemical writing by TERFs. This section will focus on three significant structures of TERF argumentation that Eliot innovated as part of his codification of the modernist trans feminine: the presentation of trans femininity as simultaneously ancient and futuristic; the contrast between the naturalness of cis bodies and the artificiality of trans bodies; and the positioning of trans womanhood in a metacritical and/or figural relation to cis womanhood, as though, in her existence, trans woman is a comment on a separate field called womanhood. In each of these cases, the modernist trans feminine was part of the cultural popularization of a foundational idea of trans femininity.

Central to Tiresias's doubleness is, as I've said, their status as both ancient and modern. TERF writing repeats this temporal frame by presenting the trans feminine as both fundamentally anachronistic and central to a bewildering quick reordering of definitions of sex. As one example of this double temporal logic, take Elinor Burkett's op-ed published in June 2015 in the *New York Times*, entitled "What Makes a Woman?" She uses reality TV star, former Olympian, and former candidate for governor of California Caitlyn Jenner as a hook. She invites her reader to consider

> Caitlyn Jenner's idea of a woman: a cleavage-boosting corset, sultry poses, thick mascara and the prospect of regular "girls' nights" of banter about hair and makeup … I have fought for many of my 68 years against efforts to put women—our brains, our hearts, our bodies, even our moods—into tidy boxes, to reduce us to hoary stereotypes … That's the kind of nonsense that was used to repress women for centuries.[10]

Burkett's editorial extrapolates from an interview with Jenner to associate trans women with the womanhood of these kinds of feminine cultural signifiers, never mind that we can look no further than Jenner's daughters to prove that plenty of cis women have similar aesthetics and ideas about gender. The editorial is accompanied by a collage graphic showing legs in fishnet stockings cut off just above the control-top line of the thigh, hands with spiky red nails, and men's legs in 1950s-style trousers that taper at the ankle, suggesting, as the essay does throughout, that trans women are in some way breaking women down into component gendered parts, as, it's implied, the patriarchy used to be able to do.[11]

Burkett then provides a litany of examples of entities that are changing policies and the language they use to include trans people in services: abortion providers referring to clients as "people" rather than women, women's colleges "contorting themselves into knots to accommodate female students who consider themselves men." She presents these changes as posing a radical new campaign of change to existing ideas about sex, which then demands change of cis women, though Burkett never explains how cis women need to change their self-concept to attain, for instance, abortion services under the identity "client." The existence of trans people in public consciousness, Burkett simply states, "[demands] that women reconceptualize ourselves." This is, in a sense, true. For trans women and other trans people to attain a place in public conversation requires cis people to see themselves as cis, though not, for instance, to cease viewing themselves as women. Such a new self-awareness entails a scary and imminent future, according to Burkett. This claim, that trans women are bound either to a regrettable past or to an insupportable future, but never dwell in the present, are never *present* in reality, is a rhetorical inheritance of the modernist trans feminine.

Another rhetorical structure that TERFs repeat is Eliot's representation of Tiresias as a doctored, false, tragic embodiment, emblematized by their "wrinkled dugs." Their writing proffers grotesquely violent descriptions of trans people's bodies and trans healthcare contrasted with proprietary claims to the naturalness of cis women's embodiment. A brief but representative sampling includes Abigail Shrier's 2020 book *Irreversible Damage: The Transgender Craze Seducing Our Daughters*. The "damage" of the title includes not only the effects she imputes to puberty-blocking hormones on future fertility, but also—as the title's meta-misgendering implies (the "daughters" Shrier refers to are trans kids seeking medical services to ease their relation to trans masculinity or trans boyhood)—the very idea of trans life and embodiment itself.[12] Germaine Greer talks in terms repeated by other TERFs about the surgical procedure of vaginoplasty as "lop[ping] off" and "chop[ping] off" "your dick," using violent verbs that could (but would not and ought not to) be applied to other contexts in which structures used to identify sex are removed from people's bodies, the breasts or uteruses of cancer patients, for example.[13] Sheila Jeffreys provides an elaborate, visceral mockery of trans women's healthcare and bodies when she writes that "newly carved-out orifices of male-bodied transgenders do not resemble vaginas; rather, they create new microbial habitats in which infections develop and cause serious smell issues for their owners."[14] This language of infection and odor, these categorical claims about the appearance of trans women's vaginas, bear no relation to reality: they simply draw shaming attention to trans women's embodiment. What person with a vagina, or genitals of any kind, would want theirs described in this kind of language? Burkett proposes that trans women must be held apart from cis women because trans women haven't "suffered" unexpected onset of menstruation, unexpected pregnancy, workplace sexualization, gender discrimination in pay, or the threat of rape, all of which she imagines the natural, if regrettable, effect of having been assigned female at birth. Of course, trans men experience the first two things and trans women (disproportionately in relation to cis women) the last three. Burkett has no interest in facts about trans life. She mobilizes her fantasy of trans life to claim the particularity of her own experience as a cis woman and to make the claim that only someone with a body like hers is a woman. She wants her reader to believe that trans women's existence is as fictional as that of a person who is magically transformed by Zeus, rather than a long historical genealogy of experience in intimate relation with that of cis women and composing part of historical category of women's experience.

The pain of the modern woman's sexualization and sex life is figured in the suffering, grotesque, body of Eliot's Tiresias, tugged between past and future. The trans feminine is made to serve as the conceptual handmaiden to the cis, clarifying, representing her experience, but also held outside of it. From Eliot to the TERFs: the trans feminine figure may be kindly and ministering. She may be threatening and frightening, a chimera. But in any case, she is apparitional, throbbing, shimmering on the threshold of being. She can be a topic, a phenomenon, a trend, a touchy subject, a problem, a first-time experience; she is a novelty, consistently, for over a hundred years. She is useful for analogy, metaphor, allegory, example, or reliable mystery, but she is not a field of investigation in her own right.[15] She cannot be real because, as Eliot suggests in his introduction to *Nightwood*, speaking of its queer and trans coterie, the abnormal is only of interest to the extent that it clarifies the general. That too has a TERF legacy: TERFs engage trans people and trans life only in relation to cis life and people.

On the Limits of Empathy, Then and Now

Modernism was part of a social process that set the terms for cis understanding of transness for the following century. This chapter is a plea to modernist scholars and teachers to distinguish among the figures of transness that cis people invent, actual trans people, and the representations trans people and communities produce. We must cease to regard trans life as an innovation of the young and bring trans ancestors, elders, and peers into the classroom discussion, if we are going to talk about trans people at all. This is more than just an imperative of good scholarly and pedagogical practice. The years 2021 and 2022 were watershed years for assaults on trans life, particularly the healthcare and well-being of trans young people, and hundreds of bills seeking to outlaw trans healthcare, criminalize doctors for providing it, remove children from their trans-affirming parents' custody, and ban trans kids from sports are being proposed and passed in states across the country.[16] These efforts represent, according to preeminent historian of American trans life Jules Gill-Peterson, a eugenicist program to disappear trans children.[17] Trans people are being erased again, setting them up to be rediscovered again, in another generation, as new, bewildering, unprecedented, confusing. Trans life has long been presented as something that cis people must strive to understand or accept, but with all those generations of investigation, understanding never seems to come. #MeToo and concordant public attention to the experiences of women and all those exposed to gendered violence makes us less harassable, less vulnerable to being held hostage by male superiors, structurally less vulnerable to rape. This is a joyous, beautiful reality. It also correlates, historically, with this rise of new attacks by cis women against trans women—a firestorm led and cheer-led by TERFs. The only response is to recognize the interrelatedness of conditions and therefore purpose among cis women and trans people, to make ourselves instruments in the "affinity of hammers" that Sara Ahmed hopes feminism is becoming.[18] When Rachel Potter argues that the depiction of "women's disordered physicality" in *The Waste Land* is "expressive of the cultural and political conflicts Eliot found troubling," we can see the resonance between that established use of the cis feminine and the use of the trans feminine.[19] Solidarity, not empathy, not interest, not fascination with difference, is the necessary relationality to end, rather than reproduce, the relation of the cis feminine to the trans feminine. If we want to talk about trans people, we should talk about trans people, then in 1922 and now in the 2020s.

Can a politically conservative, racist, geniusy Anglo-Catholic poet, dead nearly six decades, be a spur to or literary object of this project? When it comes to trans literary study, should we "Eliot" *now*? If so, *why* Eliot now and *how* should we read Eliot's trans feminine now? We must imagine that a trans feminine reader of Eliot's poem, then and now, is possible, and reorder the Eliotic relation between the perverse and the general. We can teach Eliot alongside the texts of trans feminine life that were contemporary to his poetry.[20]

Or consider another possible intertext. In the memoirs of Herculine Barbin, written and published in the 1860s, and republished and popularized by Michel Foucault in 1980, Barbin, who was assigned female at birth, lived as a girl, but was then reassigned as male in her late teens, against her will, finds a reflection of her own experience in a late classical text:

> From time to time I caught myself reading to a very late hour of the night. It was my recreation, my relaxation … I confess that I was extraordinarily shaken when I read Ovid's *Metamorphoses. Those who know them can imagine how I felt.* As the sequel of my story will clearly show, this discovery had a special bearing on my case.[21] (emphasis added)

Barbin reading Ovid's narratives of bodily transformation—Tiresias and/or Hermaphroditus, we can assume—can provide a model for us to read Eliot. Trans literary representation operates as its own lineage of both production and consumption when it's not assumed that such representations can only be understood as a commentary on or investigation of a purportedly cis general subject or cis social consensus. *The Waste Land* is a literary object in that lineage, a poem in which readers can find things that the poet may not have imagined.

Notes

1 Emma Heaney, introduction to *The New Woman: Literary Modernism, Queer Theory, and the Trans Feminine Allegory* (Evanston: Northwestern University Press, 2017).
2 Ed Madden, *Tiresian Poetics: Modernism, Sexuality, Voice, 1888–2001* (Cranbury: Rosemont, 2008); Jane Marcus, *Hearts of Darkness: White Women Write Race* (New Brunswick: Rutgers University Press, 2004), 230.
3 Cyrena N. Pondrom, "T. S. Eliot: The Performativity of Gender in *The Waste Land*," *Modernism/modernity* 12, no. 3 (September 2005): 429.
4 Matthew Scully, "Plasticity at the Violet Hour: Tiresias, *The Waste Land*, and Poetic Form," *Journal of Modern Literature* 41, no. 3 (Spring 2018): 167.
5 Janice G. Raymond, *The Transexual Empire: The Making of the She-Male* (London: Teachers College Press, 1994).
6 For an account of the development of TERFism among the powerful, public, and well-connected, see Sophie Lewis, "How British Feminism Became Anti-Trans," *New York Times*, February 7, 2019, https://www.nytimes.com/2019/02/07/opinion/

terf-trans-women-britain.html; for an account of the proliferation of the ideology among online communities of non-famous women, see Katie J. M. Baker, "The Road to Terfdom: Mumsnet and the Fostering of Anti-Trans Radicalization," *Lux* 1 (April 2021), https://lux-magazine.com/article/the-road-to-terfdom/.
7 See David F. Greenberg, *The Construction of Homosexuality* (Chicago: University of Chicago Press, 1990), 349–90.
8 Heaney, 6–13.
9 Sumita Chakraborty, "No," *Modernism/modernity* Print Plus, vol. 4, cycle 1 (March 4, 2019), https://doi.org/10.26597/mod.0096.
10 Elinor Burkett, "What Makes a Woman," *New York Times*, June 6, 2015, https://www.nytimes.com/2015/06/07/opinion/sunday/what-makes-a-woman.html.
11 For another example of such claims see Sarah Ditum, "Trans Rights Should Not Come at the Cost of Women's Fragile Gains," *Economist*, July 5, 2018, https://www.economist.com/open-future/2018/07/05/trans-rights-should-not-come-at-the-cost-of-womens-fragile-gains.
12 Abigail Shrier, *Irreversible Damage: The Transgender Craze Seducing Our Daughters* (Washington: Regnery, 2020).
13 Quoted in Cleis Abeni, "Feminist Germaine Greer Goes on Anti-Trans Rant over Caitlyn Jenner," *Advocate*, October 26, 2015, https://www.advocate.com/caitlyn-jenner/2015/10/26/feminist-germaine-greer-goes-anti-trans-rant-over-caitlyn-jenner.
14 Sheila Jeffreys, *Gender Hurts: A Feminist Analysis of the Politics of Transgenderism* (Abingdon: Routledge, 2014).
15 Chase Strangio, "When Your Existence Is Up for Debate," *Medium*, October 18, 2016, https://medium.com/stand-with-gavin/when-your-existence-is-up-for-debate-fa93a75e21f1.
16 Saeed Jones, "The Republican War against Trans Kids," *GQ*, May 5, 2021, https://www.gq.com/story/chase-strangio-on-anti-trans-laws.
17 Jules Gill-Peterson, "The Anti-Trans Lobby's Real Agenda," *Jewish Currents*, April 27, 2021, https://jewishcurrents.org/the-anti-trans-lobbys-real-agenda/.
18 Sara Ahmed, "An Affinity of Hammers," *TSQ: Transgender Studies Quarterly* 3, nos. 1–2 (May 2016): 22–34.
19 Rachel Potter, "Gender and Obscenity in *The Waste Land*," in *The Cambridge Companion to "The Waste Land"*, edited by Gabrielle McIntire (New York: Cambridge University Press, 2015), 135.
20 See Heaney, *The New Woman*, chapter 4, for some examples.
21 Quoted in *Herculine Barbin: Being the Recently Discovered Memoirs of a Nineteenth-Century French Hermaphrodite*, edited by Michel Foucault (London: Knopf Doubleday, 2013), 18.

10

Eliot in the Dadabase

Elyse Graham and Michelle A. Taylor

As the other essays in this collection suggest, this is an exciting time to be an Eliot scholar. The sudden proliferation of material available to be read—the many volumes of the *Complete Prose* and the *Letters of T. S. Eliot*—is bringing thousands of pages of new material to thousands of new readers, readers perhaps not as specialized as before, but strewn across the scholarly spectrum. This potentially overwhelming influx of material coincides with the development and proliferation of digital tools we can use to analyze it "at a distance."

Happily, at least some of those new materials are already digitized: the *Complete Prose*, currently online and being redeveloped in a "digital reborn" format; the Hale Letters, the scans of which are stored at Princeton. Yet what makes our moment so invigorating is the prospect not only of new material but also of new readers and new reading communities. The devices that allow us to read Eliot (or, as we'll discuss, *not* read Eliot) in new ways also allow us to connect in new ways, creating new forms of learning and collaboration.

What can we say right now about the *findings* of computational literary analysis on Eliot's corpus? Not much, while projects simply to digitize that corpus are still in development. Producing a machine-readable text from the scans of Eliot's letters requires a vast effort; making the *Prose* subject to faceted search is a labor-intensive process, involving collaboration across many realms of expertise, from technical to scholarly to editorial. Still, as we look ahead to the analyses that these digital projects will make possible, we have the opportunity to think a bit more abstractly about how Eliot can assist us in meeting the challenges of digital research and interpretation. In using Eliot to understand digital cultures (both academic and otherwise), we find that we come away with new perspectives on the poet, even before we've gathered and delved into the data, even while we wait to see what the future and its algorithms will bring. Perhaps, too, Eliot's example—his myth of impersonality, for one—might encourage us to address misconceptions of the possibilities offered by computational literary analysis.

We'll start by thinking about what a new group of readers—fanfiction writers—make of Eliot: how they help us to see Eliot reading and writing in the mode of a *fan*, rather than solely in the mode of a stern professional, and how they exemplify the new and unexpected literary connections that emerging technologies enable. Then, turning from the amateurish to the professional, we'll consider what Eliot can teach us in the era of "big data": how his work reflects on the myth of data prior to interpretation; how he reminds us that all data results from acts of construction, even before we subject it to interpretation. Finally, we'll discuss the avenues opening up for the computational study of Eliot's work.

Eliot's Fandom

As Megan Quigley writes in this volume, Eliot himself was a fannish reader and writer; he even belonged to literary communities that, if we wouldn't necessarily call them fandoms, nonetheless thrived in part because of their atmosphere of literary fannishness.[1] Fandom hasn't always existed as a practice (arguably, it started around the time of Charles Dickens), but the internet has certainly made it more prominent, more powerful, and more rewarding—even for fans of Eliot. At this time, Archive of Our Own (AO3), a Hugo Award–winning fanfiction platform that hosts more than nine million fan works, contains 785 pieces that use the term "T. S. Eliot" in some manner.[2] Depending on one's perspective, this number can seem both oddly high (how many poets inspire hundreds of transformative fan works?) and comparatively low in contrast to the 141,746 works that mention the name "Sherlock Holmes" or the 385,582 that contain the name "Harry Potter." Eliot's fandom, such as it is, is not the mighty industry for producing content that other fandoms are.[3] Nonetheless, we might borrow from Dr. Johnson and say that what's surprising is that Eliot has a *fandom* at all.[4]

Eliot's online fanfic writers may be drawn to what Quigley calls the "emotionally charged fan atmosphere" of Eliot's composition.[5] In their fan writings, they seem to recognize that his literariness, and even what we would describe as the modernist elements in his aesthetic, relies on modes of attachment, imitation, and interpretation that arbiters of "good reading" often regard as unscholarly. In other words, fanfic writers admire Eliot, in part, for his own fannishness. What they may be drawing from his poetry is its affinity for yoking together heterogeneous elements with a violence that John Donne would never brave but which online fandoms, with their infinite permutations of crossovers, fusions, alternate universes, and multi-fandom communities, take in stride. Usually, fans perform these acts of reckless mixing through narrative; in Eliot's case, they recognize and admire this sensibility in a different genre, lyric. Eliot's fans are noteworthy for how they manage to hybridize the unlike categories of narrative and lyric—and to put hybridity itself in the thematic foreground in ways that are exceptional even in fandom.

In general, fan texts that significantly feature Eliot's work tend to bring Eliot into conversation with a second fandom. Some writers use an Eliot poem as a template for storytelling in another fandom, associating the feelings and ideas of Eliot's "The Love Song of J. Alfred Prufrock" (for instance) with a story from *Harry Potter* or *Sherlock Holmes*.[6] Those feelings—of, helplessness, ennui, and despair—may arise from a fictional situation, but they might equally be associated with the experience of reading itself: the poem is used to channel the writer's feelings about the non-Eliot text (confusion, exasperation, enchantment) as much as to channel the feelings of characters within the narrative.[7] Still other texts, perhaps the most numerous, incorporate Eliot's work as an intertext, making allusions to his poems in a way that leverages the text as an accessory while also offering an interpretation of it.[8] In other words, these fan writers pick up on Eliot's modernist practices of citation, adaptation, and (depending on who's evaluating the reading) misprision. They understand that Eliot himself is especially interested in intertextual relations. Some fan writers, however, respond to modernist fragmentation in a reparative mode, taking Eliot's collage of impressionistic fragments and extrapolating a whole story from them: a story of trauma and attempted resolution, usually one that forges links between literary works and, sometimes, between fan writers, too. They harness Eliot's intertextuality as a healing force, rather than an ironizing or dramatic one.[9]

With his affinity for playing possum, for disappearing into a persona that rendered the real Eliot effectively anonymous, perhaps Eliot would have enjoyed an online community like AO3, where he could create multiple accounts and participate in and weave together multiple fandoms, where professional competition is supplanted by gamified play. Like these anonymous fan writers, Eliot had a private as well as a public oeuvre, based in fannish community and play. Throughout the 1930s, he wrote frequently to his friend John Hayward in a Sherlockian persona, taking solace, presumably, in converting his own personal need for secrecy and seclusion—he was literally in hiding from his wife—into a story of fictional intrigue. The Hayward Bequest of T. S. Eliot Material at the Archive Centre in King's College, Cambridge, includes an unsigned mystery story titled "The Problem of the Perplexed Publisher," starring a detective (and Geoffrey Faber stand-in) named F. C. G. Larkworthy.[10] Filed in the archive with other pieces relating to practical jokes played at Faber & Faber, this story suggests that Eliot's coterie may at times have been a fan community.[11] Certainly, Eliot enjoyed utilizing other authors' forms in his privately circulated writings.[12] In these contexts, the emotional intensity of Eliot's interpersonal attachments is channeled into the intertextual attachments that structure and enrich his coterie texts, and likewise his attachments to literary work strengthen his friendships.

Unlike many of his modernist peers, Eliot composed almost all of his correspondence—including these fan writings—on a typewriter.[13] What if the technologies that Eliot harnessed to forge these connections were not just instrumental to the work but fundamental to the kinds of connection—textual and personal—he was trying to establish? The intellectual and critical work that Eliot's fan writers do is enabled not just by affinities within Eliot's texts, the affinities they identify and explore, but also by the way that fanfic online publishing is conducted, with its story-tagging, its community-building, its gamified writing challenges. They encourage us to ask not only what Eliot's technologies enabled Eliot to make but also what our own emerging technologies will allow us to make of Eliot.

A Book-Shaped Object

Which leads us to computational text analysis, another form of digitally supported reading that claims to shed new light on beloved texts—this time in the scholarly domain of the academy, with its readings supported by long-standing hermeneutic principles, rather than the amateur domain of fandom, with its proudly, defiantly "bad" readers.

Even though practices of editing and literary criticism may present themselves as general and universal, they often quietly take their shape from engagement with a specific author. Shakespeare's influence on editorial theory and textual criticism was so profound that W. Speed Hill, a mighty figure in textual scholarship, could propose that the field would have looked entirely different if Shakespeare had died in the London plague of 1593.[14] In the early history of the digital humanities, the most prominent literary figure was Eliot's modernist colleague James Joyce, in part because the principal focus of that field was hypertext theory and modeling. Scholars interested in the capacities of digital textuality found a reflection of their own theories of text in Joyce's sprawling, non-linear, highly referential, deeply connective texts, which could seem not only to fulfill the capacities of the codex but strain them to their breaking point. Hypertext experiments based on Joyce's novel—which today are mostly lost to the ether—seemed to be the first great bloom from the cross-germination of the typographical and the digital;[15] but when hypertext theory fell out of fashion, in favor of newer digital excitements—and the Joyce estate shut down access— Joyce ceased to be the literary representative of the digital humanities.[16]

That first era having passed, we might now ask what it means for the digital humanities that T. S. Eliot is furnishing so much new material, and thus so much excitement, via the *Complete Prose* project and the digitized Hale letters at Princeton. What would a digital humanities modeled and developed with Eliot in mind look like? Analyzing the two projects just mentioned allows us to consider how Eliot might shape our approaches to digital literary study: how it may be, ironically, his conservatism that speaks most clearly to the future of digital editions and how his now-shattered myth of impersonality might guide our engagement with the myth of data that is purified of interpretation.

Eliot's paradoxical status as both a groundbreaking avant-gardist and, especially in his later career, a fundamentally conservative literary thinker (i.e., as the author of both *The Waste Land* and a poem as legible as "The Cultivation of Christmas Trees") perhaps makes him an appropriate heir to the attention once lavished on Joyce in the realm of digital literary studies. Three decades ago, the scale of hypertext editions of *Ulysses* proved to be untenable, both technologically and in terms of what copyright law permitted, and the uses they made of the possibilities of the codex were perhaps not engaging enough to hold the audience needed to sustain such resource-hungry projects.[17] Today, we might replace that technological idealism with a more conservative approach and find that the old model of the codex is crucial to the success of online scholarly apparatuses. The doctrine of revolution has been replaced with the doctrine of remediation.[18] To summarize in purely literary terms: just as dead writers feel remote from us "because we *know* so much more than they did" while also being "that which we know," older technologies, like the book, feel remote from the capacities of new tech while still determining how we prefer to read on our computers ("Tradition and the Individual Talent," *Prose2* 108). The next edition of the *Complete Prose of T. S. Eliot: The Critical Edition* on Project MUSE feels much like a digital-born effort, but it features improvements that ironically render it in many ways *more* like a print book. In fact, what is called "Prose 2.0" by the project's editorial team is the replacement of the "born digital" with the "digital reborn": the undertaking was first conceived as a print book and hosted online as a set of downloadable PDFs.

In an interview with the authors, Anthony Cuda, one of the project's editors, explained how the features and functions then under development aimed to create a reading experience that blends the foundational apparatuses of the codex with the affordances of hypertext.[19] The online XML view of the text, which is formatted for smartphone compatibility, automatically paginates itself as the reader scrolls. (Finally, a digital edition with page numbers.) The pagination is identical across all three editions: XML, print, and PDF. Rather than require a reader to move from one section to another in order to select the next section on a home page, as was the case with the original *Complete Prose*, the new iteration simply continues, like a book, from one section to the next. At the same time, hypertext (and hover-over) footnotes provide unobtrusive digital affordances while closely imitating the functionality of a print book. The creators of the new edition worked assiduously to preserve this book-like functionality, Cuda explained, because scholars demand easy, consistent citation: a conservatism that conserves scholarly effort.

Years ago, during a conversation with one of us (Graham), an editor for the *Oxford English Dictionary* described the dictionary's online platform as "a book-shaped object." Book-shaped architectures seem increasingly to be the future—the near future, at least—of online reading interfaces. In some ways, Cuda says, the technology team at Project MUSE was more wedded to the features of the codex than was the editorial team of literary scholars. When the group was designing the search function, which separates results into the categories of text, footnotes, images, and index, the tech team had to convince the editorial team to keep the "index" tab in the search results, noting that the cataloging in the index—done by editors—has a different and (at least) equal value to the cataloguing that a machine performs during a text search. (On the other hand, the editorial team had to insist that search results from the footnotes be kept separate from those from Eliot's texts: the author function remains critical to this e-text's design.)

Eliot's digital humanities can also be called conservative in the sense that this e-text tailored to his writing seeks to use its affordances to, again, *conserve*, by preserving more of, and about, the original text. This is something that the normally science-and-tech-averse Eliot would have appreciated, Cuda suggests: "I do think there's something about the historical specificity that the volumes provide and that the resources provide that would please him, and that should please any historicist … There's no way of forgetting at any point when you're reading these essays when they were published, what the context was, to whom he is speaking and responding." Eliot disliked seeing his older writing published without context: without a note, say, to let the reader know that the essay they were reading in 1959 was written four decades prior to its reprinting. Like literary tradition as Eliot envisioned it, technology is perhaps best understood not as a linear progression, with new developments replacing what came before, but rather as a mosaic, with new developments changing the position, prominence, use, and value of older ones.

Where Is the Knowledge We Have Lost in Information?

A recurring fantasy in the tech world *outside* of the digital humanities—bruited, for instance, by Chris Anderson in a 2008 *Wired* magazine article that predicted that big data would cause "the end of theory"—is what Alan Liu calls the "goal" of "tabula rasa interpretation through the hypothesis-free discovery of phenomena."[20] Politicians, lay users, and even tech writers have described computers as *objectivity machines* that present facts free from interpretation, free even from the interpretive forethought that goes into posing a question.[21] Although digital humanists have been eager to remind their readers that "designing a text-analysis program is inherently an interpretative act ... even if running the program becomes mechanistic" and that "a model is an abstraction created by human beings," still computers remain, in the public imagination, cold and sterile as a laboratory, clean of the messy trail of the human serpent.[22]

For Eliot, however, objectivity is not something born of an imaginary laboratory that sterilizes its tools of humanity. Rather, as Eliot wrote in his dissertation, "reality is a convention," shared by all and accessed by means of impersonality (*Prose1* 318). In *The Sacred Wood*, Eliot describes an impersonality that is girded by "morality" as a "convention," which provides a "framework" for emotional response that can be common across boundaries of class: the *goal* of "impersonality" is accessing common humanity and its emotional and intellectual experience, not purifying the poet or critic of the things that make us human (*Prose2* 251–2). Similarly, digital humanists (i.e., humans) develop the "frameworks" or "conventions" of computational analysis, with the goal of constructing a vision of literary culture, creation, or experience that others can access.[23] (Indeed, if there's one thing Eliot would have loved about twenty-first-century digital humanities, it's the commitment on the part of so many DH initiatives to make their projects open-access.[24]) Just as we cannot remove interpretation from the act of gathering data, mechanized or otherwise, so can we not see Eliot "objectively"—but we might be able to change the kind of object that we make him into. We might be able to use machines to displace the personality he constructs (which sometimes, but not always, consists of a charismatic *affect* of impersonality).

Rebecca Sutton Koeser, the director of a major digitization project based on the Eliot–Hale correspondence at Princeton, is doing this kind of work. When we spoke in February 2021, Koeser was in the early stages of her project. Having generated text from the scanned images of the letters, she was creating preliminary datasets comprising the dates of the letters; the names mentioned in the letters (both in the enclosures and in Eliot's own writing); and all the titular references to Eliot's works (including draft titles). Other datasets were slated for the future—for example, all the salutations Eliot uses, since his poetic imagination is especially playful in those elements. Koeser planned to write a program to find all the references Eliot makes to Hale's letters, in order to generate as complete a list as possible of Hale's side of the correspondence. When we asked whether she conceived of this project as "distant reading," Koeser said something startling: "In a way it's not even reading, because I'm not even really looking at the text right now."

In February 2021, eleven months into the Covid-19 pandemic, it felt like a bitter irony that the Hale letters were finally available but Princeton's archives were closed to outsiders; for this reason, it was shocking to imagine having onsite access to the Hale letters and not reading them. But Koeser's approach of not reading the text while preparing to read it, surely a necessity in terms of time management for such an ambitious project, can yield useful insights. It gives us the opportunity to see, if we look, an elusive version of Eliot: an Eliot who is less author than he is agent. Pulling titles, names, dates—a record of the changing routine of Hale and Eliot's decades-long epistolary relationship—brings to our attention not the man who disappears into (precisely because he constructs himself in and through) the text but rather the man who lives off the page.[25] We see a specific individual who cadges company letterhead, is forgetful about maintaining his typewriter (once, during a busy spell, he neglected to replace the ribbon for eighteen months), kisses and caresses the letters he receives, badgers his correspondent to write more often, and in other ways lives perhaps *for* the page, but not in or behind it.

This Eliot is not abstracted into prose but particularized into a record of action. Seeing the record this way reminds us that the data in our literary archives, the data that we upload to computers to rearrange using analysis tools, is left behind by individuals with flaws and biases and perversities that have affected the structure, completeness, and contents of those archives—Eliot himself tried to destroy the records of his and Hale's correspondence. The *selection* of the fragments we shore up is itself fragmentary, and often that selection betrays a storytelling impulse that precedes efforts to put those fragments in order, mosaic-like, to tell a story.

The work required to carry through the digitization of Eliot's corpus is, in many ways, what Johnson called humble drudgery: data cleaning, trial and error, script writing, the making of small but important bibliographic decisions. But the scholarly possibilities that these projects enable are remarkable. We might trace Emily Hale's movements by comparing the addresses on the envelopes in her archive; we might track how Eliot's prose allusions change, in the references he makes or how he makes them, over the course of his career; we might check Eliot's allusions against those in the publications that he read and published in, the better to trace lines of influence or canon-shaping. Even more will be possible if the online repository of the prose project expands to include other texts, such as the *Letters*.

During our interview, Cuda noted that the features currently being developed for the Eliot prose project will, in the future, be implemented across Project MUSE. The digital projects that we've described or imagined in this chapter attend closely to Eliot but also look beyond him. As a writer, Eliot exerts a tremendous force of gravity, almost planetary in scale. Perhaps one of the gifts of our emerging technologies will be—if momentarily—to escape that gravity and, on returning, to know the territory for neither the first nor the last time.

Notes

1 See pp. 212–13.
2 On July 13, 2022, there were 9,554,000 fan works on archiveofourown.org.
3 On AO3, Eliot fares as well, if not better, than his twentieth-century peers: at the time of writing, searching for "William Butler Yeats" or "W. B. Yeats" returns 362 hits; "Sylvia Plath," 625; "E. E. Cummings," 477 (note that the search is not case sensitive). "Robert Frost" takes the lead with a surprising 1,074 hits. Within Eliot's oeuvre, *Cats* is by far the most popular work, although Eliot shares that popularity with (and perhaps owes it to) Andrew Lloyd Webber: there are 459 works tagged with "Old Possum's Book of Practical Cats." (Note that the rest of the results discussed here are not pulled from tags but full-text searches, because writers do not always add tags to point to their allusions or intertexts if they do not consider their work to be contributing to a particular fandom.) Of the 444 results for "The Love

Song of," 202 mention Eliot somewhere in the text, suggesting the popularity of his "Prufrock." A total of 138 fan works mention *The Waste Land* and the name "Eliot."

4   An early examination of the difference between fan readers and other kinds of readers is Roberta Pearson, "Bachies, Bardies, Trekkies, and Sherlockians," in *Fandom: Identities and Communities in a Mediated World*, edited by Jonathan Gray, Cornel Sandvoss, and C. Lee Harrington (New York: New York University Press, 2007).

5   See p. 216.

6   "Prufrock" is especially popular for this purpose: writers often begin with Eliot's opening lines ("Let us go then, you and I") and then make substitutions that carry the poem's sentiment of helplessness and ennui into a different fictional universe. See, for example, Lanna Michaels (lannamichaels), "Call This a Love Song," *Archive of Our Own*, June 24, 2016, https://archiveofourown.org/works/96482.

7   See, for example, "Harry Potter and the Half-Blood Poet," a critique of the sixth Harry Potter novel; "He Do the Police in Different Voices," which hybridizes *The Waste Land* with the BBC series *Sherlock*; and "Unreal City," a five-chapter murder mystery crafted out of *The Waste Land*. While the writer of "He Do the Police in Different Voices" reimagines *The Waste Land*'s expression of trauma, the author of "Unreal City" translates the experience of reading the poem's obscurely connected fragments into the experience of searching for clues. Ladysisyphus, "Harry Potter and the Half-Blood Poet," *Archive of Our Own*, July 25, 2005, https://archiveofourown.org/works/799555; halloa_what_is_this, "He Do the Police in Different Voices," *Archive of Our Own*, February 4, 2015, https://archiveofourown.org/works/3289712; Neth_Smiley, "Unreal City," *Archive of Our Own*, February 9, 2018, https://archiveofourown.org/works/13619811/.

8   A particularly piquant example is the erotic *Star Wars* romance "Now, Here, Now, Always" (by the writer midwinterspring, whose username is drawn from *Four Quartets*), which relates an intimate encounter between Ben Solo and Rey Skywalker that begins with Rey reading Ben her favorite poem, *Little Gidding*. midwinterspring, "Now, Here, Now, Always," *Archive of Our Own*, July 24, 2020, https://archiveofourown.org/works/25497562.

9   "The Man Next Door" is a touching narrative (with the barest hint of homosexual frisson) whose creator writes that they "thought [Prufrock] was a bit melancholy" and that they "wanted something nice for [him]." Told from the perspective of Prufrock's neighbor, the story reframes Eliot's imagery of alienation (the overheard sounds, the choking fog) into a means of connection. "He Do the Police in Different Voices" is a story about piecing together a shattered life, its allusions to and borrowed structure from *The Waste Land* giving both the author and the character a form to work through trauma and grief. EzraNaps, "The Man Next Door," *Archive of Our Own*, June 15, 2018, https://archiveofourown.org/works/14936016.

10 Larkworthy's first three initials are Faber's initials backward.
11 Indeed, Christopher Morley, the brother of Eliot's close friend Frank V. Morley, was one of the originators of the Baker Street Irregulars.
12 For more on Eliot's coterie writings, see Michelle Taylor, "(In)discreet Modernism: T. S. Eliot's Coterie Poetics." *College Literature* 47, no. 1 (2020): 34–64.
13 For more on the thematic importance of the typewriter in *The Waste Land*, as well as a virtuoso exercise in genetic criticism that definitively establishes the chronological order of Eliot's draft fragments, see Lawrence Rainey, "Eliot among the Typists: Writing *The Waste Land*," *Modernism/modernity* 12, no. 1 (2005): 27–84.
14 W. Speed Hill, "Where Would Anglo-American Textual Criticism Be If Shakespeare Had Died of the Plague in 1593?" *Text* 13 (2000): 1–7.
15 For a full account of the life span of one such brilliant project, see Michael Groden, "Perplex in the Pen—and in the Pixels: Reflections on 'The James Joyce Archive,' Hans Walter Gabler's *Ulysses*, and 'James Joyce's *Ulysses* in Hypermedia,'" *Journal of Modern Literature* 22, no. 2 (1998–9): 225–44, and "Introduction to 'James Joyce's *Ulysses* in Hypermedia,'" *Journal of Modern Literature* 24, no. 3 (2001): 359–62.
16 See Elyse Graham, "Joyce and the Graveyard of Digital Empires," in *Debates in the Digital Humanities 2019*, edited by Matthew K. Gold and Lauren F. Klein (Minneapolis: University of Minnesota Press, 2019). Michelle Taylor, who is Team Eliot in the present collaboration as Elyse Graham is Team Joyce, notes that nothing was keeping Eliot from assuming Joyce's role during this early period, since *The Waste Land* lends itself just as much to hypertext as *Ulysses*. Graham proposes that the optimism of *Ulysses*, at least as Americans read the novel, seemed like a better fit for the optimism of the hypertext era—during the dot-com boom and the most starry-eyed era of *Wired* magazine, and following up on the utopianism of the earlier Whole Earth Network.
17 Graham, "Joyce and the Graveyard of Digital Empires."
18 Jay David Bolter and Richard Grusin, *Remediation: Understanding New Media* (Cambridge: MIT Press, 1999).
19 Anthony Cuda, interview with Michelle Taylor, November 16, 2021, Zoom recording.
20 Alain Liu, "The Meaning of the Digital Humanities," *PMLA* 128, no. 2 (2013): 414.
21 For example, in 2019, Ryan Saavedra, a reporter at the Daily Wire, posted a tweet ridiculing the idea that "algorithms, which are driven by math, are racist," implying that the presence of math in the workings of computer algorithms somehow removes bias from—for instance—functionality and training data. This is the equivalent of saying that sentences, which are driven by the linguistic rules of syntax, can't be racist.

22 Johanna Drucker, "Why Distant Reading Isn't," *PMLA* 132, no. 3 (2017): 631; Ted Underwood, "Theorizing Research Practices We Forgot to Theorize Twenty Years Ago," *Representations* 127 (2014): 69.
23 We cannot address here, but only note, the problem of digital humanities work often relying on proprietary algorithms, which makes replicability virtually impossible and prevents the audience from even seeing the full set of data being discussed.
24 On Eliot's commitment to literary work with public accessibility and reach, see David Chinitz, *T. S. Eliot and the Cultural Divide* (Chicago: University of Chicago Press, 2003), 67–70.
25 To be sure, selecting for this data carries its own presumptions: about the significance of frequency in correspondence, for example.

11

Of Corpses, Corpuses, and Career Capital: Eliot and Print Culture

Michael H. Whitworth

"I have had to write at one time or another a lot of junk in periodicals," T. S. Eliot told his literary executor, John Hayward, in February 1938; the "greater portion" of it, he advised, "ought never to be reprinted" (*Letters8* 800).[1] Eliot's writing for periodicals, now reprinted in the *Complete Prose*, is an immense gain for Eliot scholarship. But has there been a concomitant loss? The reprinting removes the essays from the print culture of their time and the materiality of the printed page: the quality and size of the paper, inking, and typesetting. The separation also removes important generic markers: the position of a review within a periodical might signal its genre or relative importance. The *Times Literary Supplement* (*TLS*), for example, clearly distinguished between leading articles on the front page, the general run of "column reviews," and the shorter notices set in a smaller typeface at the rear of the paper.[2] The reprinting of Eliot's essays also separates them from other, non-tactile forms of materiality.

The present chapter will focus on the need for a writer to earn a living and establish a reputation. In considering this aspect of print culture, I shall draw on the work of Pierre Bourdieu, and particularly his recognition that, in the market for symbolic goods such as literary artworks, economic and symbolic capital obey inverse logic. However, I tread lightly here because, as John Xiros Cooper recognized, many of Eliot's own comments demonstrate a proto-Bourdieusian understanding of the literary market.[3] Poems operate within the same logics but are further removed than essays and reviews from editorial and institutional influence, so my imminent focus is on Eliot's prose.

Male, white, educated at Harvard, the Sorbonne, and Oxford, and connected to American elites, Eliot came to the English literary scene with many advantages, yet he lacked the professional networks in England that enabled his

British contemporaries' early careers in literary journalism. Family connections facilitated Virginia Woolf's beginnings as a reviewer, for example, and Herbert Read drew on regional affiliations formed within the Leeds Arts Club.[4] Eliot's clearest account of how he built his reputation comes in a letter of advice he wrote to an inquirer in 1924. "Usually," he advised, "one begins by writing about some subject which one knows, or which one is supposed to know." His expertise in Sanskrit, he said, led to him reviewing books on "contemporary Asiatic politics," and although he neither knew nor cared about the subject, "by being supposed to have to the knowledge I got the opportunity to acquire it" (*Letters2* 487).[5] "Then," he continues, "when one is established in the minds of editors as an authority on one subject, one may gradually get the license (by another irrational process in editors' minds) to write about anything one likes." To rearticulate this in more Bourdieusian terms, through careful investment of one form of cultural capital—ideally one that has scarcity value (in London, knowledge of Sanskrit)—the young writer generates other forms of cultural capital, such as recognition as a serious thinker and punctual producer of copy. From here, the writer must lose the taint of a mere journalist: "After a time, one reprints a collection of one's essays or reviews as a book" (*Letters2* 487). Eliot also mentions the value of personal introductions to editors, though he is less specific about them (*Letters2* 488). A meeting with Bertrand Russell led to introductions to the editor of the *New Statesman* and to Sydney Waterlow, who was on the *International Journal of Ethics* board. Eliot's encounter with Russell also indicates how nonliterary factors formed part of his capital—what Bourdieu would later call "bodily hexis."[6] Russell, on first meeting Eliot, described him as "well dressed and polished, with manners of the finest Etonian type," and unfavorably contrasted another student, "an unshaven Greek" named Demos, "who earns money for his fees by being a waiter in a restaurant."[7] While Eliot's knowledge and education were the primary factors in creating his network, his ability to imitate an upper-middle-class Englishman should not be overlooked.

Eliot's advice about gathering one's essays into a book is important. Critical work on modernist print culture is dominated by a focus on periodicals, initially the "little magazines" and, more recently, the broader range of publications exemplified by the *Oxford Critical and Cultural History of Modernist Magazines* (2009–13). Books have been relatively neglected, although Lawrence Rainey's model of modernist publishing takes them into account, and Lise Jaillant's recent collection of essays deliberately redresses the balance toward book publishing. However, writing for periodicals was intertwined with the production of books. Periodicals reviewed books and took advertisements for them, and less obviously, early twentieth-century essayists and reviewers wrote with one eye on future book production. Eliot was no exception. As a form, the collection of essays can be traced back to the Victorian era, including Matthew Arnold's *Essays in Criticism* (1865, 1888) and Leslie Stephen's *Hours in a Library* (1871–9).[8] As a newcomer to the London literary scene, Eliot was also aware of more recent works such as Arnold Bennett's *Books and Persons* (1917) and Clive Bell's *Pot-Boilers* (1918).[9] The book of essays, then, takes works of "journalism" and endeavors to remove the taints of writing at speed, for an occasion, and for money. In many cases a preface or foreword attempts to disguise the miscellaneous quality by providing a rationale or context. However, it was conventional for opening pages to indicate where essays had first appeared, making the trace of journalism visible for any who wished to see. John Middleton Murry's preface to *Aspects of Literature* (1920), for instance, identifies its first chapter as a unifying essay, one that "suggests a standard of values implicit elsewhere in the book," but the same preface begins by acknowledging a debt to the periodicals in which the essays first appeared, the *TLS*, the *Nation*, and the *Athenaeum*.[10]

Eliot gained prestige within the literary marketplace by insisting that literary criticism rest on clear general principles; to foreground "prestige" is not to question the sincerity of his belief in such principles but to view them in another light. His review of Robert Lynd's *Old and New Masters* (1919) expresses disappointment at a collection of essays that failed to justify their continued existence and betrayed too many signs of their origins in weekly periodicals and a daily newspaper. Lynd did not provide a prefatory statement about his essays. Although Eliot does not mention the omission, he criticizes Lynd for the lack of clear criteria and "point of view" ("Criticism in England," *Prose2* 55, 57). Eliot acknowledges that Lynd understands the requirements of the periodical audience but chides him for failing to understand the needs of a book. Lynd begins his articles with eye-catching "curtain raisers" to attract the audience and coax them into "the proper receptive attitude":

> The periodical writer faces the risk of the reader's breaking off and turning to the next article. But if we are bold enough to publish a book we must be bold enough to presume the initial attention of the reader; the puzzle is how to maintain his attention by good substance and good manners. (55)

By contrast, in 1926, when Eliot reviewed collections of essays by Herbert Read and Ramon Fernandez, he praised both for "a unity of purpose hitherto uncommon in volumes of collected essays" and noted that both had rewritten their previously published works ("Mr. Read and M. Fernandez," *Prose2* 835).

Two years later, Eliot's own preface to *For Lancelot Andrewes* (1928) stated his "point of view": classicist, royalist, and Anglo-Catholic (*Prose3* 513).

In 1919, as he reviewed Lynd's collection, Eliot was contemplating one of his own, a "miscellany" of prose and verse, to be published in New York by Knopf. However, he had already received intimations that such a collection was unlikely to succeed (*Letters1* 284, 324). Within a month of his review of Lynd, and as a result of his *Athenaeum* articles, Eliot received an invitation from Algernon Methuen to publish a prose book (*Letters1* 369). The last nail in the coffin for the "hybrid book" came in August 1919, when John Quinn, the New York lawyer who acted, in effect, as Eliot's American literary agent at the time, reported that the form looked "too much like the literary 'remains' of a writer," or suggested a writer "who is neither one thing nor the other" (*Letters1* 389).

There are signs that Eliot, aware of the market for collected essays, shaped his contributions to the *Athenaeum* with a future book in mind. The clearest evidence comes in the titles of two reviews, "A Romantic Patrician" and "A Sceptical Patrician," which appeared on May 2 and May 23, 1919, respectively. In July 1919, in a letter to Quinn, Eliot suggested that in the hybrid book, the two articles would be grouped as a unit, "Two Types" (*Letters1* 373). Eliot also tended to frame his reviews with reference to general principles. While his opening paragraphs make free with what we might call the reviewer's deictic ("This book …"), later paragraphs turn to general reflections and considerations. In revising essays for book publication, Eliot often removed such opening deictics. The original of Eliot's "Hamlet" begins with a sentence referring to the critic under review, J. W. Robertson; revising it for *The Sacred Wood*, Eliot removed the sentence, amplifying the critical problem (*Prose2* 126, 122).[11] In several reviews, the opening sentences indicate little about the book under review, liberating the column space for general considerations that might be more easily reworked as essays in books. For example, Eliot's account of *Donne's Sermons* dispenses with the anthology itself in two sentences (*Prose2* 165), while his review of Henry Dwight Sedgwick's *Dante*, having established general principles about introductory books on "Great Authors," declares there is "not very much to say" about Sedgwick's ("Dante," *Prose2* 236).

Eliot's revisions did not, however, completely efface the origins of his prose. "The Metaphysical Poets," perhaps the most influential of Eliot's essays of the 1920s, is recognizably a book review in *Selected Essays*. Although a concluding reference to "this excellent anthology" is revised into "the excellent anthology of Professor Grierson" (*Prose2* 385, 383), Eliot retains an introductory reference to "such an anthology as this" and other references to Grierson. Unexpectedly, in polishing his review of Sedgwick's *Dante* for inclusion in *The Sacred Wood*, Eliot's revisions read more like an *Athenaeum* essay. The book version begins with reference to a recent statement by Paul Valéry as it had appeared in a review in that journal (*Prose2* 226). One can only assume the gain in geographical and temporal scope—connecting the medieval Florentine with the contemporary French poet—outweighed the need to use a periodical source. More generally, Eliot's willingness to leave traces of reviewing in the essays indicates that although he wrote these pieces with their future book context in mind, he was pragmatic and knew his readership was tolerant of such origins when he revised.

The publication of anonymous reviews was a common practice in the early nineteenth century and a crucial feature of British print culture when Eliot began publishing prose.[12] Anonymity was believed to safeguard independence because the reviewer would not suffer the social consequences of giving a bad review to an acquaintance's book. However, the converse—that a reviewer might use anonymity to cloak personal or ideological bias—was less frequently mentioned, suggesting the editor's power to moderate biases. Anonymity was believed to encourage the impersonal voice of the periodical. In 1924, Eliot's advice to Hope Clutterbuck included "studying the style and tricks of the papers one is trying to write for, and adopting its tone and prejudices" (*Letters2* 487). While such advice was not irrelevant to an author hoping to write signed pieces, its origins lay in the idea of the periodical having a unified outlook. Anonymity also enabled civil servants, barristers, and other professionals to contribute when their terms of employment would not have allowed them to express an opinion over their names in a public forum.[13] Less nobly, as George Saintsbury confessed in 1930, anonymity enabled the same reviewer to write multiple reviews of the same book in different journals.[14] The *TLS*'s adoption of anonymity lay in its origins in 1902 as a supplement to the *Times* newspaper, in which news articles were unsigned, but the practice was not unprecedented.

For a young writer seeking to establish a reputation, anonymity was a problem. It is possible that authorship was never entirely secret within the world of literary journalism, and there was certainly a great deal of curiosity about it. Eliot's letters reveal many signs of such curiosity (e.g., *Letters1* 353, 362; *Letters2* 598). However, without a signature, the writer would find it harder to establish a reputation. In a 1958 letter to the *TLS*, Eliot recognized that he had been lucky to publish over his name in the *Athenaeum* from 1919 to 1920 and anonymously in the *TLS* from 1919 onward. The *Athenaeum* had built his reputation immediately, but the investment of writing for the *TLS* took longer to mature. Eliot recalled how "the occasional deletion of a phrase, by the editorial pencil, taught me to temper my prejudices and control my crotchets and whimsies" ("The Disembodied Voice," *Prose8* 243). Writing anonymously was a source of discipline for the young critic (*Prose8* 431). No doubt such tempering generally anticipated the response of the editor, to avoid conflict. In December 1928, Eliot admitted to Bonamy Dobrée that his review of Lytton Strachey's *Elizabeth and Essex* (*Prose3* 555–61), which appeared anonymously in the *TLS*, would have been "more severe" had he been reviewing under his name (*Letters4* 356).

The collection of essays has a particular value within a culture of anonymous reviewing, allowing the reviewer to claim authorship and some of the prestige that originally belonged to the periodical. "I have been asked to write for the *Times Literary Supplement*—to write the Leading Article from time to time," Eliot reported to his mother in October 1919. "This is the highest honour possible in the critical world of literature" (*Letters1* 404). While such an honor brings immediate private rewards—income, validation, and greater self-confidence—its public benefit comes only when the preface to a collection of essays acknowledges the source.

Compared to his prose, the relation of Eliot's poetry to print culture is harder to analyze. While in the prose specific styles, tricks, tones, pronouns, and phrases have a traceable causal connection to the print context, such an analysis would not be convincing if extended to the poetry, for poetry has a high degree of autonomy from the demands of journals and editors, the only exceptions being poems commissioned for a specific occasion. The practice of friends advising on draft versions of poems in manuscript or typescript, such as Pound's editing of *The Waste Land*, is at one remove from print culture. The relation is more general: the existence of periodicals that are sympathetic to a certain mode of poetry—whether experimental or conservative—might encourage poets to work in that mode, but the relationship is very different from that of journal editors like Bruce Richmond of the *TLS* or John Middleton Murry of the *Athenaeum* to their reviewers and essayists.

What is overwhelmingly clear is that Eliot's success as a poet won him opportunities as a prose writer. As his career developed, an essay by Eliot became more attractive to periodical editors because it was, explicitly or otherwise, by the author of *The Waste Land*. However, early in his career, the relation between the scholarly reviewer and the experimental poet was not always apparent. The abandonment of the "hybrid" prose and verse book was partly due to the disjunction. Eliot was explicit about the problem in August 1920. Writing to Edgar Jepson, who had championed his poetry and Pound's, about the forthcoming *Sacred Wood*, Eliot cautioned he did not expect Jepson to like it: "I seem to have an entirely different public for my prose" (*Letters1* 491). The division between the two currencies was seen at its sharpest in 1926, when All Souls College, Oxford, rejected the proposal of Eliot for a research fellowship. While his critical prose made him a plausible candidate, his poetry was used against him. One Fellow found it "indecent, obscene, and blasphemous."[15]

Although distinct, there are certain similarities in Eliot's management of his prose and poetry oeuvres. In relation to poetry, Eliot repeatedly articulated his ideal method of establishing his importance as a poet: write "very little" but publish poems "perfect in their kind," so each new piece is "an event" (*Letters1* 338–9). When he first articulated the idea, in an April 1919 letter to J. H. Woods, he acknowledged the alternative strategy of writing prolifically and having one's writings "appear everywhere" (*Letters1* 338), but his later developments of the theme take parsimony as their starting point.[16] In relation to prose, Eliot did not aim at minimal production or making a review an "event," but he was selective, rejecting many invitations to write essays and reviews. He gave various reasons, including insufficient expertise on a particular author (*Letters2* 608) or particular form of writing (*Letters3* 295); not being able to work within the word limits (*Letters3* 144; *Letters6* 198); and not feeling sympathetic with the journal's outlook—for example, the communist *New Masses* (*Letters3* 214).

When collecting his prose, Eliot did what in February 1937 he urged the poet Ann Bowes-Lyon to do: "to select and reject with precision" (*Letters8* 486). *The Sacred Wood* is selective, but it underwent further pruning—for example, his Crashaw essay—when he created the *Selected Essays*. Similarly, in 1935, he was reluctant to allow the reprinting of what he perceived as unimportant early prose, the 1917 "Eeldrop and Appleplex" pieces from the *Little Review* (*Letters7* 664), and in 1938, as noted above, he repudiated much of his prose work as "junk" (*Letters8* 800).

Having acquired, nurtured, and preserved cultural capital, the no-longer-young writer is in a position to take a more relaxed attitude toward it and to employ it productively. In 1928, *For Lancelot Andrewes*'s jacket copy claimed that the essays therein had "a unity of their own." By 1936, in the preface to *Essays Ancient and Modern*, a more securely established Eliot could afford to look back on that claim with amusement: "I do not know whether my ideals of unity are higher, or merely my pretensions more modest, than eight years ago; I offer this book, as the title implies, only as a miscellaneous collection, having no greater unity than that of having been written by the same person" (*Prose5* 322). The impression of miscellany was what the younger Eliot had deprecated in others' collections and had been at pains to avoid in his own.

Eliot, after earning a name for himself, was poised to become, in Bourdieu's terms, a "consecrator" of others' works, one who deploys their reputation to assist other producers.[17] Writers of prefaces tread a fine line between donating their reputation and preserving it. Generosity in print toward other artists and writers was too easily mistaken for a lack of firm principles. Eliot was parsimonious, especially in the 1920s and 1930s. He gave many reasons for declining such invitations, but a recurrent one concerned the scarcity value of his endorsement and the impossibility of employing it fairly. The argument appears in a January 1934 letter to T. O. Beachcroft, who had requested a prefatory endorsement for his forthcoming collection of stories. Eliot told Beachcroft that he never wrote introductions to volumes of contemporary poetry because "if I did so for one person, it would be very difficult to refuse a dozen others." He added, somewhat cryptically, that he was also disinclined "because the whole theory seems to me bad" (*Letters7* 6). By "theory" he may have meant the belief that a prefatory endorsement would confer value. Eliot frequently invoked the opposite: that the provision of preface gave the impression that the book was not strong enough to stand on its own feet (e.g., *Letters8* 127, 147).

Throughout the 1930s, Eliot continued to be selective about endorsing others' work, and it seems likely that he continued to be cautious for the rest of his life (we await the evidence in the later volumes of the *Letters*), yet there had been a distinct and temporary softening of his attitude in the late 1920s. If his 1924 preface to Paul Valéry's *Le Serpent* may be seen as an exception and his 1926 preface to his mother's *Savonarola* as justified by family loyalty, the first phase of prefacing and introducing begins in 1927, with Eliot's introduction to Seneca, and gains pace in 1928, with introductions and prefaces to works by Wilkie Collins, John Dryden, Edgar Ansel Mowrer, and Ezra Pound (the anonymous "Publishers' Preface" to *Fishermen of the Banks* [1928] is irrelevant in Eliot's public capital because he was not underwriting the book with his name). Eliot wrote fewer prefaces and introductions in the second half of the 1930s, and his reluctance to endorse living contemporary and younger poets continued through to his death. When he resumed preface-writing in 1940, there was a discernible movement away from established classics (Seneca, Collins, Dryden, Johnson, Pascal) toward contemporary and recent thinkers, critics, and writers (D. H. Lawrence, Joseph Chiari, John Davidson, and Hugo von Hofmannsthal). Recently deceased contemporaries formed a distinct group of beneficiaries, beginning with Harold Monro in 1933, and continuing with James Joyce (1942), Charles Williams (1948), Michael Roberts (1949), among others, ending with Eliot's preface for Edwin Muir's *Selected Poems* (1964).

In his prose for periodicals, the ways that Eliot employed his reputation changed around 1928. Although his anonymous writing for the *TLS* remained constrained by the house style and the avoidance of the first-person singular, from 1928 onward his signed writings are more likely to articulate personal feelings and recollections. While earlier essays had used the first-person singular primarily to signpost the argument and to clarify—phrases like "I use the term with hesitation" (*Prose2* 764) or "as I hope to show" (*Prose3* 195)—Eliot's January 1928 review of Pound's *Personae* marks a shift. Eliot acknowledges his activity as a writer of verse: "I have, in recent years, cursed Mr. Pound often enough; for I am never sure that I can call my verse my own; just when I am most pleased with myself, I find that I have only caught up some echo from a verse of Pound's" (*Prose3* 322). A month later, his review of Baron von Hügel's *Selected Letters* expresses regret at never having met the man (*Prose3* 337). In March 1928, his "Note on Richard Crashaw" engages in subtler play with his reputation. Comparing Shelley disadvantageously to Crashaw by highlighting the vagueness of certain phrases in Shelley's "To a Skylark," Eliot not only allows himself a colloquial register previously unseen ("what the devil he means") but ironically concedes, "There may be some clue [as to the meaning] for persons more learned than I; but Shelley should have provided notes" (*Prose3* 382). The implication that Eliot is unlearned is a subtler version of his claim in his 1933 lecture "English Poets as Letter Writers" that he was "almost illiterate" and "an extremely ill-educated and ignorant man" (*Prose4* 846). In 1928 and 1933, Eliot plays against the reputation of both his poetry and prose, something that would have been impossible in his early career and that remained impossible in anonymous reviews. The reference to "notes" reads like a sly glance at *The Waste Land*.

A biographically oriented critic might attribute the change in tone in these three pieces written in October and November 1927 to Eliot's baptism and confirmation in June of that year. Taking print culture into consideration, we might attribute the change to their being written for the *Dial*, where Eliot anticipated a primarily North American readership. However, the change is not restricted to Eliot's contributions to that magazine. His preface to Mowrer's *This American World* contains a lengthy passage of reminiscence about his childhood and his sense of belonging fully neither to New England nor to Missouri (*Prose3* 491–2). In 1929, Eliot makes use of his public reputation in other ways—he writes many more letters to editors, and his review of works on Goethe implicitly draws on his authority as a publisher: "I know quite well the size of the public and the costs of production" ("Introduction to Goethe," *Prose3* 574). The published texts of his BBC broadcasts make use of direct, pedagogical address to "you," and in his July 1929 broadcast text on Donne's sermons, he refers to his being "hauled over the coals" by critics for his disparaging remarks about the dean of St. Paul's (*Prose3* 670). The causes are multiple. In March 1928, having reread *The Sacred Wood* for a new edition, Eliot noted the "stiffness" of his earlier style and his "assumption of pontifical solemnity" ("Preface to the 1928 edition of *The Sacred Wood*," *Prose3* 413). That rereading may have confirmed Eliot's decision to employ the first-person singular more freely, but the decision itself predated the rereading. The "pontifical" style had been Eliot's means of gaining critical authority, but by late 1927 it was no longer strictly necessary, even if it survived in his *TLS* essays.

To return Eliot's essays to their original print contexts does not strip Eliot of agency or imply that his style, tone, and prejudices were wholly determined by the publication for which he was writing, but it reminds us of conventions that become less visible when the text is remediated in a *Selected Essays* or *Complete Prose* and focuses attention on the ways in which Eliot accommodated his contributions within those conventions. Thinking about the relation of collections of essays to journalistic writing reminds us that, in writing for the *Athenaeum*, *TLS*, the *Dial*, or other periodicals, Eliot already had future books in mind, some of which appeared in his lifetime, others of which were never completed. When he collected his essays, Eliot transformed what might have been seen as ephemera or "junk" into something of permanent value. Evaluating Eliot's essays within their original print contexts offers insight into the evolution of his work, with the opportunity to explore how a new writer might accumulate and convert cultural capital and subsequently leverage that capital to develop stylistically.

Notes

1 For discussion of Eliot's attitude toward his prose, see pp. 23–4.
2 For the phrase "column reviews," see *Letters3* 117; for the sole shorter notice by Eliot, see his review of Agnes Mure Mackenzie (*Prose3* 184n4).
3 John Xiros Cooper, "Bringing the Modern to Market: The Case of Faber & Faber," in *Publishing Modernist Fiction and Poetry*, edited by Lise Jaillant (Edinburgh: Edinburgh University Press, 2019), 93.
4 Hermione Lee, *Virginia Woolf* (London: Chatto & Windus, 1996), 215; Tom Steele, *Alfred Orage and the Leeds Arts Club, 1893–1923* (Aldershot: Scolar, 1990), 218.

5 To Hope Clutterbuck, September 5, 1924. See "What India Is Thinking about To-day" (1916), *Prose1* 389–93.
6 Richard Jenkins, *Pierre Bourdieu* (Abingdon: Routledge, 2002), 75.
7 Bertrand Russell, March 27, 1914, quoted in Ray Monk, *Bertrand Russell: The Spirit of Solitude* (London: Jonathan Cape, 1996), 349.
8 Laurel Brake, "Literary Criticism and the Victorian Periodicals," *Yearbook of English Studies* 16 (1986), 97.
9 Eliot refers to Bennett's book in passing (*Prose2* 54); he reviewed *Pot-Boilers* (*Prose1* 723–4).
10 John Middleton Murry, *Aspects of Literature* (London: Collins, 1920), vii.
11 Similarly, see the openings of "Swinburne and the Elizabethans" (*Prose2* 119, 115) and "Swinburne as Poet" (*Prose2* 185, 181).
12 Oscar Maurer, Jr., "Anonymity vs. Signature in Victorian Reviewing," *Studies in English* 27, no. 1 (1948): 2; Robert H. Tener, "Breaking the Code of Anonymity: The Case of the *Spectator*, 1861–1897," *The Yearbook of English Studies* 16 (1986): 63.
13 Eric Barendt, *Anonymous Speech: Literature, Law and Politics* (Oxford: Hart, 2016), 26.
14 George Saintsbury, quoted by Barendt, *Anonymous Speech*, 25.
15 A. L. Rowse, diary May 28, 1926, paraphrasing Sir Charles Lucas, quoted in *Letters3* 156n.
16 For others, see Eliot's letter to W. H. Auden, August 17, 1933, *Letters6* 627; *Letters7* 246n.
17 Pierre Bourdieu, *The Rules of Art*, trans. Susan Emanuel (Stanford: Stanford University Press, 1996), 166–9.

the author can safely "affiliate" himself—a task she sees resolved, paradoxically, in the transparent persona of "Prufrock," "a strange lyric, pretending to be a dramatic monologue."[22] Notably, however, Vendler finds the moment when this pretense becomes most transparent—that is, when the "affiliation" between Eliot and "Prufrock" is strongest—in what she calls the poem's "two internal lyrics," the two passages of stanzaic verse beginning "For I have known them all already, known them all" and "And would it have been worth it, after all" (*Poems1*, 6, 8).[23] If so, the effect clearly depends upon superimposing two different senses of "lyric": the ritualistic (foregrounding "voicing," via stanzas and refrains) and the readerly (inviting intimacy with the poem's "voice"). This same association is one that Eliot's other early poems typically regard as problematic.

"La Figlia Che Piange" illustrates both the ongoing salience of the expressive subject as a problem for Eliot's poems and its link with the ritualized structures and motifs of stanzaic lyric. Composed of three irregularly rhyming stanzas, the poem begins like a quintessential Cullerian lyric, with an apostrophe to a female beloved and an incipient refrain:

> Stand on the highest pavement of the stair—
> Lean on a garden urn—
> Weave, weave the sunlight in your hair—
> Clasp your flowers to you with a pained surprise—
> Fling them to the ground and turn
> With a fugitive resentment in your eyes:
> But weave, weave the sunlight in your hair. (*Poems1* 28)

Indeed, Culler's account may be uniquely poised to describe the lyricality of a poem whose succeeding stanzas disarticulate its initial voice, shifting to a third-person vantage point, before settling upon a new "I" whom it implies to be the chastened, ironical version of the speaker of the first stanza, thus effecting a minimal overall coherence (*Poems1* 28). And yet, the very energy with which the poem seeks to disarticulate its speaker suggests that, for Eliot, the connection between lyric and subjectivity, between "voicing" and "voice," together with the expectation that the latter might be read as the voice of the poet, remained an active one, to be actively resisted.

Eliot's later insistence that "La Figlia Che Piange" was not based on experience, but on "an Egyptian carving in Italy which the poet never saw," is thus not merely redundant (*Poems1* 451). The issue is not just that, rather than disarticulating its speaker's consciousness, the poem might be seen as dramatizing his motivated evasions; instead, by the very act of marking the speech as fictional, by laying bare its constructedness, the poem invited contemplation of a still more recessed subjectivity underlying it—that of the poet. Already, then, in a minor poem like "La Figlia Che Piange," we find paradoxical intimations of what Charles Altieri has called, in Eliot, "a new immediacy, a new literalness, and a new abstract intimacy for poetry."[24] Such immediacy's afterlife in later Anglo-American poetry, Altieri suggested, would not be consummate impersonality but confessionalism, for which Eliot's poems created the conditions of possibility. By taking apart its fiction, even as it retained the armature of ritualized lyric, the poem invited readers to contemplate new principles of coherence. The experience of the poet would come, in however elusive a way, to suggest itself as that ground.

To be sure, some of Eliot's early poems seem to depart from such concerns altogether. The abrupt and discordant pieces Eliot published in 1920 under the title *Ara Vos Prec*, in England, and as *Poems*, in the United States, with their arch literary and theological allusion and their reliance on anti-Semitic and other caricatures, can seem, at best, a refinement of the spirit of the earlier "Ballade pour la grosse Lulu" and "The Triumph of Bullshit." Once again, however, the very depth of their antagonism to expressive interiority attests to its continuing salience as a problem. "Sweeney Erect," for instance, can be seen as a satire upon "overhearing" as a mode of intimate disclosure, the nineteenth-century model of the relationship of lyric utterance to audience still implicit in Eliot's later account of the "first voice" of poetry as "the poet talking to himself—or to nobody" ("The Three Voices of Poetry," *Prose7* 817). Presenting "Sweeney addressed full length to shave / Broadbottomed, pink from nape to base," the poem juxtaposes the "shriek" of Sweeney's female companion with the reaction it provokes from the "overhearing" witnesses:

> The ladies of the corridor
> Find themselves involved, disgraced,
> Call witness to their principles
> And deprecate the lack of taste
>
> Observing that hysteria
> Might easily be misunderstood;
> Mrs. Turner intimates
> It does the house no sort of good. (*Poems1* 37)

Whatever the "ladies of the corridor" profess to fear this "hysteria" being "misunderstood" *as* (scholarly conjecture ranges from unspecified "violence" to "orgasm"[25]), the poem burlesques the notion that either option implicates a profound interiority.

Yet the Eliot of *Ara Vos Prec* does not altogether dismiss concern with interiority and, with it, the prospect of being "misunderstood." The forbiddingly obscure "Ode," called by one critic Eliot's "nadir," represents in this, as in other respects, a limit case of his early exploration of lyric.[26] The only one of Eliot's printed poems never collected in his lifetime, it joins the tripartite structure of Greek choral ode to an extreme rhetoric of sexual violence and severe depersonalization. Declaring "Misunderstood / The accents of the now retired / Profession of the calamus" (*Poems1* 280), its opening strophe conjoins poetry, sexuality, dysfunction, and incomprehension; these themes return in the antistrophe, which, in a typically Eliotic contrast, sets a quintessential instance of ceremonial lyric—the chorus from Catullus's poem 61, a wedding hymn—against what Anthony Julius characterizes as "a disastrous honeymoon, and the humiliating, desperate coupling of virgins":[27]

> Tortured.
> When the bridegroom smoothed his hair
> There was blood upon the bed.
> Morning was already late.
> Children singing in the orchard
> (Io Hymen, Hymneaee)
> Succuba eviscerate. (*Poems1* 280)

"Ode" has no discernible speaker (thus either ironizing or radicalizing its "choral" template), nor are its increasingly asyndetic clauses readily legible as speech acts. So much, it seems, for the readerly lyric—unless, of course, like Julius, we interpret these absences dynamically. On this view, the poem's "intrusive use of the third person singular" becomes "a defensive, self-concealing gesture," exemplary of how "the poem is trapped between a refusal to admit responsibility for the blood, and an inability to deny it."[28] Curiously, Julius omits from his persuasive reading an element that supports it—the poem's epigraph, slightly misquoted from *Coriolanus*: "*To you particularly, and to all the Volscians / Great hurt and mischief*" (*Poems1* 280). In context, I suggest, this functions as misogynistic code: for "Volscians," read "women." Recasting the play's violence as sex and its own sex as violence, a brittle masculinity here regains its composure by presenting (unintended) infliction of pain on one woman as deliberate aggression against all women. Yet by supplying the second person addressee ("you") otherwise missing from the poem, the epigraph also hints at the otherwise absent first-person pronoun; that is, in the deleted preceding clauses from Shakespeare: "My name is Caius Marcius, who hath done."[29] Without becoming the voice of a "speaker," the poem thus reveals itself as oriented by a subject, albeit one that (via deletion) is literally outside it.

Does surmise about that subjectivity amount to "lyrical reading"?[30] Consider Eliot's November 1931 response to an inquiry from I. A. Richards about an echo of one of his own poems in *Coriolan*. Though Eliot—whose fascination with Coriolanus, in "Ode" and elsewhere, suggests various forms of investment, both personal and political[31]—acknowledged "the allusions" as "perfectly deliberate," and that it "was my intention that the reader should recognize them" (*Letters7* 731–2), he declined to elucidate them. He reminded Richards that it was "a theory of mine" that "if the reader knows too much about the crude material in the author's mind, his own reactions may tend to become at best a kind of feeble image of the author's feelings, whereas a good poem should have a potentiality of evoking feelings and associations in the reader of which the author is wholly ignorant" (*Letters5* 732). In fact, Eliot's appeal to his readers' "feelings and associations" embodies a characteristic ambivalence.[32] Where Jackson and Prins have described "lyrical reading" as replacing the "referents" shared among members of a community by public meanings, Eliot here imagines something like the reverse: public meanings (which include allusions to a notionally common "culture"[33]) are what evoke each reader's private associations. The convergence between such "feelings and associations" and those of the author is not excluded as a possibility but left indeterminate. Nevertheless, the "potentiality" of a poem to evoke readers' private feelings allows them to infer, if not specify, its derivation from the author's own.

The uncertainty of how to locate subjectivity in his poems was, in other words, something that Eliot encouraged. The crucial documents remain 1919's "Tradition and the Individual Talent" and 1921's "The Metaphysical Poets." Taken together, these essays, like the poems, do not so much eliminate as displace the "self" as a locus of poetic interest. The distinction in "Tradition" between the "man who suffers and the mind which creates" would be more easily sustained if Eliot did not place such emphasis on the pathos in creation, which is a "continual self-sacrifice" and not altogether "tranquil" (*Prose2* 109, 108, 111). Eliot's "sacrifice of himself" to "something which is more valuable" is not the theatricalization of personality that we find in, for example, Yeats's declaration that the poet "is never the bundle of accident and incoherence that sits down to breakfast; he has been reborn as an idea, something intended, complete."[34] In a sense, it was just that "bundle of accident and incoherence" that Eliot's "new wholes" preserved ("Metaphysical Poets," *Prose2* 380).[35] The literary correlate of the theatricalized self is the lyric "speaker." Eliot's "sacrifice," with the signal exception of "Prufrock," tended not so much to replace that figure with the fictive "persona" as to displace it into an implication of the poems' artistry.

The early Eliot's conflicted engagement with the expressive lyric, occasional assimilation of his work to a dramatic, fictive model, and prevailing disinclination to do so can each be read as moments in a skepticism about the value of the self; and yet, as all readers of "Tradition" will recall: "only those who have personality and emotions know what it means to want to escape from these things" (*Prose2* 111). When Eliot attributes to Dostoevsky a gift "for utilizing his weaknesses; so that epilepsy and hysteria cease to be the defects of an individual," he finds such weaknesses redeemed not in a perfected impersonality but as "the entrance to a genuine and personal universe" ("London Letter: August, 1922," *Prose2* 413). For Eliot, however, "utilize" here starts to mean something different than merely being subordinated toward some end. Poetic form, the modernist poet's ever more self-consciously employed instrument, estranges self-expression from itself.[36] Lyric is both the object of such estrangement and its result.

Notes

1 Eliot preferred to call his own explorations of the "first voice of poetry" (i.e., "the poet talking to himself, or to nobody"), "meditative verse" (*Prose7* 825). See also *The Lyric Theory Reader: A Critical Anthology*, edited by Virginia Jackson and Yopie Prins (Baltimore: Johns Hopkins University Press, 2014; hereafter *LTR*), 162–4.

2 *Eliot's Dark Angel* (Oxford: Oxford University Press, 1999), 151, 3. With the opening of Eliot's letters to Emily Hale, efforts to bypass the poet's "impersonality" seem bound to intensify. The classic statement of modernist poetry's debt to romanticism is Frank Kermode's *Romantic Image* (London: Routledge and Kegan Paul, 1957). Recent poet-critics to have displayed similar intuitions include the contributors to *The Essential T. S. Eliot*, edited by Vijay Seshadri (New York: Ecco, 2020) and Roger Reeves, "The Uses of Memory: When Ecstasy Becomes Protest," *The Yale Review* 108, no. 2 (July 2020): 23–40.

3 See especially Jonathan Culler, *Theory of the Lyric* (Cambridge: Harvard University Press, 2015); Virginia Jackson, *Dickinson's Misery* (Princeton: Princeton University Press, 2005); and *LTR*.

4 Culler, 3, 221, 1–9, 186–243.

5 *LTR*, 161 and passim. See also Jackson, *Dickinson's Misery*, 20.

6 "Abstraction," in this context, might be viewed as a negatively marked calque of the "turning away" from context attributed by Culler to apostrophe as a rhetorical trope.
7 *LTR*, 3.
8 This is not to say resolutions are impossible, only that they will not be universally accepted. Culler views historicist studies as in principle compatible with his transhistorical view of lyric, provided that the former are understood as referring to subgenres or movements within a longer lyric tradition (88).
9 For John Stuart Mill's model of (lyric) "poetry" as normatively "overheard" and its adaptation by Northrop Frye, see *LTR*, 3–4. On the distinction between expressive and dramatic utterance, see *LTR*, 5, 162–4; Culler, 2, 108–19 and passim.
10 Culler, 2, 7, and passim.
11 In this respect, Culler's argument also runs against Paul de Man's equation of lyric with "the defensive motion of the understanding" in "Anthropomorphism and Trope in the Lyric" (*The Rhetoric of Romanticism* [New York: Columbia University Press, 1984], 261), a foundational text for the new lyric studies and the source of the term "lyrical reading," if not of its historical inflection in this body of criticism. Jackson, *Dickinson's Misery*, 10, 100–9; Culler, 78–83.
12 Culler, 3, 7. Hugh Kenner, *The Invisible Poet* (New York: McDowell, Obolensky, 1959), 88.
13 Kenner, 4.
14 Culler, 6–7.
15 Instead of a "hermeneutics," Culler calls his project a "poetics" that aims to uncover "a system of possibilities that underlie the tradition and that ought to be borne in mind when reading poems that may have a relation to this tradition" (Culler, 6). See also Culler, *The Pursuit of Signs* (Ithaca: Cornell University Press, 1981), 12, 47.
16 See "A Note on Ezra Pound" (1918), where Eliot distinguishes between two relations to tradition: "an awareness and a conscious use" (*Prose1* 750).
17 To be sure, these are limits that Culler acknowledges: "Lyric, I conclude, involves a tension between ritualistic and fictional elements—between formal elements that provide meaning and structure and serve as instructions for performance and those that work to represent character or event" (7). My aim here is to show how Eliot's poetics magnify this tension.
18 I here adapt a contrast between "expressiveness" and "self-expression" borrowed by Geoffrey Hill from the choreographer Mark Morris. See Sameer Rahim, "An interview with Geoffrey Hill (1932–2016)," *Prospect Magazine* July 20, 2016. https://www.prospectmagazine.co.uk/arts-and-books/an-interview-with-geoffrey-hill-1932-2016.
19 Unlike Susan Stewart's "distressed genres," which affect orality and authenticity, Eliot's "*Waste Land* lyrics" adopt conspicuously "literary" forms. Nevertheless, their legibility as parodies likewise derives from "the reader's knowledge of the

work's contemporary status," thus highlighting the forms' archaism (see Stewart, "Distressed Genres," *Journal of American Folklore* 104, no. 411 [Winter, 1991]: 24).
20 Culler, 223.
21 For the "humiliated 'I'" in Eliot's early lyric, see Michael Levenson, *Modernism* (New Haven: Yale University Press, 2011), 167, 163–8.
22 Helen Vendler, *Coming of Age as a Poet: Milton, Keats, Eliot, Plath* (Cambridge: Harvard University Press, 2004), 111, 85. Kenner similarly praised the poem's "poised intimacy which could draw on every emotion the young author knew without incurring the liabilities of 'self-expression'" (4).
23 Vendler, 111.
24 "Eliot's Impact on Twentieth-Century Anglo-American Poetry," *The Cambridge Companion to T. S. Eliot*, edited by A. David Moody (New York: Cambridge University Press, 1994), 198.
25 Schuchard, 93; John Worthen, *T. S. Eliot: A Short Biography* (London: Haus, 2009), 80.
26 Grover Smith, *T. S. Eliot's Poetry and Plays: A Study in Sources and Meaning* (Chicago: University of Chicago Press, 1971), 38; see also *Poems1* 1177.
27 Anthony Julius, *T. S. Eliot, Anti-Semitism, and Literary Form* (Cambridge: Cambridge University Press, 1995), 20.
28 Julius, 20–1.
29 The original reads in full: "My name is Caius Marcius, who hath done / To thee particularly and to all the Volsces / Great hurt and mischief" (IV.v.66–7).
30 In "The Intentional Fallacy," W. K. Wimsatt, Jr., and Monroe C. Beardsley sought to accommodate the allusive texture of *The Waste Land* by proposing, semi-facetiously, to treat the notes as part of the poem (*LTR*, 209). Motivated initially to rescue critical judgment from appeal to biography, the normative interpretation of lyric as dramatic monologue, as Herbert F. Tucker has argued, also served the deletion of historical context by absorbing all material inside the poem within the consciousness of a speaker, with whom it ended up offering a compensatory fantasy of unmediated contact ("Dramatic Monologue and the Overhearing of Lyric" [1985], *LTR*, 151–3).
31 Writing to G. Wilson Knight on October 30, 1930, Eliot remarks, "I feel now that the political criticism, so much mentioned, is a very surface pattern; and that the real motive of the play is the astonishing study of the mother-son relation: 'he did it to please his mother.'" (*Letters5* 368).
32 Franco Moretti, *Signs Taken for Wonders: Essays in the Sociology of Literary Forms* (London: Verso, 1988), offers a Fregean reading of Eliot that privileges the (collective and intersubjective) "sense" and "associated idea" over the subjectively sensorily apprehensible "referent" (214–15).

33 Eliot would, however, complain in 1935 that "our education indeed is so chaotic that no two persons in the same company can be assumed to have their minds stocked with the same furniture; you cannot make a quotation or an allusion to which the whole of any company can respond" (*Prose5* 255).
34 W. B. Yeats, *Essays and Introductions* (London: Macmillan, 1961), 509.
35 See Kenner's inspired conflation of the claims of Eliot's two major essays: "The mind of the poet, it turns out, is the shred of platinum; itself unchanged, it catalyzes such diverse experiences as falling in love, reading Spinoza, the smell of cooking, so that they form a new whole called a poem: a reaction into which, inviolate, the catalyst does not enter" (32).
36 See Geoffrey Hill's discussion of "alienation" in Eliot and other modernists in *Collected Critical Writings*, edited by Kenneth Haynes (Oxford: Oxford University Press, 2009), 493–566.

13

Eliot's Political Theology

C. D. Blanton

The Present King of France

In 1928, "to refute any accusation of playing 'possum,'" T. S. Eliot delineated the relation of several positions sedulously assembled over a decade (*Prose3* 513). He did so in the brief preface to *For Lancelot Andrewes*—a volume of occasional reviews, gathered in oblique tribute to James I's Bishop of Winchester, the English Bible's chief architect—in a passage that came to stand as acerbic apologia:

> The general point of view may be described as classicist in literature, royalist in politics, and anglo-catholic in religion. I am quite aware that the first term is completely vague, and easily lends itself to clap-trap; I am aware that the second term is at present without definition, and easily lends itself to what is almost worse than clap-trap, I mean temperate conservatism; the third term does not rest with me to define. (*Prose3* 513)

Each term in the series presents provisional problems. The first courts contradiction. A "completely vague" classicism is no classicism at all. The last does not submit to Eliot's prerogative because he had already submitted to its. But each minimally stipulates some settled historical affiliation. Eliot's devotion was privately confirmed a year earlier, when he joined "what is called the Catholic movement" within the Anglican communion,[1] and in 1923, he had already arrayed Catholicism with Classicism to distinguish those who "believe that men cannot get on without giving allegiance to something outside themselves" and mark "the difference between the complete and fragmentary, the adult and the immature, the orderly and the chaotic" ("The Function of Criticism," *Prose2* 460-1). A year after that, he juxtaposed devotional and poetic style more explicitly still, collecting a *Homage to John Dryden* designed to salvage a cultural logic (both Catholic and Classical) since eclipsed by "the popular and pretentious verse of the Romantic Poets and their successors" ("Preface," *Prose2* 546).

As Eliot acknowledged, his homage insinuated a position captured only "in cryptogram," one that "would have led me indirectly into considerations of politics, education, and theology which I no longer care to approach in this way" (*Prose2* 546). With the "essays on style and order" offered in Andrewes's name, he grasped for that other way, sketching "certain lines of development" that gather a rough cultural history descended from a subsequently dissociated Elizabethan settlement (*Prose3* 513). The way glimpsed in "these scattered papers" comprises three volumes—*The School of Donne*, *The Outline of Royalism*, and *The Principles of Modern Heresy*—that never appeared in quite the promised form but gesture clearly enough, in the obsessions with metaphysical poetry (broadly understood) and with orthodoxy, to the familiar ground of subsequent decades. Royalism's "outline" remains harder to descry.

To be sure, neither the reactionary tendency nor the Cavalier inclination of Eliot's royalism surprises. *The Waste Land* had already marked, perhaps mourned, the fate of European dynasties. But Eliot's care to distinguish a politics beyond "temperate conservatism" ("almost worse than clap-trap") hangs on a term "at present without definition," casting beyond deposed emperors, kaisers, and tsars. The usage itself is odd. "Monarchism" would have offered a readier English usage, but it is odder still to worry the point. In 1928, few in England would have argued the apparently settled question. At its 1923 conference, before joining government (His Majesty's), even a nascent Labour Party had avoided republican temptations, deeming the monarchy hardly worth the practical politics. In that usual sense, the idea does not lack clear reference: whatever its constitutional merit, "royalism" did maintain a working sense in 1928, minimally guaranteed in George V's dull corporate person. But Eliot's unmarked stress falls on another part of the phrase, on the subtle problem of a *present* definition. Read literally, he seems to suggest that royalism's outline lies elsewhere: there exists a king, to be sure, but one insufficient to define a concept or evade conservative claptrap. The English king offers an apparent symbol, but of nothing in particular.

For the object sufficient to that political task, one needs another king. Lurking here, characteristically, is an allusion. Two decades earlier, Eliot's erstwhile mentor and persistent antagonist Bertrand Russell had worried over royalism's definition in another context, ironically seizing on *two* kings to define the problem of "definition" as such. Confronted with the need for a formal logic that referentially denotes anything at all, Russell played apparently symmetrical propositions against each other—one pointing at the present king of England

(Edward VII, in 1905), the other at the present king of France—identical in form and yet predicated in contrary ways. Straggling pretenders and interloping emperors notwithstanding, there *was* no present king of France, of course, nor had there been since the July Monarchy's 1848 collapse.

In Russell's terms, the proposition that "there is an *x*, and that *x* is the king of France" is false. Whereas the comparatively innocuous phrase "the present king of England" seems to denote unproblematically—there is such an *x*—the denoting phrase "the present king of France" retains a "meaning" (in Russell's sense) "solely in virtue of its *form*."[2] It bears an association and a historical range; it *seems* to denote. There have been kings of France, after all, and there is an available *idea* corresponding to the phrase. But it presently denotes nothing meaningfully knowable. And as Eliot insinuates, it thereby remains without meaningful definition as well. One may say that there is such an *x*. But in *this* world, the underlying proposition that such a thing *is*—that it exists at all—will always be false, symbolizing nothing.

The present king of France names a political form but lacks a body. The English one embodies no formal idea. Each is (in Russell's sense or Eliot's) half a symbol. For Eliot, royalism requires both, and by his logic, there is "at present" (ours or his) no such politics, no politics that is not false, at all. We have only its imperfect symbols. Oddly, that false politics includes the "temperate" one that Eliot disowned but later readers have insistently imposed upon him, a "conservatism" anachronistically measured in later terms. To grasp the import of Eliot's politics now, it becomes necessary to outline his royalism, give it present definition: neither conservatism nor the habituated maintenance of form for its own sake, but a Toryism of an occasionally radical type, that of the original abhorrers of 1679, unwilling to trade one king's body for another. In fact, I will suggest, Eliot's salience now lies not in the baroque and often rebarbative political theology it embraces but rather in its recognition and surreptitious critique of a political economy that remains ours to reject.

Esoteric Political Theology

A familiar history, consolidated from right and left alike, enlists Eliot in an Anglo-American conservative tradition derived from Edmund Burke. In 1960, Russell Kirk revised *The Conservative Mind* to claim Eliot as the culmination of this (largely American) "conscious conservatism," manifested in reaction to the French Revolution.[3] Kirk's "conservative as poet" absorbed the academic sobrieties of figures like Irving Babbitt, Paul Elmer More, and George Santayana, to point paradoxically to a "new" conservatism.[4] But in 1958, Raymond Williams had already contested the claim, fixing Eliot as a different end of the Burkean line: the conservative thinker who has "raised questions, which those who differ from him politically must answer, or else retire from the field," revealing "the fashionable 'New Conservatism'" and its "recovery of the bones of Burke"—rarely mentioned by Eliot, indeed a Whig—as "much too easy."[5] Those accounts converge on two premises, obvious but impossible to maintain together. The first lies in the idea of a conservatism necessarily a little vague, not always "temperate" but aspiring to temperance. Poor in explicit dogma—"characteristically inarticulate, unwilling (and indeed usually unable) to translate itself into formulae or maxims, loath to state its purpose or declare its view," in Roger Scruton's phrase—this conservatism curates pragmatic attitudes that shift more slowly over time than events themselves.[6] It amounts to what Michael Oakeshott labels mere disposition, not "necessarily connected with any particular beliefs about the universe, about the world in general or about human conduct in general."[7] Defined by its definitional imperviousness, this conservative mind comes (as Mill sneered) to refuse logical precision altogether.[8] But if so, then the second premise—that Eliot's thought embodies the "conservative" in either the staid sense or Williams's more expansive one—remains untenable. Eliot's very refusal of "clap-trap" tends to have "the effect of making complacent conservatism impossible."[9]

Williams does not quite finish the thought. Neither complacent nor conservative, Eliot's royalism follows another, sharper line, insinuated by that conceptual nullity of France's present king but difficult now to discern clearly. To position Eliot's political thought on postwar conservatism's reflexive coordinates—as a Burkean traditionalism; as some antinomic anti-communism or Hayekian chimera; as an ingenuous neoliberalism or emergent illiberalism—is to misplace it, wrenching away its context to postulate allegiances never professed and frequently scorned. Both the metic philosopher arriving in London by way of Marburg as war began and the poet absorbed in dynastic collapse and revolution were formed at the onset of what historians have sometimes termed (as Keynes had in 1919) the "European Civil War," most nearly comparable in scale to the tumultuous interludes concluded at Westphalia in 1648 or Vienna in 1815, and Eliot remained a cryptic combatant in each, summoning memories of 1649 or 1793, moments of royalism negated, to insist that any present civil war (in his time or ours) only renews older ones.[10] The result is a political philosophy founded on logical obliquity.

This "royalism" negated is a phrase that predicates but no longer denotes; it indicates a concept lacking any corresponding object and refuses present reference. It may be outlined but never quite represented. To borrow phrases from two (rather differently) reactionary contemporaries, Eliot constructs a political theology, but an esoteric one. For Carl Schmitt, notoriously, political theology names the derivation of modern state forms—structures of sovereignty, most notably—as secularized theological concepts.[11] Thrown open in the postwar crisis, such newly contested forms unseal once-resolved myths and social logics, disembedding and resurrecting archaic elements, demonstrating that politics and theology are neither neatly separable nor equivalent in weight: the former entails the latter as conceptual ground. Eliot underscored the point when, in 1936, he collected pieces from *For Lancelot Andrewes* again (under the Drydenesque title of *Essays Ancient and Modern*) and qualified his earlier pronouncement:

> I am the more careful in the matter because some years ago I made wisely or unwisely, a brief announcement of faith religious, political and literary which became too easily quotable. It may have given some critics the impression that for me all these three were inextricable and *of equal importance*. (*Prose4* 542, Eliot's emphasis)

Stipulating that the domains might prove notionally separable but separately constitute species of "faith" nonetheless, Eliot's qualification rehearses political theology's logic while disarticulating the point. Sharing none of Schmitt's confidence in theology's modern tenability *as* politics (and thus none of his patience with an actual fascism), Eliot conceals faith partially, adopting what Leo Strauss terms an esoteric mode, a politics couched in Tractarian reserve, declaimed almost inaudibly or written "between the lines"; etched indirectly, indexically, in an elliptically citational textual practice.[12] Even politics, even one's style of reading, remains a faith.

Such is the present king of France. In fact, the empty predication of an undefinable royalism specifies Eliot's esoterically intemperate Toryism quite precisely, by insisting on a world lacking present definition, recuperable only by a strange brand of elusive exegesis. The effect is felt across the *Andrewes* volume, culminating in a severe review of Babbitt (another erstwhile mentor) and his conservative "New Humanism," excoriated for abandoning theology's regulative force to a wan anthropomorphism, premised on "the inner check" of human conscience. Only with its penultimate paragraph does the review fix its real object, unfavorably comparing Babbitt with "another philosopher of the same rank," Charles Maurras ("The Humanism of Irving Babbitt," *Prose3* 461).

Eliot's fascination with the leader of Action française, the revanchist movement spawned in the Dreyfus Affair's wake as the organ of an integralist nationalism, refined as a distinctively Gallic proto-fascism still audible on the French right, is familiar enough.[13] In diction ("style and order") as in cadence (*classiciste, royaliste, catholique*), it is Maurras who patterns Eliot's self-declaration, and it was through Babbitt that Eliot first encountered Maurras. But as Eliot wrote of Babbitt and Andrewes, political Catholicism's chief exponent languished on the index, excommunicated for sundering confessional belief from political necessity. For Maurras, the church's place as the affirmative guarantor of a counterfactual legitimacy, the placeholder for an absent king, renders individual faith moot.

There is an odd contradiction nestled here. Against any cogent conservatism, Eliot summons Maurras to insinuate a belief. It is not, however, a belief in which one must particularly believe, nor even the attestation of an *existing* historical object. Maurras's Catholicism does not belong to Maurras any more than his king belongs to an actually existing France. Instead, politics is imposed as a logical postulate or necessary posture: precisely because one need not assent to a present fact, the demand retains its force. Having lapsed as extant object, royalism thus persists as coherent doctrine, but only by virtue of a theological predicate itself impervious to private judgment or valuation. With private judgment suspended, however, the possibility of a direct or (in Strauss's language) exoteric presentation, any declarative politics of a legible sort, vanishes as well. Eliot strains to declare his position not because it is not a position but because it is not properly expressible, because there exists no current political framework in which to say it. It has no sign but coheres in an index of references recalling moments of achieved historical denotation. The point is underscored in Eliot's next rejoinder to Babbitt, published a year later, when he returns to Maurras still more obliquely by mentioning his most forceful English advocate, T. E. Hulme, instead. Invoked to name what Babbitt misses even as he appears to excoriate Rousseau for expanding "an inner check into an expansive emotion,"[14] Eliot's Hulme does a double work. He embodies dogmas "which are the closest expression of the categories of the religious attitude," even while demonstrating that Babbitt "remains nearer to the view of Rousseau" in his readiness to grant redemptive power to human agency instead ("Second Thoughts about Humanism," *Prose3* 620–1).

That second insinuation is barbed. Upon Babbitt's death, Eliot confessed that it was his charge of evasion that had provoked the notorious preface (*Prose6* 187). But Eliot's citational rejoinder only confirms the charge in an evasion, distinguishing his own "point of view" from "the view of Rousseau." Babbitt is thus answered with Hulme and Maurras, so that Eliot may insist on an attitude that Babbitt has abandoned without confessing it. The specter of this "religious attitude" is drawn from Hulme's last writings, but it recalls a more primal doctrine, announced earlier in his preface to Georges Sorel's *Réflexions sur la violence*, meant to salvage socialism from the neutrally proceduralist habits in which bourgeois democracy encases it. Hulme's Sorel thus denies the postulate that "springs from Rousseau … found even in the first sentence of the Social Contract [sic]," with its blithe insistence that man is naturally free.[15] Splicing Marx with Maurras, classicism with class-war, Sorel accordingly unearths bourgeois democracy's unconfessed (and unsound) theology and answers it with another, in the claim that man is naturally sinful rather than free. Babbitt's new humanism had relied centrally on an attempt to restrain Rousseau's excess of natural imagination with the countervailing moral imagination of his "chief antagonist," Burke.[16] But it had, for Eliot, quietly absorbed Rousseau's theology as well.

That a doctrine of Original Sin anchors the most profound objection to liberal democracy is an old thought (even Reinhold Niebuhr was compelled to meet it dialectically).[17] Maurras, Hulme, Sorel—the names alone betray a recurring ideological irruption, moments at which a thought formally exiled from a secular culture returns to resonate within it. Almost syllogistically, a style implies a politics, a politics implies a theology, and together they imply a history set to converge in the vacant space of the present, on a displaced royal body figuring everything gone missing. But Eliot's oblique composite sign also resolves his volume's deeper esoteric theme, in one last indexical twist. Reviewing Arthur Symons's translations a few pieces earlier, Eliot insisted that Baudelaire "was essentially a Christian, born out of his due time, and a classicist, born out of his due time": "[t]o him the notion of Original Sin came spontaneously," even if it implied no promise of salvation ("Baudelaire in our Time," *Prose3* 76). The intermediating allusion is unvoiced, passing back silently through the Third Republic to the Second Empire and beyond, underscoring a point Eliot would make again two years later, when he invoked Hulme to quote "a paragraph which Baudelaire would have approved," insisting that "man is essentially bad" ("Baudelaire," *Prose4* 163–4). The evidence for that approval is clear enough, in every fold of Baudelaire's notion of evil. But Eliot understates it, and he radically disarticulates its source. Baudelaire discovered his doctrine not spontaneously but in the writings of Joseph de Maistre, the bloody architect of that counter-revolutionary dogma, "which explains everything and without which nothing can be explained."[18]

Unlike Rousseau and the others, Maistre is not mentioned in *For Lancelot Andrewes*. But the sequence of figures called to reassert Original Sin enshrines him as the volume's presiding intelligence, the figurehead of a dark counter-history, legible only as the effect of an ongoing style and menace. The impenetrable sectarian for whom even Burke proved too moderate, that impossible bigot (as des Esseintes calls him in *À rebours*), Maistre's specter systematically refutes Rousseau ("one of the most dangerous sophists of our century," in the Count's estimate) but, more important, answers his claims to freedom and natural reason.[19] For Isaiah Berlin, famously, Maistre stands as counter-enlightenment's ultramontane apotheosis and fascism's herald—aligned with Maurras and Eliot "for the trinity of classicism, monarchy, and the church"—and thus stands ultimately for irrationalism in purest form.[20] But the characterization stumbles over an odd confession like Baudelaire's, that this apparent irrationalism "taught me to reason," and Berlin himself strains to answer the argument that Maistre's unsparing dialectical providentialism "used the weapon of reason to defeat reason."[21] Baudelaire's lesson is more acute. Rather than resisting reason in Burkean fashion, Maistre renders it absolute by reserving it only to God, denying man's claim altogether. Original Sin stands, for Eliot and Baudelaire as for Maistre, as the reminder not only that political reason operates implacably but also that it does not belong to us.

Lying encrypted in "the present king of France" is the harder edge of Eliot's politics, stubbornly unreconciled to the bourgeois forms with which more temperate conservatisms made their peace. Politics is merely theology, misrecognized. But in the need for that encryption lies a deeper contradiction. Eliot cannot state his politics plainly, is cast instead into a chain of deferred references, for the simple reason that his politics lacks an integrated theological vehicle. His royalism is predicated on the symbolic attachment of meaning to a present body, but no such body can exist in a society where only man retains a will or claim to reason. Eliot's procedure is esoteric because it is necessarily allegorical, adapting the only style available when meaning resides somewhere else.

Incarnate Form

Along the esoteric line, through the symbolists and Baudelaire, Hulme and Sorel, from Maurras to Maistre, a coherent stance emerges, an almost categorical rejection of bourgeois culture. But it emerges only in outline, offering no affirmative program. This effect, with its insistence on our present deprivation of conceptual language, has made Eliot paradoxically ecumenical, as available, for example, to what T. J. Clark labels the "Eliotic Trotskyism" of mid-century anti-Stalinists as to Alasdair MacIntyre's Thomist variant of a related thought, by way of St. Benedict's utopian pessimism.[22] Unlike Schmitt or Strauss, Eliot prescribes no particular political system—even now, in a moment of resurgent but contradictory illiberalisms, from the neo-Catholic to the alternative right, often anxious to claim him—because he denies the coherence of any secular political ground. His unswerving principle remains wholly negative, radical rather than conservative, more Adornian than Arnoldian, simply by refusing the commodified desire that passes for affirmative political representation. It is indeed a concern with representation and its impossibility that organizes Eliot's "point of view." If Eliot's politics lacks definition, it is because representation itself has succumbed to a poetic snare and lapsed into allegory.

One of Schmitt's cardinal premises held that the European Civil War was a sign of the "depoliticization" of politics.[23] Political theology's simplest claim, that is, lies in the reassertion of politics itself as an organizing notional term, challenging a normative epistemic logic that fails to recognize its own theological inference. What Schmitt describes as "the economic thinking of our time" subordinates the theological trace within a Weberian calculus, premised on the mediated value-determination of markets, thereby deriving state authority from a shifting relative ground.[24] Masked in the command economies and party-polities of the Leninist or the fascist-corporate state, or neutrally embedded in the parliamentary democracies, a principle of exchange (x is worth y) displaces definition (x is y). For Schmitt, "[t]he understanding of every type of representation disappears with the spread of economic thinking."[25]

Schmitt's argument found sympathetic English readers in Eliot's circle, including those (like Christopher Dawson) ready to assert representative form as the (Roman) church's exclusive preserve. But Eliot grasps and radicalizes the point historically. For Schmitt, representation's disappearance exposes the social nullity of a conceptually enfeebled age: "Once the state becomes a leviathan, it disappears from the world of representations."[26] By the interwar moment, however, the world of representations as such has disappeared, and Schmitt's ambivalent Hobbesian echo concisely locates the difficulty: the "present king of France" lacks a definition because it lacks an object. The king is dead. But insofar as the present lacks a *capacity* for definition, the problem is deeper, and the present king of England little better than the French one. Or rather, the king of England presents a special case to which logic alone has no answer: a phrase that seems to retain a definition, even an apparent body, but lacks a meaning because it lacks a representational logic. Such an object exists, but insofar as it may be indifferently traded for or referred to anything else, one king restored for another, that existence secures nothing in particular. If the French king attests the loss of what Russell called meaning, the English one explains it.

At its core, Maistre's dogma of Original Sin is an answer to economics. Launched late in the Terror to refute the Pelagian postulate of Rousseau's first sentence, it exposes the romantic myth: to explain man's persistence in chains despite his natural freedom, some intervening event is required, a fall made recuperable by merely human devices. But Rousseau's answer, bequeathed *to* the French Revolution, was furnished *by* the English one, in an idea that even his former friend Hume dismissed as convenient whiggish fiction: the social contract.[27] In two essays left unfinished, Maistre undertakes to prove that man is both intrinsically sociable and naturally depraved, precisely to demonstrate the lack of any agency sufficient to underwrite a promise or guarantee a contract.[28] Taking aim at revolutionary claims to popular sovereignty, but also at its unreflective adoption of a commercial conceit, he dismisses the social contract as the representation of a will that cannot possibly exist: an agreement without standing, it pretends to ratify a compact that obtains already. A false representation by definition, the social contract equates the unlike. Properly understood, political theology is thus political economy's inverse, a critique (in a direction contrary to Marx's) of the systematized logic of representational profligacy upon which commercial society is built.

Assembled by indirection, Eliot's case against Rousseau, against economy, nonetheless summons its symbol insistently in its performative title, both an offering and an advocacy. To speak *for* Lancelot Andrewes is among other things to stand *against* Thomas Hobbes, the contract's first author, opposing in Andrewes's name an economic theory falsely cloaked as a philosophy of language and politics. As systematically as Maistre and Maurras, Eliot's Andrewes incorporates an esoteric reproach to an explicit Hobbesian sign in a series of proxies. When Machiavelli steps forth to deride Hobbes's "wholly different" statecraft—marked by "cynicism" rather than "innocence"—he adopts "the orthodox view of original sin" by telling a "truth about humanity" also attested in Andrewes's sermons ("Niccolò Machiavelli," *Prose3* 111–12, 117). Acquitted of comparisons to Napoleon and Nietzsche, Mussolini and Lenin, this Machiavelli maintains "that an established Church was of the greatest value to a State," while Hobbes is conversely damned for the "mechanistic psychology" that gave us Russell and I. A. Richards ("Niccolò Machiavelli," *Prose3* 111, 113;

"John Bramhall," *Prose3* 145). A more sustained rebuke is provided by Hobbes's antagonist John Bramhall, allowing Eliot to dismiss Hobbes's "particularly lamentable theory of the relation between Church and State"—"essentially revolutionary" and "similar to that of contemporary Russia"—a theory that "not only insists on autocracy but tolerates *unjustified* revolution" ("John Bramhall," *Prose3* 146, 148, 147). By contrast, Bramhall makes the king "a kind of symbol," substantively justified by "a double responsibility": "not merely a civil but a religious obligation toward his people" (*Prose3* 147).

In the last book of his *Lawes*, Hooker distinguishes the singularity of the English church by its dual logic of incorporation. Church and commonwealth stand as polities identical in essence, constituted by different accidental means.[29] Each names a different aspect, imposes a different obligation, but as each is vested in the same royal body, "a kind of symbol" is achieved nonetheless. The perfect coextension of church and state ensures a representational symmetry, regulated by common reference to a single corporate form, thereby solving a problem that had, in *De Monarchia*, vexed even Dante. For Eliot, that logical corporate identity forms the core of the Elizabethan Settlement, instantiated in turn by "the last of the humble Welsh family of Tudor," herself "the first and most complete incarnation of English policy"—"representative," Eliot insists, "of the finest spirit of England of the time" ("Lancelot Andrewes," *Prose2* 817).

Eliot assails Hobbes neither as a casual absolutist nor as liberalism's inadvertent architect (as Schmitt and Strauss concluded) but rather because his contract's "mutual transferring of Right" unleashes the system of broken and counterfeit signs glimpsed in Baudelaire's Paris (or Eliot's London).[30] Once referred to exchange's logic, its premise that a thing stands indifferently for another unlike it, Hobbesian society surrenders meaningful representation, trading one version of incorporation for another. Perversely, the contract's very contingency presupposes a necessary falsehood. Even the Hobbesian king, pretending what he cannot properly embody, stands instead as the accidental emblem of "a *Feigned* or *Artificiall* person."[31] The dissimulation by which even "the true God may be Personated" and a "Multitude of men ... Represented" reduces incarnation to a commercial transaction.[32]

Hobbes is not wrong, historically. With *Leviathan*'s frontispiece "already before our eyes," F. W. Maitland long ago observed the English monarchy's comical derivation from the legal fiction of the corporation sole, and even Burke pardoned politer revolutions on contractual grounds (acknowledging signatories dead and unborn).[33] But for Eliot, Andrewes models another logic, predicated not only on the coextension of an ecclesiastical polity but also on the scriptural realization that provides it a symbolic tongue. A decade earlier, Andrewes's "essential dogma" of Incarnation, reiterated over decades of Christmas sermons preached before the king, had appeared in "Gerontion" to test a mode of symbolic utterance and undissociated logical judgment irreducible to "faith religious, political and literary" because fully each at once: "The word within a word, unable to speak a word"; "Came Christ the tiger" (*Prose2* 821; *Poems1* 31). What is most political in Eliot's thought derives not from some utopian counterfactual longing for restoration, resurrection. Nor is it meaningfully conservative. It lies instead in the labor toward a symbolic style that renders definition unnecessary, by redeeming representation as present fact.

Notes

1. To Mary James Power, December 6, 1932 (*Letters6* 518).
2. Bertrand Russell, "On Denoting," *Mind*, n.s. 14:56 (October 1905): 479.
3. Russell Kirk, *The Conservative Mind: From Burke to Eliot*, rev. ed. (Chicago: Regnery, 1960), 4.
4. Kirk, 4.
5. Raymond Williams, *Culture and Society: 1780–1950* (London: Chatto & Windus, 1958), 227, 243.
6. Roger Scruton, *The Meaning of Conservatism*, 3rd ed. (South Bend: St. Augustine's, 2002), 9.
7. Michael Oakeshott, "On Being Conservative," in *Rationalism in Politics, and Other Essays* (London: Methuen, 1962), 183.
8. John Stuart Mill, *Considerations on Representative Government* (London: Parker, Son, and Bourn, 1861), 138.
9. Williams, 243.
10. John Maynard Keynes, *The Economic Consequences of Peace* (London: Macmillan, 1919), 3.
11. Carl Schmitt, *Political Theology: Four Chapters on the Concept of Sovereignty* [1934], translated by George Schwab (Chicago: University of Chicago Press, 2005), 36.
12. Leo Strauss, *Persecution and the Art of Writing* (Chicago: University of Chicago Press, 1988), 24.
13. On Maurras's proto-fascism, see Ernst Nolte, *Three Faces of Fascism*, trans. Leila Vennewitz (London: Weidenfeld and Nicolson, 1965), 54–145; on Eliot and Maurras, see Kenneth Asher, *T. S. Eliot and Ideology* (Cambridge: Cambridge University Press, 1998), 11–59.
14. Irving Babbitt, *Rousseau and Romanticism* (Boston: Houghton Mifflin, 1919), 179.

15 T. E. Hulme, translator's preface to *Reflections on Violence*, Georges Sorel (London: Allen & Unwin, 1916), ix; Jean-Jacques Rousseau, *"The Social Contract" and Other Later Political Writings*, 2nd ed., edited and translated by Victor Gourevitch (Cambridge: Cambridge University Press, 2019), 43.
16 Babbitt, *Democracy and Leadership* (London: Constable, 1924), 119.
17 Reinhold Niebuhr, *The Children of Light and the Children of Darkness: A Vindication of Democracy and a Critique of Its Traditional Defence* (New York: Scribner, 1944), 15–33.
18 Joseph de Maistre, *St Petersburg Dialogues, or Conversations on the Temporal Government of Providence*, translated by Richard A. Lebrun (Montreal: McGill-Queen's University Press, 1993), 33.
19 Huysmans, J.-K., *À rebours* (Paris: Pour le Cent Bibliophiles, 1903), 154; Maistre, 34.
20 Isaiah Berlin, "Joseph de Maistre and the Origins of Fascism," in *The Crooked Timber of Humanity: Chapters in the History of Ideas*, 2nd ed., edited by Henry Hardy (Princeton: Princeton University Press, 2013), 93.
21 Charles Baudelaire, *"My Heart Laid Bare" and Other Texts*, trans. Rainer J. Hanshe (New York: Contra Mundum, 2020), 160; Berlin, *Crooked Timber*, 164.
22 T. J. Clark, "Greenberg's Theory of Art," *Critical Inquiry* 9, no. 1 (1982): 143; Alasdair Macintyre, *After Virtue: A Study in Moral Theory* (London: Duckworth, 1981), 244–5.
23 Schmitt, *Roman Catholicism and Political Form* [1923], translated by G. L. Ulmen (Westport: Greenwood, 1996), 25.
24 Schmitt, *Roman Catholicism*, 13.
25 Schmitt, *Roman Catholicism*, 25.
26 Schmitt, *Roman Catholicism*, 22.
27 David Hume, "Of the Original Contract" [1748], in *Political Essays*, edited by Knud Haakonssen (Cambridge: Cambridge University Press, 2006), 186–201.
28 Maistre, *Against Rousseau*, translated and edited by Richard A. Lebrun (Montreal: McGill-Queen's University Press, 1996).
29 Richard Hooker, *Of the Laws of Ecclesiastical Polity*, edited by Arthur Stephen McGrade (Cambridge: Cambridge University Press, 2004), 129.
30 Thomas Hobbes, *Leviathan* (London: Penguin, 1985), 192.
31 Hobbes, 217.
32 Hobbes, 220.
33 F. W. Maitland, "The Crown as Corporation," in *State, Trust and Corporation*, edited by David Runciman and Magnus Ryan (Cambridge: Cambridge University Press, 2003), 35; Edmund Burke, *Reflections on the Revolution in France*, in *Revolutionary Writings: Reflections on the Revolution in France and the First Letter on a Regicide Peace*, edited by Iain Hampsher-Monk (Cambridge: Cambridge University Press, 2014), 100–1.

14

The Perfect *Post*-Critic?

Sumita Chakraborty

To suggest that T. S. Eliot's approach to the art of criticism resembles post-critique may seem to be a perverse provocation, especially given that Eliot is best known for promoting "a pure contemplation from which all the accidents of personal emotion are removed" ("The Perfect Critic," *Prose2* 269). Remarks like this make it difficult to imagine Rita Felski's equally axiomatic question as one that bears upon Eliot's critical program: "Why are we so hyperarticulate about our adversaries and so excruciatingly tongue-tied about our loves?"[1] Also contributing to the seeming perversity is the distinction between Eliot's literary moment and our contemporary moment, in which, according to Felski,

> After decades of heady iconoclasm, after the bacchanalian joys of ripping up New Critical attitudes and scoffing at Leavisite platitudes, we are left nursing a Sunday morning hangover and wondering what fragments, if any, can be retrieved from the ruins.[2]

Eliot, of course, was not "after" New Criticism but pivotal to it, as much as he resisted the name itself and as much as his critical impulses differed substantially from New Critical maxims even as the New Critics turned to his material for inspiration. Post-critique emerges from a post-poststructuralist investment in what Felski calls "the rarefied air of metacommentary."[3] To put it broadly, scholars working in post-critique seek ways of engaging textual objects that differ from analytical methods that Eve Sedgwick once termed the "hermeneutics of suspicion." Where Sedgwick largely sought to interrogate trends in queer theory, however, post-critics see the hermeneutics of suspicion as a much wider phenomenon, describing the academy as an institution that solely privileges a readerly disposition of "distance and dislike" toward the textual object and what it might hold, as opposed to other affects that one might have toward a text, like love and intimacy.[4] As Felski and Elizabeth S. Anker write, to post-critics, "the intellectual or political payoff of interrogating, demystifying, and defamiliarizing"—critical gestures that post-critics perceive as, cumulatively, the sine qua non of "critique"—"is no longer quite so self-evident."[5]

Eliot makes an unlikely—and surprisingly flattering—cameo in Felski's *Hooked*. Although Felski conflates Eliot with New Criticism, describing him as "a byword for modernist impersonality and austere formalism," she turns to him as an example of how post-critical attitudes can be useful in pedagogical practice. Eliot was "deeply engaged with his working-class students at the University of London extension school," where he "revised assignments to speak to their interests, drew on anecdotes to render literature more accessible, and made connections between the labor of writing and his students' working lives."[6] Still, this example insinuates a distinction between Eliot's approach to literature on the page and in the classroom, insofar as it assumes that Eliot would have to revise, open, and build bridges to and from his own relation to literature to be viable in a classroom. There is a massive discrepancy between the critical inclinations attached to Eliot's critical legacy and those for which post-critics advocate most fiercely.

Yet I cannot stop hearing Eliot's voice in Felski's question about what "fragments, if any, can be retrieved from the ruins," especially considering the way this phrase alludes to the end of *The Waste Land*. In surprising ways, post-critique's methodological weariness echoes the fatigue of a poem emblematic of the catastrophic destruction of the First World War. Consider, too, the famous beginning of Bruno Latour's "Why Has Critique Run Out of Steam?," an essay now considered foundational for post-critical thought: "Wars. So many wars."[7] Latour shares with Eliot a sense of apprehension at a scale of global violence that, in each writer's moment, was unprecedented, altering the coordinates of what each thought warfare could look like (for Latour, September 11, 2001), and both are thus inspired to express exhaustion with conflict itself.

In what follows, I trace parallels between Eliot's approach to literary criticism and the aims of post-critique, first with an examination of the discrepancy between the statements with which Eliot's criticism is most commonly associated and the many other varied commitments found within his critical program, including his perhaps surprising affinity for joy and pleasure. I'll then examine how Eliot's investment in unity via literature parallels some of the projects of post-criticism. Finally, I'll consider the extent to which Eliot's proto-post-critical tendencies illuminate some limits of post-critique, particularly for those who believe that for their intellectual and political projects, critique has quite a bit of steam left in it.

The essays we now most commonly associate with Eliot—including "Tradition and the Individual Talent," "Hamlet," and "The Metaphysical Poets"—were written and published within two years (1919 for the first two, 1921 for the third), early in Eliot's career. This period represents a transitional zone between Eliot's juvenilia and early scholarship and his ascendance to literary fame and cultural celebrity, not to mention his confirmation in the Church of England in 1927 and his increased estrangement from his first wife. These essays have had such extraordinary afterlives that "extraordinary" somehow sounds like an understatement. As Anthony Cuda and Ronald Schuchard describe, they "furnish us with the signal concepts and phrases that have made Eliot's criticism a permanent feature of our monographs, syllabi, and anthologies, including the 'extinction of personality,' the 'objective correlative,' the 'dissociation of sensibility,' and the 'mythical method'" (*Prose2* xiii). But the full scope of the *Collected Prose* reveals—perhaps for the first time, in such an acute manner— that the extent to which they have come to synecdochally stand in for all of "Eliot's criticism" obscures the breadth, variety, and shifts of and within Eliot's body of work.

Eliot's views on impersonality, objectivity, and a depersonalized approach to criticism were much more varied than these early essays imply. While comprehension of the text remains Eliot's primary concern, on several occasions, the goal is not to attain an impersonalized mastery over the mysteries of the text but to experience an affect: joy. As Eliot grants in a 1956 essay, "The Frontiers of Criticism," understanding is the key to joy. Yet, as he also adds, it is futile to attempt understanding the textual object without also having experienced joy in response to it. He creates a chiastic circular logic that entangles pleasure and criticism: "It is certain that we do not fully enjoy a poem unless we understand it; and on the other hand, it is equally true that we do not fully understand a poem unless we enjoy it" (*Prose8* 115). Eliot's conviction regarding the importance of pleasure in critical inquiry is both remarkably nuanced and firm. He grants joy complexity, acknowledging, for example, that the concept does not mean one single thing, but rather "varies" depending on "the object inspiring joy." And while he acknowledges that literature can inspire negative emotions, only joy and its kin are granted a central role in the creation of literary criticism (*Prose8* 115). With this broader context in mind, it does seem Eliot believes literary criticism should be hyper-articulate about, and informed by, our loves.

I say this not to imply that the entirety of Eliot's critical orientation chimes well with the affective relationships to literature post-critique advocates. There is no easy way to characterize "the entirety of Eliot's critical orientation." For

Richard Shusterman, for example, "Eliot's early attack on impressionistic criticism was directed at exposing and correcting" the notion that enjoyment is possible without comprehension—an assertion that would not suit a post-critical agenda. But, as Shusterman (also citing from "The Frontiers of Criticism") continues, Eliot's "later theorizing warns against" the idea that enjoyment can be removed from interpretation, an admonition directed at "the one-sidedly narrow search for 'scientific' interpretive knowledge pursued by both historico-biographical criticism and 'the lemon-squeezer school' of New Criticism."[8] Just as a few select early critical principles have come to stand synecdochally for Eliot in a way that fails to fully reflect the scope of his prose writings, "Eliot" has also come to inaccurately stand in for a "New Critical" attitude toward literary criticism. Eliot's early essays began to influence New Critics *after* he had already turned toward a "moral theory of literature," into which, as Iman Javadi, Jayme Stayer, and Schuchard note in their introduction to the fifth volume of the *Complete Prose*, "the New Critics would not follow Eliot" (*Prose5* xxix). Not only are these single essays not "Eliot," but "Eliot" is also not "New Criticism."

Further, Eliot was also consistently willing to reassess his former views—even those views that drew New Critics to his work and have now become synonymous with his name. By 1931, for example, Eliot was distancing himself from his arguments regarding the "dissociation of sensibility" in the work of the metaphysical poets, following criticism about his "historical generalizations," electing not to pursue publishing the Clark Lectures, in which he broached those theses (*Prose4* xvii). By 1937, he'd even reassessed his earlier objections to *Hamlet* (*Prose5* xxx). "The Frontiers of Criticism" is, fundamentally, a comprehensive reevaluation: it begins with Eliot looking back at his earlier essay "The Function of Criticism" (written thirty-six years prior) and finding it "impossible to recall to mind the background of [his] outburst" (*Prose8* 121). He is relieved to find "nothing positively to contradict [his] present opinions," yet he finds himself unfamiliar with the premises of a "number of statements" he had made "with assurance and considerable warmth" (*Prose8* 121). (Perhaps the way this later essay finds him unable to recall his earlier discontents—and perfectly capable of recalling his lifelong affinities—is yet another demonstration of his preference for pleasure rather than conflict as a critical impetus.) The spirit of reevaluation also inspires him to reconsider his prior approach to "understanding," bluntly installing even more space between his preferences and New Critical tendencies: "I do not think that most poetry ... requires that sort of dissection for its enjoyment and understanding," he writes, even if, he admits, he himself as a poet has sometimes "led critics into temptation" (*Prose8* 127). And as for his understanding of his own critical merits, it comes from neither an alliance with New Criticism nor an association with the signal concepts that have since become famous (which he describes as "a few notorious phrases which have had a truly embarrassing success in the world") but rather from his "private poetry-workshop; or a prolongation of the thinking that went into the formation of [his] own verse" (*Prose8* 124). Eliot believes he is at his best when he is writing about "poets and poetic dramatists who had influenced [him]" (*Prose8* 124). The work of which Eliot is the proudest is not impersonal at all. It is a cumulative record of having been moved, throughout his life, by art.

When Eliot wrote to J. H. Woods, his supervisor at Harvard, in July 1915, to inform him he was resigning from doctoral study, he described his decision in relation to two different "wars," a metaphor that provides another—and much more pernicious—connection to post-critique. (By way of preview, recall Latour's weary "Wars. So many wars.") One of those wars was his decision to "start the battle" of "engag[ing] in literary work" in London; the other was the First World War, which "hastened" his marriage to Vivien Haigh-Wood and partially inspired his decision to stay in London (*Letters1* 117). From the beginning of Eliot's career, war—as both a material, historical event and a metaphor for his work and ambitions—was indispensable to his understanding of his literary career (*Letters1* 117). It's worth adding, too, that this conflation was also deeply practical: Eliot and Vivien's financial well-being was affected by Eliot's literary ambitions and the war, as he bluntly explains in an August 1915 letter to Conrad Aiken: "What I want is MONEY!$!£!! We are hard up! War!" (*Letters1* 121). After this eruption, he includes two lists in the style of Wyndham Lewis: one to "BLAST" Kaiser Wilhelm, Sir Edward Grey, the American ambassadors, and the Democrats and the other to "BLESS" Constantinople, himself, Harriet Monroe, and two military leaders.[9]

One of those leaders is Pierre François Joseph Benoit Rosalvo Bobo, a Haitian politician who opposed the United States' influence in Haiti and led a rebellion against the United States' sympathetic Haitian president Vilbrun Guillaume Sam. The other is Harold W. Blot, a US Marine Corps general who participated in the United States' subsequent invasion of Haiti, which lasted for approximately two decades, wreaking substantial havoc on the populace. These two figures are not simply "on different sides" of a conflict; their positions are antithetical, with one advocating for the independence of his people—a struggle with a long history— and the other fighting on behalf of yet another colonialist power that sought dominion over a non-white nation in the interests of its own global dominance.

Eliot's tendency to think of opponents as two sides of the same coin makes it difficult to assess his stance on war and his precise convictions in ideological or political conflicts. Eliot was famously one of the "Men of 1914"—Lewis's nickname linked to the pressures of the First World War, for himself, Eliot, James Joyce, Ezra Pound, and T. E. Hulme—and *The Waste Land* resonated widely as an expression of an anguished, war-torn world. But Eliot's correspondence is full of contradictions. To his mother in June 1918, he describes the war as a cataclysmic event: "The strain of life is very great and I fear it will be for the rest of the lives of anyone now on earth. I am very pessimistic about the world we are going to have to live in after the war" (*Letters1* 267). Eleven years later, though, in an August 1929 letter to E. M. Forster, he addresses the meaning of *The Waste Land*: "I only think that you exaggerate the importance of the War in this context. The War crippled me as it did everyone else; but me chiefly because it was something I was neither honestly in nor honestly out of" (*Letters4* 573). This slipperiness regarding warfare also extends to a resistance against expressing ideological or political allegiances. Later, as has been the subject of much discussion, Eliot seems to approach fascism and communism with equal anxiety (*Prose5* xviii–xix). And as Vincent Sherry points out, Eliot—like many of his modernist compatriots—increasingly resisted the language of "reason" that dominated English Liberal rhetoric.[10] As Eliot moved more deeply into his conviction in his faith, he became increasingly suspicious of liberalism and capitalism—as well as "ineffective democracy and secularism" (*Prose5* xx). Certainly, it makes a great deal of sense that anyone might find little in the business of nation-states that accord with one's ethical vision; yet, it is uncommonly and uncomfortably difficult for a reader to come away with a clear sense of Eliot's own convictions.

While Eliot often appears to resist taking a position on any side of any given conflict or antagonism, he *does* consistently advocate for a vision of unity via literature. During the final years of and following the Second World War, much of his literary energy went to holding various positions dedicated to unifying the Western world around, and with, literature. These efforts include his work as president of Books Across the Sea, which was initially established as a countermeasure to the distribution of Nazi propaganda and then morphed, in the final years of the war, into a method of unifying British and American literary cultures.[11] Following the Second World War, Eliot's "earlier 'idea' of a Christian society ... had developed into the 'idea' of a European society, and his vision of the essentials of cultural unity would soon find completion in *Notes towards the Definition of a Culture*," in which Eliot advocates for an unconscious unity among people (*Prose7* xi). Eliot champions unity (and uniformity) of purpose rather than difference (or conflict). Eliot's insistence on joy is also a part of this vision of unity, his stance mirroring the "happily diverse" self-ideation of the British Empire, which Sara Ahmed describes as "a project of social description: to see happily is not to see violence, asymmetry, or force."[12] The ability to include both Bobo and Blot on the same line—a line that calls for both to be "blessed," no less—is coterminous with a vision of a world unified by Western literature, and both hold at their heart a belief in joy as the dominant reason for literary engagement.

In both a modernist context and our contemporary critical moment, this emphasis on unity—and literature's role in building it—is driven by the advent of new vistas of warfare. Marina MacKay notes that "the history of aerial bombing overlaps almost entirely with the history of modernism itself," including not only the most iconic bombings of the Spanish War and the Second World War but also "the fact that aerial bombing had been sanctioned thirty years earlier in a range of imperial contexts, British, French, and Italian."[13] (The occupation of Haiti by the US military was, in fact, one early example.) Eliot's response to this traumatic history calls to mind the post-critical response to recent political catastrophes. One could imagine a niche game show in which contestants were asked to guess whether the author of the following sentences was T. S. Eliot or Bruno Latour: "Should we be at war, too, we, the scholars, the intellectuals? Is it really our duty to add fresh ruins to fields of ruins?"[14] For that matter, could such a game be played with Felski's articulation that criticism should help literary studies find answers to the question "Why, after all, should literature matter?"[15] In a conflict-riven world, such views hold that disagreement is a much less worthy project than building unity.

This resistance to division is a consistent feature of post-critique, which is unified by the conviction that we ought to turn our attention to figuring out how to rebuild, cohere, and energize ourselves in response to contemporary assaults on the humanities and progressive politics alike. (Their conflation of "literary war" with actual war parallels Eliot's own.) As Felski and Anker put it, "The concern is that a pervasive mood of suspicion, ennui, or irony, in this regard, can easily become debilitating, both intellectually and politically."[16] In turn, it is thought that such "debilitation" requires a cure, that that cure entails the construction or creation of something else, and that this cure cannot come from any methodology that has ever been used to deconstruct something. Of the modes of analysis Felski offers as alternatives to critique, the most important practice appears to be "composing," which shares with Latour an investment in putting down the hammer (or the sledgehammer) and in picking up some other tool that can make sense of the rubble. Shall we at least set our lands in order?

While sympathetic to some of post-critique's aims, I struggle with it intellectually and politically. Critiques of post-critique with which I resonate have been written by Sheila Liming, Eleni Coundouriotis and Lauren M. E. Goodlad, David Kurnick, Anna Kornbluh, and, especially, Sangeeta Ray.[17] I referenced the relation between Latour's "Why Has Critique Run Out of Steam?" and the post-9/11 moment from which it comes; Ray incisively points out that understandings of that moment and its demands diverge starkly along the lines of subject positions and of the scholar's ethical commitments (including whether or not to accept the narrative of "9/11-as-event"). I am compelled by Ray's skepticism regarding how Latour's understandable dismay with far-right rhetoric has led to some rather questionable conclusions: "Living in his small French village, he is appalled by conspiracy theories regarding acts of terror, especially 9/11, and urges us to understand that … 'our critical equipment deserves as much scrutiny as the Pentagon budget' (really!!)."[18] In fact, a great deal of post-critical work has reacted to right-wing appropriations of critique's interpretive strategies precisely by suggesting that literary critics should take up the work of dismantling (or at least deprioritizing) those interpretive moves themselves, as if the project of critique were responsible for right-wing malfeasance and ill faith. I find this conclusion questionable. Eliot's affinities with post-critique might help recast its liberatory aspirations in a light that reveals how it reinforces the hierarchies it aims to combat.

While Eliot's penchant for unity has often been read as an understandable effect of his religious faith, his letter to Conrad Aiken in 1915—"GEN. BOBO GEN. BLOT"—indicates that a form of "both sides"–ism, the gnarlier cousin of the idea of "unity" (and one that has gained right-wing traction in the 2020s), was a part of Eliot's thinking from his earliest days, well before his religious conversion. His unwillingness to differentiate between these two persons and their contexts, and, more still, his decision to designate them both as worthy of blessings, is as hard of a (red?) pill to swallow when considered in Eliot's historical context, in which the United States' occupation of Haiti was about to begin, as it is in our own, in which Haiti is again facing an instability that is the product of the States' (and France's, and Spain's) long-standing colonialist violence. Accordingly, Eliot's proto-post-critical impulses offer a stark example of how, to borrow a phrase from Patricia Stuelke, "repair is entangled with the very history and practices of neoliberal empire and the settler colonial carceral state."[19] An awareness of the relationship between colonialism and literary publishing also puts a less optimistic sheen on Books Across the Sea. It is far from groundbreaking to point out that the export of literature and the English language has long been a fundamental colonial weapon. The history of Books Across the Sea is a perfect example: the English-Speaking Union (ESU) took over the organization in 1947 and continues its project until this day in a vastly expanded form, dedicated to the notion that "people who shared a common language would soon discover that they also shared similar values, whatever their differences in nationality or background."[20]

And while we can see that Eliot's investment in outreach fits into an admirable lifelong pattern of literary citizenship outside of the academy, which is a fundamental tenet of post-critique's ambitions, his counter-institutional work also helps us to see that when we define "institution" largely in terms of higher education, we run the risk of taking our most sinister institutions—such as racism and misogyny—along with us as we flee to allegedly safer ground. For example: Eliot's rebellion from the too-stifling halls of academe also took place in letters and in poems, and often in the form of what Michael North describes as "racial ventriloquism."[21] Eliot's identity as "Old Possum" (a nickname found not only in his letters and in the title *Old Possum's Book of Practical Cats* but also in the signature line of some of his public prose)—a guise in which he crawls and climbs mischievously, lovingly, and joyously through his poetry and prose alike—is not so much immune from the ailments of the institution as it is contingent on a shared language of racist rhetoric. If people who share a common language share a common set of values, as the ESU claims, then the language of Eliot's noninstitutional literary community—with which he collaborated, argued, refined his thinking, and developed his sense of what literature and literary criticism can do—demonstrates that fetishizing the flight from the institution and its predilections may be as dangerous as fetishizing the institution.

Eliot's post-academic writing frequently exudes the joy for which he advocates in reading poetry. His racist pantomimes do, too. Which brings me back to the sentence from "The Frontiers of Criticism" I earlier cited: "I do not think that most poetry … requires that sort of dissection for its enjoyment and understanding." Here, as in many post-critical works, "dissection" and "enjoyment" are opposed to one another. I'm reminded of a point Jane Gallop has most recently, and most persuasively, made: "If we look at critique not in the theoretical abstract but in its historical effectiveness, we can see that rather than alternating between a critique moment and an appreciation moment, to effect real change we have needed both at the same time."[22] If one sees taking a position within a conflict, or laboring to fight an institution, as indispensable to one's work—especially, as Gallop also notes, if one is committed to "struggles against racism, homophobia, and ableism"—it's worth holding onto the example that many minoritarian critics have set of simultaneously embracing dissection *and* enjoyment.[23] I'm empathetic with both Eliot's and post-critics' desire to feel as though they're building something rather than tearing things down. But, and at the risk of sounding like the enemy of all pleasure, Eliot's weariness with conflict in all forms and the racist pantomimes that sustain his "shadowy antitype of the institution" show that plenty of occasions perfectly well call for a hammer or a sledgehammer, which are, after all, also tools made for building.

Notes

1. Rita Felski, *The Limits of Critique* (Chicago: University of Chicago Press, 2015), 12.
2. Felski, 15.
3. Felski, 15.
4. Sheila Liming, "Fighting Words," *Los Angeles Review of Books*, December 14, 2020.
5. Elizabeth S. Anker and Felski, introduction to *Critique and Postcritique* (Durham: Duke University Press, 2017), 1.
6. Felski, *Hooked: Art and Attachment* (Chicago: University of Chicago Press, 2020), 155.
7. Bruno Latour, "Why Has Critique Run Out of Steam? From Matters of Fact to Matters of Concern," *Critical Inquiry* 30 (Winter 2004): 253.
8. Richard Shusterman, "T. S. Eliot on Reading: Pleasure, Games, and Wisdom," *Philosophy and Literature* 11, no. 1 (April 1987), 4.
9. Eliot contributed two poems to the second and final issue of Lewis's *BLAST*, which was published a few months before this letter to Aiken. His lists parody the Vorticist manifesto published in the magazine's first issue.
10. Vincent Sherry, *The Great War and the Language of Modernism* (Oxford: Oxford University Press, 2003).
11. See, for example, "Presidential message to Books Across the Sea" (*Prose6* 418) and David Chinitz and Ronald Schuchard's introduction of Eliot's wartime criticism (*Prose6* xxviii).
12. Sara Ahmed, *The Promise of Happiness* (Durham: Duke University Press, 2010), 131–2.
13. Marina MacKay, *Modernism, War, and Violence* (London: Bloomsbury, 2017), 136.
14. Latour, "Why Has Critique Run Out of Steam?," 253.
15. Felski, *Limits*, 14.
16. Anker and Felski, introduction to *Critique and Postcritique*, 20.

17 In order, the pieces to which I refer are Eleni Coundouriotis and Lauren M. E. Goodlad's "What Is and Isn't Changing?," *Modern Language Quarterly* 81, no. 4 (December 2020): 399–418; David Kurnick's "A Few Lies: Queer Theory and Our Method Melodramas," *ELH* 87, no. 2 (Summer 2020): 547–72; and Anna Kornbluh's "Extinct Critique," *South Atlantic Quarterly* 111, no. 4 (October 2020): 767–77. Liming's is in my first note. For Sangeeta Ray's, please see the following note.
18 Sangeeta Ray, "Postcolonially Speaking?" *MLQ* 81, no. 4 (December 2020): 555.
19 Patricia Stuelke, *The Ruse of Repair: US Neoliberal Empire and the Turn from Critique* (Durham, NC: Duke University Press, 2021), 17.
20 "About Us." Mission & History, English-Speaking Union, accessed July 7, 2021, https://www.esuus.org/esu/about/mission/.
21 Michael North, *The Dialect of Modernism: Race, Language, and Twentieth-Century Literature* (Oxford: Oxford University Press, 1998), 8.
22 Jane Gallop, "Has Postcritque Run Out of Steam?," *symploke* 28, nos. 1–2 (2020): 535.
23 Gallop, 535.

Part III

Looking Ahead

15

T. S. Eliot and the Humanities to Come

Simon During

The future is not an easy topic for scholarship. After all, there is nothing there—yet—to be scholarly about. Eliot himself went further. In a 1927 review he declared that "To be interested in 'the future'" is "a symptom of demoralization and debility," only to qualify his condemnation by making a useful distinction ("Charleston, Hey! Hey!," *Prose3* 25). There are two kinds of future, Eliot suggested. On the one side, there is "the future of the present," which is the future that we plan for. On the other, "the future of the future," which is the "future beyond our power" and which Eliot further dismissed because we can only conceive of it in "dreams" (25). Or, as he might have added, in prophecy.

The distinction between the present present and present future is less clear than Eliot claimed, which becomes quickly apparent when one is thinking about the future of the humanities today. As we all know, the humanities are being rapidly transformed. They are becoming detached from the canons, hierarchies, legitimations, and authority in which they were established in Europe over centuries. The sense that the high humanities, whose past stretches back to the classical era, are vital to the status and flourishing of society (a sense which has long been under stress) is now vanishing.[1] In this situation, the humanities' present future is so opaque that it might as well be a future future. Planning and prophecy merge. Unsurprisingly, my remarks here belong more to prophecy than to planning.

The humanities' transformation is happening under pressures that seem to be intensifying. As we know, the academic literary humanities have had to endure the embrace of business models and managerialism by academic administrators—a creeping side effect of the global economy's opening after 1989 and the consequent drive to impose market relations upon all productive forces. At the same time, large-scale technological changes have marginalized print and print culture—the received humanities' life blood. In addition, the high humanities are being reshaped by the movement toward decolonization, which not just provincializes Europe's heritage but often situates it as fundamentally racist, imperialist, and white. In the end, these pressures need not be thought of as independent of each other. In complex ways they feed off each other, various wills for emancipation combining with the will to extend productivity and market mechanisms.

The current dissolution of the humanities affects literature and English departments especially powerfully. In the period between about 1920 and 1980, English was the most popular humanities discipline of them all, but over recent decades that has changed.[2] English departments are shrinking. They are cutting courses, especially graduate programs. With less demand, there are thus fewer avenues for professional careers. My own view is that the most important of the various reasons for this change has been the emergence of digital technologies rather than anything more ideological: young people's interest in and familiarity with literature is decreasing largely because the internet, social media, and so on offer more intensity, speed, reach, interchange, and connectivity than do books. Yet, the survival of English departments depends on their continuing appeal to adolescents.

There is very little we can do about the diminished appeal of English, and it isn't clear to me that, from a dispassionate point of view, it is even worth deploring. However, this depletion of traditional literary desire does not mean that students will no longer want to study literature, just that fewer will. Those students who do remain will surely expect to analyze literature in new ways and contexts, which means that English departments will have to evolve. My prophetic argument: Eliot can help us plan this development.

Eliot's remarks about planning and prophecy also downplay his own lifelong interest in time. Across his career as a poet and as a critic, he was driven by the ambition to realize ways of thinking about time and history other than the linear and historicist one in which a knowable present constantly advances toward an unknowable future, leaving a known past in its wake. Eliot aimed to dynamize relations among past, present, and future so that the past and future continually change as the present changes. That, famously, was a point of "Tradition and the Individual Talent" as well as, more obliquely, of *The Waste Land*. After his conversion to Anglicanism, and in another spirit, Eliot attempted to create artifacts of language in which eternity might intersect with the human, fallen, temporal order. That was a point of *Four Quartets* and his verse dramas.

Eliot's assaults on linear and progressive time may not help us much in thinking about the future of the humanities right now. It is worth reminding ourselves, however, that absorbing those assaults on linear/progressive time has been, and still might be, of value to the humanities, even if only by admonishing them. There is a sense in which Eliot's mystical commitment to the idea that, as he phrased it in *Burnt Norton*,

> Time present and time past
> Are both perhaps present in time future,
> And time future contained in time past.
> If all time is eternally present
> All time is unredeemable

might make us sensitive to the possibility that the attraction of his own work may be bound to its unredeemability (*Poems1* 177).

Any more down-to-earth thinking about Eliot and the future of the humanities has to begin with one extraordinary fact. By the end of the Second World War, Eliot had become "the most important figure in twentieth-century English language literary culture," as Louis Menand recently put it—and indeed, as John Xiros Cooper has reminded us, not just the Anglophone humanities either.[3] But in an amazing reversal, by about 1990 Eliot was if not exactly a persona non grata, at least one of those formerly august figures who most clearly represented the authority and hierarchy of the old, received high humanities, and thus too their whiteness, patriarchalism, and Eurocentrism. Let me put it this way: more than just about anyone, Eliot came to represent all that the liberatory spirit of 1968, in its various forms and aftermaths, sought to overturn.

This is not the place to try to account for this reversal, although it is worth remembering that Eliot, for all his immediately postwar authority, had always been denounced by the Left—let George Orwell's (admittedly rather idiosyncratic) review of *Notes towards the Definition of Culture* (1948), which concentrated on the impracticality of Eliot's defense of inherited class difference, stand as an example.[4] A more substantial backlash began in the mid-1950s in Raymond Williams's *Culture and Society* (1958), which, while praising (and absorbing) Eliot's concept of culture as a "whole way of life" and also his understanding that culture happens at different levels (in "sub-cultures"), complained that Eliot had "closed almost all the existing roads" toward the future.[5] Already for Williams, future thinking needed to leave Eliot behind.

Williams's critique of Eliot was elaborated by the new Left's next generation. Terry Eagleton, Francis Mulhern, John Fekete, and Chris Baldick all expanded it.[6]

No less tellingly, Edward Said, who did more than anyone to trigger the internal critique of the received humanities' Eurocentrism, but who was also among the first major literary intellectuals to recognize the threat that managerialism, decolonization, and identity politics posed to the received humanities, was never reconciled to Eliot's legacy, regarding him to the end as the agent of "austere canonizations of European monuments."[7] More recent writers like Stefan Collini and Mark Greif, who have little truck with radicalism and might be expected to be more open to Eliot's legacy, also do not apply the full extent of their sympathies to him. Collini, for instance, accuses Eliot of "wilful elusiveness," "ambitious self-fashioning," "fastidious nose-holding," "mock humility," and so on, and he cites Ezra Pound's famous bon mot, according to which Eliot had "arrived at the supreme Eminence among English critics largely through disguising himself as a corpse."[8]

In the face of all this, I want to argue that Eliot can and should retain a place in the humanities but—here's the catch—that can happen only in a very particular, perhaps counterintuitive, way.

Even were we to lift the siege mentality in which the study of canonical white men now so often proceeds, Eliot's work would still be available in the academy only in small historically based courses and research fields—at least to the degree that they continue to exist at all. Eliot has already become for Anglophone modernism something like what Coleridge is for Anglophone romanticism, a controversial figure from quite another era. Both Johns Hopkins University Press's recent eight-volume scholarly edition of Eliot's *Complete Prose* and Christopher Ricks and Jim McCue's annotated edition of the collected and uncollected poems are pinnacles of erudition and will be extraordinarily useful to those who work in the field. But they are also emblems of pious monumentalization. This monumentalized Eliot is not the Eliot who can offer most for the future of the humanities.

My hunch is that Eliot's early literary criticism is what will retain practical vital power. It can be called on to help us reshape the English department in ways that might allow that institution to survive under conditions that are difficult now and that will surely only become harsher. The English department is pivotal to Eliot's future, because without strong English departments it is unlikely that even Eliot as a poet will be much remembered.

During his lifetime, Eliot was successful as a man of letters in a variety of modes. He was, of course, first and foremost a poet, in both the experimental mode of his first period and the more vatic and theological mode that followed after *Ash-Wednesday* (1927). He was, second, a literary critic, whose groundbreaking magazine essays after 1917 presented methods and concepts that formed a basis for the (popular) twentieth-century English department up until about 1970. Third, after his conversion to Anglicanism in 1926, Eliot became a conservative Christian social/cultural critic, who helped spur on even the Left cultural studies that was early to reject him. Fourth, in the 1940s and 1950s, he was a successful dramatist, extending a fashion for serious verse-drama. Fifth, he was editor of the *Criterion* (1922–39), the journal that most nearly approached the gravitas and sway of the great nineteenth-century quarterlies. Last, as a director of Faber & Faber, he was the outstanding British literary publisher of his time.

To understand why, of these various contributions, it is Eliot's early criticism that might best help keep his work alive and provide a tool for restructuring English departments, we must remind ourselves what that criticism was, as well as to reexamine the context in which it appeared.

Eliot's intervention into the Anglophone literary world was just about as revolutionary in his criticism as in his poetry. In the essays collected in *The Sacred Wood* (1920), as well as in the not-there-included essay "A Brief Treatise on the Criticism of Poetry," published that same year in the *Chapbook*, Eliot outlined a program for criticism that broke with received models.

Eliot's first move was to make a firm distinction between criticism and reviewing, the latter of which he thought of as the sharing of "impressions" as well as a kind of "discreet advertisement" (*Prose2* 206). Unlike reviewing, criticism attends to the poem as a constructed artifact, a work of art, and as nothing else. (In these essays Eliot focused on poems and "poetry," a word which for our purposes can stand for literary texts of any genre.) Unlike reviewing too, criticism is not based on a personal, affective response to a work. It is not "sentimental." Nor is it sociological. A literary text might indeed be a "social document," but that too is of no interest to criticism proper (204). The critic's interests in texts are not philosophical or moral or historical, and when critics do think about literature philosophically or historically or morally, they are writing as philosophers or historians or are doing critique (as we would say), not writing as critics. Critics are no more psychologists or aestheticians. A significant section of "The Perfect Critic," one of Eliot's more trenchant statements of purpose, is devoted to condemning Edmund Gosse's psychologistic definition of poetry as "the most highly organized form of intellectual activity" (*Prose2* 262), a formulation that would soon be echoed by I. A. Richards in *The Principles of Literary Criticism* (1924), where poetry is said to offer one of those "most valuable states of mind" that involve "the most comprehensive co-ordination of activities."[9] For Eliot, criticism had no relation to pseudo-scientific formulations of this kind.

What skills might a critic bring to bear so as to respond fully just to words on the page?

The first of Eliot's key arguments is that the perfect critic is probably also a poet:

> You cannot understand the technique of poetry unless you are to some extent capable of performing this operation ... The critic of poetry needs the same professional equipment as the poet: the same knowledge of poetry, the same enjoyment of it, the same ear and eye, the same philology, the same general education.[10]

For Eliot, to appreciate how a poem works you need to have tinkered with constructing one yourself.

The second of Eliot's key arguments is vaguer. What the critic brings to bear on the poem are not private emotional associations or a store of facts or, of course, an ideological or moral program and interest, but simply "intelligence."[11] This intelligence is not innate. It is a function of "sensibility" formed by the long accumulation of "impressions" that have (somehow) become a "structure."[12] I suspect that what this rather obscure formulation means is that critics need to have lived sufficiently intensely and broadly, and also to have read enough, for their responses to be sufficiently coherent and for as little as possible of each work's presence, order, and force to be lost.

The critic's experienced, trained, and focused intelligence also takes the form of an "enquiry," but not one that asks, "what does this poem mean?" Eliot is not interested in interpretation. Rather it asks: "how does this text work? How was it put together?" And then, "does it succeed and if so why?"

The third of Eliot's important early arguments was that the success of a text may be judged by this crucial standard: "Permanent literature is always a presentation: either a presentation of thought, or a presentation of feeling by a statement of events in human action or objects in the external world" ("The Possibility of a Poetic Drama," *Prose2* 280). A presentation, *not* a representation. Good (or "permanent") literature is literature in which abstraction and emotion—the stringencies of thought and the contingencies of subjectivity—are constrained in being expressed in events or objects.

It should already be clear that Eliot's program for criticism was skeptical and subtractive. He insisted on what we (but not he) would call the "autonomy" of the text and did so by rejecting almost all the forms of writing about literature then current. His positive program was minimalist and atomistic. It took each text on its own terms and paid attention to its construction and to its qualities—that is, to the force and reality of its (impersonal) presentation of the world.

For our purposes, Eliot's last significant argument was that writing literature and writing criticism were mutually dependent. On the one hand, strong creative writing needed a critical sense, that is, the kind of knowledge and experience proper to the critic. On the other hand, criticism was a mode of writing that had to be constructed and that required flair and skill. This point is key to my argument to come.

Before considering why this critical program might be useful to the future English department, it is relevant to sketch briefly the academic and intellectual context in which Eliot's program was invented. Eliot's early criticism is perhaps best understood as a response to what was happening at the time in academic philosophy, and more concretely, it turned the principles and findings of what would soon become analytic philosophy on to another field—literary criticism. Eliot invented a new form of criticism basically by shunting analytic philosophy's original program onto the study of literature, if in a different tone and rhetoric.

Eliot had been a PhD student in philosophy in the period when a completely new mode of philosophizing was making its way into the discipline.[13] This new mode was invented by Gottlob Frege, G. E. Moore, Bertrand Russell, and Ludwig Wittgenstein, among others. In the form in which it would become canonical, it broke with both idealism and pragmatism, allowing it to develop a radical, if more modest, understanding of what philosophy could do. Eliot was familiar with this new analytic mode: he attended Russell's classes outlining a version of the new philosophy at Harvard (indeed he taught it to undergraduates) and, on coming to Oxford on a scholarship, was invited to present a paper in Russell's rooms at Trinity College, Cambridge—the movement's very center, where Russell had met Wittgenstein. Eliot's own PhD thesis had been on the post-Hegelian idealist philosopher F. H. Bradley. It contended with, but did not embrace, the new thought. But if, as a philosopher, Eliot did not sign up to the new method, his early literary criticism is, in my view, profoundly shaped by it nonetheless.

The core of this new philosophy was based on the argument that truth was not a function of the relation between ideas and the world but of the relation between statements and states of affairs. A proposition was true if and only if what it stated was a fact out there in reality. Truth did not come into question in relations between mind and world but only between propositions and facts, so that, for instance, the statement "x is y" is true if and only if x is y. So for the new philosophy (at first called the "new realism" in the United States), instead of the world existing in the traces that it leaves on and in our private consciousness, there existed an external world out there. And instead of mind and consciousness, there was language.[14]

At the heart of this shift lay Frege's new transformational logic that substituted a "function-argument" analysis for a "subject-predicate" one, so that, for instance, a sentence like "Jenny is a child" is not parsed as grammatical structure in which "Jenny" is the subject and "a child" the predicate but as an *instance* of the general function "x is a child."[15] "Is" no longer denotes a (problematic) relation: it denotes membership of a set. And the old idealist understanding that members of a set share an essential quality was replaced by the concept that a set consisted only of whatever was counted into it. Instead of essences, instances. Representation is replaced by instantiation as the framework for truth procedures.

This revision of philosophy had a profound ripple effect on the academy. It stimulated Eliot's program, which would form the basis of the twentieth-century English department. It also stimulated a new field established by A. O. Lovejoy, who, like Eliot, was a refugee from the Harvard battles between the new realists, the idealists, and the pragmatists. Lovejoy's "history of ideas" attempted to reduce philosophy's conceptual power by placing ideas in time's flow. At Oxford, R. G. Collingwood was another refugee from these struggles, and in his escape he too attempted a "rapprochement between philosophy and history," as he put it.[16] Collingwood provided the intellectual basis for what would later become the "Cambridge School" of intellectual history. That school would openly jettison the concept of "ideas" and replace it by discursive acts performed in various contexts. More speculatively, I'd suggest that, if early analytic philosophy did not actually influence, it did prepare the way for Lewis Namier's "prosography," which used data about individuals to explain political events seemingly organized around parties, values, and communities. Namier's revisionism ushered in that revolution in historical research, which would change the discipline's relation to the archive.[17] In sum: these ripples out from Fregian analytic philosophy as devised by Moore, Russell, and Wittgenstein would help shape the twentieth-century humanities by forming what we might call a *modernist* stream within them, across various disciplines.

Eliot's early criticism belongs to this movement most obviously in that it was primarily focused on *language*, not "meaning" or consciousness or beauty, for instance. It was analytical in the sense that it was interested in how words were put together to form literary works. And it shared the new philosophy's realism: its commitment to the external world as the test of truth. As we have seen, it judged literary works not by how they represented the world or by their impact on their readers but by the ways in which they used language to present the (or *a*) world. Finally, just as the new philosophy undermined the basis of idealism, not least in its Kantian and Hegelian forms with their moral, quasi-theological implications, Eliot's criticism was positioned not only against romanticism (affective subjectivism unbound, as he viewed it) but against Arnoldian/Humboldtian *Bildung*, with its own progressivist moral freight.

Most trenchantly, if less concretely, Eliot's criticism was, like analytic philosophy, intellectually modest in the sense that it did not claim to offer a vision, to inspire with ideals, or to ground cultural values. Analytic philosophy merely offered a mode of analysis of, and a limitation on, what could be said to be true. Eliot's criticism was modest that way too. It offered a method by which those interested in literature, for whatever reason and from whatever background, might learn to write and judge more astutely.

The English department of the future will, I believe, need to be post-ideological in that way. It will welcome students from various cultures and backgrounds, with various "identities" attaching to different values and interests, who hold various political and religious views. What will bring them into the department is not a shared ethical/cultural program (a shared essence in philosophical terms) but an interest in reading and writing. They will want to lower the barriers among communication, creative writing, reviewing, and criticism, while also clarifying what those barriers are. In the new English department, students will be trained to write in all these genres. They will understand that these genres, and especially creative writing and criticism, have mutual dependencies as well as defining differences.

Crucially, the English department to come will welcome young people whose primary interest is to *write* (creatively, journalistically, whatever) and then bind them to literary criticism. Students will be led to understand that if you are to judge whether you are writing well, you need to have read a great deal, not least canonical texts. The new English department will disparage professionalism and "research." All this, Eliot's program not just allows but encourages. It is, as we have begun to see, a program of criticism for that minority who want to write, especially creatively, and who thus take writing seriously enough to study its various modes and times—but who need not wish to make large collective claims for literature's social, moral, or political sway. The English department's ethos will succor enquiry and experimentation.

In this modest form, the English department might survive the dissolution of the old humanities and the waning of interest in high literature and so, among much else, keep Eliot's own contributions alive in an era that will have little tolerance of, for instance, the Christian conservatism of his later work, such as

The Idea of a Christian Society (1940). But one feature of Eliot's later thought will remain pertinent: his insistence that *institutions* matter—not the orthodox Christian Church, which was of course the institution to which he was loyal, but rather the modest, marginalized English department. Not, then, the English department as the Church's spiritual successor, a (Leavisite) possibility about which Eliot was scornful. Indeed, he could not even reconcile himself to the ways in which the criticism that he had pioneered was being academically institutionalized. But he would have accepted, I think, the English department that I am imagining here: the English department as a bolt hole for writing nerds.

Of course, Eliot's program for criticism faltered in the end, as did the various modernist disciplinary formations to which it was loosely allied. It may be that English departments cannot consistently be as modest as Eliot's early criticism proposed. It may be that they will always be tempted to assign political, moral, cultural, and spiritual purposes to themselves. Perhaps, practically speaking, the study of writing can never separate writing from the messy world that it engages. In *The Idea of a Christian Society* and elsewhere, Eliot himself came to think that the culture (and the humanities and literary criticism most of all) could not maintain its social power unless it was legitimated and ordered by religious orthodoxy, a skeptical view that does not contradict his earlier critical program—and one that it is still too soon to prove wrong. Whatever the case in this regard, accepting Eliotic criticism's institutional, conceptual, and cultural fragility is no reason not to call on it to inspire the reshaping of the English department in times when the humanities and the enormous academic/bureaucratic apparatus built up around them are in startling decline.

Notes

1 The argument that tensions over the humanities' social function date back at least to Wilhelm von Humboldt's period is made in Paul Reitter and Chad Wellmon, *Permanent Crisis: The Humanities in a Disenchanted Age* (Chicago: University of Chicago Press, 2021).

2 Modern literary criticism's intellectual energy and institutional success were often overlooked between about 1970 and 2000, the period of theory's emergence and the canon wars. There are now signs, however, that it is once again being acknowledged. See, for instance, Timothy Aubry, *Guilty Aesthetic Pleasures* (Cambridge: Harvard University Press, 2018); Joseph North, *Literary Criticism: A Concise Political History* (Cambridge: Harvard University Press, 2017); and the 2014 *Modern*

Language Quarterly special issue on the history of literary criticism, under the title "Lessons from the Past." For the English department's popularity, see Julie A. Reuben, *The Making of the Modern University: Intellectual Transformation and the Marginalization of Morality* (Chicago: University of Chicago Press, 1996), 202.

3 Louis Menand, *The Free World: Art and Thought in the Cold War* (New York: Farrar, Straus and Giroux, 2021), 457; John Xiros Cooper, *T. S. Eliot and the Ideology of "Four Quartets"* (Cambridge: Cambridge University Press, 1995), 28ff.

4 George Orwell, "Review of *Notes towards the Definition of Culture*," in *The Collected Journalism and Letters of George Orwell, vol IV: In Front of Your Nose 1945–1950* (London: Secker & Warburg, 1969), 455–7.

5 Raymond Williams, *Culture and Society: Coleridge to Orwell, 1780–1950* (1958; London: Hogarth Press 1993), 175.

6 See, for instance, Terry Eagleton, *The Function of Criticism* (London: Verso, 1984), 100; Francis Mulhern, *Culture/Metaculture* (London: Routledge, 2000), 51–4; John Fekete, *The Critical Twilight: Explorations in the Ideology of Anglo-American Literary Theory from Eliot to McLuhan* (London: Routledge, 1977), 29–31; Chris Baldick, *The Social Mission of Literary Criticism, 1848–1932* (Oxford: Oxford University Press, 1983), 109–24.

7 Edward W. Said, *Reflections on Exile and Other Essays* (Cambridge: Harvard University Press, 2000), 132.

8 I have drawn these phrases from Stefan Collini, *Absent Minds: Intellectuals in Britain* (Oxford: Oxford University Press, 2006), 304–22. The Pound citation is taken from William Chace, *The Political Identities of Ezra Pound and T. S. Eliot* (Stanford: Stanford University Press, 1973), 221. See also Mark Greif, *The Age of the Crisis of Man: Thought and Fiction in America, 1933–1973* (Princeton: Princeton University Press, 2015), 70–1.

9 I. A. Richards, *Principles of Literary Criticism*, 2nd ed. (1926; London: Routledge, 2004), 53.

10 Richards, 204.

11 Richards, 268.

12 Richards, 269–70.

13 There is, of course, a substantial scholarly literature on Eliot's relation to philosophy, going back at least as far as Hugh Kenner's *The Invisible Poet: T. S. Eliot* (New York: McDowell, Obolensky, 1959)—one of whose canonical moments is Richard Wollheim's "Eliot and F. H. Bradley: an Account," in *Eliot in Perspective*, edited by Graham Martin (London: Macmillan, 1970), 168–93. Perhaps the most thoroughgoing analysis remains Walter Benn Michaels's "Philosophy in Kinkanja: Eliot's Pragmatism," *Glyph* 8 (1980): 170–202. Among the recent literature, I have found Jewel Spears Brooker's *T. S. Eliot's Dialectical Imagination* (Baltimore: Johns Hopkins University Press, 2018) and Eric Sigg's *The American*

T. S. Eliot: A Study of the Early Writings (Cambridge: Cambridge University Press, 1989) especially useful for my purposes. Much of this scholarship argues that Bradley is the key figure in Eliot's philosophical orientation; see, for instance, Piers Gray's exhaustive *T. S. Eliot's Intellectual and Poetic Development 1909–1922* (Brighton: Harvester, 1982) and Louis Menand, *Discovering Modernism: T. S. Eliot and His Context*, 2nd ed. (Oxford: Oxford University Press, 2007), 43–53. But that consensus was interrupted, I think rightly, by Richard Shusterman in *T. S. Eliot and the Philosophy of Criticism* (New York: Columbia University Press, 1988), which brought Bertrand Russell into the picture.

14 In 1912 a collection of essays by American academics titled *The New Realism* introduced what we now call the analytic turn to the United States. See Edwin B. Holt et al., *The New Realism: Cooperative Studies in Philosophy* (New York: Macmillan, 1912).

15 Michael Beaney, "The Analytic Revolution," in *The History of Philosophy*, edited by Anthony O'Hear (Cambridge: Cambridge University Press, 2016), 229.

16 R. G. Collingwood, *"An Autobiography" & Other Writings*, edited by David Boucher and Teresa Smith (Oxford: Oxford University Press, 2013), 147.

17 See D. W. Haydon, *Conservative Revolutionary: The Lives of Lewis Namier* (Manchester: Manchester University Press, 2019), 154.

16

Eliot, Brexit, and the Idea of Europe

Jason Harding

T. S. Eliot held strong beliefs that are opposed to Brexit. In 1962, Eliot weighed the pros and cons of the UK's application to join the six nations—France, Italy, West Germany, Belgium, Luxembourg, and the Netherlands—that formed the European Economic Community (EEC), or "Common Market." Wary of a referendum and reserving judgment on the intricacy of the economic, political, and legal issues, Eliot declared:

> I have always been strongly in favour of close cultural relations with the countries of Western Europe. For this reason my personal bias is in favour of Britain's entering into the Common Market. And I have not been impressed by the emotional appeals of some of those who maintain that to take this course would be a betrayal of our obligations to the Commonwealth. ("Going into Europe," *Prose8* 529)

This statement was consistent with Eliot's long-standing faith in the idea of Europe, "the idea of a common culture of western Europe" ("A Commentary [Apr. 1926]," *Prose2* 778), a belief that outweighed support for empire and the economic complications of the UK redirecting its balance of trade. (In 1962, the UK saw 43 percent of exports heading for Commonwealth countries and 16 percent to those within the Common Market.) Nor was Eliot concerned by a loss of UK sovereignty. Increased political and economic union through a centralized bureaucracy might be the implied corollary of his vision of European unity. A few weeks later, in January 1963, Charles de Gaulle used his veto to keep the UK out of the EEC, dealing a huge blow to British Europhiles. Eliot would not live to see Britain join the European Union.

Eliot's contribution to the symposium "Going into Europe" was published in the London monthly magazine *Encounter*. When the journal was launched in 1953, Eliot had declined an invitation from Stephen Spender to contribute on the grounds of its American backing. Little did he know that the money for *Encounter* came, via a front organization, from the CIA, using funds covertly siphoned from the Marshall Plan, or "European Recovery Program." Spender, who later pleaded ignorance of *Encounter*'s funding, protested to the man who secured the checks, Michael Josselson (a CIA agent in Paris), about a "reputation we have to try and live down of being a magazine disguising American propaganda under a veneer of British culture."[1] *Encounter* was a sophisticated intellectual journal promoting an American ideal of liberal democracy based upon what one scholar identifies as "the common heritage of the European Enlightenment, the rule of law, Wilsonian internationalism, pragmatism, and urban cosmopolitanism."[2] Eliot disliked liberal traditions and was scathing about Woodrow Wilson's interventions in European politics during the Versailles Treaty negotiations. Nevertheless, the issue of Britain's entry to the Common Market was sufficiently weighty for Eliot to offer a public statement in favor of European unification.

One can imagine the delight of *Encounter*'s American sponsors at securing a wholehearted endorsement from a Nobel laureate firmly in accord with the ambitions of US foreign policy. The editors of *Encounter* complained to Denis de Rougemont (a Swiss writer who obtained Eliot's support for his 1948 Hague Congress on a European union): "Unhappily, our audience is overwhelmingly *not* Europeans. The British, when they speak of Europe, do not say 'we' but 'they.'"[3] Eliot's view of a common European culture was not commonplace in Britain after the Second World War. Europeans often overlook the crucial role the United States of America played in strengthening commitment in Britain toward a united states of Europe.

Eliot's idealized conception of the unity of European culture was forged as a student in the classrooms of Harvard University and cemented in London in the tumultuous years of the First World War. In January 1918, Eliot extrapolated from his obituary reflections on Henry James the extraordinary observation that it is "the consummation of an American to become, not an Englishman, but a European—something which no born European, no person of any European nationality, can become" ("In Memory of Henry James," *Prose1* 648). Months after the armistice bells rang out, Eliot brooded upon Paul Valéry's lament for the destructive forces that had led to a disabling crisis for many European intellectuals: "From an immense terrace of Elsinore which extends from Basle to Cologne, and touches the sands of Nieuport, the marshes of the Somme, the chalk of the Champagne, the granite of Alsace, the Hamlet of Europe looks upon millions of ghosts."[4] In "Tradition and the Individual Talent" (1919), Eliot offered a timely meditation on how the voices of the dead speak eloquently through the voice of a living tradition, "the mind of Europe" (*Prose1* 107) which has apparently superannuated nothing since Homer. Eliot's concept of tradition was quite different from those European avant-garde movements—Italian and Russian Futurism, or the revolt of Dada—concerned with sweeping away the past and starting afresh.

John Maynard Keynes's objections to the Versailles Treaty profoundly affected Eliot. Keynes resigned from the British delegation to warn the public that the vindictive and punitive terms imposed on the defeated powers, Germany and Austria-Hungary, would cause economic and political shock waves threatening another European war. In his work at Lloyds Bank, Eliot dealt with German war reparations, tracking foreign-currency fluctuations and noting hyperinflation in Germany and Eastern Europe as a result of the terms of the Versailles Treaty. Economic collapse would eventually bankrupt Germany and leave its political arena ripe for violent extremism. The enforced dismemberment of the Austro-Hungarian Empire enacted by the Versailles Treaty concerned Eliot. He thought national territories had been defined by narrow ethnic lines. Eliot believed that European civilization's cultural and spiritual values transcended these artificial frontiers. Worse still, the Russian Revolution of October 1917 had created a Communist state fomenting world revolution and an implacable hostility toward Western Europe.

Critics have recognized *The Waste Land* as, albeit in a coded way, an anguished commentary on the fragmentation of postwar Europe; or, as Eliot put it in a 1923 review of James Joyce's *Ulysses*, "the immense panorama of futility and anarchy which is contemporary history" (*Prose2* 478). In April 1921, he told Richard Aldington, "The whole of contemporary politics etc. oppresses me with a continuous physical horror like the feeling of growing madness in one's own brain" (*Letters1* 550). Europe's fate was intimately linked to his own well-being. When Eliot composed *The Waste Land*, he was officially a "resident alien" in London. He confided to his brother, Henry, in July 1919: "It is damned hard work to live with a foreign nation and cope with them—one is always coming up against differences of feeling that make one feel humiliated and lonely. One remains always a foreigner" (*Letters1* 370).

In the opening movement of *The Waste Land*, the sudden interpolation of words and then a sentence in German interjects foreign elements, disorientating and defamiliarizing. A German place name (Starnbergersee) is reinforced by talk of Munich's Hofgarten and an archduke from the collapsed Austro-Hungarian Empire, raising unsettling questions about the macabre section title "The Burial of the Dead" and its relation to the vitality of civilization in postwar Europe. In the cosmopolitan exchanges of modern city life, peopled with refugees dispersed by the Versailles Treaty, miscommunication is inevitable: "Bin gar keine Russin, stamm' aus Litauen, echt deutsch" (*Poems1* 55) says a shadowy presence. "I am not Russian, I come from Lithuania, a real German" (my translation). But to translate is to make oneself deaf to the "tonal recesses of foreignness," as Christopher Ricks writes, "the complications of foreignness and whether a Lithuanian be Russian or German or even perhaps simply Lithuanian?"[5] The newly independent Lithuania was only fully established as a republic in 1922, after fighting free of over a century of Russian domination—a national identity encouraged by Germany and German-speaking Lithuanians, immediately threatened by the world revolution spearheaded by Bolshevik Russia.

Eliot completed *The Waste Land* in Lausanne, where he was undergoing a rest cure at the sanatorium of the Swiss psychiatrist Dr. Roger Vittoz, during a leave of absence following a nervous breakdown. "At least there are people of many nationalities," Eliot wrote to his brother Henry in December 1921, from cosmopolitan, multilingual Switzerland (*Letters1* 614). Here, in the center of Europe, he conceived an apocalyptic vision of imperial collapse: "What is the city over the mountains / Cracks and reforms and bursts in the violet air / Falling towers / Jerusalem Athens Alexandria / Vienna London" (*Poems1* 69). His pencil draft named the "Polish plains" invaded by swarming "hooded hordes" (*Poems1* 344), a nightmare of the Russian Revolution and a premonition of Soviet Russia's invasion of Poland in 1939.

In the notes added to *The Waste Land*, Eliot transcribed a passage in German from his copy of Hermann Hesse's *Blick ins Chaos* ("Glimpse into Chaos"): "Already half of Europe, already at least half of Eastern Europe, is on the way to chaos, drives drunkenly in holy delusion along the edge of the abyss, singing drunkenly, singing hymns, as Dmitri Karamazov sang. The offended bourgeois laughs at the songs; the saint and seer hear them with tears" (*Poems1* 76, my translation). Hesse's reflections in *Blick ins Chaos* on Dostoevsky as a sick man and a prophet, whose novel *The Brothers Karamazov* dramatizes and foretells Europe's downfall and the chaos in at least half of present-day Europe, struck a deep chord with Eliot. In 1922, both Hesse's *Siddhartha* and *The Waste Land* looked to Hindu and Buddhist texts to heal the trauma inflicted by the bursting of the overripe fruits of European civilization.

In March 1922, Eliot wrote Hesse: "I find in your *Blick ins Chaos* a seriousness that has not yet arrived in England" (*Letters1* 645, my translation). Eliot published Hesse's gloomy survey of "Recent German Poetry" in the first issue of

Criterion alongside *The Waste Land*. It concluded: "These poets feel, or seem to feel, that there must first be disintegration and chaos, the bitter way must first be gone to the end, before new settings, new forms, and new affinities are created."[6] Hesse was one of several important European authors recruited to strengthen the internationalist dimensions of Eliot's review. In retrospect, Eliot claimed that the beginning of his "adult life" could be dated from "the period ... marked by *The Waste Land*, and the foundation of *The Criterion*, and the development of relations with men of letters in the several countries of Europe" ("Brief über Ernst Robert Curtius," *Prose8* 147).

In July 1922, Eliot explained to Ernst Robert Curtius that the "great aim" of the *Criterion* was "to raise the standard of thought and writing in [England] by both international and historical comparison" (*Letters1* 710). Curtius, a professor of Romance languages, recalled that in the 1920s "A Europe of the mind—above politics, in spite of all politics—was very much alive. This Europe lived not only in books and periodicals but also in personal relations."[7] In the 1920s, this cosmopolitan spirit was characterized by the *entretiens* held in the abbey church at Pontigny, where Paul Desjardins oversaw thematic discussions between a select group of European intellectuals, and by the signing of the Locarno Treaty in 1925 between France and Germany, an indication that a half-century of struggle and warfare might have been disarmed. In the 1920s, European union was the best way to prevent another ruinous war.

In August 1927, Eliot used his editorial in the *Criterion* to define and defend his vision of "The European Idea." His remarks deserve to be quoted at length:

> Nine years after the end of the War we are only beginning to distinguish between the characteristics of our own time and those inherited from the previous epoch. One of the latter was Nationalism. We have been for nine years reminded, by the facts and fancies of the press, of the growth of the spirit of nationalism, of the greater number of nationalities, and of the multiplicity of the reasons which all these nations have for failing to get on with each other. Instead of a few "oppressed minorities," the oppressed minorities seem to be almost in a majority; instead of a few potential Sarajevos, we seem to have dozens. But the *Idea* of Nationality is no longer the same idea that it was for Mrs. Browning or Swinburne; like most of Woodrow Wilson's ideas it was aged when he discovered it; it will not explain fascism any more than it will explain bolshevism. Not how Europe can be "freed," but how Europe can be organized, is the question of the day. (*Prose3* 156)

Eliot went on to argue that "The European Idea" was illustrated by Henri Massis's defense of the Catholic West and Romain Rolland's socialist internationalism, as well as Oswald Spengler's and Paul Valéry's reflections on the decline of western Europe. He concluded:

> [T]he most important event of the War was the Russian Revolution. For the Russian Revolution has made men conscious of the position of Western Europe as (in Valéry's words) a small and isolated cape on the western side of the Asiatic Continent. And this awareness seems to be giving rise to a new European consciousness … We are beginning to hear mention of the reaffirmation of the European tradition. It will be helpful, certainly, if people will begin by believing that there is a European tradition; for they may then proceed to analyse its constituents in the various nations of Europe; and proceed finally to the further formation of such a tradition. (*Prose3* 156–7)

It is essential to recognize that Eliot's idea of Europe constituted a rejection of liberal and socialist internationalism in the defense of a conservative Latin-Catholic tradition. In his 1929 essay *Dante*, Eliot asserted: "In Dante's time Europe … was mentally more united than we can now conceive" (*Prose3* 702). The patrimony of the Holy Roman Empire to modern Europe lay behind the *Criterion*'s advocacy of a cultural "conversative revolution" in the interwar period.[8] Eliot found backing for this ideology in a book by the right-wing historian Christopher Dawson, *The Making of Europe: An Introduction to the History of European Unity* (published in 1932 by the Catholic firm Sheed & Ward), which contended that the Church of Rome was the cornerstone of European civilization. Dawson's myth of Europe is marked by exclusion and reaction: his political and spiritual unity of Europe in the medieval period had resisted the threat of "barbarian tribes" and the "expansion of Moslem culture."[9] In 1936, Eliot once again used his editorial in the *Criterion* to defend his faith in European unity against a polemic by the American critic Joseph Wood Krutch provocatively titled *Was Europe a Success?* Eliot was incredulous that Krutch downplayed the role of Christianity in shaping Europe's destiny: "He does not appear to think that Christianity had very much to do with the development of European civilization, except to obstruct it" (*Prose5* 359).

It is significant that Curtius, one of the *Criterion*'s valued collaborators, began to express his doubts about Eliot's credentials as a leader of a conservative intellectual movement. In a 1929 article in German, Curtius criticized Eliot for the declaration that he was a "classicist in literature, royalist in politics, anglo-catholic in religion" ("Preface to *For Lancelot Andrewes*," *Prose3* 513), since it represented to Curtius a retreat from what he called "European universal-history," the 2,500-year-old legacy of humanistic tradition.[10] During the 1930s, the *Criterion*'s network of European contributors disintegrated. In 1936, Eliot observed: "[T]here seem to be fewer and fewer writers who are speaking not only to their own countrymen but to Europe as a whole" ("Tradition and the Practice of Poetry," *Prose5* 308). As rival European ideologies took to armed conflict during the Spanish Civil War, Eliot declined to voice public support for the anti-fascist Popular Front of Communists, Socialists, and Liberals. Yet this stance does not represent any sympathy with the British policy of appeasement toward Nazi Germany's demands for territorial gains in Europe, which Eliot declared in January 1939 engendered in him a depression of spirits so deep that it represented a new emotion. In his bleak January 1939 editorial "Last Words," Eliot closed down the *Criterion* with the sad conclusion: "The 'European Mind,' which one had mistakenly thought might be renewed and fortified, disappeared from view" (*Prose5* 661).

One of the most fascinating recent developments in Eliot scholarship is a recognition of Eliot's efforts in the 1940s to rebuild Britain's cultural and diplomatic links with European countries. Some of his most important work was conducted on behalf of the British Council, which had been established to promote a sympathetic understanding of British foreign policy overseas. In 1942, Eliot was approached by the British Council to form part of a high-level strategic diplomatic mission to neutral Sweden, where he delivered lectures and readings over five weeks. Wartime travel to and from Sweden was difficult. Still, Eliot felt that it was necessary to use the soft power of cultural diplomacy to counteract German military pressure to maintain vital Swedish exports of war materials. Eliot's radio broadcasts also helped to stimulate cultural relations after the fractures of war. In a message broadcast on the BBC European Service after the liberation of Rome in June 1944, Eliot affirmed it is "the tradition of Latin culture which we have in common, together with our common religion, that created the European consciousness, the common mind in which we are Europeans" (*Prose6* 508). In March 1946, Eliot delivered three BBC radio broadcasts to occupied Germany on the subject of "The Unity of European Culture," repeating his appeal to a shared European legacy, a "common *tradition* of Christianity which has made Europe what it is," adding tendentiously that "[a]n individual European may not believe that the Christian Faith is true, and yet what he says, and makes, and does, will all spring out of his heritage of Christian culture and depend upon that culture for its meaning" (*Prose6* 718–19).

In the postwar wreckage of Germany, whose cities had been devastated by Allied bombing, Curtius listened to Eliot's broadcasts on "The Unity of European Culture" with a grim forbearance. In July 1945, Stephen Spender had traveled to the occupied Rhineland, documenting the destruction of Cologne, where the RAF estimated that 61 percent of the city had been decimated. "In the destroyed German towns," wrote Spender, "one often feels haunted by the ghost of a tremendous noise. It is impossible not to imagine the rocking explosions, the hammering of the sky upon the earth, which must have caused all this."[11] In Bonn, Spender talked with his mentor, Curtius, circumventing a ban on fraternization with the Germans due to an official Allied drive to the denazification of notable intellectuals. Spender realized that Curtius sold his library to survive during the war. Curtius's 1948 magnum opus, *European Literature and the Latin Middle Ages*—which he described as his intellectual alibi under Nazism—is preoccupied with preserving and transmitting the European literary canon to the postwar world. It is striking, however, that in Curtius's contribution to a *Festschrift* celebrating Eliot's Nobel Prize for Literature in 1948, old grievances resurface. With more irritation than gratitude, Curtius chastised Eliot's Latinate idea of Europe for its "exclusion of Germany, her language and her culture … His judgment shows that criticism can also be an expression of politics."[12]

One aspect that may surprise contemporary commentators on Brexit is the significance accorded to the pronouncements of public intellectuals in the realm of European politics. Throughout the 1940s, Eliot repeatedly spoke of the responsibility of the "man of letters" to inform and influence "an international fraternity of men of letters, within Europe" ("Die Einheit der europäischen Kultur," *Prose6* 715). Eliot had sought to do this through his editorship of the *Criterion* until totalitarianism and war throughout Europe rendered this aim impossible. In "The Responsibility of the Man of Letters in the Cultural Restoration of Europe," written shortly after the Allied landings in Normandy, Eliot was cautious about endorsing cultural propaganda, remarking: "The man of letters as such, is not concerned with the political or economic map of Europe; but he should be very much concerned with its cultural map … But the man of letters should know that uniformity means the obliteration of culture, and that self-sufficiency means its death by starvation" (*Prose6* 520). This observation led Eliot to formulate some political dangers for the European intellectual:

> The primary aim of politics, at the end of a great war, must be, of course, the establishment of a peace, and of a peace which will endure … At the end of the last war, the idea of peace was associated with the idea of independence and freedom: it was thought that if each nation managed all its own affairs at home, and transacted its foreign political affairs through a League of Nations,

peace would be perpetually assured. It was an idea which disregarded the *unity* of European culture. At the end of this war, the idea of peace is more likely to be associated with the idea of *efficiency*—that is, with whatever can be *planned*. This would be to disregard the *diversity* of European culture ... and there is a danger that the importance of the various cultures may be assumed to be in proportion to the size, population, wealth and power of the nations. (*Prose6* 521)

In his October 1944 broadcast for the BBC World Service, titled "The Responsibility of the European Man of Letters," Eliot opined: "Europe, if it is to recover health, must be a unity of diverse nations in a European culture" (*Prose6* 542).

When they met in Paris in May 1945, Paul Valéry told Eliot: "*L'Europe est finie*" (*Prose6* 754). A year later, in his preface to a book documenting the wartime destruction of Poland, Eliot wrote: "For a European, the problem is whether Europe can survive ... At the present time, every country of Western Europe has within itself germs of decay and elements of discord" ("Preface to *The Dark Side of the Moon*," *Prose6* 745). The survival of intellectual freedom across Europe felt precarious. Eliot's defense of European cultural unity was as invaluable during the Cold War as during the Second World War. In December 1947, Eliot traveled on behalf of the British Council in another exercise of cultural soft power, offering two lectures and a reading in Rome, amid a Communist-backed general strike orchestrated to topple Italy's Christian Democrat–led coalition. When Melvin Lasky launched the anti-Communist monthly magazine *Der Monat* in Berlin in 1948, his founding aspiration had been to fulfill the mission that Eliot voiced in his postwar broadcasts to occupied Germany: the creation of "a network of independent reviews, at least one in every capital of Europe," on the principle that "their cooperation should continually stimulate that circulation of influence of thought and sensibility, between nation and nation in Europe, which fertilises and renovates from abroad the literature of each one of them" (*Prose6* 713–14). In 1962, Lasky, now chief editor of *Encounter* magazine in London, approached Eliot for a statement for the symposium on "Going into Europe" disseminating the opinions of prominent British intellectuals.

I began by suggesting that T. S. Eliot held strong beliefs that are opposed to Brexit. His vision of the "Idea of Europe" was an expression of his conservatism: deeply pro-Christian and anti-Communist, antagonistic to liberal individualism and secular pluralism. The complications of Eliot's politics and theology make it a moot point how he might have voted in the 2016 UK referendum on continued membership of the European Union. In his speech as vice president of the Fédération britannique des comités de l'Alliance française delivered on June 2, 1951, Eliot emphasized loyalty to the distinctive inflections that the culture and language of a country contribute to Europe:

> In short, it is not only not true that to be a good European it is necessary to be less an Englishman, or a Frenchman, or any other nationality; it is also not true that to be a good European one must have an equal and impartial affection for every other European country. There is always a danger that some enthusiastic supporters may envisage European culture as something which could be completely unified, which should obliterate regional and national differences: and that could only lead to a condition in which we should have nothing to gain from each other. For if the native of the shore of the Mediterranean was identical with the native of the shore of the North Sea in thought, sensibility and behaviour, there would be no longer any point in either one crossing Europe to meet the other. They might both just as well stop at home and talk to their next door neighbour. (*Prose7* 618)

In this sense, one can be a good European without believing that national differences should be eradicated in a European Union seeking ever closer political and economic integration. In a little-known contribution to a Portuguese journal, Eliot wrote: "[T]he ultimate unity of Europe cannot come through identity of political organisation, or a legal-political federation ... but from the unity of the Christian Faith" ("To the Editor of *Aventura*" *Prose6* 414). In 1993, in a climate of bitter political divisions occasioned by the Maastricht Treaty on European Union, A. D. Moody remarked: "I have to confess that I cannot see how Eliot's thought and theory ... [are] likely to be of much use or influence in today's efforts to construct a united Europe."[13] Yet, as Brexit continues to reshape the contemporary context, Eliot's historically conditioned ideological, theological, and personal beliefs still offer a compelling example of a utopian ideal: "the unity of European culture."

Notes

1 Quoted in Jason Harding, "'Our Greatest Asset': *Encounter* Magazine and the Congress for Cultural Freedom," in *Campaigning Culture and the Global Cold War: The Journals of the Congress of Cultural Freedom*, edited by Giles Scott-Smith and Charlotte A. Lerg (London: Palgrave Macmillan, 2017), 109.

2 Michael Hochgeschwender, "A Battle of Ideas: The Congress for Cultural Freedom (CCF) in Britain, Italy, France, and West Germany," in *The Postwar*

Challenge: Cultural, Social, and Political Change in Western Europe, 1945–1958 (Oxford: Oxford University Press, 2003), 326.

3 Quoted in Harding, "'Our Greatest Asset,'" 102.
4 Paul Valéry, "Letters from France," *Athenaeum* (April 11, 1919), 184. Eliot recalled Valéry as "a figure symbolic of the Europe of our time" (*Prose6* 753).
5 Christopher Ricks, *T. S. Eliot and Prejudice* (London: Faber, 1988), 191–2.
6 Hermann Hesse, "Recent German Poetry," *Criterion* (October 1922): 90.
7 Ernst Robert Curtius, *Essays on European Literature*, trans. Michael Kowal (Princeton: Princeton University Press, 1973), 170.
8 Jason Harding, *"The Criterion": Cultural Politics and Periodical Networks in Interwar Britain* (Oxford: Oxford University Press, 2002), 216–17.
9 See Christopher Dawson, *The Making of Europe: An Introduction to the History of European Unity* (New York: Sheed & Ward, 1932). In a lecture on "The Idea of a European Society," delivered in Hamburg in 1949, Eliot praised Dawson for "a wealth of scholarship which I can only admire" (*Prose7* 409).
10 For Eliot's supposed retreat from "europäischer Universalgeschichte," see Ernst Robert Curtius, "T. S. Eliot als Kritiker," *Die Literatur* (October 1929): 11–15.
11 Stephen Spender, *New Selected Journals 1939-1995*, edited by Lara Feigel and John Sutherland (London: Faber, 2012), 35.
12 Ernst Robert Curtius, "T. S. Eliot and Germany," in *T. S. Eliot: A Symposium*, edited by Richard March and Tambimuttu (London: Poetry London, 1948), 122.
13 A. D. Moody, "The Mind of Europe" (1993), in *Tracing T. S. Eliot's Spirit: Essays on His Poetry and Thought* (Cambridge: Cambridge University Press, 1996), 69.

17

Mature Fans Steal: Eliot's Fictions

Megan Quigley

A thought experiment: what might we learn about Eliot's poetry *and* Eliot scholarship if we read them through the lens of fanfiction? Yes, fanfiction—known best through the huge online world of Sherlock Holmes, Harry Potter, and Twilight unauthorized stories. Fanfic, fondly known as "playing in someone else's sandbox," is an immense and growing literature.[1] It can be kinky or perverse, although it is often just intellectually rogue as fans pen new versions of previously published texts.[2] If fanfic is what Balaka Basu recently called "amatory" writing, which blurs the relationship between canon and new text in order to *get the story right*, here is one possible theory: the extremely scholarly and astutely annotated two volumes of *The Poems of T. S. Eliot* are a kind of fanfiction.[3] The editors take up Eliot's characteristic ideas, tone, and arguably even his "characters," if we read *The Waste Land* as a kind of *Pale Fire* narrative with an idiosyncratic editor annotating a lyric poem, which I do, and … they keep the story going. They even create a new "composite" version of *The Waste Land*, which imagines a possible version of the poem that never could have existed.[4]

But *Poems* is just one, if the most cerebral, fannish text inspired by Eliot's work and life. There are many contemporary fictionalized accounts of T. S. Eliot's poetry and his life, both in biofictions and fanfictions.[5] While biofiction (based on the biographies of historical figures) and fanfiction or fanfic (which is usually collaborative, amateur work "poaching" off real historical figures' lives or previously published stories) are discrete categories, they differ mostly in degree rather than in kind, particularly in distinction to traditional academic studies.[6] Both biofiction and fanfiction share what many academics might find a kind of unrestrained attachment to a literary text or personage and a blurring of the line between author and reader. I would like to suggest that this kind of earnest, and even unseemly, reappropriation of literary texts, symbols, and figures is perhaps not all that different from Eliotic modernism. Why does it matter if we see Eliot as an obsessive fan and his carefully crafted "impersonal" and erudite reputation as just a scholarly fiction?

Let's begin at the end, with some burnt love letters.

Part 1: *The Aspern Papers*—in Reverse

One reason that now, more than ever, scholars need to think about Eliot's life and work in relationship to fiction is the opening of the Emily Hale papers. The archive of 1,131 letters that Eliot wrote to Hale, his longtime American love, over the course of twenty-six years, was unsealed with great excitement in January 2020. In a note set to be released at the same time by the Houghton Library, Eliot revealed he had burnt Hale's side of the correspondence. The Hale papers, and Eliot's response from beyond the grave, have undermined any remaining attempts to read Eliot's poetry as impervious to biographical critique. They reveal that Eliotic impersonality, renowned from "Tradition and the Individual Talent" (1919), was always a sham or, as I would prefer to see it, a kind of fiction-making project, a desire to free the poetic voice from its sources in the poet's experiences and secrets.

Eliot's private life and opinions have, of course, not stayed out of the academic or public eye since his death in 1965. Whether in books about his anti-Semitism, articles bemoaning his reactionary politics or questioning his sexuality, or even the award-winning film on his relationship with his first wife, Vivien, Eliot's private life did not remain private. Ann Pasternak Slater's *The Fall of a Sparrow: Vivien Eliot's Life and Writings* (along with the digital version of Vivien's diaries and short fiction) and the new color facsimile of *The Waste Land* are but two of the recent works that help us to think through the ways Eliot's life shaped his verse, and they support the notion that rather than a singly authored text, *The Waste Land* was a collaborative effort with Pound and Vivien.[7] The fanfiction and biofiction archive of Eliot also shows an eager readerly interest in imagining the personal domain inhabited by the "possum."

Yet the Hale archive is different in its relationship to Eliot's own theory of impersonality, reading, and sources. The letters show us Eliot, in his own words, citing biographical sources, even presenting a kind of roman à clef for several poems. As Frances Dickey has shown, "one of the stunning takeaways of his letters to Hale is the consciously autobiographical nature of his poetry."[8] In these letters, Eliot points out the sources of figures in poems and calls *Burnt*

Norton a love poem dedicated to Hale. He also revises our understanding of when Eliot and Hale first met and the extent of their love affair (he talks of the smell of her hair and her perfume). Hale, we learn from the correspondence, contributed to his religious passions and inspired many of his most renowned poetic achievements. No one, Eliot wrote, would ever understand some of his poems but Hale, and he wanted to preserve this archive of letters as a guide to later readers. Why would preserving the letters matter if his poetry's sources in his life weren't important? The letters act like a little impersonality bomb that Hale (and Eliot) set off fifty years after her death.

One small detail of Eliot's 1963 missive at the Houghton, his allusion to a story by Henry James, further troubles any easy division of the poet and his poetry and confirms Eliot's investment in fiction. Eliot summarizes Hale's decision to donate his letters to Princeton as "*The Aspern Papers* in reverse."[9] With those words, Eliot opens the door for us to read his actual life as one would a Jamesian fiction. In her insightful biography of Eliot, Lyndall Gordon lay the groundwork for understanding Eliot's indebtedness to the ghost of Henry James, and the newly published materials help us to think further about Eliot as a James "fan."[10]

Perhaps it ought not to be surprising that someone who entitled poems "Portrait of a Lady" and "Bellegarde"—both references to novels by James— would refer to a James story in a note, but the weighty circumstances of that public-facing statement at the Houghton, an attempt to circumscribe a potentially defining biographical moment, make the allusion seem strange. In this note, after spelling out why confessional or autobiographical writing was so antithetical to his spirit, Eliot promises to keep his narrative short while he explains the history of the letters. Although he admits that he and Hale had always intended to donate their correspondence to a research library, the timing of Hale's donation was disconcerting to him. Because both parties were still alive at the time of Hale's gifting, Eliot feared prying librarians' eyes, especially as he was about to be remarried. He writes that, "it seemed to me that her disposing of the letters in that way at that time threw some light upon the kind of interest which she took, or had come to take, in these letters," and then summarizes, "*The Aspern Papers* in reverse."

In *The Aspern Papers*, written in 1888, a nameless narrator recounts his efforts to get his hands on the papers of the famous poet Jeffrey Aspern by ingratiating himself with the old muse of Aspern's famous poems, the now decrepit Juliana, and her equally decrepit niece Miss Tita, in their still more decrepit palazzo in Venice.[11] Full of intrigue (what would the papers reveal?), lies (the narrator takes on a fake identity), and romance (what about Julia's eyes bewitched Jeffrey

Aspern?), the story also revels in a sense of evil that can never quite be spelled out, though it seems connected with the unknowable limits to which our narrator will go to obtain these desired papers. When the narrator refuses, finally, to give himself to Miss Tita in exchange for the papers, Tita burns all of Aspern's papers in retaliation:

> "Oh, I don't know. I have done the great thing. I have destroyed the papers."
> "Destroyed them?" I faltered.
> "Yes; what was I to keep them for? I burnt them last night, one by one, in the kitchen."
> "One by one?" I repeated, mechanically.
> "It took a long time—there were so many." (James, 320)

The narrator is reduced to merely echoing in horror.

In writing "*The Aspern Papers* in reverse," Eliot suggests that out of similarly scorned pride Hale has donated his letters to Princeton library for posterity and publicity, instead of burning the correspondence. She has preserved what Tita determined to burn but under a similar impulse: revenge for unrequited love. It is impossible, however, to know that this is exactly what Eliot means, because of the vagueness of his diction: "her disposing of the letters in that way at that time threw some light upon the kind of interest which she took, or had come to take, in these letters." Eliot's repetitive phrasing and indeterminate diction (what kind of light, on what kind of interest in what time?) echoes Jamesian circumlocutions and refuses specificity. Another way to read "*The Aspern Papers* in reverse" is that Eliot has acted as the irate former lover who has burned the correspondence in an act of vengeance. The note specifically highlights (in added blue pen) that he instructed a colleague to burn the correspondence. Is Eliot the self-deluding mechanical narrator or the hysterical letter-burning woman? By asking a colleague to burn the letters rather than doing it himself, perhaps he distances himself from the act, because, unlike Tita, he couldn't be bothered to burn them, or on the contrary, perhaps he reveals he is unwilling to burn the treasured letters himself. Eliot's cover note suggests that Hale's decision to donate the letters to the library at that time was wrong. Yet his allusion to *The Aspern Papers* also redirects the implied criticism back at himself, a person who feverishly desires to control the reputation of a poet by burning up the evidence.

Nearly thirty years earlier, in his lecture notes to a course on "Contemporary English Literature" delivered in spring 1933 to Harvard undergraduates, now published in Volume 4 of *The Complete Prose*, Eliot lay out his method for analyzing *The Aspern Papers*; he was simultaneously discussing his lecture plans in a letter to none other than Hale. In his James lectures, he planned to explain that "Nobody has ever found the writing of fiction more exciting than did James" and that "it is impossible to get the most out of James without taking seriously his devotion to his art" (*Prose4* 769). He also established that James was central to Eliot's own vision of contemporary writing, arguing that James, along with Conrad, was "much more important" than the other writers he would discuss (771).

To Hale, Eliot writes on March 6, 1933, that he will "try to give a good lecture tomorrow morning," because "the Aspern papers is not so difficult." Then, and this a crucial but opaque section of his letter, he writes:

> I can't expect these boys to get the intensity that I get and have got [from the story], ... this quite apart from the personal and private significance which *The Aspern Papers* has come to have for me: but I was fascinated by it long before that. (Eliot–Hale)

Is Eliot here quite simply implying to Hale that *The Aspern Papers* has a particularly intimate significance for him because he is also the poet writing secret love letters to his beloved that will one day be a source of literary value? He has become Jeffrey Aspern. And isn't it odd that he's writing that within the love letters themselves? And if he is revealing, within this letter, that he and Hale know they are reenacting *The Aspern Papers* scene of correspondence between a poet and his secret muse, then his Houghton statement, thirty years later, becomes posthumously more intimate. When Eliot writes, "*The Aspern Papers* in reverse," apparently indicting Hale for all of posterity as poetry-killing and fame-seeking, he is simultaneously still (even in note perhaps dictated to his second wife Valerie) in a conversation with Hale, pointing at the way they have continued to play out their roles from James's haunting tale, as he and she together knew they always were.

While we cannot know exactly why Eliot chose to allude to a famous novella in his note at the Houghton, or even if he remembered discussing it earlier with Hale, the reference is in keeping with the manifold allusions to James in his writing and, more important, his modeling of his own life on that of James. Eliot called James, author of *The Portrait of a Lady*, "The Turn of the Screw," *The Ambassadors*, and many other works, and forty-five years Eliot's senior, "the most intelligent man of his generation" ("In Memory of Henry James," *Prose1* 650). Eliot began his literary career boasting of their similarities, writing proudly, in a letter to his mother in March 1919, that "I really think that I have far more *influence* on English letters than any other American has ever had, unless it be Henry James" (*Letters1* 331), and his late great work *Four Quartets* grew from the nexus of images joining *Burnt Norton*, *Murder in the Cathedral*, and the poem "Bellegarde."[12] James's influence spread across Eliot's poetic career. James presented the perfect example of the artist-critic, and recalling Eliot's own decision between philosophy and poetry as a career, we can see him throwing in his lot with Henry, rather than William, James.

Eliot's fannish relationship to James is solidified by another document in Volume 1 of the *Complete Prose*. In "The Two Unfinished Novels" by Henry James, the putative author "Enrique Gomez" thanks "Miss Anna Louise Babson, of New York, for revising the English version of this review" (*Prose1* 655). Enrique is fascinated by James's final, incomplete novels because their plans show James had been intending to forgo his usual social studies and (as we could say of the style of much of the later James) aimed to "obliterate" any outlines of normal storytelling. For Enrique, the novel's plan shows James "audaciously and unconquerably reaching out toward something Jamesian beyond James" (*Prose1* 653). The editors of Volume 1 of Eliot's prose point out similarities between Eliot's other writing on James and this review, and they posit that Enrique Gomez and Miss Babson, for that matter, are both most likely pseudonyms for Eliot, who admits to his mother in January 1918 that he "had to write most of the Henry James number of the *Egoist*" (*Letters1* 248). Enrique Gomez, a "Hispanicized version" of Henry James's own name, was, they argue, "partly inspired by the Spanish lessons" Eliot had been taking, and Eliot invented this pseudonym to make it less obvious that he authored many of the James articles himself (655). Writing as Enrique, Eliot notes that in the unfinished novel there was "to have been a masterly turn of the screw later," but sadly the novel was never itself completed (*Prose1* 655). Here in this review, we see Eliot identifying so thoroughly with Henry James that he both names himself after him and also seems, in his letter-writing hoax, to finish "turning the screw" for James. We can almost hear Eliot laughing to himself as he notes that James (or he, in this review) is attempting something "so difficult that one holds one's breath still at the terrifying risk of the experiment" (653).

Was Eliot's interest in James really a kind of fandom? Fans, according to *The Fan Fiction Studies Reader*, are often defined by their desire to pretend, resemble, imitate, or copy an original.[13] In the examples above, Eliot adopts James's words and characters for his own usage without appropriate citation, blurs the line between author and literary text, and even invents a fictionalized version of the author (perhaps with a wink to his community of readers) in "reviewing" the author's texts. He fudges the distinction between himself and the beloved writer.

Vivien Eliot, in desperation after Eliot's decision to leave her, renamed herself in her diary Daisy Miller, a Jamesian character, reflecting her own understanding of James's influence on her life with Eliot. Lyndall Gordon notes that Eliot and John Hayward moved into the same block of flats that James had once lived in. She observes that "It is curious—unprecedented—how often Eliot's letters refer to [his] essay on James" and adds, "As he wrote it he took up the mantle of the Master."[14] Eliot also enacts a near definition of fan transcendence when he alleges his "special knowledge" and twins himself and James.[15] He writes: "I do not suppose that anyone who is not an American can *properly* appreciate James," but Eliot understands: "It is the final perfection, the consummation of an American to become, not an Englishman, but a European—something which no born European, no person of any European nationality, can become" ("In Memory of Henry James," *Prose1* 648).

While I believe we can conclusively call Eliot a James "fan," I do not wish to overstate Eliot's investment in James, because I think Eliot was a fan of other writers as well, and even of Sherlock Holmes, who is a prime, if not the prime, subject for contemporary fanfiction. But why does it matter if we see Eliot as often enacting a kind of fan impulse?

Part 2: Bring On the Fanfic

Fanfiction is usually defined as "derivative amateur fiction" based on another text or a real historical person; it "poaches," to use Henry Jankin's well-known term, off previously published fiction, other media (like TV or movies), or real life to create new, unauthorized texts. Beyond that, the definition becomes a bit hazy; you can go to podcasts like *Fansplaining* to hear arguments about whether fanfic must be anonymous, transformative, or free.[16] While fictions derived from other texts have obviously existed as long as literature itself, fanfic has a specific history, culture, reputation, and, most important, affect.[17] It is often written by women, or *Star Trek* fans, or perhaps queer women who are *Star Trek* fans; misogyny and homophobia against the preponderantly female writers and readers contribute to fanfiction's low reputation. Fans' "interest, fascination, and even obsession with their beloved objects" can be affirmative, in which case they collect knowledge about the objects or extrapolate the stories of their fandom, or transformative, in which case they seek to remake the objects of interest through their own narratives.[18] Fanfic of Eliot spans from the personal (a reimagining of Eliot and Jean Verdenal as lovers who go camping) to the literary—a story of

Prufrock's concerned neighbor reaching out to let him know he is not alone, or new takes on *Cats*, or (my personal favorite) Prufrock written as spoken by the director Joss Whedon.[19]

The fanworld is huge, and as Kavita Mudan Finn recently reminded us, fan studies is also "a capacious and often cacophonous field." She bemoans academics who "discover and seize upon fan studies terminologies, frameworks, and critical lenses without paying sufficient attention to their larger contexts."[20] In order not to do that here, I will be clear: while those stories about Eliot are fanfic, Eliot's poetry and scholarship aren't actually fanfic. Biofiction is also not fanfic. These texts are not anonymous, not collaborative, not amateur (writers make money off them), and the texts help to establish reputations. In juxtaposing fanfic and biofictions with scholarship of Eliot, however, I hope to call attention to two points: first, the comparison helps us see that fannish fiction and biofiction of Eliot were sometimes as "right" about Eliot's sources and personal life as the scholarly record. Second, highlighting Eliot's own fannish impulses in both his life and his writing shows that Eliot's modernist allusiveness can be read through the lens of fans' emotional obsessions with previous texts and specific writers. Handing Eliot back to his "fans" may be the best way to keep him relevant to readers in the twenty-first century.

It is essential to note, in connection with the first point, that newly available archival sources do not always confirm the truisms of mainstream scholarship on Eliot. At times, the new information validates the more inventive and unapologetically affective gestures typical of Eliot's biofic and fanfic. For instance, in a letter from the Hale archive dated August 18, 1932, Eliot asserts that he believed he met Hale in 1905. Frances Dickey argues this is plausible, since Eleanor Hinkley, Eliot's cousin, and Hale were classmates from childhood, and if true, it means that Eliot had known Hale since she was really an adolescent: fourteen years old. If Eliot is right, his and Hale's relationship was longer than even Lyndall Gordon had imagined—over half a century.

Most scholarly editions and biographies date Eliot's meeting Hale to 1912. In contrast, the biofics imagine the young pair meeting at a much earlier date. In *The Archivist*, Martha Cooley posits that they'd known each other since adolescence, age sixteen or so, and in Sara Fitzgerald's *The Poet's Girl*, they connect in 1913 but acknowledge that they already know each other: "We had met once before, probably at one of those debutante parties the season Eleanor came out."[21] Indeed, if Eleanor was about sixteen at her Boston debutante ball, the date would be around 1907. Both biofictions thus come closer than the scholarship, to Eliot's date of 1905. This astonishing fact encourages us to reassess the value of creative types of criticism as it undermines the stark hierarchies of scholarship and biography in relation to biofiction, throwing off Eliot's often own charismatic edicts but keeping his work alive and vital for ourselves and our students.

Second, let's imagine what it would mean to read Eliot's allusions as from a "shy proto-fan" in his poetry, as Stephanie Burt names him in "The Promise and Potential of Fan Fiction." Eliot's assertion that Blake's "early poems show what the poems of a boy of genius ought to show, immense power of assimilation" is a fit description of Eliot's own early method, evidenced by the allusions, borrowings, and foreign epigraphs permeating *Prufrock and Other Observations* and *Poems* (1920), and epitomized in *The Waste Land* ("William Blake," *Prose2* 187). When, in "Philip Massinger," Eliot differentiates between versions of assimilation, declaring "Immature poets imitate; mature poets steal; bad poets deface what they take, and good poets make it into something better, or at least something different" he could practically be writing a manifesto for fanfic (*Prose2* 245). Laura Heffernan and Rachel Sagner Buurma's work on modernist pedagogy has shown that Eliot's extension lectures shaped his particular canon.[22] Much of Eliot's repertoire of allusions was built specifically by the work he put into preparing paid lectures with strict parameters and expectations. Rather than reading Eliot's modernist allusiveness as fulfilling his fantasy of a traditional writer's "historical sense"—the sense of one who writes with the knowledge of the "whole of the literature of Europe from Homer and within it the whole of the literature of his own country"—if we see it as fannish, it shows how Eliot's canon was always already personal, somewhat pragmatic, and idiosyncratic ("Tradition and the Individual Talent," *Prose2* 106).

Recognizing how Eliot's personal and idiosyncratic canon—typified by his "Aspern Papers" remark—manifests in his poetry changes the way we approach his allusiveness itself. As illustration, consider how Jamesian and other allusions work in one of Eliot's most densely allusive poems. "Burbank with a Baedeker: Bleistein with a Cigar" demonstrates the way Eliot's fascination with *The Aspern Papers* translates into his poetry. In this complex quatrain poem from 1919, James's story appears in the epigraph, where, amid six allusions to Gautier, Browning, Shakespeare, etc., Eliot cites, "the gondola stopped, the old palace was there, how charming its gray and pink" (*Poems1* 34, 488). The allusion to an aesthetically beautiful vision of Venice from James's story joins a combined reference to *Othello* and Browning's "Toccata of Galuppi's": "goats and monkeys, with such hair too!" The epigraph juxtaposes images of animalistic ribaldry and lost beauty, degenerate sexuality and historic grace. Eliot's vision of paradoxical literary Venice, both beautiful and always already repulsive, incarnate in the epigraph, seems to mirror the two different visions of visiting Venice embodied in Burbank with his guidebook and Bleistein with his cigar.

In a powerful essay, Ronald Bush argues that we misunderstand Eliot's allusions, in "Burbank" in particular but as a general technique, if we depend entirely upon our literary knowledge in the hope of getting to the heart of Eliot's meaning. "The aims of Eliot's allusions are often conflicted," he argues, "torn between clarifying the reader's understanding and preserving a deliberate obscurity that is not (as student readers sometimes assume) accidental or perverse but essential."[23] Bush traces Eliot's Harvard lecture notes to show that Eliot describes allusion as not entirely a conscious process for writer or reader and maintains that allusions exist for the "'sake of the emotional aura which they bring,'" and that often their "unfathomability ... is part of their *raison d'être*."[24] Bush implies that notes for the reader are unnecessary, since the allusions are about "the emotional charge attached" to "a real deeper emotional current of life" rather than being clarified by discovering a source.[25] His point gains support from Eliot's explanatory letter to Hale, in 1933, that although he will aim to explain mathematically how his poem and James's story are connected stylistically, his students could never truly understand his allusion due to its personal and private significance.

Although at first glance Eliot's difficult poetry and contemporary fanfiction have little in common, seeing Eliot as a fan permits us to read his poetry as yoking characters, allusions, authors, and works into his own emotionally charged fan atmosphere. It further undermines any kind of "impersonal" or autotelic claims for his work and instead marks it as intensely personal, idiosyncratic, and of its place and time. The Hale papers invite us to see a new Eliot, who imagined himself as explaining through love letters many of the sources and themes of his work. The "Eliot" envisioned by years of scholarship was often as much a product of fanfiction as that more obviously incarnate in the many biofictions and fanfictions of his life and work. Thus reading Eliot's verse, life, and scholarship through the lens of fanfiction can teach us to see a new Eliot whose celebrated impersonality may have been his own greatest fiction. Understanding "Eliot" as having many fictional afterlives (in fanfic, biofic, scholarship), all variously valuable, invites us to rethink the importance of "fiction" for understanding and teaching Eliot today. For me, it also importantly wrestles Eliot away from the ivory tower and puts him back into readers' hands, where they can write him, rewrite him, borrow his language, and rethink his canon, just as he did with the writers he adored.

In an *Aspern Papers* fanfic called "What is to give light must endure burning," the author, tigriswolf, reimagines James's novella as if told by the spurned female protagonist, Tina. Here, Tina admits she feels some "vindictive joy" in burning the letters, while insisting her goal is really to preserve her aunt's privacy.[26] Changing the narrative point of view and reversing who has the last word about why the letters were destroyed, tigriswolf takes ownership of the story and undercuts the misogyny of James's narrator. While we cannot write a feminist version of the actual Hale–Eliot story, we can, like tigriswolf or like T. S. Eliot, retell James's story and give it whatever ending we choose.

Notes

1 Anne Jamison, *Fic: Why Fanfiction Is Taking Over the World* (Dallas: Smart Pop, 2013), 17.
2 Stephanie Burt, "The Promise and Potential of Fan Fiction," *New Yorker* (August 23, 2017). https://www.newyorker.com/books/page-turner/the-promise-and-potential-of-fan-fiction.
3 Balaka Basu, panelist, in "Fan Fiction, Fan Studies, and Literary Studies," 2022 Modern Language Association Conference (January 6, 2022).
4 "*The Waste Land*: An Editorial Composite," *Poems*1: 321–46.
5 Biofictions include Michael Hastings's *Tom and Viv* (London: Oberon, 2006), Martha Cooley's *The Archivist* (Boston: Little Brown, 1998), Steven Carroll's *The Lost Life* (London: 4th Estate, 2009), Llywelyn Jones's *Tiresias* (Devon Llywelyn Jones, 2013), and Sara Fitzgerald's *The Poet's Girl* (New York: Thought Catalog, 2020). Eliot's own contemporaries, often to his chagrin, also included barely fictionalized versions of Eliot in their works. See Richard Aldington's *Stepping Heavenward* (Garden City: Doubleday, 1931), Virginia Woolf's *The Waves* (New York: Harcourt, 1931), and D. H. Lawrence's *Women in Love* (London: Martin Secker, 1921). For fanfic see Archive of Our Own (AO3): there are approximately 750 stories that are about, refer to, quote, or rewrite T. S. Eliot.
6 Henry Jenkins, "Textual Poachers," in *Textual Poachers: Television Fans and Participatory Culture* (London: Routledge, 1992), 24–49.
7 Ann Pasternak Slater, *The Fall of a Sparrow Vivien Eliot's Life and Writings* (London: Faber, 2020), and T. S. Eliot, *The Waste Land: A Facsimile and Transcript of the Original Drafts Including the Annotations of Ezra Pound*, edited by Valerie Eliot (London: Faber, 2022). See also Robert Crawford, *Eliot after "The Waste Land"* (London: Jonathan Cape, 2022), and Lyndall Gordon, *The Hyacinth Girl: T. S. Eliot's Hidden Muse* (New York: Norton, 2023).
8 Frances Dickey, "May the Record Speak: The Correspondence of T. S. Eliot and Emily Hale" (*Twentieth-Century Literature* 66, no. 4, 2020): 443.

9 "Statement by T. S. Eliot on the opening of the Emily Hale letters at Princeton University" (*Prose8* 597 and Eliot–Hale).
10 Lyndall Gordon, *T. S. Eliot: An Imperfect Life* (New York: Norton, 2000).
11 Henry James, *Complete Stories* Vol. 3 (New York: Library of America, 1999), 228–320.
12 Gordon, 548–50.
13 Nicholas Abercrombie and Brian Longhurst, "Fans and Enthusiasts," in *The Fan Fiction Studies Reader*, edited by Karen Hellekson and Kristina Busse (Iowa City: University of Iowa Press, 2014), 173–5.
14 Gordon, 103.
15 Transcendence is "the breakdown of the boundary between the self and the star as the audience member fantasizes about becoming the star and feeling the motions of the star" (Abercrombie and Longhurst, 174).
16 Flourish Klink, "Towards a Definition of 'Fanfiction,'" *Fansplaining*, May 30, 2017, https://www.fansplaining.com/articles/towards-a-definition-of-fanfiction.
17 "Fanfiction" as a term is relatively new, probably stemming from 1944 (Hellekson and Busse, 5). Some academics call even the *Iliad* and the *Odyssey* the "earliest version" of fanfiction as the oral mythologies predated Homer's versions; some critics point to the need for copyright laws for fanfiction to exist as a genre because fandom needs a canon from which to be derivative; some critics believe once writing aims to make a profit it can no longer be called fanfic. Most academics use a "narrowly defined" approach to fanfiction, which requires "rewriting of shared media" stemming from 1960s science-fiction fandom (Hellekson and Busse, 6–10).
18 Hellekson and Busse, 3.
19 EzraNaps, "The Man Next Door," *Archive of Our Own*, June 15, 2018, https://archiveofourown.org/works/2610134; WarnerHedgehog, "Echidna Touchstone's Pamphlet of Impractical Cats," *Archive of Our Own*, April 24, 2023, https://archiveofourown.org/works/14936016, https://archiveofourown.org/works/7593577/chapters/17279875; crowleyshouseplant, "The Love Song of Joss Whedon," *Archive of Our Own*, May 5, 2014, https://archiveofourown.org/works/1573454.
20 Kavita Mudan Finn, panelist comments in "Fan Fiction, Fan Studies, and Literary Studies," 2022 Modern Language Association Conference (January 6, 2022). Since the first volume of *Transformative Works and Culture*, the primary scholarly journal of fanfiction, scholars and fans have debated the relationships and ethics of scholars of fandom; see Dana L. Bode, "And Now, a Word from the Amateurs," *Transformative Works and Cultures* 1 (2008), https://doi.org/10.3983/twc.2008.051.
21 Fitzgerald, 9.
22 Laura Heffernan and Rachel Sagner Buurma, *The Teaching Archive: A New History for Literary Study* (Chicago: University of Chicago Press, 2020).

23 Ronald Bush, "'Intensity by association': T. S. Eliot's Passionate Allusions," *Modernism/modernity* 20, no. 4 (2013): 709.
24 Bush, 710.
25 Bush, 722.
26 L. E. Williams ("tigriswolf"), "What Is to Give Light Must Endure Burning," *Archive of Our Own*, September 8, 2011, https://archiveofourown.org/works/250757.

18

Afterword: Strange God—Eliot, Now

Urmila Seshagiri

Bombs are falling over Kyiv today. Fatal, incandescent, each one the monstrous afterbirth of ambition, the work of a twenty-first-century Mr. Kurtz who "wanted to swallow all the air, all the earth, all the men before him."[1] How might we travel from the specter of a future wasteland back to the centenary of an earlier one? In my end, perhaps, is my beginning: I open this afterword with a return to the titular phrase "Eliot now." The editors' deceptively simple declaration "Eliot now is Eliot new" serves as an exhortation to action.[2] It insists that we attend to the interconnected processes whereby words gather and release meaning, processes as complex in a single instant as over the passage of decades. With Eliotic elegance, Quigley and Chinitz's statement creates possibilities through a subtle prosodic distinction: "now" and "new," separated by a single vowel, suggest conditions of being equivalent and yet unrelated. That rich paradox lends momentum to the essays collected in *Eliot Now*, whose key questions about the poet and his career we might trace back to Virginia Woolf's reaction to hearing Eliot read *The Waste Land* one hundred years ago: "It has great beauty & force of phrase: symmetry; & tensity. What connects it together, I'm not so sure … One was left, however, with some strong emotion."[3] In eighteen chapters that variously investigate "what connects it together," scholars and poets moved by "strong emotion" demonstrate that T. S. Eliot remains, in Chinitz's words, "more interesting than either his past enthusiasts or detractors cared to admit."[4] Chinitz and Quigley's collection galvanizes our scrutiny of Eliot and sheds new light on how a century of readers have (or have not) reconciled the enduring brilliance of Eliot's poetry with the uneven relevance of his critical-philosophical thought. Further, and perhaps of greater significance for our disciplinary future, these eighteen chapters offer robust models for how and why we should continually and self-consciously justify our commitments to literature's histories and canons.

What, then, can modernism mean in the time of the twenty-first century? How does T. S. Eliot's oeuvre—literary, critical, published, unpublished, as-yet unread—aid our conception of this historical moment? These are difficult paths to tread, and Eliot (unlike, for example, James Baldwin, whose righteous visionary genius burns brighter with each passing decade) refuses to make it easy. Academic conversations about Eliot's prejudices acquire a different complexion in the third decade of this century, when nations around the world are reckoning with the entrenched racisms constitutive of their character. Set aside, for the moment, Bolo, Bleistein, and murderous-pawed Rachel; set aside the poet's characterization of his own spoken English (in an April 1928 letter to Herbert Read) as a putatively humiliating Southern "nigger drawl" (*Letters4* 137). We will return to these embattled instances shortly. Rather, consider that Eliot's Page-Barbour Lectures, later published as *After Strange Gods*, were delivered in 1933, in the same Charlottesville that would be bloodied by a rally of white supremacists convinced, in 2017, that "[t]he population should be homogeneous." To gather under the banner "Unite the Right" was to deem "any large number of free-thinking Jews undesirable" (*After Strange Gods*, *Prose5* 20) and to march for the crudest version of what Ann Marie Jakubowski calls Eliot's "yearning for an integral identity, with cohesive religious, national, and racial attributes."[5] In the United States, the post-Charlottesville spate of violent attacks against Jewish, Muslim, Hindu, and Sikh people, indigenous and Black and Latinx and Asian American people, citizens as well as immigrants from near and far, would seem ample reason to unseat last century's Anglo-American poet-genius. Our current historical self-scrutiny has emboldened us to remove monuments and rename buildings and deaccession museum holdings. Perhaps T. S. Eliot's place in the literary firmament that he was instrumental in creating ought now to be treated like statues of Robert E. Lee, Cecil Rhodes, King Leopold, Edward Colston, Theodore Roosevelt, and Thomas Jefferson, relocated to more fitting domains. Should we continue our efforts to separate Eliot's poetic speakers from Eliot's own convictions, to draw what Chinua Achebe calls a *cordon sanitaire* between the artist and the critic?[6] The poets all say, resoundingly, *yes*.

The six poets who speak about *The Waste Land* at its centenary approach the *now* and the *new*, the present and the unprecedented, with an intimate understanding of how Eliot's craftsmanship reverberates in today's world. Their conversation comes alive through its engagements with contemporary literature and politics; they show us a T. S. Eliot as prophetic and as blind as the Tiresias he reveres. James Longenbach's and Craig Raine's pieces situate Eliot as the colossus of English poetry, a figure to whom subsequent poets are indebted and whose heir has yet to be born. Concentrating his attention on the micro-nuances of verse-punctuation, Longenbach points out that Eliot "would insist that in poetry, punctuation includes the absence of punctuation marks, and in this regard we are still learning to be Eliot's contemporaries."[7] Raine, too, regards Eliot as an artist without peer and pronounces that "The two central modernist texts are *Ulysses* and *The Waste Land* ... They are, and have been for nearly a century, impossible as models. Both are without progeny."[8] Carl Phillips, who shares Longenbach's and Raine's love of the "architecture and sense of order and sheer beauty" of Eliot's poems, nevertheless counters their claims by citing Hayden and Hughes, Ashbery and Graham: "[T]here are so many other texts available from which I can learn and teach what *The Waste Land* presents at the level of craft."[9] Alison C. Rollins's life as a "Black, queer woman" and a "descendant of the enslaved" adds indelible historical layers to Eliot's work: *The Waste Land*'s shortest section, "Death by Water," Rollins suggests, leaves her "forced to reckon with the Middle Passage."[10] Lesley Wheeler, too, points to the dark violence pervading the poem: "The risk and reality of sexual predation are everywhere ... Eliot's repetition and allusion mimic trauma as well as depicting it. Further, and more disturbingly to sexual assault survivors, it uses rape as a metaphor for other kinds of damage."[11] And Hannah Sullivan articulates what Phillips describes as the "conundrum" of *The Waste Land*:

> [I]t is a poem that could have only been written at this specific moment in literary history, a decade after the term "free verse" came into common use but a couple of decades before poets and their readers lost their sense of verse as a native language. I usually teach it near the beginning of any course on modernism or twentieth-century literature, but I have a fantasy of teaching it as the last poem in a course on English poetry, as an elegy.[12]

Sullivan's question about *The Waste Land*—is it bound to its exact history or always breaking its own chrysalis to wing past the present moment?—carries me to "The Love Song of J. Alfred Prufrock," a work whose expressive depths contain our *now* with breathtaking prescience. As a professor of modernism, I had become accustomed to students treating "Prufrock" as a relic of the early twentieth century, the poem's self-absorbed speaker and his Western masculine antecedents increasingly remote from the young citizens of today's world. But suddenly, every *volta* of Eliot's poem maps the cultural turns of our time. Unlike *The Waste Land*, whose aesthetic fragments and temporal largesse unlock human catastrophe across plural histories, the narrower ambit of "The Love Song of J. Alfred Prufrock" limns the exceptional circumstances of *this* catastrophic moment. Let us revisit Eliot's familiar, scalpel-precise lines and appreciate the newness afforded by their now-ness.

In our time, myriad life-threatening risks haunt the simple proposition "Let us go then, you and I" (*Poems1* 5). To go anywhere (public places, institutional spaces, the natural world, the internet) means exposing oneself not only to a potentially deadly virus but also to

> The eyes that fix you in a formulated phrase,
> And when I am formulated, sprawling on a pin,
> When I am pinned and wriggling on the wall,
> Then how should I begin
> To spit out all the butt-ends of my days and ways?
> And how should I presume? (*Poems1* 7)

A "formulated phrase" transmitted everywhere instantly may "force the moment to its crisis" (7). Black Lives Matter. Make America Great Again. Critical Race Theory. Fake News. #MeToo. But what happens when the "eyes that fix you in a formulated phrase" belong to artificial intelligence? Confined to our Zoom squares and screens, we resemble the "lonely men in shirt-sleeves, leaning out of windows" in Prufrock's desolate world, "pinned and wriggling" while AI reconstitutes human individuality as patterned, predictable fields of data (7). Time turns into a sequence of uneasy intervals between a moment of action and the moment "when I am formulated" by machine-generated algorithms. (It is darkly comic to find our fears of a sentient algorithm articulated in Pound's famous words about Eliot: "He has actually trained himself *and* modernized himself *on his own*."[13]) The algorithms, "singing, each to each," have written history: and because I "do not think that they will sing to me," I, too, await the moment when "human voices wake us" (9).

J. Alfred Prufrock's own voice takes on an expansiveness befitting today's roiling cultural currents. The austerity of his dramatic monologue gives way to loud and diversely figured *prosopopoeiae*, a contemporary chorus that joins Prufrock in asking, "And how should I presume?" and "Do I dare?" (*Poems1* 6). This chorus includes Black people wondering if they will find themselves assaulted, "pinned and wriggling," while presuming to enjoy daily life. It includes women wondering what awaits them—unprecedented power? low wages? barriers to health care?—in rooms where they dare to "come and go, / Talking" (*Poems1* 6). It includes sexually intimate partners wondering what might ensue if one person says, "That is not what I meant, at all" (8). It includes trans people wondering if choosing to "wear white flannel trousers" or "part my hair behind" will make them targets of violence (9). It includes dispossessed refugees and migrants who have "squeezed the universe into a ball" as they dare to uproot and transplant their entire lives (8). And it includes a generation terrified to live on this ailing planet, asking, "Do I dare to eat a peach? / ... and walk upon the beach" in a place where "yellow fog" causes each evening to "spread out against the sky / Like a patient etherized upon a table" (9, 5).

Etherized patients: above all, the poem anatomizes the recent global pandemic.[14] I find that I am no longer teaching Eliot to young people unable to imagine a world scarred by mass death, no longer urging students to cultivate the faculty of sympathy for anonymous millions lost to war and disease. Each of my students now comes to this poem having had cause to say, "I have seen the eternal Footman hold my coat, and snicker, / And in short, I was afraid" (*Poems1* 8). A new register of fear spreads through Eliot's words, as though aerosolized particles of coronavirus and its Greek-lettered variants were infecting the speaker's lyrical aspirations. Prufrock ventriloquizes the grotesque calculations weighing human life against profit: "And would it have been worth it, after all, / ... / Would it have been worth while?" (8). His injunction "Oh, do not ask, 'What is it?'" (5) performs the willful indifference to scientific knowledge that has devastated communities everywhere. Perhaps most chillingly, Prufrock's "yellow fog" and "yellow smoke" recall President Trump's phrase "China virus," that alarmist synecdoche for a Yellow Peril said to have originated in Wuhan wet markets, where contagion "lingered upon the pools that stand in drains" until it "made a sudden leap" across Western borders (5). Prufrock excoriates the public figures complicit with this insidious fiction who chose to remain

> Deferential, glad to be of use,
> Politic, cautious, and meticulous;
> Full of high sentence, but a bit obtuse;
> At times, indeed, almost ridiculous—
> Almost, at times, the Fool. (9)

Through the pandemic's transformative optic, fragmented utterances that we have long associated with Prufrock's self-defeating solipsism gather the clarion strength of a global community's outward-facing outrage.

A startling literalism descends on the poem's metaphors. "To prepare a face to meet the faces that you meet"—a line famously evocative of urban anomie—now captures the practice of masking (or not masking) one's face in the company of other people (*Poems1* 6). Ever-advancing medical technologies illuminate the body's disease-ravaged systems, "as if a magic lantern threw the nerves in patterns on a screen" (8). Prufrock himself, afflicted by pandemic-era symptoms of stress ("They will say: How his hair is growing thin!" … "But how his arms and legs are thin!"), experiences the eeriness of lockdown ("certain half-deserted streets, / The muttering retreats / Of restless nights"). He knows the world-shrinking monotony of quarantining at home in a time of scarcity and terror:

> For I have known them all already, known them all:
> Have known the evenings, mornings, afternoons,
> I have measured out my life with coffee spoons;

and the sound of deaths mounting in hospital wards closed off to loved ones:

> I know the voices dying with a dying fall
> Beneath the music from a farther room. (6)

And the lines we have erstwhile attributed to fears of feminine mobility now shape themselves into an ekphrastic verse about bodies slipping from life to death, lying motionless in operating theaters, autopsy chambers, morgues, or coffins:

> And I have known the arms already, known them all—
> Arms that are braceleted and white and bare
> (But in the lamplight, downed with light brown hair!)
> Is it perfume from a dress
> That makes me so digress?
> Arms that lie along a table, or wrap about a shawl. (7)

This verse ends by posing the harrowing question raised by the pandemic's commencement as well as its recession: "And how should I begin?" To learn to live again after practicing not-dying means, perhaps, sharing Prufrock's refusal of Hamlet and his preference for Lazarus.

More than a century after its composition, "The Love Song of J. Alfred Prufrock" has sprung to life as an uncanny documentary of shared conditions of being, and as this pandemic passes into memory, Eliot's poem will stand alongside newer arts to provide retrospective points of entry into the particulars of suffering from 2020 onward. But—to return to Bolo and Bleistein, Rachel and "unity of religious belief"—how should we reconcile the affective power of the poetry with the poet's often troubling worldview? And haven't we posed this question over and over? What new answers might we expect to find? Today, the distance between Eliot's poetics and his politics gapes like a wound. Mapping that distance, and continuing to remap it with newly visible coordinates, reveals the stakes of valuing a difficult artist's difficult art.

Perhaps we should ask a question that T. S. Eliot taught us to ask, even (or especially) though our answers might not satisfy him: "What is a Classic?" In a 1991 lecture bearing a title identical to Eliot's 1944 essay, J. M. Coetzee investigates Eliot's adulation for Virgil, tracing it to the desire to "claim a cultural-historical unity for Western European Christendom, including its provinces, within which the cultures of its constituent nations would belong only as parts of a greater whole."[15] Speaking on or around the time when Eliot's misogyny, anti-Semitism, and coarse anti-Black language had swum into unavoidable view, Coetzee offers two competing readings of Eliot's techniques for intellectualizing "cultural-historical unity." These readings forecast not only the contours of subsequent scholarship about Eliot and the development of twentieth-century poetry but also burgeoning theories of transnational modernism and postwar institutional formation. On the one hand, Coetzee applauds Eliot for envisioning culture as a self-regulating phenomenon, "an entirely transpersonal order" whose immanent capacity for advancement ensures that subsequent generations, not Eliot himself, will decide what "classic" denotes. Less sympathetically, however, Coetzee frames Eliot's career as

> the essentially magical enterprise of a man trying to redefine the world around himself—America, Europe—rather than confronting the reality of his not-so-grand position as a man whose narrowly academic, Eurocentric education had prepared him for little else but life as a mandarin in one of the New England ivory towers.[16]

Coetzee shows us the necessity of acceding to the truths of both characterizations; it is neither inconsistent nor hypocritical to understand the detached philosopher as an anxious aspirant.

Coetzee's concluding postulate—"The classic defines itself by surviving"—yields a method for reading lines of Eliot's thought and poetry:

> The classic defines itself by surviving. Therefore the interrogation of the classic, no matter how hostile, is part of the history of the classic, inevitable and even to be welcomed. For as long as the classic needs to be protected from attack, it can never prove itself classic.
>
> One might even venture further along this road to say that the function of criticism is defined by the classic: criticism is that which is duty-bound to interrogate the classic. Thus the fear that the classic will not survive the decentering acts of criticism may be turned on its head: rather than being the foe of the classic, criticism, and indeed criticism of the most skeptical kind, may be what the classic uses to define itself and ensure its survival.[17]

Coetzee's injunction to critics to "interrogate the classic" allows for neither evasion nor apology. It catapults us into our own fiery, world-spanning debates over how art and history dwell in the architectures of collective memory. Where Eliot is concerned, our scholarly generation enters into these debates with access to an ever-greater quantity of the poet's own writings and, further, with a clear-eyed understanding of the self-reinforcing and exclusionary tactics that buttress different forms of traditional authority.

Eliot's *East Coker* gifts us the logic for revisiting ostensibly settled questions with fresh curiosity:

> And what there is to conquer
> By strength and submission, has already been discovered
> Once or twice, or several times, by men whom one cannot hope
> To emulate—but there is no competition—
> There is only the fight to recover what has been lost
> And found and lost again and again: and now, under conditions
> That seem unpropitious. But perhaps neither gain nor loss.
> For us, there is only the trying. The rest is not our business. (*Poems1* 191)

If we continue "the fight to recover what has been lost / And found and lost again and again," we might revive a decades-old experiment as a test of whether we can metabolize the resistance of our poet-playwright-critic-editor-publisher-Nobel laureate to the idea that all people are created equal.

Consider (or reconsider) how Eliot's post-conversion critical program looks against a broad timeline of twentieth-century racial and religious violence. In 1933, Hitler had become the chancellor of Germany when Eliot gave the Page-Barbour lectures at the University of Virginia, arguing, as I have stated—but these words demand repeating—that "reasons of race and religion combine to make any large number of free-thinking Jews undesirable." In 1935, Germany created the Nuremberg Laws that would culminate in the Holocaust, and Eliot's essay "Religion and Literature" railed against the corruptions of secularism, opining, "What I want is a literature which should be *un*consciously, rather than deliberately and defiantly, Christian" (*Prose5* 221). In 1939, the year Hitler invaded Poland, Eliot delivered the Cambridge University lectures that would become *The Idea of a Christian Society*, declaring that "the only hopeful course for a society which would thrive and continue its creative activity in the arts of civilisation, is to become Christian" (*Prose5* 694). In 1941, as Hermann Goering set the Nazis' Final Solution in motion, Eliot wrote in September 1941 to his fellow Christian intellectual J. H. Oldham, "To suggest that the Jewish problem may be simplified because so many will have been killed off is trifling: a few generations of security and they will be as numerous as ever" (*Letters9* 915). And in 1948, after the Holocaust and the end of the Second World War, after Apartheid laws were established in South Africa, and amid ongoing bloodshed in the partition following India's independence from Great Britain, Eliot wrote the following impassioned sentences in *Notes towards the Definition of Culture*:

> It is against a background of Christianity that all our thought has significance. An individual European may not believe that the Christian Faith is true, and yet what he says, and makes, and does, will all spring out of his heritage of Christian culture and depend upon that culture for its meaning … The Western world has its unity in this heritage, in Christianity and in the ancient civilizations of Greece, Rome and Israel, from which, owing to two thousand years of Christianity, we trace our descent. (*Prose7* 277)

This sequence of excerpts might compel us to demand, as George Bornstein, riffing on *The Waste Land*, did a quarter century ago, "What was Eliot thinking? What thinking? What?"[18] Surely there can be little of the "classic" in such sentiments, which neither were neutralized by Eliot's characterization of his 1948 Nobel Prize as "primarily an assertion of the supra-national value of poetry" nor, in the current day, possess enough integrity to endure what Coetzee calls "the decentering acts of criticism" ("Response to the Toast at the Nobel Banquet," *Prose7* 467). The self-replenishing seas of meaning in "Prufrock," *The Waste Land*, and *Four Quartets* affirm Pound's dictum that "Literature is news that STAYS news."[19] In sharp contrast, Eliot's post-1927 philosophies of culture—however erudite, however eloquent, however comparatively less fascistic than Pound's—often discredit themselves.

As scholars and students of literature, we live in the postwar house that T. S. Eliot built, and to reexamine the foundations of our house is inevitably to discover where it has been inhospitable. To read Eliot's writings as vestigial evidence of bygone modes of thought ignores their affinities with eruptions of anti-Semitism in our present moment. As bombs rain down on Kyiv and more than ten million Ukrainians flee their homeland, the country's democratically elected Jewish president, Volodymyr Zelensky, a descendant of Holocaust victims and survivors, fights alongside other Ukrainian citizens to defend his nation from the near-fascist Russian government that would annex it. It is a related fact that in the United States in 2022, a Tennessee school board successfully banned Art Spiegelman's Pulitzer Prize–winning graphic novel *Maus*, the story of a Jewish Holocaust survivor and his family. Rather than risk the dangerous amnesia of sidelining the unpalatable elements of Eliot's race-thought, we can connect those elements more fully to sociopolitical contexts across different temporalities. What the scholar and poet Gabrielle McIntire observes about Eliot's poetics holds equally true for Eliot studies: "memory, like an Other, manifests a separate and ongoing *coming-into-being* that demands a ceaseless reopening to the work of its translation and transfiguration."[20] Reopened, translated, transfigured: who might Eliot be, now?

The essays in Quigley and Chinitz's collection illuminate the complex poetic worlds of Eliot and his successors, celebrating what Hannah Sullivan hails as Eliot's "polyvocal, democratic" art. In so doing, they perform multilayered refutations of Eliot's own claim that "It is against a background of Christianity that all our thought has significance." The backgrounds and foregrounds that these new essays make available heighten our understanding of the authoritative traditions that Eliot brought into existence within and without the academy. In my beginning is my end. Returning to Virginia Woolf's response to *The Waste Land*, I find fertile terrain for our ongoing study of Eliot's career: "It has great beauty & force of phrase: symmetry; & tensity. What connects it together, I'm not so sure ... One was left, however, with some strong emotion." Affirming J. M. Coetzee's pronouncement that "criticism, and indeed criticism of the most skeptical kind, may be what the classic uses to define itself and ensure its survival" (16), the scholars and poets in *Eliot Now* hold Eliot's writings up to twenty-first-century modes of scrutiny, revealing anew the "beauty & force of phrase" of his words.

Notes

1 Joseph Conrad, *Heart of Darkness*, 5th ed., edited by Paul B. Armstrong (New York: Norton, 2017), 59.
2 See p. 8. Also Megan Quigley, "#MeToo, Eliot, and Modernist Scholarship," *Modernism/modernity* Print Plus, vol. 5, cycle 2 (September 28, 2020), https://doi.org/10.26597/mod.0163.
3 Virginia Woolf, *The Diary of Virginia Woolf, Vol. 2: 1920–1924*, edited by Anne Olivier Bell (San Diego: Harcourt, 1978), 178.
4 David E. Chinitz, "A Vast Wasteland? Eliot and Popular Culture," in *A Companion to T. S. Eliot*, edited by Chinitz (Malden: Wiley-Blackwell, 2007), 67.
5 See p. 98.
6 Chinua Achebe, "An Image of Africa," in *Hopes and Impediments: Selected Essays* (London: Penguin, 2019).

7 See p. 235.
8 See p. 242.
9 See p. 236.
10 See p. 249.
11 See p. 240.
12 See p. 247.
13 Quoted in Humphrey Carpenter, *A Serious Character: The Life of Ezra Pound* (London: Faber, 1988), 258.
14 On modernist literature and the influenza pandemic of 1918, see Elizabeth Outka, *Viral Modernism* (New York: Columbia University Press, 2019).
15 J. M. Coetzee, *Stranger Shores: Literary Essays 1986–1999* (New York: Viking, 2001), 5.
16 Coetzee, 7.
17 Coetzee, 16.
18 George Bornstein, "T. S. Eliot and the Real World," review of *T. S. Eliot, Anti-Semitism, and Literary Form*, by Anthony Julius, and *Inventions of the March Hare: Poems 1909–1917*, by T. S. Eliot, *Michigan Quarterly Review* 36, no. 3 (1997): 494–505.
19 Ezra Pound, *ABC of Reading* (New York: New Directions, 1934), 29.
20 Gabrielle McIntire, *Modernism, Memory, and Desire: T. S. Eliot and Virginia Woolf* (Cambridge: Cambridge University Press, 2007).

The Waste Land Centenary: Poets on Eliot

In memory of James Longenbach (1959–2022)

The Points of Poetry

James Longenbach

"Why, my dear More," wrote T. S. Eliot in October 1930 to the critic Paul Elmer More,

> are you so foolish as to discuss seriously with a mere ignoramous [*sic*] like myself questions of philosophy and theology, and then go for me on the one subject on which I know more than almost anyone living. I am quite aware that I am a minor romantic poet of about the stature of Cyril Tourneur, that I have little knowledge and no gift for abstract thought; but if there is one thing I do know, it is how to punctuate poetry. (*Letters5* 361)

Professor More persisted in seeing erratic punctuation as evidence of the state of Western civilization, while Eliot deployed punctuation in poetry as he might deploy meter or rhyme or line itself as a way of managing a poem's syntax, making us hear syntax in one way but not in another. Poetry, wrote Eliot in the *TLS* two years before he composed his 1930 letter to More, is "itself a system of punctuation" ("Questions of Prose," *Prose3* 495).

When *The Waste Land* turned fifty, the critic A. Walton Litz began his lectures by saying that *The Waste Land* is a museum of verse forms. Sticking just to "The Fire Sermon," the third of the poem's five movements, he'd point out the free verse, the pentameters, the couplets, the quatrains, the Shakespearean sonnet (beginning "The time is now propitious"), and the Petrarchan sonnet (beginning "Trams and dusty trees") (*Poems1* 64, 65).[1] Now, another fifty years later, the poem's punctuation seems as vivid, because of what poets are doing now. For anyone who makes poems in English, punctuation marks are as important as the letters of our alphabet.

It wasn't always this way. When the eighth- or ninth-century poem we call "The Seafarer" was inscribed in the Exeter Book, it was unlineated and unpunctuated;

it looks there like Joycean prose.[2] The poems of Horace and Homer were also written down this way; we didn't need to see the lines to understand their organization. Even after the rise of print culture, the lines of Shakespeare ("Let me not to the marriage of true minds") or of Williams ("so much depends") end where they do because of how they sound, not how they look.[3] Today, there aren't many unpunctuated prose poems (Michael Palmer has written a few, and of course there's Joyce); after we've given up rhyme, meter, line, and punctuation of any kind, what's left to direct syntax?

We have no idea how Shakespeare punctuated his plays (we've learned to trust editors), and his predecessor Sir Thomas Wyatt, whose poems exist in handwritten manuscripts as Shakespeare's don't, was used to reading the twenty-one-line poem we call "They Flee from Me" with only one punctuation mark. Wyatt's rhythmically various lines are thrilling as he saw them ("It was no dreme I lay brode waking"), and the first line of "They Flee" sports that one slash or virgule ("They fle from me / that sometime did me seke"), a punctuation mark employed today by poets such as Jos Charles, who also changes spelling.[4] It wasn't until the eighteenth century that English punctuation became regularized, along with the English spelling of words.[5]

This is why Eliot said that poetry is itself a system of punctuation. In other words, like meter or rhyme or line, punctuation is a way of organizing a poem's syntax, and in this sense, meter or rhyme or line are themselves kinds of punctuation. Every kind of punctuation can be found in *The Waste Land*, as can every kind of syntax, and most important, its fifth and final movement is largely (in the conventional sense) unpunctuated. Yet Eliot's unpunctuated lines sound like this—

> If there were rock
> And also water
> And water
> A spring
> A pool among the rock (*Poems1* 68–9)

—and like this—

> Sweat is dry and feet are in the sand
> If there were only water amongst the rock (*Poems1* 68)

—and also like this:

> Falling towers
> Jerusalem Athens Alexandria

>   Vienna London
>   Unreal (*Poems1* 69)

Eliot needs us to work through more conventional punctuation to get to these lines, which seem spoken by no one (*seem* being the important word). He would insist that in poetry, punctuation includes the absence of punctuation marks, and in this regard, we are still learning to be Eliot's contemporaries. Is that regard very small or very large?

Throughout the twentieth century, we associated an absence of punctuation in poetry more with Williams or Cummings than with Eliot, and beginning with his 1963 book *The Moving Target*, their heir W. S. Merwin wrote conventionally unpunctuated poems for the next fifty years.

>   The future woke me with its silence
>   I join the procession
>   An open doorway
>   Speaks for me[6]

Merwin's lineation often substitutes for conventional punctuation, parsing the syntax into clearly consumable pieces. But in the unpunctuated poems of *Headwaters*, published in 2013, Ellen Bryant Voigt doesn't let line function that way:

>   first frail green in the northeast the forest around us no longer
>   a postcard of Christmas snow clotting the spruce or worse
>   fall's technicolor beeches sumac sugar maple death
>   even the death of vegetation should never be
>   so beautiful it is unseemly I prefer the cusps[7]

Rather than emphasizing the grammatical shape of clauses or phrases, Voigt's lines shape our experience of the poem's syntax: avoiding any consistent alignment of syntax and line, either violating the grammatical integrity of the clauses or running them together, she creates variable rhythms within the lines.

Eliot of course used line for both purposes in *The Waste Land*, a poem that is also punctuated in several ways, metered in several ways, and rhymed in several ways. Does that variety reflect cultural chaos, or does the variety reflect lunch? Does language reflect?

Any aspect of poetry means what it means in a particular place at a particular time, and Paul Elmer More thought Eliot's varied punctuation raised questions of theology and philosophy. At the same time, Eliot thought of himself as a romantic poet of the stature of Tourneur. That's a great thing to have been.

The Waste Land Now

Carl Phillips

What is the influence of T. S. Eliot's *The Waste Land in* 2023? Let me start with an unlikely and potentially unpromising confession: I haven't taught this poem in at least twenty years. That doesn't mean, however, that the poem isn't influential and relevant (which are two different things). I consider *The Waste Land* seminal to an understanding not just of modernism but of so much of the poetry that's been written (in English) in modernism's long, more-restless-than-not wake. Though strategies like collage, associative leaping, and apparent non sequitur existed earlier—in jazz, for example, or *The Pillow Book* of Sei Shōnagon—*The Waste Land* stands as one of the first poems to align those strategies with psychology; in particular, Eliot brings together public and private psychology, sees them as intertwined, even as Freud analogously sees our private anxieties as inseparable from those of civilization itself.

Though *The Waste Land* does at one point address the "Gentile or Jew" as if to imply a lack of bias (that is, as if to say, Whoever you are, Reader, I'm talking to you), anyone who's read Eliot's earlier poems (and presumably his private correspondence)—let alone the internet—knows of Eliot's anti-Semitism and the ways some critics and scholars have tried to separate the poem from the maker's politics—something which, as a queer, biracial writer and reader, I'm not willing to do (*Poems1* 67). As the saying goes, where there's smoke, there's fire—so why wait for proof by getting burnt oneself eventually?

This doesn't mean that the poem isn't influential. Because it's so seminal, *The Waste Land* has been hugely influential and continues to be so today. But because of its influence, there are so many other texts available from which I can learn and teach what *The Waste Land* presents at the level of craft. The poem's filmic jump cutting is mirrored, for example, in Robert Hayden's "Middle Passage," in Langston Hughes's *Montage of a Dream Deferred*, or pretty much anything by John Ashbery or Jorie Graham. And because my students look almost nothing like those who filled a typical university classroom in Eliot's day—by which I mean that my students are decidedly more diverse, racially and in terms of sex and gender, many coming from groups largely excluded from education in the past—it seems at best an unfairness, at worst a heartlessness, to ask my students to spend substantial time with a poem complicated not only by Eliot's politics but by the fascism of Ezra Pound, to whom the poem is dedicated right from the start; that's a lot to bracket for the sake of literary appreciation.

And yet—teaching aside—I return to *The Waste Land* often enough as a reader. I do so as I've returned, over the years, to what's left of the Roman Forum and the Colosseum, whose architecture and sense of order and sheer beauty can make it easy to forget that the same people who conceived of these structures conquered and colonized any people who *weren't* Roman, even imposing Latin on them as the official language and replacing their gods with Roman gods. When I was studying Julius Caesar's *Gallic Wars* in high school, it didn't occur to me that this was a version of fascism, any more than it seemed wrong that all the books from which I learned to read English as a child were filled exclusively with white people. That no one like me was there felt, if not correct, then ordinary, as much so as my being the only Black kid in my class or seeing no Black people on TV.

I keep returning to *The Waste Land* as to the broken detritus of what was once considered the height of empire and human civilization. The poem is itself built from fragments that can seem haphazardly juxtaposed, though the speaker confirms a certain deliberateness: "These fragments I have shored against my ruins"—I take the ruins to refer equally to the self and to the broken remnants to which the world seems, by the twentieth century, irreparably reduced, a landscape of sterility ("dry sterile thunder without rain"), communion reduced to mere sexual exchange, dead pastoral ("The nymphs are departed"), romance replaced by power and duty (what Elizabeth chooses over love in the form of the Earl of Leicester) (*Poems1* 71, 68, 62).

And yet—. And yet, throughout Eliot's poem, there's an impulse toward continuance that feels like hope, or the belief in possibility, despite the ruins—the beating of wings, the beating of oars, the various questions whose very utterance, like prayer, resembles faith in, at the very least, an other who might respond and, in doing so, provide that connection without which we've only ourselves for company in the ruined (yet unpredictably lovely, as if that were the point of ruin, not so much to disclose as to throw into starker relief a loveliness when, like a self-sustaining form of persistence, it discloses itself) psychological landscape that is *The Waste Land*. Or maybe not ruined—instead, strewn with ruins. For the poem does end with rain bringing something like relief to a parched landscape. And it begins with spring rain, bringing the "dull roots" to life again, "breeding / Lilacs out of the dead land" (*Poems1* 55). I used to wonder how this made April the cruelest month—back when those opening lines were still the only ones that I could actually "translate," moving quickly past the part about memory and desire, unaware that the roots could be a way of thinking *about* memory and desire. If the rain brings relief, it also means we remember—not just the joys, presumably, but the losses, the disappointments—and it also means we desire again, just when we thought restlessness was a stage we might outgrow; we might rest, at last. For me, this is the chief reason why *The Waste Land* still matters. It speaks from, and to, conundrum. Isn't this conundrum how life, in fact, still is? One very hot summer, years ago, when I was touring the Roman Forum for the very first time, it began to rain, though the sky was cloudless.

Glossing *The Waste Land*

Lesley Wheeler

It's too soon to see what poets make of the new Eliot editions. Yet contemporary poets, like scholars, are busy reannotating Eliot. As in recent symposia in *Modernism/modernity*, some focus on Eliot's representations of sexual violence, especially in *The Waste Land*.[8] In the process, they reject critical objectivity—a shift away from traditional scholarship that has come to shape my writing, too.

Jeannine Hall Gailey's first collection, *Becoming the Villainess*, revisits myths about sexual assault, including the stories of Little Red-Cap, superheroes, and, most prominently, Philomel, working through Ovid toward Eliot. The poem "Remembering Philomel," about the author's rape at six by a male babysitter, begins with the line, "The professor asks, what is the scene here, class?"[9] His assignment requires writing from Philomel's point of view. In the classroom, imagining Philomel's experience is an intellectual exercise discussed in distanced terms. Gailey reframes it to root her reading and her writing in personal trauma.

There are no references to Eliot within "Remembering Philomel," but in the endnotes, Gailey describes how "the nightingale in T. S. Eliot's *The Waste Land* sings 'Tereu, Tereu.'"[10] Gailey does engage modernism openly in "Her Nerves," a poem beginning with the epigraph, "*My nerves are bad tonight. Yes, bad.*" Its speaker addresses a husband who is condescending and anxious about his wife's writing:

> You are afraid—not just of me,
> but what I see and hear that you don't—
> the crusts of blood, slippery dirt-gorged voices.
> You like it when I curse creatively,
> hate it when paper piles like excrement around me.[11]

Imagery of waste and mental disintegration recalls Eliot's poem and Vivien Eliot's contributions to it. (Gailey reports studying the facsimile edition of *The*

Waste Land and reading about the Eliots' marriage.[12]) "Her Nerves" can't be a historical persona poem from Vivien Eliot's perspective—it refers to Sylvia Plath—but like Eliot, Gailey finds analogues among mythic and contemporary figures. Throughout *Becoming the Villainess*, women suffer predatory violence, then take revenge, often through words.

"Her Nerves" echoes and counters "A Game of Chess," riffing on Eliot's language and motifs, layering perspectives and temporalities. Eliot's allusive poetry becomes subject to allusion, emphasizing how rape underlies, even initiates, literary resonance. A later collection, Paisley Rekdal's *Nightingale*, highlights this point: "I have spent my life devoted to an art whose foundational symbol is one of unspeakable violence."[13] Like Gailey, Rekdal moves from Ovid to Eliot, interweaving refractions of their work with the story of her sexual assault. Unlike Gailey, whose diction tends to be straightforward, Rekdal imitates Eliot in her display of erudition.

Section II of *Nightingale* begins with a free-verse narrative, "Philomela," about a granddaughter excluded from her grandmother's will.[14] By itself, the poem parallels rather than alludes to Eliot. The lyric essay that immediately follows, however, testifies to aborted literary inheritance, implying Rekdal's ambivalence about the august tradition Eliot helped construct. The essay, "Nightingale: A Gloss," consists of brief prose meditations on "Philomela" and its themes of violence, silence, and art as a kind of speech. In the essay's present, Rekdal works in an artists' colony, omitting parts of the myth that are "too grotesque" from her poem and ignoring advice to take walks in the woods.[15] She also describes how her younger self was attacked by a stranger: "It's 1992 and I'm hiking near Loch Ness." A passing fisherman attacks, and "I do not use my voice."[16] The essay, unlike Rekdal's Philomel poem, depicts violence graphically, although for years, Rekdal "resisted speaking about it."[17]

"Nightingale: A Gloss" critiques how Ovid and other poets shift emphasis from "empathy to spectacle" by "positioning an implicitly male audience in the consciousness of a raving, raped woman."[18] Evoking *The Waste Land* as well as her work, she observes: "Madness to insist on narrative cohesion when the story is one of fragmentation, chaos."[19] Like Eliot's "Notes to *The Waste Land*," Rekdal's scholarly account of her writing process bristles with quotes, translations, and references, as in a citation from "'The Waste Land,' II, 27": "('Jug jug,' Eliot croons)" (*Poems1* 58).[20] A faint echo of Eliot's line "the heart of light, the silence" also appears in Rekdal's speculation that "that the heart of poetry was only silence" (*Poems1* 56).[21] She shifts from formal citation to echo as if transforming from dutiful scholar to a poet who can "whistle back" to a disturbing tradition.[22]

Insight comes from oscillating between different approaches to texts, allowing personal experience to inform interpretation.

The Waste Land, as Megan Quigley writes, is replete with "visceral displays of violence against women."[23] Recent scholarship explains its prevalence in terms of literary antecedents, which is certainly valid—Eliot's poem has scholarly dimensions. Biographer Robert Crawford, for instance, posits that the references are "reincarnations of some underlying, disturbing myth," with no basis in Eliot's life beyond awareness of "seedier goings on around Crawford Mansions."[24] Yet the women in Eliot's circle, whether or not they experienced assault, probably constrained their activities in fear of it, like Rekdal at her artists' colony. Eliot understood this, even if women never confided in him and even if he never read "22 Hyde Park Gate," Virginia Woolf's story of sexual abuse shared with the Memoir Club in November 1920.[25] The risk and reality of sexual predation are everywhere and always have been.

There are many ways to gloss *The Waste Land*. I've written before about the persistence of Eliot's rhythms in the poetries of Kim Addonizio, Major Jackson, Robert Sullivan, and others.[26] *The Waste Land* first haunted me through its sounds, then through its otherworldliness, Eliot's "Unreal City" reverberating through my book *Heterotopia*. For some, it also remains a poem about rape, and not just thematically. As Rekdal writes, "lyric time is not progressive but fragmentary and recursive," therefore working like trauma, "the *now* of terror repeatedly breaking back through the crust of one's consciousness."[27] Eliot's repetition and allusion mimic trauma as well as depicting it. Further, and more disturbingly to assault survivors, it uses rape as a metaphor for other kinds of damage.

Yet my students are beginning to find new saliences in *The Waste Land*. It feminizes mental illness, they note; nervous breakdown has become neurodivergence.[28] There can be no definitive edition of a text with so many past and possible meanings. "Eliot now" will always be an impermanent condition.

T. S. Eliot's *The Waste Land* Now

Craig Raine

In his introduction to his *Choice of Kipling's Verse*, Eliot refers several times to Kipling's story "'The Finest Story in the World'" (in *Many Inventions*, 1898), where the clerk and would-be author Charlie Mears has had previous lives, which are inadvertently revealed in stories Charlie tells but is unable to write: "The

Fates," says the Kipling narrator-figure, "that are so careful to shut the doors of each successive life behind us had, in this case, been neglectful, and Charlie was looking, though that he did not know, where never man had been permitted to look with full knowledge since Time began." Eliot refers to this story three times, lastly praising its historical imagination: "The historical imagination may give us an awful awareness of the extent of time, or it may give us a dizzy sense of the nearness of the past" (*Prose6* 229). Isn't there a congruence between Eliot's phrase "an awful awareness of the extent of time" and Kipling's "to look with full knowledge since Time began"?

"HURRY UP PLEASE ITS TIME" is a radical piece of doubling—simultaneously a pub announcement of imminent closing and Eliot's way of saying that time is one and indivisible, an omnipresent (*Poems1* 60). "Memory and desire" are mixed (*Poems1* 55). Past and future are fused. *The Waste Land* is a poem predicated on this assumption and the assumption of reincarnation, of previous lives.

We understand, then, the structure of Eliot's poem, its thematic organization.

But it is a poem famous for its surface lack of structure, its absence of transitions, its abrupt juxtapositions, its rapid switches of tone, its hectic dynamic—for its smash cuts from a recognizably poetic high style to the spoken voice, from the hieratic to the demotic. From "Son of man. / You cannot say or guess, for you know only / A heap of broken images" to "If you see dear Mrs. Equitone, / Tell her I bring the horoscope myself" (*Poems1* 55, 56).

The two central modernist texts are *Ulysses* and *The Waste Land*. Eliot's great poem derives from Joyce's novel. In his essay "*Ulysses*, Order and Myth" (1923), Eliot acclaims Joyce's structural engine—metempsychosis, the transmigration of souls. The use of the past—Ulysses and Homer's *Odyssey*—as a way of organizing the chaos of the contemporary has, Eliot says, the importance of a scientific discovery. So Eliot learned from Joyce.

Can poets now learn from *The Waste Land*?

In his essay on Marlowe, Eliot refers to the Chinese wall of Milton—an exclusion and a barrier. In "The Classics and the Man of Letters," he says, "Milton's was certainly a style fatal to imitators: that is just as true of the style of James Joyce, and the influence of a great writer upon other writers can neither add to nor detract from his title to honour" (*Prose6* 299). Of Shakespeare (in "To Criticize the Critic"), Eliot says, "A poet of the supreme greatness of Shakespeare can hardly influence, he can only be imitated" (*Prose8* 462). Again, in "Milton II": "For a long time after an epic poet like Milton, or a dramatic poet like Shakespeare, nothing can be done" (*Prose7* 25). After Milton, we have

Miltonics—for example, Coleridge's "Religious Musings" and Wordsworth's "Descriptive Sketches" and "The Evening Walk"—all failed attempts to follow the Miltonic example, which sink into slavishness, before Wordsworth and Coleridge invent themselves—Coleridge with his Conversation poems, Wordsworth with his epic of the growth of a poet's mind. Half a century on, Hopkins says of Milton's genius that one should admire "and do otherwise."

This is true of both *Ulysses* and *The Waste Land*. They are, and have been for nearly a century, impossible as models. Both are without progeny. In Scott Fitzgerald's *Tender Is the Night*, the talentless and touchy McKisco has his lack of originality broadcast by his wife, Violet: "'It's on the idea of *Ulysses*,' continued Mrs. McKisco. 'Only instead of taking twenty-four hours my husband takes a hundred years. He takes a decayed old French aristocrat and puts him in contrast with the mechanical age.'" McKisco is tetchy about his presumed originality: "Oh, for God's sake, Violet, don't go telling everybody the idea … I don't want it to get all around before the book's published."[29] There are no novels that are outgrowths from *Ulysses*—or none that have survived.

For example, Orwell's *A Clergyman's Daughter* (1935) in chapter 3 has a scene set in Trafalgar Square, featuring the homeless and rootless. It features the aleatoric dialogue of the down-and-outs: "*Deafie* (singing): 'With my willy willy, *with* my willy willy—.'"[30] A Nighttown jumble fatally indebted to the "Circe" episode of *Ulysses*. Only Orwell completists remember this justly forgotten felony.

Nor are there any poems remotely like *The Waste Land*—one of the shortest long poems in the English language. It cannot be copied. It is too famous, too well-known, too distinctive, too original to be imitable. Hollywood turns out replicas and reproductions apace: Brad Pitt is a retread of James Dean, Catherine Zeta-Jones a high-street copy of Ava Gardner's haute couture. But literature laughs at copies of its iconic texts. *The Waste Land* is too exact, too tight a mosaic, too perfect to be copied.

Which is ironic because its perfection is partly accidental. Valerie Eliot's facsimile edition of the poem's manuscript demonstrates not only the flawed genius of Eliot but also the perfect editorial genius of Ezra Pound. The dynamic I've already alluded to is the direct result of Pound's interventions, his unerring ability to identify the inert in Eliot's original drafts. There is nothing Pound cut that we would want to restore. Had Eliot proceeded without Pound's assistance, we would be reading the depressing and otiose *The Waste Land: An Editorial Composite*, wished on us by Christopher Ricks and Jim McCue—a text unabridged too far. Eliot undone (*Poems1* 321–46).

In a 2018 interview with Hermione Lee, Tom Stoppard was explaining that the final text was available for last-minute alteration, that this was what Stoppard *loved* about theater. "You mean," she said, "that you're willing to change anything." "Yes," he replied, "but only if I'm the one making the changes."[31] The text confected, as if it were viable, by Ricks and McCue is a hubristic act of editorial officiousness. Of course, it is likely to be welcomed by the Eliot industry—and play to the sentimental idea that great art is inexhaustible—but it contravenes Eliot's decisions. All poetry in the end surrenders its difficulty. There is no longer quite the same pressing need, for instance, for the foundation of a Browning Society.

In his autobiography, *Something of Myself,* Kipling outlines his method: his Anglo-Indian tales "were originally much longer than when they appeared, but the shortening of them, first to my own fancy after rapturous re-readings, and next to the space available, taught me that a tale from which pieces have been raked out is like a fire that has been poked."[32] Pound did a good deal of poker work. Eliot accepted his judgments. As a result, *The Waste Land* seems to be a poem of collage and accretion, a long poem of fragments. It looks and reads as if it has come into being gradually, section by section, rather like "The Hollow Men" and *Ash-Wednesday*—which is partially, superficially, the case. Yet it feels quite different. Fundamentally, the poem is far from gradual—swift, pell-mell, strobe-lit—and this unsettling vitality is largely created by Pound's radical surgery, which left an anthology of great moments. One smashing tune after another. Like Mussorgsky's *Pictures at an Exhibition* or Tchaikovsky's *Nutcracker*. It will take a poet of comparable invention to rival Eliot's bravura conjuration or clear Joyce's high bar.

Techniques for Cohesion

Hannah Sullivan

There's *The Waste Land* that I teach (no, not *The Wasteland*: two words). Ezra Pound might have called it the "longest poem in the English langwidge," but for teaching purposes, it's conveniently short, a fraction of the length of a single episode of *Ulysses*, and conveniently capacious, touching on most of the major topics of modernism. In its 433 lines, we've got the Great War, jazz, a gramophone, riffs on tradition, anxiety about the future, the tarot pack, a typist eating food in tins, a solicitation to a Brighton hotel, Eliot's relationship to Pound, early twentieth-century print culture, and, via the facsimile edition, a whole set of questions about editing. It's the paradigmatic modernist text, and it's fun to teach, polyvocal, democratic. *Poems* (1920) produces a lot more "hot" moments in the classroom.

Then there's *The Waste Land*. For poets—beginning with Ezra Pound, who wrote "Complimenti, you bitch. I am wracked by the seven jealousies"—the poem provokes more complicated feelings. My own are commingled admiration, envy, and a kind of seat-gripping sympathetic performance anxiety, every time, about whether it will come off. As the facsimile edition shows, Eliot was not especially in control of his materials: having formed the desire to write a long, four-part poem about London at different historical periods, he was slow to get to it, and having produced a number of short and disjunctive sections, he was far from clear on how to fit them together.

This is where the admiration begins. Compared to other modernist long poems—Pound's *Hugh Selwyn Mauberley*, Hope Mirrlees's *Paris*, Nancy Cunard's *Parallax*—*The Waste Land* is both remarkably polyphonic and highly cohesive. On the one hand, we have clearly delineated individuals speaking in quite precise idiolects (I can't think of many contemporary poets who would risk the banality of "I didn't mince my words"); on the other, a series of methods for transitioning between them that makes the exact break point between voices hard to pin down. As Eliot's original title for the poem's first section made clear, this is a poem for one voice—but a voice that can perform, camp, mold into many. "He Do the Police in Different Voices" is a tag from *Our Mutual Friend*—a description of the lively way that the orphan Sloppy reads the newspaper aloud, not all in his own voice, but with "different" voices for the different characters. In this respect, the scene at the end of "A Game of Chess" functions, in microcosm, as a model for the speech act of the whole poem: "And if you don't give it him, there's others will, I said. / Oh is there, she said. Something o' that, I said" (*Poems1* 60).

When Eliot recorded this section, his voice was gesturally colloquial without attempting precise mimicry of a working-class London accent (a contracted "ma" for "my" in "I didn't mince my words," a soft glottal stop in "he's been in t' army four years") throughout; he then uses slight changes of pitch to suggest a doing of voices within a doing of voices, as the narrator switches between telling the story and giving us Lil's and Albert's words directly. Could a contemporary poet do this? Even someone with the ability to notate the speech of three working-class characters as precisely as Eliot (with some help from Vivien) would likely balk at the acting involved in "doing" the voices. It would be too difficult for anyone other than a trained professional; there would be anxieties about being inauthentic, patronizing, and culturally appropriative. One of the legacies of confessionalism in contemporary poetry is a po-faced literalism about "doing" any voice other than one's own: either, we tend to assume, someone is speaking "authentically" or they're speaking entirely inauthentically, merely acting a part. Fiona Shaw's performance (available on *The Waste Land* app) goes in the direction of full theatricality. At each of the "jump cuts" (her term), she rearranges herself, alters her mannerisms and facial expressions, and modulates her voice. After a while, this becomes exhausting and more than a little unnerving, as if someone with multiple personality disorder is undergoing a rapid series of switches. It is also a misunderstanding of the relationship between the voices. We might not be entirely convinced by Eliot's note to line 218 explaining that all of the "personages" in the poem are united in Tiresias, but the idea that each character "melts into" the next is fundamental. The whole is more than the parts.

Now we come to jealousy. In one of the many passages of self-recrimination in the *Cantos*, Pound wrote, "And I am not a demigod, / I cannot make it cohere."[33] This is the experience of many writers of long poems. But for at least some of the time that Eliot was working on *The Waste Land*, Eliot was a demigod, fashioning his separately composed passages into a whole via a series of subtle sound modulations as well as various (logically illicit, in many cases) forms of semantic and syntactic cohesion.

Take the opening, for example. "April *is* the cruellest month" is followed by three participial clauses of explanation ("breeding lilacs out of the dead land," "mixing memory and desire," "stirring dull roots with spring rain") before being paralleled by a second sentence about a season (*Poems1* 55). "Winter kept us warm" is also followed by two (longer) participial clauses (*Poems1* 55). When the third sentence then begins, "Summer surprised us," it appears as if the run-through of the seasons is continuing: four seasons, four sentences (*Poems1* 55). And the syntactic parallelism continues, because summer is also qualified by a participial clause: "coming over the Starnbergersee" (*Poems1* 55). At the same time, two things have changed dramatically. The "us" in "winter kept us warm" is most naturally understood as an inclusive pronoun: this is something that winter does for all of us at any point in time. But the "us" surprised by summer "coming over the Starnbergersee" cannot be taken inclusively because the location is bewilderingly specific and obscure ("the Lake of Starnberg" receives a cursory mention in Baedeker's 1879 *The Eastern Alps*; the German name is used in only a handful of English-language publications before 1922). So who is speaking? The fact that it *can't be the poet*, a man called Thomas Stearns Eliot, born in St. Louis in 1888, only becomes fully apparent a few lines later as Marie provides more specific details about her identity. For now, "us" bridges across the voice shift, spuriously cohesive with the previous "us," in fact marking out a change of referent.

The other warning sign of a shift of speaker is a change in the rhythm. The opening lines are close to being in the traditional song meter of English, a trochaic line of seven ("catalectic") or eight syllables: "Go and catch a falling star," "Fear no more the heat o' the sun." Eliot's lineation, with the participles running down the right-hand margin (also a way to establish a pattern, set up a rule, which the voice shift breaks), obscures this, but not much rewriting is needed to produce something quite regular:

> April is the cruellest month
> Breeding lilacs out of [the] dead land
> Mixing memory and desire
> Stirring dull roots with spring rain
> Winter kept us warm and covered
> O'er the earth forgetful snow [cf. "O'er the earth the flowers grow"]
> Fed a little life dried tubers.

In the next line, however, the pattern completely breaks down: "Summer," like "April" and "winter," is a good trochaic noun, but the two-syllable verb "surprised" is, like almost all two-syllable verbs in English, an iamb. Eliot could have kept the trochaic pattern behind the arras going with another one-syllable verb, such as "shocked," but instead, he deliberately abandons it, moving into longer and freer lines, including a line of untranslated German.

This paves the way for a larger, less subtle shift of voice and tone at the beginning of the new verse paragraph. Now, for the pair of rhetorical questions, "what are the roots that clutch, what branches grow / Out of this stony rubbish?" (*Poems1* 55). Eliot moves into the magniloquence of blank-verse pentameter. The prepositional verb ("grow out of") is broken across the line break, producing the distinctive double clot of stress: "grow" is already stressed, as the final syllable of the line, but by the nuclear-stress rule, "out" is more stressed again. Wordsworth achieves the same effect at the start of Book VII of the *Prelude* with a Miltonic simile, "like a torrent bursting / From a black thunder cloud," but Eliot probably had, at the back of his mind, God's rebuke to Adam in *Paradise Lost* Book VI:[34]

> In the sweat of thy face shalt thou eat bread,
> Till thou return unto the ground; for thou
> Out of the ground wast taken, know thy birth,
> For dust thou art, and shalt to dust return.[35]

The Waste Land is often said to be in free verse. In fact, much of it is metrical. But it is a poem that could have only been written at this specific moment in literary history, a decade after the term "free verse" came into common use but a couple of decades before poets and their readers lost their sense of verse as a native language. I usually teach it near the beginning of any course on modernism or twentieth-century literature, but I have a fantasy of teaching it as the last poem in a course on English poetry, as an elegy.

When Thunder Speaks: Writing Freely between Sight and Sound

Alison C. Rollins

Christina Sharpe's *In the Wake: On Blackness and Being* devotes an entire chapter to "The Weather." Sharpe writes of weather as a pervasive anti-Black climate and draws a connection between lungs and weather, questioning, "But who has access to freedom? Who can breathe free?"[36] In the "damp gust" of Eliot's *The Waste Land* we know rain is on the way. The two seemingly simple words "Bringing rain" point to what I hope to deliver to the reader in my lyric—my sterile silence broken with the spittle of words uttered.

When writing poetry, I like to think I occupy the time and space between the *sight* of lightning and the *sound* of thunder. Thunder is heard *after* a lightning flash; lightning, a cloud's visible electrical discharge, occurs *before*. Sight comes before sound because light is much faster than sound. If we speak in terms of linear time, the accurate order of events is first, second, third, or past, present, future. The lightning of the past or present serves as forebear to the future thunder. Through this lens, thunder exists in the future tense. In this vein, I view my subject position as poet as that of a betwixt-and-between seer, and the poem as a portal of future possibility.

When I wrote the poem "Self-Portrait of Librarian with T. S. Eliot's Papers," the year 2020 was still in the future. The poem begins, "In the year 2020, T. S. Eliot's papers will be unsealed."[37] At the present moment, the future 2020 of that poem now resides in the past, for as Heraclitus posits, change is the only constant.

What does this imply for me as I reflect on the centenary of T. S. Eliot's *The Waste Land*? What does this mean for you, reader, as you encounter this essay here and now? In the preface to *Queer Times, Black Futures,* Kara Keeling argues, "Every *now* harbors chaos and, therefore, a capacity for change."[38] In the midst of chaotic change, I have come to see my work in conversation with Eliot's *The Waste Land*. My work is steeped in a belief that poetry carries out the impossible, or that, as Keeling states, "Poetry is a way of entering the unknown and carrying back the impossible; it is productive of ideas or knowledges that were incomprehensible and unacceptable before their distillation as such via poetry."[39]

In 2019, Naomi Shihab Nye selected "Self-Portrait of Librarian with T. S. Eliot's Papers," from my debut collection *Library of Small Catastrophes*, for republication in the *New York Times Magazine*, stating, "Alison C. Rollins makes use of imagery relating to archives, texts, figures from history, card catalogs, classifications—libraries as evocative troves of imagery, blurring eras, familiar phrases and identities."[40] Nye's phrase "blurring eras" best captures my fascination with how time functions in my own work and in *The Waste Land*. In "What the Thunder said," each of the first three lines starts with the word "After." In the *after* of visible lightning, we are met with lyric representations of thunder's voice:

> After the torchlight red on sweaty faces
> After the frosty silence in the gardens
> After the agony in stony places
> The shouting and the crying (*Poems1* 68)

First comes the lightning flash as forewarning, followed by thunder or the sound of "shouting and crying." Much of my work is fixated upon the ways we order events. I am obsessed with the blurring or queering of temporal notions such as *after* and *before*. Another of the poems in *Library of Small Catastrophes*, titled "Free Radical," takes the form of a list with almost every phrase repeating the word "before."[41]

As a writer, I never walk alone. As artists, the living, the dead, and the yet-to-exist walk side by side with us, in our creative endeavors. This is how I choose to interpret Eliot's mentioning of "the third" in "What the Thunder said":

> Who is the third who walks always beside you?
> When I count, there are only you and I together
> But when I look ahead up the white road
> There is always one walking beside you (*Poems1* 69)

I read "the third" as a figure who stands in for the future, embodying what it means to "look ahead." To "look ahead," however, is also simultaneously steeped in looking back or behind. Thus, the poem exists as a trinity—an amalgam of the past and present situated in the future. To write poetry in the present is to look ahead while also looking back; thus, poems come in threes, manifesting as nods to the past, present, and future.

The opening stanza of "What the Thunder said" ends with a remark on the relationship between life and death:

> He who was living is now dead
> We who were living are now dying
> With a little patience (*Poems1* 68)

As a Black, queer woman, I find patience, even "a little patience," a fraught concept. I think of Martin Luther King, Jr., who, as president of the Montgomery Improvement Association, declared, "For many years we have shown an amazing patience … But we come here tonight to be saved from that patience that makes us patient with anything less than freedom and justice."[42] In league with King, I reflect on Phillis Wheatley, the first "African American" author of a published book of poetry. Regarding slavery, Wheatley—born in West Africa—writes in a 1774 letter, "in every human breast, God has implanted a Principle, which we call Love of Freedom; it is impatient of Oppression, and pants for Deliverance."[43] Faced with a trinity of life, death, and patience, perhaps I have learned to reject Eliot's third term.

Since the section that precedes "What the Thunder said" is titled "Death by Water," it is only fitting to consider thunder's connection with water. As a descendant of the enslaved, I am consistently forced to reckon with the Middle Passage. In the preface to *Undrowned: Black Feminist Lessons from Marine Mammals*, Alexis Pauline Gumbs posits: "I am talking about the middle passage and everyone who drowned and everyone who continued breathing. But I am troubling the distinction between the two."[44]

Although I share the birthplace of St. Louis, Missouri, with Eliot, I reside now in the city of Colorado Springs. I write this essay from a rented blue house surrounded by the mountains of Colorado. Each day, when I go outside, I reconcile my Black body with Marie's line from the opening stanza of *The Waste Land*: "In the mountains, there you feel free" (*Poems1* 55). To trouble the notion of "silence" and the urgent need for water, Eliot writes, "Here is no water but only rock":

> Dead mountain mouth of carious teeth that cannot spit
> Here one can neither stand nor lie nor sit
> There is not even silence in the mountains
> But dry sterile thunder without rain (*Poems1* 68)

Later, in "What the Thunder said," Eliot returns water to the reader in the form of rain, writing:

> Only a cock stood on the rooftree
> Co co rico co co rico
> In a flash of lightning. Then a damp gust
> Bringing rain (*Poems1* 70)

I find poetry the medium most adept for holding the complexity and nuance of my survival. In a 1982 interview with Claudia Tate, the "Black lesbian feminist warrior poet" Audre Lorde articulates, "I have a duty to speak the truth as I see it and share not just my triumphs, not just the things that felt good, but the pain, the intense, often unmitigated pain. It is important to share how I know survival is survival and not just a walk through the rain."[45] As long as I have breath in my body, I have a duty to share the multifaceted dimensions of my existence and lived experience. As weathered writer, I sit in the rain and speak my truth through poems. In the bright flash of lightning that pierces the sky, one can spot the cock of Eliot's *The Waste Land* as it stands on my shoulder. The cock's cry of *Co co rico co co rico* defies the impossible. It is the poem's never-ending call for freedom.

Notes

1 A. Walton Litz, *Eliot in His Time* (Princeton: Princeton University Press, 1973), 7–8.
2 James Longenbach, *The Art of the Poetic Line* (Minneapolis: Graywolf, 2008), 83–7.
3 William Shakespeare, *Shakespeare's Sonnets*, edited by Stephen Booth (New Haven: Yale University Press, 1977), 100; William Carlos Williams, *Collected Poems*, edited by A. Walton Litz and Christopher MacGowan (New York: New Directions, 1988), vol. 1, 224.
4 Richard Harrier, *The Canon of Sir Thomas Wyatt's Poetry* (Cambridge: Harvard University Press, 1975), 131–2. See Jos Charles, *Feeld* (Minneapolis: Milkweed, 2018). See also Peter Murphy, *The Long Public Life of a Short Private Poem* (Palo Alto: Stanford University Press, 2019).
5 M. B. Parkes, *Pause and Effect: An Introduction to the History of Punctuation in the West* (Berkeley: University of California Press, 1993).
6 W. S. Merwin, *Collected Poems 1952–1993*, edited by J. D. McClatchy (New York: Library of America, 2013), 264.
7 Ellen Bryant Voigt, *Headwaters: Poems* (New York: Norton, 2013), 14.
8 "Reading *The Waste Land* with the #MeToo Generation," edited by Megan Quigley, *Modernism/modernity* Print Plus, vol. 4, cycle 1 (March 4, 2019), https://doi.

org/10.26597/mod.0094; and "#MeToo and Modernism," *Modernism/modernity* Print Plus, vol. 5, cycle 2 (September 28, 2020), https://doi.org/10.26597/mod.0163.
9   Jeannine Hall Gailey, *Becoming the Villainess* (Bowling Green: Steel Toe, 2006), 7.
10 Gailey, *Becoming the Villainess*, 80.
11 Gailey, 54.
12 Gailey, email message to the author, May 12, 2021.
13 Paisley Rekdal, *Nightingale* (Port Townsend: Copper Canyon, 2019), 54.
14 Rekdal, 35–7.
15 Rekdal, 38.
16 Rekdal, 40.
17 Rekdal, 43.
18 Rekdal, 46.
19 Rekdal, 45.
20 Rekdal, 53.
21 Rekdal, 54.
22 Rekdal, 54.
23 Megan Quigley, "#MeToo, Eliot, and Modernist Scholarship" in "#MeToo and Modernism," edited by Quigley.
24 Robert Crawford, *Young Eliot: A Biography* (New York: Farrar, Straus and Giroux, 2015), 364.
25 Hermione Lee, *Virginia Woolf* (New York: Vintage, 1999), 153. Lee also describes Woolf discussing the abuse with friends as early as 1911.
26 Lesley Wheeler, "Undead Eliot: How 'The Waste Land' Sounds Now," *Poetry* 204, no. 5 (September 2, 2014), https://www.poetryfoundation.org/poetrymagazine/articles/70143/undead-eliot-how-the-waste-land-sounds-now.
27 Rekdal, *Nightingale*, 51.
28 Lesley Wheeler, "Hurry Up Please Its Time," *Modernism/ modernity* Print Plus, vol. 5, cycle 2 (September 28, 2020), https://doi.org/10.26597/mod.0165.
29 F. Scott Fitzgerald, *Tender Is the Night* (New York: Scribner, 1962), 17.
30 George Orwell, *A Clergyman's Daughter* (San Diego: Harcourt Brace Jovanovich, 1970), 154.
31 Hermione Lee, "Tom Stoppard, interviewed by Hermione Lee," *YouTube*, uploaded by The 92nd Street Y, New York, October 17, 2018, https://www.youtube.com/watch?v=OvZ53Vm-ZoM.
32 Rudyard Kipling, *Something of Myself: For My Friends Known And Unknown* (San Francisco: Tannenberg, 2014), 94.
33 Ezra Pound, *The Cantos of Ezra Pound* (London: Faber, 1975), 796.
34 William Wordsworth, *The Poems of William Wordsworth: Collected Reading Texts from the Cornell Wordsworth Series* (Penrith: Humanities-Ebooks, 2014), 238.
35 John Milton, *Paradise Lost* (Richmond: Alma, 2019), 273.

36 Christina Sharpe, *In the Wake: On Blackness and Being* (Durham: Duke University Press, 2016), 112.
37 Alison Rollins, *Library of Small Catastrophes* (Port Townsend: Copper Canyon, 2019), 22.
38 Kara Keeling, *Queer Times, Black Futures* (New York: New York University Press, 2019), ix.
39 Keeling, xii.
40 Naomi Shihab Nye, "Self-Portrait of Librarian with T. S. Eliot's Papers," *New York Times Magazine* (December 1, 2019), 12.
41 Rollins, 30.
42 Martin Luther King Jr., *Stride toward Freedom: The Montgomery Story* (Boston: Beacon, 2010), 50.
43 Phillis Wheatley, *The Writings of Phillis Wheatley*, edited by Vincent Carretta (Oxford: Oxford University Press, 2019), 120.
44 Alexis Pauline Gumbs, *Undrowned: Black Feminist Lessons from Marine Mammals* (Chicago: AK Press, 2020), 1.
45 Claudia Tate, "Audre Lorde," in *Black Women Writers at Work*, edited by Tate (New York: Continuum, 1985), 104.

Selected Bibliography of Recent T. S. Eliot Scholarship

Note: This list includes monographs, edited collections, and forums highlighting T. S. Eliot since 2000. For further resources we recommend the periodically updated bibliographies on the website of the International T. S. Eliot Society (tseliotsociety.org). *The T. S. Eliot Studies Annual* (listed below) and the website of the T. S. Eliot Foundation (tseliot.com) also provide useful primary and secondary sources.

Asher, Kenneth. *Literature, Ethics, and the Emotions*. Cambridge: Cambridge University Press, 2017.

Avery, Todd. *Radio Modernism: Literature, Ethics, and the BBC, 1922–1938*. Aldershot: Ashgate, 2006.

Badenhausen, Richard. *T. S. Eliot and the Art of Collaboration*. Cambridge: Cambridge University Press, 2004.

Beasley, Rebecca. *Theorists of Modernist Poetry: T. S. Eliot, T. E. Hulme, Ezra Pound*. London: Routledge, 2007.

Blanton, C. D. *Epic Negation: The Dialectical Poetics of Late Modernism*. Oxford: Oxford University Press, 2015.

Boll, Tom. *Octavio Paz and T. S. Eliot: Modern Poetry and the Translation of Influence*. London: Legenda, 2012.

Booth, Allyson. *Reading "The Waste Land" from the Bottom Up*. New York: Palgrave Macmillan, 2015.

Brinkman, Bartholomew. *Poetic Modernism in the Culture of Mass Print*. Baltimore: Johns Hopkins University Press, 2017.

Brooker, Jewel Spears, ed. *T. S. Eliot and Our Turning World*. New York: St. Martin's, 2001.

Brooker, Jewel Spears. *T. S. Eliot's Dialectical Imagination*. Baltimore: Johns Hopkins University Press, 2018

Brooker, Jewel Spears, ed. *T. S. Eliot: The Contemporary Reviews*. Cambridge: Cambridge University Press, 2004.

Brown, Janice. *The Lion in the Waste Land: Fearsome Redemption in the Works of C. S. Lewis, Dorothy L. Sayers, and T. S. Eliot*. Kent: Kent State University Press, 2018.

Cameron, Sharon. *Impersonality: Seven Essays*. Chicago: University of Chicago Press, 2007.

Camlot, Jason. *Phonopoetics: The Making of Early Literary Recordings*. Stanford: Stanford University Press, 2019.

Carver, Beci. *Granular Modernism*. Oxford: Oxford University Press, 2014.
Childs, Donald J. *From Philosophy to Poetry: T. S. Eliot's Study of Knowledge and Experience*. London: Athlone, 2001.
Childs, Donald J. *Modernism and Eugenics: Woolf, Eliot, Yeats, and the Culture of Degeneration*. Cambridge: Cambridge University Press, 2001.
Chinitz, David E., ed. *A Companion to T. S. Eliot*. Oxford: Wiley-Blackwell, 2009.
Chinitz, David E. *T. S. Eliot and the Cultural Divide*. Chicago: University of Chicago Press, 2003.
Cianci, Giovanni, and Jason Harding, eds. *T. S. Eliot and the Concept of Tradition*. Cambridge: Cambridge University Press, 2007.
Cohen, Debra Rae, Michael Coyle, and Jane Lewty, eds. *Broadcasting Modernism*. Gainesville: University Press of Florida, 2009.
Cole, Sarah. *At the Violet Hour: Modernism and Violence in England and Ireland*. Oxford: Oxford University Press, 2012.
Collini, Stefan. *Common Writing: Essays on Literary Culture and Public Debate*. Oxford: Oxford University Press, 2016.
Collini, Stefan. *The Nostalgic Imagination: History in English Criticism*. Oxford: Oxford University Press, 2019.
Comentale, Edward P. *Modernism, Cultural Production, and the British Avant-Garde*. Cambridge: Cambridge University Press, 2004.
Cooper, John Xiros. *The Cambridge Introduction to T. S. Eliot*. Cambridge: Cambridge University Press, 2006.
Cooper, John Xiros. *Modernism and the Culture of Market Society*. Cambridge: Cambridge University Press, 2004.
Cooper, John Xiros, ed. *T. S. Eliot's Orchestra: Critical Essays on Poetry and Music*. New York: Garland, 2000.
Crawford, Robert. *Eliot after "The Waste Land."* London: Jonathan Cape, 2022.
Crawford, Robert. *Young Eliot: From St. Louis to "The Waste Land."* London: Jonathan Cape, 2015.
Cuda, Anthony. *The Passions of Modernism: Eliot, Yeats, Woolf, and Mann*. Columbia: University of South Carolina Press, 2010.
Cuddy, Lois. *T. S. Eliot and the Poetics of Evolution: Sub/Versions of Classicism, Culture, and Progress*. Lewisburg: Bucknell University Press, 2000.
Däumer, Elisabeth, and Shyamal Bagchee, eds. *The International Reception of T. S. Eliot*. London: Continuum, 2007.
Diaper, Jeremy. *T. S. Eliot and Organicism*. Clemson: Clemson University Press, 2018.
Dickey, Frances. *The Modern Portrait Poem: From Dante Gabriel Rossetti to Ezra Pound*. Charlottesville: University of Virginia Press, 2012.
Dickey, Frances, and John D. Morgenstern, eds. *The Edinburgh Companion to T. S. Eliot and the Arts*. Edinburgh: Edinburgh University Press, 2016.
Diepeveen, Leonard. *The Difficulties of Modernism*. New York: Routledge, 2003.

Donoghue, Denis. *Words Alone: The Poet T. S. Eliot.* New Haven: Yale University Press, 2000.
Douglass, Paul, ed. *T. S. Eliot, Dante, and the Idea of Europe.* Newcastle upon Tyne: Cambridge Scholars, 2011.
DuPlessis, Rachel Blau. *Genders, Races, and Religious Cultures in Modern American Poetry, 1908–1934.* Cambridge: Cambridge University Press, 2001.
DuPlessis, Rachel Blau. *Purple Passages: Pound, Eliot, Zukofsky, Olson, Creeley, and the Ends of Patriarchal Poetry.* Iowa City: University of Iowa Press, 2012.
Eliot, T. S. *The Waste Land: A Facsimile and Transcript of the Original Drafts.* Centenary ed. Edited by Valerie Eliot. New York: Norton, 2022.
Ellis, Steve. *British Writers and the Approach of World War II.* Cambridge: Cambridge University Press, 2015.
Ellis, Steve. *T. S. Eliot: A Guide for the Perplexed.* London: Continuum International, 2009.
Epstein, Josh. *Sublime Noise: Musical Culture and the Modernist Writer.* Baltimore: Johns Hopkins University Press, 2014.
Esty, Jed. *A Shrinking Island: Modernism and National Culture in England.* Princeton: Princeton University Press, 2004.
Faber, Toby. *Faber & Faber: The Untold Story.* London: Faber, 2019.
Faltejskova, Monika. *Djuna Barnes, T. S. Eliot and the Gender Dynamics of Modernism: Tracing "Nightwood."* New York: Routledge, 2010.
Geary, Matthew. *T. S. Eliot and the Mother.* New York: Routledge, 2021.
Ghosh, Ranjan. *Transcultural Poetics and the Concept of the Poet: From Philip Sidney to T. S. Eliot.* New York: Routledge, 2016.
Gordon, Lyndall. *The Hyacinth Girl: T. S. Eliot's Hidden Muse.* New York: Norton, 2023.
Gordon, Lyndall. *The Imperfect Life of T. S. Eliot.* Rev. ed. London: Virago, 2012.
Graham, T. Austin. *The Great American Songbooks: Musical Texts, Modernism, and the Value of Popular Culture.* New York: Oxford University Press, 2013.
Griffiths, Matthew. *The New Poetics of Climate Change: Modernist Aesthetics for a Warming World.* London: Bloomsbury, 2017.
Hadjiyiannis, Christos. *Conservative Modernists: Literature and Tory Politics, 1900–1920.* Cambridge: Cambridge University Press, 2018.
Harding, Jason. *"The Criterion": Cultural Politics and Periodical Networks in Inter-War Britain.* Oxford: Oxford University Press, 2002.
Harding, Jason, ed. *The New Cambridge Companion to T. S. Eliot.* Cambridge: Cambridge University Press, 2017.
Harding, Jason, ed. *T. S. Eliot in Context.* Cambridge: Cambridge University Press, 2011.
Hargrove, Nancy Duvall. *T. S. Eliot's Parisian Year.* Gainesville: University Press of Florida, 2009.
Hart, Henry. *The Living Moment: Modernism in a Broken World.* Evanston: Northwestern University Press, 2012.

Hepburn, Allan. *A Grain of Faith: Religion in Mid-Century British Literature.* Oxford: Oxford University Press, 2018.
Hollis, Matthew. *"The Waste Land": A Biography of a Poem.* New York: Norton, 2022.
Jacobs, Alan. *The Year of Our Lord 1943: Christian Humanism in an Age of Crisis.* Oxford: Oxford University Press, 2018.
Jaffe, Aaron. *Modernism and the Culture of Celebrity.* Cambridge: Cambridge University Press, 2005.
Jaillant, Lise. *Cheap Modernism: Expanding Markets, Publishers' Series and the Avant-Garde.* Edinburgh: Edinburgh University Press, 2017.
Jones, Susan. *Literature, Modernism, and Dance.* Oxford: Oxford University Press, 2013.
Julius, Anthony. *T. S. Eliot, Anti-Semitism and Literary Form.* New ed. London: Thames and Hudson, 2003.
Kennedy, Sarah. *T. S. Eliot and the Dynamic Imagination.* Cambridge: Cambridge University Press, 2018.
Laity, Cassandra, and Nancy K. Gish, eds. *Gender, Desire, and Sexuality in T. S. Eliot.* Cambridge: Cambridge University Press, 2004.
Leavitt, June. *Esoteric Symbols: The Tarot in Yeats, Eliot, and Kafka.* Lanham: University Press of America, 2007.
Lehman, Robert. *Impossible Modernism: T. S. Eliot, Walter Benjamin, and the Critique of Historical Reason.* Stanford: Stanford University Press, 2016.
Levenson, Michael. *Modernism.* New Haven: Yale University Press, 2011.
Lewis, Ethan. *Modernist Image.* Newcastle upon Tyne: Cambridge Scholars, 2010.
Ley, James. *The Critic in the Modern World: Public Criticism from Samuel Johnson to James Wood.* London: Bloomsbury, 2014.
Llorens-Cubedo, Dídac. *T. S. Eliot and Salvador Espriu: Converging Poetic Imaginations.* Valencia: Universitat de València, 2013.
Lockerd, Benjamin G., ed. *T. S. Eliot and Christian Tradition.* Madison: Fairleigh Dickinson University Press, 2014.
Longenbach, James. *The Lyric Now.* Chicago: University of Chicago Press, 2020.
MacDiarmid, Laurie. *T. S. Eliot's Civilized Savage: Religious Eroticism and Poetics.* New York: Routledge, 2003.
MacKay, Marina, *Modernism and World War II.* Cambridge: Cambridge University Press, 2007.
Madden, Ed. *Tiresian Poetics: Modernism, Sexuality, Voice, 1888–2001.* Cranbury: Rosemont, 2008.
Maddrey, Joseph. *The Making of T. S. Eliot: A Study of Literary Influences.* Jefferson: McFarland, 2009.
Mallinson, Jane. *T. S. Eliot's Interpretation of F. H. Bradley: Seven Essays.* Dordrecht: Springer, 2002.
Manganaro, Marc. *Culture, 1922: The Emergence of a Concept.* Princeton: Princeton University Press, 2002.

Matthews, Steven. *T. S. Eliot and Early Modern Literature*. Oxford: Oxford University Press, 2013.
Matthews, Steven. *"The Waste Land" after One Hundred Years*. Woodbridge: D. S. Brewer, 2022.
McCabe, Susan. *Cinematic Modernism: Modernist Poetry and Film*. New York: Cambridge University Press, 2005.
McDonald, Peter. *Serious Poetry: Form and Authority from Yeats to Hill*. Oxford: Clarendon, 2002.
McIntire, Gabrielle, ed. *The Cambridge Companion to "The Waste Land."* Cambridge: Cambridge University Press, 2015.
McIntire, Gabrielle. *Modernism, Memory, and Desire: T. S. Eliot and Virginia Woolf*. Cambridge: Cambridge University Press, 2008.
McLaughlin, Joseph. *Writing the Urban Jungle: Reading Empire in London from Doyle to Eliot*. Charlottesville: University of Virginia Press, 2000.
Melaney, William D. *After Ontology: Literary Theory and Modernist Poetics*. Albany: State University of New York Press, 2001.
Menand, Louis. *Discovering Modernism: T. S. Eliot and His Context*. 2nd ed. Oxford: Oxford University Press, 2007.
Meyer, Kinereth, and Rachel Salmon Deshen, eds. *Reading the Underthought: Jewish Hermeneutics and the Christian Poetry of Hopkins and Eliot*. Washington: Catholic University of America Press, 2010.
Miller, Andrew John. *Modernism and the Crisis of Sovereignty*. New York: Routledge, 2007.
Miller, James E., Jr. *T. S. Eliot: The Making of an American Poet, 1888–1922*. University Park: Pennsylvania State University Press, 2005.
Morra, Irene. *Verse Drama in England, 1900–2015: Art, Modernity and the National Stage*. London: Bloomsbury, 2016.
Moses, Omri. *Out of Character: Modernism, Vitalism, Psychic Life*. Stanford: Stanford University Press, 2014.
North, Michael. *Reading 1922: A Return to the Scene of the Modern*. New York: Oxford University Press, 2001.
Oser, Lee. *The Ethics of Modernism: Moral Ideas in Yeats, Eliot, Joyce, Woolf and Beckett*. Cambridge: Cambridge University Press, 2007.
Oser, Lee. *The Return of Christian Humanism: Chesterton, Eliot, Tolkien, and the Romance of History*. Columbia: University of Missouri Press, 2007.
Patterson, Anita. *Race, American Literature and Transnational Modernisms*. Cambridge: Cambridge University Press, 2008.
Perloff, Marjorie. *21st-Century Modernism: The "New" Poetics*. Malden: Blackwell, 2002.
Pinkerton, Steve. *Blasphemous Modernism: The 20th-Century World Made Flesh*. New York: Oxford University Press, 2017.
Pollard, Charles W. *New World Modernisms: T. S. Eliot, Derek Walcott, and Kamau Brathwaite*. Charlottesville: University of Virginia Press, 2004.

Pryor, Sean. *Poetry, Modernism, and an Imperfect World*. Cambridge: Cambridge University Press, 2017.
Query, Patrick R. *Ritual and the Idea of Europe in Interwar Writing*. Burlington: Ashgate, 2012.
Quigley, Megan, ed. "#MeToo and Modernism." Forum. *Modernism/modernity* Print Plus, vol. 5, cycle 2 (September 28, 2020). https://doi.org/10.26597/mod.0163.
Quigley, Megan, ed. "Reading *The Waste Land* with the #MeToo Generation." Forum. *Modernism/modernity* Print Plus, vol. 4, cycle 1 (March 4, 2019). https://doi.org/10.26597/mod.0094.
Raine, Craig. *In Defence of T. S. Eliot*. London: Picador, 2000.
Raine, Craig. *T. S. Eliot*. Oxford: Oxford University Press, 2006.
Raine, Kathleen. *Defining the Times: Essays on Auden and Eliot*. London: Enitharmon, 2002.
Rainey, Lawrence. *Revisiting "The Waste Land."* New Haven: Yale University Press, 2007.
Ramazani, Jahan. *Poetry and Its Others: News, Prayer, Song, and the Dialogue of Genres*. Chicago: University of Chicago Press, 2014.
Ramazani, Jahan. *Poetry in a Global Age*. Chicago: University of Chicago Press, 2020.
Ramazani, Jahan. *A Transnational Poetics*. Chicago: University of Chicago Press, 2009.
Rasula, Jed. *What the Thunder Said: How "The Waste Land" Made Poetry Modern*. Princeton: Princeton University Press, 2022.
Richards, Joshua. *T. S. Eliot's Ascetic Ideal*. Leiden: Brill, 2020.
Ricks, Christopher. *Decisions and Revisions in T. S. Eliot*. London: British Library, 2003.
Ridler, Anne. *Working for T. S. Eliot: A Personal Reminiscence*. London: Enitharmon, 2000.
Rosenthal, Edna. *Aristotle and Modernism: Aesthetic Affinities of T. S. Eliot, Wallace Stevens and Virginia Woolf*. Eastbourne: Sussex Academic, 2008.
Rzepa, Joanna. *Modernism and Theology: Rainer Maria Rilke, T. S. Eliot, Czesław Miłosz*. Cham: Palgrave Macmillan, 2021.
Sherry, Vincent. *The Great War and the Language of Modernism*. New York: Oxford University Press, 2003.
Sherry, Vincent. *Modernism and the Reinvention of Decadence*. Cambridge: Cambridge University Press, 2015.
Sicari, Stephen. *Modernist Humanism and the Men of 1914: Joyce, Lewis, Pound, and Eliot*. Columbia: University of South Carolina Press, 2011.
Slater, Ann Pasternak. *The Fall of a Sparrow: Vivien Eliot's Life and Writings*. London: Faber, 2020.
Smart, John. *Tarantula's Web: John Hayward, T. S. Eliot and Their Circle*. Norwich: Michael Russell, 2013.
Soud, W. David. *Divine Cartographies: God, History, and Poiesis in W. B. Yeats, David Jones, and T. S. Eliot*. Oxford: Oxford University Press, 2016.
Spurr, Barry. *"Anglo-Catholic in Religion": T. S. Eliot and Christianity*. Cambridge: Lutterworth, 2010.

Stasi, Paul. *Modernism, Imperialism, and the Historical Sense*. Cambridge: Cambridge University Press, 2012.

Stayer, Jayme. *Becoming T. S. Eliot: The Rhetoric of Voice and Audience in "Inventions of the March Hare."* Baltimore: Johns Hopkins University Press, 2021.

Stayer, Jayme, ed. *T. S. Eliot, France, and the Mind of Europe*. Newcastle upon Tyne: Cambridge Scholars, 2015.

Sullivan, Hannah. *The Work of Revision*. Cambridge: Harvard University Press, 2013.

Surette, Leon. *Dreams of a Totalitarian Utopia: Literary Modernism and Politics*. Montreal: McGill-Queen's University Press, 2011.

Surette, Leon. *The Modern Dilemma: Wallace Stevens, T. S. Eliot and Humanism*. Montreal: McGill-Queen's University Press, 2008.

Swigg, Richard. *Quick, Said the Bird: Williams, Eliot, Moore, and the Spoken Word*. Iowa City: University of Iowa Press, 2012.

Tearle, Oliver. *The Great War, "The Waste Land" and the Modernist Long Poem*. London: Bloomsbury, 2019.

Terblanche, Etienne. *T. S. Eliot, Poetry, and Earth: The Name of the Lotos Rose*. London: Lexington, 2016.

Thaventhiran, Helen. *Radical Empiricists: Five Modernist Close Readers*. Oxford: Oxford University Press, 2015.

Trevelyan, Mary, and Erica Wagner. *Mary and Mr Eliot: A Sort of Love Story*. London: Faber, 2022.

Trotter, David. *Cinema and Modernism*. Oxford: Blackwell, 2007.

T. S. Eliot Studies Annual. 5 vols. Clemson: Clemson University Press; Liverpool: Liverpool University Press, 2017–23.

Vanheste, Jeroen. *Guardians of the Humanist Legacy: The Classicism of T. S. Eliot's "Criterion" Network and Its Relevance to Our Postmodern World*. Leiden: Brill, 2007.

Vendler, Helen. *Coming of Age as a Poet: Milton, Keats, Eliot, Plath*. Cambridge: Harvard University Press, 2004.

Viney, William. *Waste: A Philosophy of Things*. London: Bloomsbury, 2014.

Wexler, Joyce. *Violence without God: The Rhetorical Despair of Twentieth-Century Writers*. New York: Bloomsbury, 2017.

Whittier-Ferguson, John. *Mortality and Form in Late Modernist Literature*. Cambridge: Cambridge University Press, 2014.

Woelfel, Craig. *Varieties of Aesthetic Experience: Literary Modernism and the Dissociation of Belief*. Columbia: University of South Carolina Press, 2018.

Worthen, John. *T. S. Eliot: A Short Biography*. London: Haus, 2009.

Ziolkowski, Theodore. *Classicism of the Twenties: Art, Music, and Literature*. Chicago: University of Chicago Press, 2015.

Index

Achebe, Chinua 104 n.15, 222
Ackroyd, Peter 77 n.13, 78 n.19
African Americans. *See also* race
  and racism
  Black dialect in Eliot 93–4, 95
  Eliot's speech as racially marked 95, 222
  influence of Eliot on African American writers 93–4
After Strange Gods
  anti-Semitism in 56, 80, 104 n.9, 222, 228
  and heresy 54
  as ill-tempered 34
agriculture, Eliot's criticism of 73–6
Ahmed, Sarah 116, 175
Aiken, Conrad 18, 39
allusions. *See also* annotations and footnotes
  and common culture 150
  effect of new resources on 3–6, 208–11
  Eliot on 4, 216
  and fanfiction 215
  Waste Land allusions in modern poetry 238–40
Altieri, Charles 148
"American Literature and the American Language" 96
Anabasis 17, 82
Anglo-Catholicism, Eliot's conversion to. *See also* baptism; Christianity
  and continuity 97–9
  declaration of 54, 134, 155–6, 200
  effect on prose 28, 139
  and legitimacy of institutions 192
  and marriage to Vivien 43–4
  and political theology 155–66
  process of 97
  and prolific period 44
  and race 56–7, 93–9
  reactions to 55, 56
  and validity 94, 97–8
  and whiteness 93–9

Anker, Elizabeth S. 169–70, 175
annotations and footnotes
  by Eliot 16
  Eliot on 13–14
  in *Inventions of the March Hare* 11, 21
  in *Poems* (2015 collection) 14–16, 21
  as unneeded 216
Anthropocene 67–76
anti-Semitism
  in *After Strange Gods* 56, 80, 104 n.9, 222, 228
  in *Ara Vos Prec / Poems* (1920) 148
  as challenge for Eliot scholarship 222, 227, 228–30, 236
  in "Dirge" 17, 146
  Eliot's opposition to 6, 56–7
  in "Gerontion" 6
  in Hale letters 6
  and Holocaust 228–9
  and Jewish writers' interest in Eliot 80
  present-day 229–30
apostrophe 143–4, 146, 147
Ara Vos Prec 16, 148–50. See also *Poems* (1920)
Archive of Our Own 120, 217 n.5
Arnold, Matthew 53–4, 58, 61, 133
artificial intelligence 224. *See also* digital humanities
Ash-Wednesday 44, 243
Athenaeum essays 133, 134, 135, 140

Babbitt, Irving 54, 159–61
Bagchee, Shyamal 82
Baldwin, James 222
"Ballade pour la grosse Lulu" 16, 148
baptism 97, 99, 139
Barbin, Herculine 117
Barnes, Djuna, *Nightwood* 115
Baudelaire, Charles 30, 34, 161, 162
"Baudelaire" 161
"Baudelaire in our Time" 161
BBC. *See* radio broadcasts

Beachcroft, T. O. 138
Beardsley, Monroe C. 153 n.130
Beasley, Rebecca 79, 83
Bell, Clive 133
Bell, G. K. A. 26
"Bellegarde" 209, 212
Bellow, Saul, "The Song of Songs of Mendel Pumshtok" 79–81, 88
Benda, Julien 52, 55
Bennett, Arnold 133
Bergonzi, Bernard 60
Berlin, Isaiah 162
Betjeman, John 59
Bible, translations of 61
bibliographies on Eliot 25–6, 27, 81, 82
biofiction 207–8, 213, 214–15, 216
Blake, William 215
"The Blameless Sister of Publicola" 12
BLAST 16, 178 n.9
Blot, Harold W. 173, 175, 176
Bobo, Pierre François Joseph Benoit Rosalvo 173, 175, 176
body
  in "Sweeney Erect" 148–9
  trans body 109, 110–12, 113–14
Books Across the Sea 174, 177
Bourdieu, Pierre 131, 132, 138
Boyden, Michael 80
Bradley, F. H. 60, 189
Bramhall, John 165
Brexit 195, 203–4
"A Brief Treatise on the Criticism of Poetry" 187
British Council 201, 203
British Soil Association 73
Brooker, Jewel Spears 47 n.2, 48 n.9, 193 n.13
Brooks, Gwendolyn 94
Browne, Martin 46
Browning, Robert 19–20, 215
Buddhism 83, 84, 102, 198
"Burbank with a Baedeker: Bleistein with a Cigar" 33, 215–16
"The Burial of the Dead" 197–8
Burke, Edmund 157–8
Burkett, Elinor 113–14, 115
Burnt Norton
  and desire 18
  and Hale relationship 45, 208–9

  influence of James on 212
  placement in *Collected Poems* (1936) 13
  and time 185
  and translation 81
Bush, Ronald 216
Buurma, Rachel Sagner 215
Buxton, Noel 26
Byatt, A. S. 63 n.23

canon
  and critic's role in defining classics 227–8
  Eliot's place in 7, 25, 222
  influence of fandom on 215
  as undeclared translations 84
capitalism. *See* economics
Catholicism. *See* Anglo-Catholicism, Eliot's conversion to; Christianity
Cats. *See* *Old Possum's Book of Practical Cats*
Catullus 149
Chakraborty, Sumita 112
Chapman, George 26
charity and lectures 32
Charles, Jos 234
"Charleston, Hey! Hey!" 183
Chiari, Joseph 138
Chinitz, David E. 48 n.21, 93, 130 n.24, 221, 230
Choice of Kipling's Verse 240–1
Christianity. *See also* Anglo-Catholicism, Eliot's conversion to
  and intellectualism 52–3, 56, 58–61
  and masochism 18–20
  political theology 155–66
  and race 56–7, 93–103
  and royalism 59–62
  and translations by Eliot 82–3
  and unity 8, 56–7, 58, 200, 201, 203, 204, 226–30
Churchill, Winston 58
CIA 196
classicist, Eliot as
  and Classicism 155–6
  criticism of 11, 60, 200
  declaration of 54, 134, 155, 200
  and Joyce 33
  and Maurras 160, 161, 162
"The Classics and the Man of Letters" 241

clerisy 52
Clutterbuck, Hope 135
Coetzee, J. M. 227–8, 229, 230
Coleridge, Samuel Taylor 52, 242
Collected Poems 13, 16, 19
collections. See also *specific titles*
   and career capital 131–40
   Eliot's control of 13–14, 21–2, 23–4, 25, 131, 137
   role in publishing market 132–3
Collingwood, R. G. 190
Collini, Stefan 51, 186
Collins, Wilkie 138
colonialism 173, 176–7
Columbo and Bolo verses (*The Columbiad*) 11, 17–18, 94
The Complete Prose of T. S. Eliot. See also criticism by Eliot
   chronological arrangement of 27–9, 124–5
   digitization of 35 n.6, 123–4
   materials gathering 24–6
   origins and organization of 25
   pagination 124
   and print culture 131–40
   as resource 4, 23–34, 186
   size of 27, 171
Connolly, Cyril 13
Conrad, Joseph 96
"Contemporary English Prose" 33
continuity
   and conversion to Anglo-Catholicism 97–9, 102
   and race 97–8, 99, 101
   and royalism 157
conversion. See Anglo-Catholicism, Eliot's conversion to
Cooley, Martha 214
Cooper, John Xiros 185
Coriolan 55–6, 150
"Cousin Nancy" 40
Covid-19 pandemic 224, 225–6
Crashaw, Richard 139
Crawford, Robert 105 n.23, 240
Criterion
   and agriculture 73
   closure of 28, 201
   and European unity 198–201, 202
   finances 43

   first issue 27
   influence and impact of 42, 187
   and royalism 55
   time spent on 24, 44, 54
   and Vivien 42
criticism
   and anonymity 135–6
   Coetzee on 227–8, 229, 230
   eco-criticism 68–9
   Eliot's advice on 132, 135
   poet as critic 55
   relation to poetry 187–8
   vs. reviewing 187
   and unity 174–8
   as writing skill 189–90
criticism by Eliot
   areas of interest 29–30
   authoritative tone in 27–8
   career capital 131–40
   and context 28–9
   eco-criticism 68–9
   Eliot on collecting and reprinting 23–4
   fannishness in 120, 121–2, 209–13, 215–17
   and impressionistic criticism 172, 187
   influence and impact of 6, 23, 171, 186–92
   and joy 171–2, 177–8
   and language 190–1
   lectures and classes by Eliot 5, 33–4, 44–5, 210–11, 215–17
   post-critique 169–78
   and public intellectualism 53–4
   restraint in 23
   revising and reevaluation 29, 172–3
   skepticism in 31
   volume of 23, 25, 27, 171
"Criticism in England" 133
Crutzen, Paul 68
Cuda, Anthony 124, 127
Culler, Jonathan 143–7
"The Cultivation of Christmas Trees" 123
cultural diplomacy by Eliot 201–3
"Cultural Diversity and European Unity" 57
culture. See European culture; Jewish culture
"Culture and Anarchy" 55
Cummings, E. E. 68–9, 127 n.3, 235

Cunard, Nancy 53
Curtius, Ernst Robert 85–8, 199, 200, 201–2

Dadaism 29
Dante 14, 29–30, 39, 43, 44, 165
"Dante" (1920) 30, 42, 134, 135
"Dante" (1929) 14, 29–30, 200
Däumer, Elisabeth 82, 87
Davidson, John 138
Dawson, Christopher 163, 200
"Death by Water" 223, 249
"The Death of Saint Narcissus" 18–19, 145
"The Death of the Duchess" 17
decolonization and humanities 7, 184, 186
"Dedication II" 17, 18
"A Dedication to My Wife" 13
Dial 39, 139, 140
Diaper, Jeremy 68, 73
Dickey, Frances 5, 69, 94, 208, 214
"Die Einheit der europäischen Kultur" 202
"Difficulties of a Statesman" 56
digital humanities
    and *Complete Prose* 35 n.6, 119, 123–4
    computational literary analysis 119–20, 122–7
    effect on scholarship 119–27
    and Hale letters 119, 123, 126–7
"Dirge" 17, 145–6
"The Disembodied Voice" 136
dissociation of sensibility 171, 172
divorce 44, 45
Donne, John 29, 31, 54, 140
"Donne in Our Time" 31
"Doris's Dream Songs" 18
Dostoevsky, Fyodor 43, 151, 198
dramatic works 44, 45, 147, 151, 184, 187
Dryden, John 138, 155–6
The Dry Salvages 46, 77 n.6
DuPlessis, Rachel Blau 93

East Coker 15, 17, 73–6, 100–3, 228
Eco, Umberto 80
ecocriticism 68–9
economics
    European Economic Community 195–6
    and humanities 183–4
    and political theology 163–4
    and print culture 131–40, 184

education
    of Eliot 37, 39–40, 60, 137, 173, 189
    Eliot on 154 n.33
"Eeldrop and Appleplex" 137
Egoist 212
elegy 146, 223, 247
"Elegy" 145–6
Eliot, Andrew 100
Eliot, Charlotte 38–9, 69
Eliot, T. S. *See also* criticism by Eliot; influence and impact of Eliot; poetry; scholarship, Eliot; *specific titles*
    British naturalization 58
    childhood 37–9
    education 37, 39–40, 60, 137, 173, 189
    expatriation 38–9, 197
    finances 43, 173
    health 198
    marriage to Valerie Fletcher 12, 47
    marriage to Vivien Eliot 40–4, 173
    in other authors' fiction 217 n.5
    relationships to contemporaries 33–4
Eliot, Valerie
    dedications to 13, 17, 18
    as literary editor 24, 25, 242
    marriage to 12, 47
Eliot, Vivien
    addiction 40–1
    Criterion writings 42
    death of 46
    marriage to 40–4, 173, 213, 238–9
    mental health 40–1, 43–4
    scholarship on 37, 208
    separation from 45
    and *The Waste Land* 208, 244
Elizabethan Age
    Eliot's interest in 29, 30
    and Eliot's political theology 156, 165
Elizabethan Essays 25
Elyot, Thomas 58, 101
Emerson, Ralph Waldo 16
Encounter 195–6, 203
English departments 7, 184, 186–92
"English Poets as Letter Writers" 4, 139
English-Speaking Union (ESU) 177
environmentalism 67–76
epideictic, lyric as 144
Essays Ancient and Modern 137, 159
Esty, Jed 99, 101

"European Civil War" 158, 163
European Common Market 52, 195–6
European culture
　absorption of other cultures into 83–5
　and agriculture 73–6
　and allusions 150
　and Eliot's conversion to Ango-Catholicism 98–9
　and racism 56–7
　religion as legitimizing 192
European unity
　and Christianity 8, 200, 201, 203, 204, 228–9, 230
　and cultural diplomacy by Eliot 201–3
　and culture 56–61, 174–8, 195–204, 226–8
　and racism 8, 56–7
"Exequy" 17, 145–6
expatriate, Eliot as 38–9, 58, 197
"Eyes that last I saw in tears" 18

Faber, Geoffrey 17, 122
Faber & Faber
　Eliot's work at 24, 43, 122, 187
　files as resource 26, 34
fanfiction
　biofiction 207–8, 213, 214–15, 216
　defined 207, 212, 213
　and desire to work with original 212
　of Eliot 120–2, 213–17
　Eliot as fan 120, 121–2, 209–13, 215–17
fascism
　Eliot's resistance to 159, 174, 201
　and Maurras 55, 57, 160–2
　and nationalism 199
　and Pound 229, 236
　prefigurations of 160, 161, 237
Feinsod, Harris 82–3
Felski, Rita 169–70, 175
femininity in *The Waste Land* 107–17
Fernandez, Ramon 133
"The Fire Sermon" 71, 84, 85, 108–17, 233
First World War 173–5, 197, 200
Fitzgerald, F. Scott 242
Fitzgerald, Sara 214
Fletcher, Valerie. *See* Eliot, Valerie
Flores, Ángel 85, 86, 87
For Lancelot Andrewes
　editorial unity in 137
　preface and declarations 54, 56, 134, 155–6, 159–62, 164–6, 200
Foucault, Michel 117
Four Quartets. See also *Burnt Norton*; *The Dry Salvages*; *East Coker*; *Little Gidding*
　environmentalism in 67, 73–6
　Hindu and Buddhist thought in 83, 102
　influence of James on 212
　patriotism 53
　pollution and waste in 67
　time in 184
　whiteness in 93, 99–103
free verse 223, 233, 247
Frege, Gottlob 189, 190
Freud, Sigmund 88, 107, 236
"The Frontiers of Criticism" 171–3, 177
Frost, Robert 127 n.3
"The Function of Criticism" 172

Gailey, Jeannine Hall
　"Her Nerves" 238–9
　"Remembering Philomel" 238
Gallop, Jane 177–8
Gallup, Donald 25–6, 27, 32, 81, 82
"A Game of Chess" 42, 239, 244
Gates, Henry Louis, Jr. 98
gender. *See also* women
　cis and trans femininity 107–17
　and misogyny 213, 217, 226–7
"Gerontion" 3–6, 15, 16, 39, 41–2, 55, 166
Gish, Nancy 85
Goethe, Johann Wolfgang von 139
"Going into Europe" 195–6
Gordon, Lyndall 43, 209, 213
Gosse, Edmund 187
Greer, Germaine 114
Greif, Mark 186
Grierson, H. J. C. 134–5
Gumbs, Alexis Pauline 249

Haffenden, John 6, 37
Haigh-Wood, Vivien. *See* Eliot, Vivien
Haiti, occupation of 173, 175, 176
Hale, Emily
　first meeting 39, 214
　as muse 40, 42, 44–6, 209
　relationship with 37, 40, 43, 44–7, 209, 214

Hale letters
  anti-Semitism in 6
  destruction of 127, 208
  digitization of 119, 123, 126–7
  effect on Eliot studies 4–6, 37
  Eliot's response to donation 27, 37, 40, 209–10, 211
  and fanfiction 208–13
  as resource on allusions 208–11
  start of correspondence 41
  unsealing of 4, 27, 126, 208
"Hamlet" 42, 134, 171, 172
Harvard College
  Eliot as student 30, 39–40, 53, 173, 189
  lectures and classes by Eliot 5, 33–4, 44–5, 210–11, 215–17
Hayward, John 17, 19, 121–2, 213
Heffernan, Laura 215
Heraclitus 45
Hesse, Eva 80–1, 84, 85–8
Hesse, Hermann 198–9
Hill, W. Speed 122
Hinduism 83, 102, 198
Hinkley, Barbara 39
Hinkley, Eleanor 39, 214
Hobbes, Thomas 164–5
Hofmannsthal, Hugo von 138
"The Hollow Men" 18, 43, 243
Holocaust 228–9
Homage to John Dryden 155–6
Homer 84, 218 n.17, 234, 241
"Hommage à Charles Maurras" 57
homosexuality and the homoerotic. *See also* trans
  Eliot's interactions with 5, 12
  and fanfiction 213
  in *The Waste Land* 12, 88, 108, 111, 112
Hooker, Richard 165
Horace 234
"How the Tall Girl's Breasts Are" 12
"How to Read Poetry" 32
Hügel, Friedrich von 139
Hughes, Ted 25
Hulme, T. E. 160, 161
"The Humanism of Irving Babbitt" 159
humanities
  and decolonization 7, 184, 186
  future of 183–92
Hume, David 164

Huxley, Aldous 48 n.16
hypertextuality 122–4

The Idea of a Christian Society 25, 52, 58, 63 n.24, 192, 228
"The Idea of a European Society" 205 n.9
idiolects 244–5
"If I Were a Dean" 26
impersonality, theory of
  and anonymity 135
  and criticism 125, 170, 171, 173, 187, 189, 208
  and digitization of corpus 120, 123, 125, 126
  and Hale letters 208–9, 216
  and lyric theory 145, 148, 151
influence and impact of Eliot
  on African American writers 93–4
  and *Criterion* 42, 187
  on criticism 6, 23, 171, 186–92
  and future of humanities 185
  on Jewish writers 80
  overview of 6–8
  and *The Waste Land* 223, 236–8, 241–3
"In Memory of Henry James" 196, 211–12, 213
International Student Service 32
intertextual relations and fanfiction 120–1
"Introduction to Goethe" 139
"Introduction to *Nightwood*" 115
Inventions of the March Hare 11, 16–17, 20–1, 24, 145, 146
Italy, Eliot's travels to 203

Jackson, Virginia 143, 150
Jaillant, Lise 132
James, Henry 5, 33, 209–13, 215–17
Jarrell, Randall 11
Javadi, Iman 172
Javadizadeh, Kamran 95
jazz 93, 236, 243
Jeffreys, Sheila 114
Jenner, Caitlyn 113
Jepson, Edgar 136–7
Jewish culture 79–81, 88
"John Bramhall" 165
"John Marston" 34 n.2
Jonson, Ben 29
Josselson, Michael 196

journalism, disdain for 132, 133
joy 171–2, 175, 177–8
Joyce, James
   Eliot on 33, 138, 197
   and hypertextuality 122–3
   influence and impact of 223, 241, 242, 243
Julius, Anthony 56–7, 149
Julius Caesar 237

Keeling, Kara 247
Kenner, Hugh 145, 153 n.22, 154 n.35, 193 n.13
Kermode, Frank 25
Keynes, John Maynard 158, 197
King, Martin Luther, Jr. 249
Kipling, Rudyard 30, 240–1, 243
Kirk, Russell 157–8
Knowledge and Experience in the Philosophy of F. H. Bradley 60, 189
Koeser, Rebecca Sutton 126
Koestenbaum, Wayne 12
Krutch, Joseph Wood 200

"La Figlia Che Piange" 46, 147–8
Laforgue, Jules 20–1, 39
Larkin, Philip 59–60
Lasky, Melvin 203
"Last Words" 201
Latour, Bruno 170, 173, 175–6
Lawrence, D. H. 33, 138, 217 n.5
Leavis, F. R. 13
Lefevere, André 80
Léger, Alexis 83
Lehan, Richard 71
"Le Roman anglais contemporain" 33
"Let quacks, empirics, dolts debate" 51
Lewis, Amanda 93
Lewis, Wyndham 16, 33, 173, 174
Leyris, Pierre 91 n.39
"Lines for Cuscuscaraway and Mirza Murad Ali Beg" 52
"The Literature of Fascism" 55
Little Gidding 18, 37, 100, 102–3
Litz, A. Walton 233
Liu, Alan 125
Lloyd, Marie 53
Lloyds Bank 34, 42, 197
"London Letters" 53

Longenbach, James 8, 222–3, 233–5
Longfellow, Henry Wadsworth 16
Lorde, Audre 250
Lovejoy, A. O. 190
"The Love Song of J. Alfred Prufrock"
   annotations for 15
   and "The Death of Saint Narcissus" 19
   and fanfiction 127 n.3, 128 n.6, 128 n.9, 214
   parodied in "The Song of Songs of Mendel Pumshtok" 79–81, 88
   as part of prolific period 39
   pollution and waste in 69–70, 72
   and the posthumous 13
   Pound on 22
   and "Prufrock's Pervigilium" 19, 38
   recordings 15
   relevance to modern readers 223–4
   translations 79–81
"The Love Song of St. Sebastian" 18–20
Lynd, Robert 133
Lyon, Ann Bowes 137
lyric theory 143–51

MacCabe, Colin 60–1
MacGreevy, Thomas 55
Machiavelli, Niccolò 164
MacKay, Marina 175
Madden, Ed 107
Maistre, Joseph de 161–2, 164
Maitland, F. W. 165
man of letters 4, 53, 186–7. *See also* public intellectualism
Marcus, Jane 107
Margul-Sperber, Alfred 87
"Marina" 15
marriages 12, 40–4, 47, 173
Marshall Plan 196
Marx, Karl
   Marxist response to post-critique 176–8
   and political theology 161, 164
masochism 18–20
Massis, Henri 199
Maurras, Charles 54, 55, 56, 57, 159–60, 161
McCue, Jim. See *The Poems of T. S. Eliot*
McIntire, Gabrielle 69, 71, 94, 230
McVey, Christopher 84
Menand, Louis 57, 185

Menasce, Jean de 91 n.39
mental illness, feminization of 240
Merwin, W. S. 235
"Message on Charles Maurras" 57
Mesterton, Erik 82
"The Metaphysical Poets" 83, 134–5, 150–1, 171
Methuen, Algernon 134
#MeToo movement 116, 224
Middle Passage 223, 249
Mill, John Stuart 152 n.9, 158
Milton, John 30, 241–2, 246
Milton Academy 39
minstrelsy, blackface 38
misogyny. *See also* gender; women
  as challenge for Eliot readers 6, 226–7
  and fanfiction 213
The Modern Dilemma 58
modernism
  cross-disciplinary 190, 192
  Eliot's place in canon 6, 7, 170, 186
  and environmentalism 68–9, 70
  and fanfiction 120, 121, 208, 214, 215
  and future of humanities 222–3, 227
  and Gailey 238
  and homosexuality 12
  and lyric 143, 151
  and print culture 132–3
  and trans femininity 107–17
  and translation 79–80, 83, 84, 88
  and unity 175
  The Waste Land as paradigmatic text 236, 241, 243–4
"Modern Tendencies in Poetry" 26, 28, 29
Monro, Harold 138
Moody, A. D. 204
Moore, G. E. 189, 190
morality 30, 31, 125
More, Paul Elmer 233, 235
Morley, Christopher 129 n.10
Morrison, Toni 95–6
Mosley, Oswald 6
Mowrer, Edgar Ansel 138, 139
"Mr. Read and M. Fernandez" 133
"Mr. Reckitt, Mr. Tomlin, and the Crisis" 58
Muir, Edwin 138
Murder in the Cathedral 45, 212

Murry, John Middleton 133
"The Music of Poetry" 24, 61
mythical method 54, 71, 171

Namier, Lewis 190
St. Narcissus 18, 19
nationalism
  Eliot on 57, 199
  and Maurras 55, 160
"A Neglected Aspect of Chapman" 26, 43
Neruda, Pablo 88
New Criticism
  Eliot as pivotal to/stand-in for 169, 170, 172–3
  and "Gerontion" 3
  and lyric theory 144
  and translation 83
"New Humanism" 159
"Niccolò Machiavelli" 164
Nobel Prize 28, 202, 229
North, Michael 93, 95, 177
"Note of Homage to Allen Tate" 51–2
"A Note of Introduction to *In Parenthesis*" 144
"Note on Ezra Pound" 152 n.16
"Note on Richard Crashaw" 139
Notes Towards the Definition of Culture 58–9, 73, 83, 174–5, 185, 229
Nye, Naomi Shihab 248

objective correlative 11, 171
"Ode" 149–50
Old Possum's Book of Practical Cats 17, 127 n.3, 177, 214
"On Christianity and a Useful Life" 32
On Poetry and Poets 25
"On the Place and Function of the Clerisy" 52
organicist movement 73, 74–5, 76
Original Sin 161, 162, 164
Orwell, George 185, 242
Ovid 238, 239
"The Oxford Jonson" 29
Ozick, Cynthia 7

Paris, Eliot's travels to 39
parody
  of literary forms in *The Waste Land* 152 n.19

"The Song of Songs of Mendel
    Pumshtok" 79–81, 88
pastoral 67, 68, 71–2, 75–6, 237
patriotism 53
Patterson, Anita 93
Paz, Octavio 88
"The Perfect Critic" 42, 187
Perse, Saint-John 82–3
"Philip Massinger" 42, 67, 215
Phillips, Carl 223, 236–8
philosophy
    and Eliot 37, 39, 40, 53, 60, 158,
        189–91, 221
    and role of critic 187
Pillat, Ion 82
Plath, Sylvia 127 n.3, 239
Poems (1920) 148–50, 215, 244. See also
    Ara Vos Prec
The Poems of T. S. Eliot
    annotations in 14–16, 21
    as fanfiction 207
    overview of volumes 16–18
    as resource 4, 11–22, 186
Poems Written in Early Youth 11, 19
poetry. See also *The Poems of T. S. Eliot*
    Eliot on 13–14, 67, 83, 144, 145,
        150, 233
    Hale as muse 40, 42, 44–6, 209
    hybrid book proposal 134, 136–7
    influence and impact of 6, 223,
        236–8, 241–3
    and lyric theory 143–51
    and punctuation 223, 233–5
    relation to criticism 187–8
    Richards on 187
    sexually explicit pieces 12–13
    as between sight and sound 247–50
    volume of 16
    Yeats on 150
politics
    depoliticization of 163
    political theology 155–66
    role of public intellectual 53, 202–3
pollution and the Anthropocene 67–76
Pondrom, Cyrena 107
popular culture 93
"Portrait of a Lady" 39, 209
post-critique 169–78
"The Post-Georgians" 33

Potter, Rachel 116
Pound, Ezra
    and Black dialect 95
    Cantos 245
    and "The Death of Saint Narcissus"
        submission 19
    on Eliot 12, 22, 186, 244, 245
    Eliot on 139, 152 n.16
    and fascism 229, 236
    on literature 229
    Personae 139
    and *The Waste Land* 136, 208, 242, 243
    "Preface to *The Dark Side of the Moon*"
        203
"Preludes" 39
Prichard, Matthew 4–6, 39
Prins, Yopie 143, 150
print culture and career capital 131–40,
    184
privacy 12–13
"The Problem of the Perplexed Publisher"
    122
Project MUSE 35 n.6, 123–4, 127
prose. See criticism by Eliot
Prufrock and Other Observations 146–7,
    215
"Prufrock's Pervigilium" 19, 38
public intellectualism
    and Christianity 52–3, 56, 58–61
    Eliot as intellectual 32, 51–62, 139
    influence and impact of 202–3
    and man of letters role 4, 53, 186–7
    and royalism of Eliot 54–9
    and unity 56–62
punctuation 223, 233–5

Quigley, Megan 120, 221, 230, 240
Quinn, John 21, 134

race and racism. See also African
    Americans; anti-Semitism; whiteness
    and Anglo-Catholicism 56–7, 93–103
    Black dialect and Black culture in Eliot
        93–4, 95, 177
    blackface minstrelsy 38
    and Bolo poems 17–18, 94
    as challenge for Eliot scholarship and
        readers 222, 224, 226–30
    and conversion 94, 98

and Covid-19 pandemic 225
Eliot's speech as racially marked 95, 222
and royalism 56–7
and segregation in St. Louis 38, 94
and unity 8, 56–7, 177–8
and universality 95–6, 99
and validity 94, 98–9, 100
and whiteness 19, 93–103
radio broadcasts 30, 58, 59, 140, 201–3
Raine, Craig 222–3, 240–3
Rainey, Lawrence 132
rape and sexual violence
in "The Death of Saint Narcissus" 19
in "The Love Song of St. Sebastian" 20
and male audience 238, 239
in "Ode" 149–50
in *Sweeney Agonistes* 20
and trans women 115, 116
in *The Waste Land* 110, 223, 238–40
Raymond, Janice 108
Read, Herbert 132, 133
recordings by Eliot 15, 244–5
"Reflections on Contemporary Poetry" 21, 28
"Reflections on *Vers Libre*" 53, 61
Rekdal, Paisley
"Nightingale" 239–40
"Philomela" 239
religion. *See* Anglo-Catholicism, Eliot's conversion to; baptism; Buddhism; Christianity; Hinduism; Unitarianism
"Religion and Literature" 228
representation
vs. instantiation 190
and political theology 163–4
vs. presentation 188
"The Responsibility of the European Man of Letters" 31
"The Responsibility of the Man of Letters in the Cultural Restoration of Europe" 53, 202–3
Revised Psalter 61
"Rhapsody on a Windy Night" 19, 38
Richards, I. A. 150, 187
Ricks, Christopher. See also *The Poems of T. S. Eliot*
and *Inventions of the March Hare* 11, 21, 24

on translation 198
ritual
and lyric 144–5
and royalism 59
and social unity 54
Roberts, Michael 138
Robertson, J. W. 134
Rolland, Romain 199
Rollins, Alison C. 223, 247–50
"Free Radical" 248
"Self-Portrait of Librarian with T. S. Eliot's Papers" 247–48
"The Romantic Generation, If It Existed" 28
romanticism 151 n.2, 186, 191
"A Romantic Patrician" 134
Rosenfeld, Isaac, "The Song of Songs of Mendel Pumshtok" 79–81, 88
Rougemont, Denis de 196
Rousseau, Jean-Jacques 160, 161, 162, 164
royalism
and Christianity 59–62
and conservatism 156–8
declaration of 54, 134, 155, 200
and Maurras 54, 55
and political theology 155–66
and public intellectualism 54–9
"Royalism and Socialism" 54
Russell, Bertrand 41, 132, 156–7, 189
Russian Revolution 197, 200

The Sacred Wood
editing of essays in 134, 135, 137
Eliot on style of 140
and impersonality 125
influence and impact of 25, 187
as part of prolific period 42
and public intellectualism 53–4
voice of compared to Eliot's poetry 136–7
Said, Edward 186
Saintsbury, George 135
Samarrai, Ghanim 81
Sandburg, Carl 33
Sanskrit, Eliot's knowledge of 132
Sanz Irles, Luis 85–8
Save the Children Fund 26
Sayyab, Badr Shakir al 81
"A Sceptical Patrician" 134

Schmitt, Carl 159, 163, 165
scholarship, Eliot
   challenge of racism and anti-Semitism in 222, 227, 228–30, 236
   and digitization 119–27
   effect of new resources on 3–8, 34
   future of 221–30
   and future of humanities 183–92
   as product of fanfiction 216
   and recently published works 6
Schuchard, Ronald. See also *The Complete Prose of T. S. Eliot*
   on Hale 43
   and prose collection 25, 171, 172
   on recently published works 6
   and *The Varieties of Metaphysical Poetry* 24
Schuster, Joshua 70
scrutiny and modern life 224
Scully, Matthew 107–8
"The Seafarer" (Old English poem) 233–4
St. Sebastian 18
"Second Thoughts about Humanism" 160
Second World War
   appeasement policy 201
   effect on prose 28
   and European unity 201–3
   and Hale relationship 46
   Holocaust 228–9
   lectures 32
   and post-critique 175
Sedgwick, Eve 169
Sedgwick, Henry Dwight 134, 135
Selected Essays 23, 25, 28, 134, 137
The Selected Prose of T. S. Eliot 23, 25
Seneca 138
A Sermon Preached in Magdalene College Chapel 39
Seshagiri, Urmila 97–8
sex and sexuality. *See also* homosexuality and the homoerotic; rape and sexual violence; trans
   in Bolo and Columbo poems 17–18
   Eliot's sexually explicit poems 12–13
   and masochism 18–20
   and modernity 112
   and Prichard 5, 39
   and St. Louis mores 38

   in *The Waste Land* 12, 85, 88, 108, 109–10, 111, 112, 238–40
Shakespeare, William
   Coriolanus 12, 55, 149–50
   Eliot on 241
   influence on textual criticism 122
   Othello 215
   and punctuation 234
Shama'a (journal) 26
Sharpe, Christina 247
Shaw, Fiona 245
Shelley, Percy Bysshe 45, 139
Sherry, Vincent 174
Shusterman, Richard 172
Sinclair, May 33
skepticism 31
Slater, Ann Pasternak 37, 41, 208
slavery and Middle Passage 223, 249
"Sleeping Together" 12
smog and smoke 67, 69–70, 72
social contract 164–5
"The Social Function of Poetry" 61
soil 73, 74–5, 76
"Some Thoughts on Braille" 32
"Song" 13, 145–6
Southam, B. C. 16
Spanish Civil War 53, 175, 201
speech and pronunciation
   Eliot's speech as racially marked 95, 222
   idiolects 244–5
   recordings 15
   voices 244–7
Spender, Stephen 195–6, 201–2
Spengler, Oswald 200
Spenser, Edmund 71–2, 75
Spiegelman, Art 229
Spurr, Barry 98, 99
Squire, J. C. 33
"Statement by T. S. Eliot on the opening of the Emily Hale letters at Princeton University" 27, 37, 40, 209, 211. *See also* Hale letters
Stayer, Jayme 5–6, 172
Stead, William Force 97–9
Stephen, Leslie 133
St. Louis
   influence on Eliot 37–8
   pollution and waste in 69–70
   segregation and racism in 38, 94

Stoermer, Eugene 68
Stoppard, Tom 243
Strachey, Lytton 136
Strauss, Leo 159, 163, 165
Sullivan, Hannah 223, 230, 243–7
Sweden, travels to 201
Sweeney Agonistes 20, 38, 44
"Sweeney Erect" 15, 148–9
Swinburne, Algernon Charles 30
Symons, Arthur 161

Tall Girl poems 12–13, 17
Taylor, Michelle A. 94
technology
    digitization of Eliot's works 35 n.6, 119–27
    and fanfiction 120–2
    and objectivity 125
    and scrutiny 224
    and time 224
Terblanche, Etienne 69
TERFs (trans exclusionary radical feminists) 108, 113–16
Thames, pollution of 67, 71–2
Thayer, Scofield 16, 39, 40
theology
    political theology 155–66
    and validity 97, 102–3
"Those Who Need Privacy and Those Whose Need Is Company" 32
"Thoughts After Lambeth" 56
"The Three Voices of Poetry" 31
thunder/lightning 247–9, 250
time
    Eliot's interest in 184–5
    and technology 224
    and timelessness of cis/trans femininity 111, 113, 114
    and *The Waste Land* 184, 241, 247–9
Times Literary Supplement
    and anonymity 135
    importance to Eliot's career 24, 135–6
    placement of articles 131
    style of essays in 139
Tiresias, in *The Waste Land* 107–17
To Criticize the Critic (collection) 25
"To Criticize the Critic" (lecture) 28–9, 241
"Tradition and the Individual Talent"
    and absorption of other cultures 83–4, 85
    and digital technologies 123
    and impersonality 208, 215
    as part of prolific period 42, 171
    place within corpus 14, 28
    subjectivity of 150–1
    and time 184
    and unity of European culture 3, 196–7
"Tradition and the Practice of Poetry" 201
trans
    cis and trans femininity 107–17
    and modern readers 224–5
    and TERFs 108, 113–16
translation
    by Eliot 82–3
    of Eliot 79–82, 83–8
    limitations of 198
    and parodies 79–81, 88
trauma
    in Eliot 5, 18, 39, 121, 175, 198, 223, 240
    in Gailey 238
    and Vivien 41
"Triumphal March" 55
"The Triumph of Bullshit" 16, 148
T. S. Eliot Studies Annual 69
Twain, Mark 95–6
"Two Studies in Dante" 30
"The Two Unfinished Novels" 212
typewriters 122, 126

Ukraine war 221, 229
Ulysses (Joyce) 33, 122–3, 197, 223, 241, 242, 243
Unitarianism 39, 45, 97, 99
unity. *See also* European unity
    and anti-Semitism 228–9
    as challenge for scholarship 226–30
    and Christianity 8, 56–7, 58, 200, 201, 203, 204, 226–30
    and criticism 174–8
    and culture 56–61, 174–8, 195–204, 226–8
    and joy 175
    and post-critique 175–6
    and public intellectualism 56–62
    and race 8, 56–7, 177–8
    and royalism 54

"The Unity of European Culture" 201
universality and race 95–6, 99
Upton, Edward 83, 84
The Use of Poetry and the Use of Criticism 13–14

Valerie's Own Book 12, 17
Valéry, Paul 135, 138, 196, 200, 203
validity 94, 96–100, 102–3
"The Value and Use of Cathedrals in England Today" 59–60
The Varieties of Metaphysical Poetry 24, 54
Vendler, Helen 146–7
Verdenal, Jean 39
verification *vs.* validity 102
Versailles, Treaty of 197, 198
"Verse Pleasant and Unpleasant" 33
"Views and Reviews: Journalists of Yesterday and Today" 58
violence. *See* rape and sexual violence
Virgil 227
Voigt, Ellen Bryant 235

Wagner, Richard, *Tristan und Isolde* 40, 42
war. *See also* First World War; Second World War
  "European Civil War" 158, 163
  and modernism 175
  and post-critique 170, 175
  and royalism 158
  Spanish Civil War 53, 175, 201
  Ukraine 221, 229
  and unity 174–5, 200, 201–3
  and *The Waste Land* 174, 197
The Waste Land
  allusions to in modern poetry 238–40
  and anti-Semitism 17, 146
  Buddhist and Hindu thought in 83, 84, 198
  cadence of 52
  centenary 8, 222–3, 233–50
  cohesion techniques 243–7
  drafts 11, 17
  as elegy 223, 247
  facsimile editions 24, 208, 242, 243–4
  fanfiction in 215
  fanfiction of 128 n.3, 128 n.7, 128 n.9, 207
  and free verse 223, 233, 247
  future of 247–9
  and Hale 40
  hypertextuality of 129 n.16
  influence and impact of 223, 236–8, 240–3
  length of 242, 243
  and lyric theory 145–6
  and modern readers 236–8
  mythical method in 54
  opening lines 18
  parody forms in 152 n.19
  poets on 222–3, 233–50
  pollution and waste in 67, 71–2
  and post-critique 170
  publishing history 145
  and punctuation 233–4
  reception and reviews of 42, 88, 244
  recordings and performances 244–5
  sex and sexuality in 12, 85, 88, 108, 109–10, 111, 112, 238–40
  teaching 236, 243–4, 247
  and time 184, 241, 247–9
  and trans femininity 107–17
  translations of 80–1, 83–8
  verse forms in 233
  and war 174, 197
  and weather 247–50
  Woolf on 221, 230
  working title 244
Waterlow, Sydney 132
Wells, H. G. 58
"What the Thunder said" 248–9, 250
Wheatley, Phillis 249
Wheeler, Lesley 223, 238–40
whiteness. *See also* race and racism
  and conversion to Anglo-Catholicism 93–9
  in "The Death of Saint Narcissus" 19
  in *Four Quartets* 93, 99–103
  and identity 93–103
  and universality 95
  as unmarked marker 103 n.1
  and validity 94, 99, 100
Whitman, Walt 16, 70
Whittier, John Greenleaf 16
will and social contract 164
"William Blake" 215
Williams, Charles 138
Williams, Raymond 158, 185

Williams, William Carlos 69, 234, 235
Wilson, Woodrow 196, 199
Wimsatt, W. K., Jr. 153 n.130
women
  cis and trans femininity 107–17
  cities as escape for 76
  feminization of mental illness 240
  misogyny and fanfiction 213, 217
  misogyny as challenge for Eliot scholarship 226–7
  as muses 46, 209, 211
  in translations of *The Waste Land* 87
Woolf, Virginia
  correspondence with 26
  Eliot on 33
  environmentalism of 68–9
  fictionalization of Eliot 217 n.5
  professional network of 132
  "22 Hyde Park Gate" 240
  on *The Waste Land* 221, 230
Wordsworth, William 242, 246
works. *See* collections; criticism by Eliot; dramatic works; poetry; *The Complete Prose of T. S. Eliot*; *The Poems of T. S. Eliot*; *specific titles*
Wright, Richard 94
Wyatt, Thomas 234

Yeats, William Butler 127 n.3, 150